Cooking Light

COOKBOOK 1996

Cooking Light
COOKBOOK 1996

Oxmoor House®

Copyright 1995 by Oxmoor House, Inc.
Book Division of Southern Progress Corporation
P.O. Box 2463, Birmingham, Alabama 35201

Library of Congress Catalog Number: 87-61020
ISBN: 0-8487-1456-3
ISSN: 1043-7061

Manufactured in the United States of America
First Printing 1995

Be sure to check with your health-care provider before making any changes in your diet.

Editor-in-Chief: Nancy Fitzpatrick Wyatt
Senior Foods Editor: Katherine M. Eakin
Senior Editor, Editorial Services: Olivia Kindig Wells
Art Director: James Boone

Cooking Light® Cookbook 1996

Editor: Caroline A. Grant, M.S., R.D.
Foods Editor: Deborah Garrison Lowery
Copy Editors: Donna Baldone, Holly Ensor,
    Jacqueline Giovanelli
Editorial Assistant: Lisa C. Bailey
Designer: Faith Nance
Director, Test Kitchens: Kathleen Royal Phillips
Assistant Director, Test Kitchens: Gayle Hays Sadler
Test Kitchen Home Economists: Molly Baldwin,
    Susan Hall Bellows, Julie Christopher,
    Michele Brown Fuller, Natalie E. King,
    Elizabeth Tyler Luckett, Iris Crawley O'Brien,
    Jan A. Smith
Senior Photographer: Jim Bathie
Photographer: Ralph Anderson
Senior Photo Stylist: Kay E. Clarke
Photo Stylist: Virginia R. Cravens
Publishing Systems Administrator: Rick Tucker
Director of Production and Distribution: Phillip Lee
Associate Production Manager: Theresa L. Beste
Production Assistants: Valerie Heard,
    Marianne Jordan Wilson
Recipe and Menu Developers: Pat Coker;
    Linda West Eckhardt; Karen Levin;
    Karen Mangum, M.S., R.D.; Susan Reeves, R.D., L.D.;
    Jane Ingrassia Reinsel; Patricia Schmidt;
    Marie Simmons; Elizabeth J. Taliaferro
Text Consultants: Maureen Callahan, M.S., R.D.;
    Helen Anne Dorrough, R.D.; Office of the Vice
    President of Health Affairs, University of Alabama in
    Birmingham: Julius Linn M.D., Executive Director, and
    Lisa Mahaffey, Associate Editor; Christin Loudin, R.D.;
    Tracey Minkin; Elizabeth J. Taliaferro; Emily Walzer;
    Marion Winik

Cover: *Tortellini-Basil Soup (page 225)*
Back cover: *Lemon Cream Pie (page 242)*
Page 2: *Banana Pudding Cheesecake (page 242)*

Contents

pages 74 and 75

Introduction   6

The Way to Wellness

News You Can Use   10
Know Your Nutrition Needs   13
Profiles in Fitness   14
A Dozen Ways to Pamper Yourself   16
What's New in the Marketplace   18
How to Perfect Chicken Pot Pie   21
Uncork the Virtues of Vinegar   22

Light and Healthy Meals

Breakfast and Brunch   23
Quick and Easy   35
That's Entertaining   49
Holiday Celebrations   65

Light Recipes

Appetizers and Beverages   83
Breads   95
Fish and Shellfish   107
Grains and Pastas   119
Meatless Main Dishes   133
Meats   147
Poultry   163
Salads and Salad Dressings   175
Sandwiches and Snacks   189
Sauces and Condiments   199
Side Dishes   209
Soups and Stews   221
Desserts   231

page 93

page 98

Menus and More

Eat Great to Lose Weight   246
Calorie/Nutrient Chart   250
Recipe Index   263
Subject Index   270
Acknowledgments and Credits   272

Welcome to
Cooking Light 1996

This year *Cooking Light Cookbook* may throw you a few surprises. But, I promise, you'll like every one of them. That is if you like spending an hour or so in a hammock—for your health. Or getting advice from a personal exercise trainer—without paying the price. Or learning how you can live longer—really.

Our exercise and health section takes on a whole new face with this latest edition of *Cooking Light*. You'll notice the difference beginning on page 10. Look for these new features:

• **News You Can Use.** This section (formerly called "Update") is an at-a-glance look at the past year's hottest nutrition and fitness issues. The title is fitting because a short synopsis beneath each headlined article tells how the information directly applies to you.

• **What's New In the Marketplace.** These pages are meant to short-circuit your shopping time for the newest food and fitness products. See pages 18 and 19 to find out which fat-free deli meat we deemed the best or to learn about the benefits of a neat new off-trail walking shoe.

• **Profiles in Fitness.** Do you swim, golf, garden, or run? Then meet someone who's probably a lot like you on pages 14 and 15. We asked fitness writer Emily Walzer to find four health-conscious people of various ages, fitness levels, and interests to introduce to you. They share their exercise triumphs and goals; then, exercise physiologist Carol Garber tells them how to achieve these aspirations which may mirror yours.

• **A Dozen Ways to Pamper Yourself.** I'm not kidding. Your state of mind is just as critical to your overall health as your diet and exercise habits. So we enlisted the pro of self-pampering, witty writer and regular National Public Radio contributor, Marion Winik, to share a few of her best secrets for staying mentally fit.

I researched the phenomenon of a moderate amount of self-indulgence this past year at a resort and spa on Sanibel Island, Florida. After a few days of relaxation, I felt a burst of rejuvenation much like the physical one I feel after a good morning run. Fortunately, you don't have to go to a spa for a mental lift—see pages 16 and 17 for a dozen other suggestions.

Great Recipes and Menus—As Usual

One thing that hasn't changed about *Cooking Light Cookbook* is that it's still jam-packed with more that 300 terrific-tasting recipes and 20 menus that fit into a healthy diet. Each recipe comes with a complete nutritional analysis so you can keep up with calories, fat, and other diet concerns. Here are some of our favorites:

- Tangy Marinated Tomatoes (page 75)
- Brie-Filled Pork Chops with Apple Stuffing (page 159)
- Country Chicken Pot Pie (page 168)
- Fudgy Mint Brownie Dessert (page 237)

Besides recipes, look for these added benefits:

• **Menus made easy.** Find preplanned menus (all photographed) for entertaining, special holidays, and even times when you need something quick and easy.

• **A week's worth of calorie-controlled menus.** If you're following a 1200- or a 1600-calorie-a-day diet to lose, gain, or maintain weight, you'll love the 7-day eating plan we devised for you beginning on page 246.

• **Tips and mini-articles about fitness, food, and nutrition.** Scattered among the recipes are some helpful hints for saving time, cooking techniques, and health and fitness updates. So what's an article about in-line skating safety doing on a page of recipes? The answer's simple—it's a graphic illustration of the way you should live your life for a healthy balance. Your diet, fitness activities, and health practices should work as related components that combine for a healthy lifestyle.

The secret to maintaining good health is to keep your lifestyle exciting and *fun.* We've tried to show you how in this edition of *Cooking Light Cookbook;* I think we've succeeded. So turn the page and let the fun begin....

All the Best to You,

Caroline Grant

Caroline A. Grant, M. S., R.D.

The Way to Wellness

News You Can Use

This year's reports on health studies and findings further confirm what we thought might be true: that we all need to exercise more, to eat more fruits and vegetables, and to increase the amount of calcium in our diets.

It's Never Too Late

Starting an exercise program even in the golden years can help you live longer and feel better. And you don't have to have a rigorous routine; we're talking about walking the dog, planting flowers, or lifting a few dumbbells.

So you've never exercised before in your entire life. You may find it hard to believe, but even if you're already up in years, you'll feel better, get stronger, and reduce your health risks if you start moving now. By moving, we mean doing something—anything—that counts as moderate exercise such as walking, gardening, and the like. Even better news is that you can accumulate the time over the course of the day. Some yard work here, a quick bike ride there, and presto—you've logged in your life-enhancing half hour.

As proof that it's never too late to start exercising, one study found that lifting a few weights helped one group of 72- to 98-year-olds double their muscle strength in just 10 weeks. The participants worked on weight-lifting machines for 45 minutes, three times a week. Besides gaining added strength, they increased walking speed and the ability to climb stairs. Participants also said that they felt less depressed.

The increased muscle strength occurred because strength training exercises actually prevent and even reverse the natural deterioration of muscle mass regardless of age. The exercises also build bone strength—a crucial issue for aging women and men who battle osteoporosis as well as joint injuries.

Need to know more pluses of exercise before you pick up the dumbbells? Then consider that it also promotes a loss of body fat, boosts energy and self-confidence, gives you a greater sense of physical and emotional power, and reduces risk of heart disease, cancer, and diabetes.

Work Out Harder, Live Longer

Although just 30 minutes of moderate activity each day can reduce the risk of disease, some studies show that the harder you work out, the longer you may live.

That was the discovery in one 20-year Harvard study where men who worked out vigorously and regularly had a substantially lower mortality rate than men who engaged in only very moderate exercise. In fact, the more active the participant was, the longer he was likely to live.

The men who had the lowest mortality rates walked at a quick clip (4 to 5 mph) for 45 minutes, five times a week; ran at a 6 to 7 mph pace for a total of three hours per week; cycled for one hour, four times a week; or played one hour of singles tennis, three times a week.

HIGH CHOLESTEROL: WHEN (NOT) TO WORRY

If you're over 70, with high cholesterol and no other symptoms of heart disease, then diet and exercise, instead of drugs, may be the best medicine for you. But for the younger crowd with consistently high cholesterol levels, cholesterol-lowering drugs may be a lifesaver. See how to determine what's right for you.

Keep your blood cholesterol level at 200 milligrams per deciliter (mg/dL) at least until more research is conducted say most experts, including those at the American Heart Association. But new studies suggest that older adults with no other risk factors (such as heart disease, diabetes, or high blood pressure) may not have as much to fear from high cholesterol readings. The key phrase here is *no other risk factors*.

Results from a Yale University study indicate that men and women aged 70 and older with cholesterol readings of 240 (mg/dL) were no more likely to die of heart disease or to be hospitalized with a heart attack or chest pain than those whose cholesterol ranked in the "desirable" range of 200 or less. These findings reinforce those of the Framingham Heart Study which also found no relationship between cholesterol levels and heart attack risk in older adults.

What this means for people over age 75 with consistent cholesterol levels over 240mg/dL *and* no history of coronary artery disease is that simple measures for reducing cholesterol may prove more helpful than the regimented routine recommended for a person in his forties. Daily walks, eating less saturated fat, and eating more fresh produce may be an easier prescription to swallow for these people than the cholesterol-lowering drugs that also may have side effects.

How To Know When You Need Medicine

If you're under 75, take note: Before you decide that you can forego cholesterol-lowering medication, talk to your doctor. More than likely, if your blood cholesterol level is over 220, you exercise, you've adopted a diet of less fat and cholesterol and more high-fiber foods, and your cholesterol level is still high after six months, you'll need to take the medicine.

If that's the case, we now have proof that the medicine can do more than reduce your risk of heart attack—it may save your life. A recent study shows that taking the medicine may add years to your life. A news-breaking Scandinavian study showed a 42 percent lower coronary death rate and a 30 percent lower overall death rate among people who took a cholesterol-lowering drug than those who took a placebo.

> *Walk for Life*
>
> If every American who is currently sedentary would walk, work around the house, or even dance for a total of 30 minutes daily, 250,000 lives could be saved from cancer, heart disease, and diabetes every year.

A *Little* Wine Remains Divine...

You've heard that *moderate* alcohol consumption may protect against heart disease. For those who do drink, that translates into one drink a day for women and one or two drinks a day for men for the heart-protective effect. (One drink equals 12 ounces of beer, 4 ounces of wine, or 1½ ounces of 80-proof spirits.) And, despite red wine's reputation as being "better for you," protective properties against coronary artery disease are about the same in beer, wine, or spirits.

Why Vegetarians Are Healthier

Vegetarians eat more fruits and vegetables, and the payoff is better health. Here's why.

If you need one more piece of evidence to convince you that a diet high in fruits and vegetables is good for you, here it is: According to British scientists, vegetarians are 20 percent less likely to die of heart disease and 40 percent less apt to die of cancer than people who eat meat.

In a Harvard study, middle-aged men who ate a lot of fruits and vegetables were significantly less likely to suffer strokes than other men. In fact, increasing produce intake to three servings a day equals a 20 percent drop in the risk of stroke. These results parallel findings reported a few years ago about women who ate a diet high in spinach, carrots, and other fruits and vegetables rich in antioxidant nutrients; they had a 54 percent lower risk of stroke than other women.

Experts say that the clearest benefit of a vegetarian diet appears to be a reduced risk of coronary artery disease, which can be attributed to vegetarians' lower blood cholesterol levels and lower blood pressure. It helps that vegetarians tend to stay at healthier weights than do nonvegetarians, another factor that reduces heart disease risk. In fact, research at the University of California at San Francisco found that switching to a very low-fat vegetarian diet may even help reverse the effects of atherosclerosis.

HOW TO GET MORE CALCIUM

Last year the National Institute of Health told us to consume more calcium to curb the osteoporosis epidemic. Here's how much you need and where to get it.

If we're to rid an aging population of osteoporosis, then we need to start consuming more calcium at an earlier age; but even consuming more later in life can help.

Remember, to absorb calcium, you need an adequate amount of vitamin D. You'll find it in four glasses of vitamin-D-fortified milk and most ordinary multivitamins, or from 10 to 15 minutes of exposure to sunlight.

According to the National Institute of Health, here's how much calcium you need each day.

• Children and young adults ages 11 through 24 years: 1,200 to 1,500 milligrams (mg)

• Men 25+ and women 25 to 50+: 1,000 mg

• Postmenopausal women and all women 65+: 1,000 to 1,500 mg (Postmenopausal women not taking estrogen supplements need 1,500 mg.)

Best Calcium Sources:

• Low-fat milk, cheese, and yogurt. Three (8-ounce) glasses of skim milk a day give you 900 mg calcium.

• Green leafy vegetables.

• Broccoli, beans, canned sardines, canned salmon (with bones), fortified citrus juices, and molasses.

Easy Ways to Add Calcium

Here are four quick and easy ways to get a little more calcium in your diet:

1. Add powdered milk to mashed potatoes, casseroles, sauces, and soups.

2. Eat more yogurt. Yogurt has about 100 mg more calcium per 8 ounces than milk.

3. Cook oatmeal in low-fat milk instead of water.

4. Drink calcium-fortified orange juice every morning.

Know Your Nutrition Needs

How to Make Our Recipes Work for You

You've seen the handy nutrient grid with each recipe. By using the grid in combination with the Daily Nutrition Guide numbers below, you'll find it easy to follow a healthy eating plan.

DAILY NUTRITION GUIDE			
	Women Ages 25 to 50	Women Over 50	Men Over 24
Calories	2,000	2,000 or less	2,700
Protein	50g*	50g or less	63g
Fat	67g or less	67g or less	90g or less
Saturated Fat	22g or less	22g or less	30g or less
Carbohydrates	299g	299g	405g
Fiber	25g to 35g	25g to 35g	25g to 35g
Cholesterol	300mg** or less	300mg or less	300mg or less
Iron	15mg	10mg	10mg
Sodium	3,300mg or less	3,300mg or less	3,300mg or less
Calcium	800mg	800mg	800mg

* grams is abbreviated throughout the book as g
** milligrams is abbreviated throughout the book as mg

Just remember that calorie requirements may vary according to your size, weight, and activity level; the recommendations in the chart are simply an estimate of the number of calories you need to maintain your present weight. If you use the chart's calorie guide yet gain weight, decrease your calorie intake over time in 500-calorie increments until your weight levels off. To gain weight, do the opposite—just increase calories in your daily diet by 500-calorie increments until you reach your goal.

The calorie calculation and nutrient values in the nutrient grid with each recipe are taken from a computer analysis based on U.S. Department of Agriculture figures and the following guidelines:

• We use the lesser amount of an ingredient for nutrient calculation when a range (such as 3 to 4 cups flour) is given.

• The analysis reflects the fact that some alcohol evaporates during cooking.

• Only the amount of marinade absorbed by the food is used to determine nutrient values.

• We don't include garnishes or optional ingredients in the analysis.

Count Your Grams

We now know that for optimum health, limiting your fat intake is as important as keeping up with the calories you eat. One easy way to keep up with your fat intake is to count fat grams. To do this, first determine your appropriate calorie level. Use the calorie level listed in the Daily Nutrition Guide (left) or multiply your present weight by 15 for an estimate. Then check the Daily Fat Limit chart below to find out the maximum number of fat grams you should consume daily based on the number of calories you eat. Then start counting.

To find out how much fat you're eating, check the number of grams in the nutrient grid following each recipe in this book. See the Calorie/Nutrient Chart (pages 250-262) for fat gram figures for individual food items.

DAILY FAT LIMIT	
Calories Per Day	Grams of Fat
1,200	40
1,500	50
1,800	60
2,000	67
2,200	73
2,500	83
2,800	93

Profiles in Fitness

Take a tip from these folks—they've found the key to fitness: activities they love. To help each of them reach their personal fitness goals, we asked for suggestions from Carol Garber, Ph.D., exercise physiologist and director of training and testing for cardiovascular fitness at Memorial Hospital in Rhode Island. Perhaps you'll find inspiration for your own fitness fun in these profiles.

Gung-Ho Gardener, Amy Cuthbert

This 43-year-old freelance graphic designer lives with her husband and young daughter in a Chicago suburb and is a passionate gardener. Amy gardens every day—spring, summer, and fall. And in winter, gardening is a "mental workout" as she plans for next season. When she's not gardening, she and her husband work on renovating their home, which involves tearing down walls, bagging plaster, and cutting wood. Amy's daily exercise includes keeping up with her active 4-year-old, doing housework with vigor, and walking instead of driving whenever possible.

Amy's Fitness Goals: To be healthy, to maintain her weight, and to stay in shape.

Her Fitness Benefits: Bending, lifting, and stretching from gardening and renovating her house keep Amy's muscles toned and flexible. She gets aerobic benefits from using a push-mower, dragging bags of peat moss, and walking at a good clip. And Amy says that the relaxation gardening provides lowers her blood pressure.

Fitness Prescription:
• Start a formalized walking program of three 30-minute walks a week to boost fitness and to provide more intensive cardiovascular exercise.
  • Work out at home on an exercise bike or treadmill during winter months.
  • Do stretching exercises for the back, shoulders, and legs before digging, lifting, and hauling to relieve muscle stress.

Weekend Warrior, Bob Delano

At 52, this executive, who lives near Boston with his wife and college-age son, finds himself on the links with a golf club in hand every weekend. He plays 18 holes on Saturday and Sunday, and gets in a quick nine holes early on Friday mornings in the summer months. As a devoted walker, he always walks the golf course and also walks about six miles a week with his wife. When Bob isn't golfing or walking, he rounds out his exercise regimen with half-hour workouts on stair-climber and treadmill machines.

Bob's Fitness Goals: To maintain a routine he enjoys and to lose 20 pounds.

His Fitness Benefits: Walking and using the stair-climber and a treadmill tones Bob's leg muscles and improves his cardiovascular endurance. Golfing also improves the flexibility in Bob's arms and shoulders.

Fitness Prescription:
• To lose weight, add a daily, 30-minute calorie-burning workout such as three miles of brisk walking or a half-hour on the exercise equipment on nongolfing days.
• Add 10 minutes each on a ski machine and a stationary bike, and add some upper body exercises to make gym workouts more interesting.

All-Around Active, Peg Gignoux

Peg is a 37-year-old artist who lives in Chapel Hill, North Carolina, with her husband and two children, ages nine and ten. Already a lifetime recreational swimmer, Peg took her swimming to the next level four years ago when she began working out for one hour, three times a week with the North Carolina Aquatic Masters swim team at the University of North Carolina at Chapel Hill Natatorium. She rounds out her exercise regimen with family activities like rollerblading, gardening, walking, and renovating the school playground.

Peg's Fitness Goals: To build lower body strength and to compete in the swimming portion of a triathalon.

Her Fitness Benefits: Peg's exercise routine has helped her to lose 20 pounds and to increase her upper body strength in the past year. Swimming at the competitive level has given her a sleek physique and a great lung capacity, "especially for someone who smoked for 10 years."

Fitness Prescription:
• Begin cycling or walking for 30 minutes at least twice weekly to increase leg strength and to add to her cardiovascular training.
• Work to build walking speed and increase cycling proficiency to improve endurance needed for a triathalon.

Elite Exerciser, Heidi Zimmerman

This single 32-year-old sales representative living in northern California is a super-active athlete. As a trail runner, she gets in four 40-minute runs during the week and a 90-minute run on Sundays. Her weekly athletic agenda also includes two full-body weight workouts at the gym and playing roller hockey. She goes mountain biking a couple of times a month, completes one marathon every year, and snow skis.

Heidi's Fitness Goals: To stay fit and to complete a 50-kilometer run in eight to ten hours.

Her Fitness Benefits: By balancing aerobic activities and strength training, Heidi stays strong, toned, and fit enough to try any sport. Heidi says the year-round training also relieves stress which counters her "hyper" personality.

Fitness Prescription:
• Gradually increase the length of daily runs.
• Try water running at the gym for an additional cardiovascular workout without risk of injury.
• Add a few minutes of stretching after warm-ups, paying particular attention to legs, ankles, and hips, to lessen chances for injury.

A Dozen Ways to Pamper Yourself

The secret of success with any self-improvement program is to do it out of self-love, not self-loathing. When you put on eye cream, do it because you love your skin, not because you hate your wrinkles. Think of pampering as making a fuss over yourself, and soon you'll find the habits of staying fit and taking care of yourself infused with pleasure.

1 Get a massage—The deep release from a massage is not only physical, but also mental and emotional, as is the feeling of well-being that comes in its wake. One hour on the table of a skilled masseuse will show you why massage is an essential part of the daily routine at upscale health spas.

2 Have a facial—Treat yourself to the feeling of gentle fingertips smoothing lotions and potions onto your face; to cool, rich creams and fragrant clouds of steam; to an hour of peace and luxury. You'll feel like a movie star, and your skin will glow for days.

3 Try Aromatherapy—Good smells work subtle magic on your psyche. Boil a pot of water on the cooktop, and drop in a bag of cinnamon tea or loose potpourri to steep. Dab a little essential oil on your throat. Have the interior of your car cleaned and scented. Buy a bouquet of fresh flowers—tuberoses, freesia, and gardenias are among the most fragrant.

4 Spruce up your meals—Whatever you eat, make it beautiful. Buy yourself a gorgeous, oversized plate. Garnish your meal with edible flowers like nasturtiums and violets. Drink iced tea from a goblet. Use a cloth napkin, even if (especially if) you're dining alone.

5 Buy the best—Whether your choice is fresh-roasted coffee beans, organic vegetables, or fresh-squeezed juice, giving yourself the best makes food seem like a luxury. So splurge and buy a bottle of fancy imported mineral water to drink with dinner. Sound too extravagant? Just remember—you're worth it.

9 *Get fashion fit*—Remember how you felt about new sneakers when you were a kid? Well, it still works. A pair of pristine white running shoes, snazzy new aerobics or biking shorts, or a bright-colored warm-up suit really does make you feel like kicking up your heels.

10 *Go for glamour*—Get your hair cut, colored, permed, or Frenchbraided. Have a manicure and a pedicure, whether it's for a special night out on the town, for a big meeting, or just for fun.

6 *Take a bubble bath*—A moisturizing bubble bath is an inexpensive, readily available way to relax. Light a candle, pour a glass of white wine (if you wish), get a novel or the latest issue of your favorite magazine, and put on some relaxing music. Is there a more luscious way to spend an hour alone?

11 *Buy yourself a present*—Set aside a few dollars to buy yourself a sensual, nonfood treat: a silk chemise, bath salts, or bright lipstick. How about satin sheets (or maybe you prefer flannel) or a superlarge, extraplush bath towel?

7 *Find a new place to relax*—Serve yourself breakfast in bed on a tray that's complete with the daily newspaper and a bud vase, or grab a tall, refreshing drink along with the latest best-seller, and escape to a porch swing or hammock.

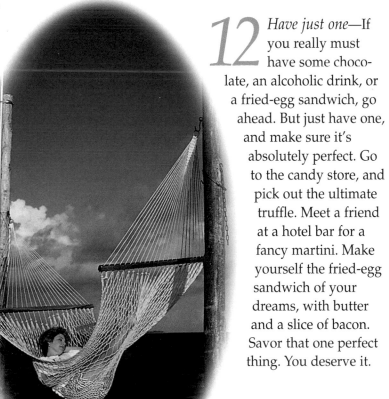

12 *Have just one*—If you really must have some chocolate, an alcoholic drink, or a fried-egg sandwich, go ahead. But just have one, and make sure it's absolutely perfect. Go to the candy store, and pick out the ultimate truffle. Meet a friend at a hotel bar for a fancy martini. Make yourself the fried-egg sandwich of your dreams, with butter and a slice of bacon. Savor that one perfect thing. You deserve it.

8 *Make a fitness date*—Call a friend you haven't seen for a while or one you spend hours gabbing with on the phone, and make plans to walk or ride bikes in the early morning or during your lunch hour. This is such a pleasant, easy way to work out that it just may become a weekly ritual.

What's New in the Marketplace?

SHOES FOR WALKING OFF THE BEATEN PATH

If you'd rather do your walking on country roads, greenways, rock-strewn paths, or other unpaved surfaces, then check out the new walking shoe designed for the rugged road you travel. Rugged Walkers, made by Merrell Footwear, are waterproof shoes designed for greater stability and traction than traditional sneakers. But they don't have the stiff, cumbersome feel of hiking boots. Models for men and women come in several styles and range in price from $70 to $120. And as an added bonus, the company provides charts that not only help you measure your fitness level, but also help you plan walking exercise programs tailored to your determined fitness level. The charts are free, and they'll send them to you upon request. Just write to Merrell Footwear, P.O. Box 4249, Burlington, VT 05406.

BURGERS THAT COULD FOOL A VEGETARIAN

Now you can invite a vegetarian friend over for burgers. Green Giant's Harvest Burger or Boca Burger Company's Boca Burger (made primarily from soy protein) are now in the freezer section of most major grocery stores. These 100% meatless specialty burgers boast only 4.5 grams or less of fat per patty. That's compared to the average 11 grams of fat in a 3-ounce turkey burger.

We sampled the burgers and other dishes made from the bulk form of the Boca product in our test kitchen. Here are our verdicts.

• The Boca Burger original was our favorite.

• Green Giant's Italian-style and Southwestern-style Harvest Burgers are pretty good, too.

• Grilled or pan-fried (both brands) is better than baked or microwaved.

• Boca Burger Company's bulk form of the product is a good replacement for ground beef in tacos and spaghetti. In fact, we hardly knew the beef was missing in our Boca-stuffed tacos.

Is Fat-Free Margarine Better?

Generally speaking, no. Most of the fat-free margarines we tried got a quick thumbs down. But one—Fleishmann's Fat-Free Low-Calorie Spread—was worth a second sampling. Unlike the others, which were too salty and had a chemical taste, this one possessed a pleasant sweet-salty blend of flavors, spread well on toast or pancakes, and mixed well with potatoes and other vegetables.

Look for Fleishmann's fat-free spread in the dairy case in most grocery stores. Just remember to use it (and other fat-free brands you may like) only for a flavor topping. It won't work for baking or frying.

For a lower-fat alternative for sautéing, there is a fat-free choice with I Can't Believe It's Not Butter! Spray. It has 0 grams fat in 4 full sprays. Use it for basting or pump it right onto a bowlful of popcorn. You can find it in the dairy case in most supermarkets.

LUNCHEON MEATS GO FAT FREE
(Really)

It really happened. Now you can put sausage in your grocery cart, throw hot dogs on the grill, and slap bologna on a sandwich without guilt. Some of the new fat-free luncheon meats taste pretty good and won't bust your fat and calorie budget.

We were a bit skeptical about these products, so we shipped in some to taste for ourselves. Several passed our critical tastebuds. But if you're watching sodium in your diet, you need to know that these meats are just as high or higher in sodium than higher-fat counterparts.

Our favorites were Oscar Mayer's fat-free oven-roasted turkey, and Butterball's fat-free hot dogs, fat-free bologna, and fat-free smoked sausage and kielbasa sausage. The sausages tasted salty, but you could use either in a recipe like red beans and rice, and the flavor would be just fine.

EGGS ON THE PANTRY SHELF

Worried about the dangers of undercooked eggs? You'll welcome Just Whites, a shelf-stable all-natural egg white powder that can be used to replace eggs or egg whites in recipes. The powder is pasteurized, so there's no need to cook it to reduce the risk of salmonella.

But the real test is how well it works in recipes. Here's what we found in our kitchens.

• It works great in muffins.

• It makes a nice meringue. When mixed with water, it whips up to a high volume and looks pretty on top of a pie. Some of our tasters did detect a slight citrus flavor in the meringue, though.

• Think twice before using the powder in soufflés or chiffon mixtures. We tried it in a soufflé and a chiffon pie, and both developed a dense, custard-like layer at the bottom.

Just Whites is available in 8-ounce canisters, and will keep up to 5 years on the shelf. You can order by mail from Deb-El Foods, 2 Papetti Plaza, Elizabeth, NJ 07206, or call 800-773-8822 for a catalog source.

How to Perfect Chicken Pot Pie

Can chicken pot pie taste like Mom's without all the fat and calories?
You bet! Read on to see how.

We turned this traditionally high-fat family favorite into a healthier one by making simple substitutions and by using low-fat cooking techniques that you can use in your own recipes. Here's what we did.

• Substituted a low-fat biscuit topping for a fat-laden double crust to cut 288 calories, 26 grams of fat, and 7.5 grams of saturated fat from each serving. (The low-fat biscuit and baking mix does have the same amount of sodium as the regular mix, so if you're watching your sodium, see the low-sodium biscuit topping idea on page 168.)

• Used skinned chicken breast halves instead of a broiler-fryer and skimmed the fat from the broth used for the sauce to reduce fat.

• Replaced butter with evaporated skimmed milk in the sauce mixture to shave 6 grams of fat from each serving. This substitution boosts the calcium from 45 milligrams to 191 milligrams per serving.

• Decreased the salt in the chicken-vegetable mixture.

• Added potato, onion, and celery to the filling to make it heartier and more flavorful.

Before   Chicken Pot Pie

1	(3- to 3½-pound) broiler-fryer, cut up		8	to 10 tablespoons cold water
9	cups water		¼	cup butter
1	(20-ounce) package frozen mixed vegetables		½	cup all-purpose flour
3¾	cups all-purpose flour		1½	teaspoons salt
1¼	teaspoons salt		¼	to ½ teaspoon pepper
1¼	cups shortening		⅛	teaspoon ground nutmeg
			1	tablespoon butter, melted

Calories: 727
Percentage of Calories from Fat: 51%

Cholesterol: 74mg
Sodium: 966mg

After   Country Chicken Pot Pie

2	pounds skinned chicken breast halves		1	(10-ounce) package frozen mixed vegetables
4	sprigs fresh parsley		⅔	cup all-purpose flour
3	stalks celery, cut into 2-inch pieces		1	(12-ounce) can evaporated skimmed milk, divided
1	small onion, quartered		½	teaspoon poultry seasoning
1	bay leaf		½	teaspoon salt
5	cups water		¼	teaspoon pepper
	Vegetable cooking spray		¼	teaspoon dried thyme
1	cup chopped onion		2	cups low-fat biscuit and baking mix
¾	cup diced celery		2	tablespoons chopped fresh parsley
1½	cups peeled, cubed potato		¾	cup 1% low-fat milk

Calories: 384
Percentage of Calories from Fat: 8%

Cholesterol: 55mg
Sodium: 796mg

Look for the complete recipe for Country Chicken Pot Pie on page 168.

Uncork the Virtues of Vinegar

Lots of flavor, no fat. With that winning combination, it's worth paying a little extra for a bottle of flavored vinegar or taking the time to make your own.

It's a flavor secret professional cooks have used for years—a splash of raspberry vinegar in salad dressing, a spoonful of herbed vinegar in beef stew. Until recently, flavored vinegars have seemed too "gourmet" for the average cook. You could buy them only from cooks' catalogs or specialty food shops. But now the secret's out. Fruit and herb vinegars line the shelves in most supermarkets. You pay a little more for them than for regular distilled vinegars, but the flavor's worth it. Once flavored vinegars become a staple in your kitchen, you'll want to make your own since you'll save money and the process can take as little as 10 minutes. Turn to page 208 to see how.

Turn to page 208 to see how.

Ways to Use Flavored Vinegars

- Use in marinades to tenderize and flavor meats.
- Substitute for plain vinegar in salad dressing or vinaigrette recipes.
- Splash over steamed or stir-fried vegetables.
- Substitute for lemon juice.
- Toss fresh berries with a few tablespoons of sugar and a sprinkle of fruit vinegar.
- Use to marinate cucumber slices and carrot slices overnight in the refrigerator.
- Combine with nonfat or low-fat mayonnaise, sour cream, or yogurt to make a fast dip.
- Enliven soups and stews with a dash of herb vinegar.
- Blend equal parts of fruit vinegar and honey for a quick dressing for melon.
- Accent Bloody Marys or chilled tomato juice with a dash of herb vinegar.
- Add a dash of herb vinegar instead of salt to cooked beans or peas.

Warm Peaches and Cream Cereal and Sausage-Cheese Muffins (Menu begins on page 24.)

Breakfast
& Brunch

A Country Inn Breakfast

Warm Peaches and Cream Cereal
Swiss Muesli
Chocolate Chip Streusel Cake
Sausage-Cheese Muffins
Vanilla-Glazed Fruit
Orange Juice

Serves 6

Maybe your family or house guests are like guests that check into bed-and-breakfast inns—they wander to the kitchen in shifts. If so, here's a meal that's ready when they are.

Let them choose one of the cereals or the streusel cake. With either of these choices a muffin, fruit, and ½ cup orange juice completes a meal that contains an average of 450 calories. So keep the coffee hot and the kitchen open . . . breakfast is served anytime.

Vanilla-Glazed Fruit (page 26) and Chocolate Chip Streusel Cake

Warm Peaches and Cream Cereal

(pictured on page 23)

1   (16-ounce) can sliced peaches in juice, undrained
3   cups skim milk
2   tablespoons sugar
⅛   teaspoon salt
¾   cup farina, uncooked
¼   cup firmly packed brown sugar
¼   cup vanilla low-fat yogurt
1½ tablespoons finely chopped pecans, toasted

Drain peaches, reserving ¾ cup juice. Combine juice, half of sliced peaches, and milk in container of an electric blender; cover and process until smooth. Set aside remaining sliced peaches.

Combine pureed peach mixture, 2 tablespoons sugar, and salt in a saucepan; bring to a boil. Add farina in a slow, steady stream, stirring constantly; reduce heat, and simmer, stirring constantly, 2 minutes or until thickened.

Spoon cereal mixture into 6 (10-ounce) custard cups. Sprinkle brown sugar over cereal mixture. Place cups on a baking sheet. Broil 5½ inches from heat (with electric oven door partially opened) 1 minute or until sugar melts.

Spoon reserved peaches over each serving; top each serving evenly with yogurt and pecans. Serve immediately. Yield: 6 servings (240 calories per serving).

Per Serving:

Fat 2.6g	Carbohydrate 46.6g	Fiber 1.2g
saturated fat 0.4g	Cholesterol 3mg	Iron 8.2mg
Protein 7.7g	Sodium 200mg	Calcium 291mg

Swiss Muesli

Muesli is European-style granola. Mix it with milk and let it sit overnight to create a creamy texture similar to cooked oatmeal.

2¼   cups regular oats, uncooked
2¼   cups skim milk
3   tablespoons brown sugar
3   tablespoons raisins
¼   teaspoon salt
1½   cups vanilla low-fat yogurt
3½   tablespoons chopped pecans

Combine first 5 ingredients in a medium bowl, stirring well. Cover and chill 8 hours. Stir in yogurt. Spoon into individual bowls; sprinkle with chopped pecans. Yield: 6 servings (271 calories per ¾-cup serving).

Per Serving:

Fat 6.3g	Carbohydrate 43.9g	Fiber 3.7g
saturated fat 1.2g	Cholesterol 5mg	Iron 1.7mg
Protein 11.3g	Sodium 187mg	Calcium 236mg

Chocolate Chip Streusel Cake

¼   cup plus 2 tablespoons firmly packed
       brown sugar
¼   cup plus 1 tablespoon all-purpose flour
1   teaspoon ground cinnamon
1½   tablespoons margarine
¼   cup plus 2 tablespoons semisweet
       chocolate mini-morsels
⅓   cup margarine, softened
¾   cup sugar
¾   cup frozen egg substitute, thawed
3   cups sifted cake flour
2   teaspoons baking powder
¼   teaspoon salt
¾   cup skim milk
2½   teaspoons vanilla extract
       Vegetable cooking spray

Combine first 3 ingredients in a small bowl; cut in 1½ tablespoons margarine with a pastry blender until mixture resembles coarse meal. Add mini-morsels; toss well. Set aside.

Beat ⅓ cup margarine at medium speed of an electric mixer until creamy. Gradually add ¾ cup sugar, beating well. Add egg substitute; beat well.

Combine cake flour, baking powder, and salt; add to margarine mixture alternately with skim milk, beginning and ending with flour mixture. Mix after each addition. Stir in vanilla.

Pour half of batter into an 8-inch springform pan coated with cooking spray. Sprinkle half of brown sugar mixture over batter. Pour remaining batter over brown sugar mixture in pan; top with remaining brown sugar mixture. Bake at 350° for 50 minutes or until cake springs back when lightly touched. Cool in pan 10 minutes; remove sides of pan, and let cake cool completely on a wire rack. Yield: 18 servings (191 calories per serving).

Per Serving:

Fat 5.8g	Carbohydrate 31.7g	Fiber 0.5g
saturated fat 1.6g	Cholesterol 0mg	Iron 1.9mg
Protein 3.3g	Sodium 106mg	Calcium 57mg

Sausage-Cheese Muffins

(pictured on page 23)

Vegetable cooking spray
⅓ pound freshly ground raw turkey
    breakfast sausage
¼ cup chopped green pepper
¼ cup chopped green onions
1 cup all-purpose flour
¼ cup cornmeal
1 teaspoon baking soda
¼ teaspoon salt
⅛ teaspoon ground red pepper
1 cup nonfat buttermilk
2 teaspoons margarine, melted
1 egg, beaten
⅓ cup (1.3 ounces) shredded reduced-fat
    sharp Cheddar cheese

Coat a nonstick skillet with cooking spray.
Place over medium heat until hot. Add sausage,
green pepper, and green onions. Cook until
sausage browns, stirring until it crumbles; drain,
if necessary.

Combine flour and next 4 ingredients in a bowl;
make a well in center of mixture. Combine buttermilk, margarine, and egg; add to dry ingredients,
stirring just until dry ingredients are moistened.
Gently fold in sausage mixture and cheese.

Spoon batter into muffin pans coated with
cooking spray, filling two-thirds full. Bake at 400°
for 20 minutes or until golden. Remove muffins
from pans immediately. Yield: 12 muffins (96 calories each).

Per Muffin:		
Fat 3.1g	Carbohydrate 11.6g	Fiber 0.7g
saturated fat 1.0g	Cholesterol 28mg	Iron 0.9mg
Protein 5.6g	Sodium 309mg	Calcium 60mg

Vanilla-Glazed Fruit

1 small cantaloupe, peeled and thinly
    sliced
1 vanilla bean, split lengthwise
¼ cup low-sugar apple spread
2 tablespoons unsweetened apple juice
1½ cups fresh strawberries, halved
2 plums, pitted and thinly sliced
1 kiwifruit, peeled and cut into 12 wedges

Arrange cantaloupe slices on individual serving
plates; cover and chill.

Scrape seeds from vanilla bean into a medium
bowl; set aside.

Combine apple spread and apple juice in a
small saucepan, stirring well. Cook mixture over
low heat until apple spread melts, stirring frequently. Add apple mixture to vanilla seeds, stirring well.

Add strawberries, plums, and kiwifruit to apple
mixture; toss gently to coat. Cover and chill thoroughly. To serve, spoon glazed fruit over cantaloupe slices. Yield: 6 servings (95 calories per
serving).

Per Serving:		
Fat 0.7g	Carbohydrate 22.6g	Fiber 3.5g
saturated fat 0.2g	Cholesterol 0mg	Iron 0.5mg
Protein 1.7g	Sodium 12mg	Calcium 25mg

Don't Blame the Genes

According to new research from the Center for
Developmental and Health Genetics at Pennsylvania
State University, low-fat diets and active lifestyles
make a bigger impact on cholesterol levels among
middle-aged people than does their genetic profile.

Mountain Breakfast

Silver Dollar Pancakes
Sugared Turkey Bacon
Blueberry Applesauce
Spiced Fruit Tea

Serves 6
TOTAL CALORIES PER SERVING: 470
(Calories from Fat: 12%)

The mountain air is crisp and inviting, and you're geared up for a day out-of-doors. Fuel up first with a hearty breakfast that will keep you going strong until lunchtime.

Arrange 6 pancakes on each plate and dust them with powdered sugar; top each serving with 2 tablespoons of Blueberry Applesauce. A slice of Sugared Turkey Bacon and a mug of hot tea round out the meal.

Silver Dollar Pancakes and Blueberry Applesauce (page 28)

Silver Dollar Pancakes

2   cups all-purpose flour
1   tablespoon baking powder
⅛   teaspoon salt
2   tablespoons sugar
1¼   cups skim milk
½   cup low-fat sour cream
2   egg whites, lightly beaten
1   egg, lightly beaten
   Vegetable cooking spray
1   tablespoon sifted powdered sugar
   Fresh blueberries (optional)

Combine first 4 ingredients in a medium bowl; make a well in center of mixture. Combine milk, sour cream, egg whites, and egg. Add milk mixture to dry ingredients, stirring just until dry ingredients are moistened.

Coat a nonstick griddle with cooking spray, and preheat to 350°. For each pancake, pour 1 heaping tablespoon batter onto hot griddle. Cook pancakes until tops are covered with bubbles and edges look cooked; turn pancakes, and cook other side. Sprinkle pancakes with powdered sugar. Garnish with fresh blueberries, if desired. Yield: 36 (2½-inch) pancakes (40 calories each).

Per Pancake:

Fat 0.6g	Carbohydrate 6.9g	Fiber 0.2g
saturated fat 0.3g	Cholesterol 8mg	Iron 0.4mg
Protein 1.5g	Sodium 19mg	Calcium 38mg

Sugared Turkey Bacon

1   tablespoon brown sugar
1   tablespoon frozen egg substitute, thawed
1½ teaspoons low-sodium Worcestershire sauce
1½ teaspoons spicy brown mustard
6   slices turkey bacon
½   cup fine, dry breadcrumbs

Combine first 4 ingredients in a shallow bowl, stirring well. Dip each slice of bacon into sugar mixture; dredge in breadcrumbs. Place bacon slices on rack of a broiler pan.

Bake at 350° for 20 to 25 minutes or until bacon is crisp. Yield: 6 slices (78 calories each).

Per Slice:

Fat 2.6g	Carbohydrate 9.0g	Fiber 0.4g
saturated fat 0.6g	Cholesterol 10mg	Iron 0.7mg
Protein 3.6g	Sodium 307mg	Calcium 25mg

Blueberry Applesauce

For chunky applesauce, process less than six seconds.
For smooth, process longer.

2 cups peeled, diced cooking apple
1 cup fresh or frozen blueberries, thawed
⅓ cup unsweetened orange juice
2 tablespoons sugar
1 teaspoon grated orange rind

Combine all ingredients in a medium saucepan, stirring well. Bring to a boil; cover, reduce heat, and simmer 15 minutes or until apple is tender. Cool slightly.

Position knife blade in food processor bowl; add apple mixture. Process 8 seconds or until almost smooth. Transfer mixture to a bowl. Cover and chill thoroughly. Yield: 1¾ cups (12 calories per tablespoon).

Per Tablespoon:

Fat 0.1g	Carbohydrate 3.0g	Fiber 0.4g
saturated fat 0.0g	Cholesterol 0mg	Iron 0mg
Protein 0.1g	Sodium 0mg	Calcium 1mg

Spiced Fruit Tea

2   cups unsweetened orange juice
2   cups unsweetened pineapple juice
¼   cup honey
¾   teaspoon whole cloves
¼   teaspoon whole allspice
2   (3-inch) sticks cinnamon, broken in half
2   cups water
3   regular-size tea bags
   Orange wedges studded with cloves (optional)

Combine first 3 ingredients in a saucepan, stirring well. Place cloves, allspice, and cinnamon sticks in a 6-inch square of cheesecloth; tie with string. Add spice bag to fruit juice mixture. Bring to a boil; cover, reduce heat, and simmer 30 minutes. Remove and discard spice bag.

Bring 2 cups water to a boil in a medium saucepan. Add tea bags; remove from heat. Cover and steep 15 minutes. Remove and discard tea bags. Combine tea and juice mixture, stirring well. Serve warm. Garnish with orange wedges studded with cloves, if desired. Yield: 6 cups (128 calories per 1-cup serving).

Per Serving:

Fat 0.1g	Carbohydrate 32.4g	Fiber 0.2g
saturated fat 0.0g	Cholesterol 0mg	Iron 0.4mg
Protein 0.9g	Sodium 2mg	Calcium 22mg

Seasoned Alaskan Salmon (page 30), Poached Pineapple in Yukon Jack (page 31), Sourdough and Mushroom Strata (page 30), and Cranberry-Orange Cider (page 31)

An Alaskan Brunch

Seasoned Alaskan Salmon
Sourdough and Mushroom Strata
Poached Pineapple in Yukon Jack
Cranberry-Orange Cider

Serves 4
TOTAL CALORIES PER SERVING: 609
(Calories from Fat: 14%)

America's last frontier may be rugged territory, but you can use its finest flavors for an elegant brunch menu. Fresh Alaskan salmon, sourdough bread, Yukon Jack (orange liqueur), and fresh cranberries combine to make a hearty menu as grand as the region itself.

Add a little fun to the Alaskan theme of your party. Check out a book about the state from the library, and scribble little-known facts on the backs of placecards. Let each guest share their own tidbit about Alaska while sampling the state's indigenous flavors.

Seasoned Alaskan Salmon

1   (12-ounce) salmon fillet
¼   teaspoon cracked black pepper
⅛   teaspoon salt
⅛   teaspoon paprika
⅛   teaspoon ground red pepper
    Vegetable cooking spray
⅓   cup thinly sliced shallots
1   ounce reduced-fat, low-salt ham, cut into
        ¼-inch-wide strips
¾   cup canned no-salt-added chicken broth,
        undiluted
1   tablespoon dark brown sugar
    Fresh thyme sprigs (optional)

Cut salmon fillet into 4 equal pieces. Sprinkle cracked pepper, salt, paprika, and ground red pepper evenly over salmon pieces, and set salmon aside.

Coat a large nonstick skillet with cooking spray; place over medium-high heat until hot. Add shallots and ham; sauté 2 minutes or until shallots are tender. Add salmon fillets to skillet; cook 4 minutes. Turn fillets, and cook 2 minutes; add broth and brown sugar. Bring to a boil; cook 4 minutes or until fish flakes easily when tested with a fork. Transfer fillets to individual serving plates. Spoon ham mixture evenly over fillets. Garnish with fresh thyme sprigs, if desired. Yield: 4 servings (151 calories per serving).

Per Serving:

Fat 5.9g	Carbohydrate 4.4g	Fiber 0.1g
saturated fat 1.0g	Cholesterol 50mg	Iron 0.9mg
Protein 18.5g	Sodium 168mg	Calcium 17mg

Sourdough and Mushroom Strata

6   (1¾-ounce) sourdough rolls, divided
2   tablespoons grated Parmesan cheese
1   cup sliced fresh crimini mushrooms
1   cup sliced fresh shiitake mushrooms
¼   cup sliced green onions
⅓   cup canned no-salt-added chicken broth,
        undiluted
1   tablespoon finely chopped fresh thyme
2   cloves garlic, minced
    Vegetable cooking spray
1   tablespoon all-purpose flour
1   cup skim milk
¼   cup frozen egg substitute, thawed
¼   teaspoon salt
¼   teaspoon freshly ground pepper

Tear 1 sourdough roll into small pieces. Position knife blade in food processor bowl; add sourdough roll pieces. Process until crumbs form. Combine 2 tablespoons breadcrumbs and Parmesan cheese in a large bowl, stirring well; set aside. Reserve remaining breadcrumbs for another use. Cut remaining 5 rolls into 1-inch cubes. Add bread cubes to breadcrumb mixture; set aside.

Combine crimini mushrooms and next 5 ingredients in a large nonstick skillet. Bring to a boil over medium-high heat. Cover, reduce heat, and simmer 5 minutes. Uncover and simmer 5 minutes or until liquid evaporates; remove from heat. Add mushroom mixture to bread mixture, tossing gently. Spoon bread mixture into a 1-quart casserole dish coated with cooking spray, and set aside.

Combine flour and milk, stirring until smooth. Stir in egg substitute, salt, and pepper.

Pour milk mixture over bread mixture in casserole dish. Cover and bake at 325° for 20 minutes. Uncover and bake 20 minutes or until set. Let stand 5 minutes before serving. Yield: 4 servings (231 calories per serving).

Per Serving:

Fat 2.8g	Carbohydrate 38.8g	Fiber 3.0g
saturated fat 0.6g	Cholesterol 3mg	Iron 2.7mg
Protein 13.8g	Sodium 453mg	Calcium 140mg

Poached Pineapple in Yukon Jack

If Yukon Jack is unavailable, substitute Triple Sec or another orange-flavored liqueur.

1 small fresh pineapple, peeled and cored
3 tablespoons firmly packed brown sugar
3 tablespoons Yukon Jack
2 tablespoons water
½ teaspoon grated orange rind
¼ cup fresh blueberries
¼ cup fresh raspberries

Cut pineapple into 12 (¼-inch-thick) slices, and set aside. Reserve remaining pineapple for another use.

Combine sugar, Yukon Jack, and water in a large nonstick skillet; cook over low heat, stirring constantly, until sugar dissolves. Add pineapple slices and orange rind; bring to a boil. Cover, reduce heat, and simmer 10 minutes, turning pineapple once.

Arrange 3 pineapple slices on each individual serving plate; top each serving with 1 tablespoon blueberries and 1 tablespoon raspberries. Drizzle syrup evenly over each serving. Yield: 4 servings (84 calories per serving).

Per Serving:

Fat 0.5g	Carbohydrate 21.3g	Fiber 2.7g
saturated fat 0.0g	Cholesterol 0mg	Iron 0.6mg
Protein 0.5g	Sodium 4mg	Calcium 16mg

Cranberry-Orange Cider

You can also serve this cider over crushed ice for a cool, refreshing beverage.

2 cups fresh or frozen cranberries, thawed
4 cups water
6 whole cloves
2 (3-inch) sticks cinnamon
½ cup sugar
¼ cup frozen orange juice concentrate, thawed
2 tablespoons lemon juice

Combine first 4 ingredients in a medium saucepan; bring to a boil. Cover, reduce heat, and simmer 25 minutes; let cool. Pour mixture through a cheesecloth-lined wire-mesh strainer into a bowl; press with back of spoon against the sides of the strainer to squeeze out juice. Discard pulp, seeds, cloves, and cinnamon stick remaining in strainer.

Combine cranberry juice mixture, sugar, orange juice concentrate, and lemon juice in saucepan. Place over low heat, and cook, stirring constantly, until sugar dissolves. Serve immediately. Yield: 4 cups (143 calories per 1-cup serving).

Per Serving:

Fat 0.1g	Carbohydrate 36.7g	Fiber 0.5g
saturated fat 0.0g	Cholesterol 0mg	Iron 0.1mg
Protein 0.6g	Sodium 1mg	Calcium 9mg

Farmer's Market Brunch

Vegetable Omelets
Dillweed Rolls
Fresh Berries with Creamy Peach Topping
Spicy Tomato Cocktail

Serves 6
TOTAL CALORIES PER SERVING: 535
(Calories from Fat: 22%)

Celebrate summer's bountiful harvest with a brunch featuring fresh vegetables, fruits, and herbs. Head to the farmer's market to do your shopping.

Make the tomato cocktail and the roll dough first. The dough needs plenty of time to rise, but you don't have to knead it. Serve guests an extra roll, since menu calories allow for 2 per person.

Vegetable Omelets

3   small round red potatoes
    Vegetable cooking spray
1½ teaspoons vegetable oil
1   cup sliced fresh mushrooms
¾   cup chopped fresh broccoli
½   cup chopped onion
½   cup chopped sweet red pepper
1   tablespoon chopped fresh basil
¼   teaspoon freshly ground pepper
1   cup frozen egg substitute, thawed
2   tablespoons unsweetened orange juice
2   egg whites
1   tablespoon all-purpose flour
¾   cup (3 ounces) shredded reduced-fat sharp
        Cheddar cheese, divided
    Fresh basil sprigs (optional)

Cook potatoes in boiling water to cover 15 minutes or just until tender. Drain; let cool. Cut potatoes into thin slices.

Coat a nonstick skillet with cooking spray; add oil. Place over medium-high heat until hot. Add mushrooms and next 3 ingredients; sauté 6 minutes or until vegetables are tender. Add potato slices, chopped basil, and ¼ teaspoon pepper; cook 1 minute. Set aside, and keep warm.

Combine egg substitute and orange juice; beat at medium speed of an electric mixer until foamy. Beat egg whites at high speed of an electric mixer until soft peaks form. Add flour; beat until stiff peaks form. Gently fold egg white mixture into egg substitute mixture. Coat a medium-size nonstick skillet with cooking spray; place over medium heat until hot. Add one-third of egg mixture to skillet; spread evenly. Cover; cook 4 minutes or until set.

Spoon one-third of vegetable mixture over half of omelet. Sprinkle with ¼ cup cheese. Loosen omelet with a spatula; carefully fold in half. Slide omelet onto a serving platter; set aside, and keep warm. Repeat procedure twice. To serve, cut each omelet in half. Garnish with fresh basil sprigs, if desired. Serve warm. Yield: 6 servings (125 calories per serving).

Per Serving:

Fat 4.2g	Carbohydrate 11.2g	Fiber 1.5g
saturated fat 1.8g	Cholesterol 9mg	Iron 1.7mg
Protein 10.9g	Sodium 186mg	Calcium 153mg

Vegetable Omelets, Fresh Berries with Creamy Peach Topping (page 34), and Dillweed Rolls (page 34)

Dillweed Rolls

This no-fuss bread doesn't require kneading. Simply let the dough rise, spoon it into muffin pans, let it rise again, and bake.

1½   cups skim milk
⅓   cup margarine
3¾   cups all-purpose flour, divided
¼   cup sugar
2   tablespoons chopped fresh dillweed
½   teaspoon salt
1   package active dry yeast
¼   cup frozen egg substitute, thawed
    Vegetable cooking spray

Combine milk and margarine in a saucepan; heat until margarine melts, stirring occasionally. Cool to 120° to 130°. Combine 1½ cups flour and next 4 ingredients in a large bowl. Gradually add liquid mixture to flour mixture, beating well at low speed of an electric mixer. Beat 2 additional minutes at medium speed. Add egg substitute, and beat well. Gradually stir in enough of the remaining 2¼ cups flour to make a soft dough. (Dough will be sticky.)

Cover and let rise in a warm place (85°), free from drafts, 45 minutes or until doubled in bulk. Stir dough down to remove air bubbles. Spoon dough into muffin pans coated with cooking spray, filling two-thirds full. Cover and let rise in a warm place, free from drafts, 30 minutes or until doubled in bulk.

Bake at 400° for 15 minutes or until golden. Remove from pans immediately. Serve warm. Yield: 1½ dozen (146 calories each).

Per Roll:		
Fat 3.7g	Carbohydrate 23.9g	Fiber 0.8g
saturated fat 0.7g	Cholesterol 0mg	Iron 1.4mg
Protein 3.9g	Sodium 121mg	Calcium 34mg

Fresh Berries with Creamy Peach Topping

1   cup sliced fresh or frozen peaches, thawed
¼   cup low-fat sour cream
1   tablespoon brown sugar
½   teaspoon lemon juice
3   cups fresh strawberry halves
1   cup fresh blackberries
    Fresh mint sprig (optional)

Combine first 4 ingredients in container of an electric blender; cover and process until smooth.

Place berries in a serving bowl. Serve with peach mixture. Garnish with fresh mint, if desired. Yield: 6 servings (64 calories per serving).

Per Serving:		
Fat 1.6g	Carbohydrate 12.9g	Fiber 4.3g
saturated fat 0.8g	Cholesterol 4mg	Iron 0.5mg
Protein 1.1g	Sodium 5mg	Calcium 32mg

Spicy Tomato Cocktail

4   cups no-salt-added tomato juice
2   cups spicy hot vegetable juice
3   tablespoons lemon juice
2   teaspoons low-sodium Worcestershire sauce
¼   teaspoon ground celery seeds
¼   teaspoon hot sauce

Combine all ingredients in a large pitcher, stirring well. Cover and chill thoroughly. Yield: 6 cups (54 calories per 1-cup serving).

Per Serving:		
Fat 0.0g	Carbohydrate 12.8g	Fiber 0.6g
saturated fat 0.0g	Cholesterol 0mg	Iron 1.3mg
Protein 2.2g	Sodium 320mg	Calcium 16mg

Green Beans with Basil, Baked Halibut Provençal, and Oven-Roasted Potato Slices (Menu begins on page 42.)

Quick
& Easy

Mexican Beef Salad

A Salad Luncheon That Says "Olé"

Mexican Beef Salad
Citrus-Jicama Salad
Chilled Mexican Coffee

Serves 6
TOTAL CALORIES PER SERVING: 534
(Calories from Fat: 23%)

Enjoy this festive Mexican menu as a complete meal, or serve the beef salad alone as a meal in itself. It's a menu you can make for company or family without much effort.

Cupping the salad in tortilla bowls adds to the south-of-the-border flair, but the edible bowls are optional. Instead, you may prefer to serve the salad along with with crisp-baked tortilla chips. Just cut each tortilla into 6 wedges, place them on an ungreased baking sheet, and coat them with cooking spray. Then bake at 350° for 8 to 10 minutes or until the chips are crisp.

Mexican Beef Salad

1 pound lean boneless top round steak
1 tablespoon chili powder
½ teaspoon onion powder
½ teaspoon ground oregano
½ teaspoon ground cumin
¼ teaspoon garlic powder
¼ teaspoon ground red pepper
2 teaspoons vegetable oil
1 (8-ounce) carton low-fat sour cream
2 tablespoons canned chopped green chiles
1 teaspoon chili powder
¼ teaspoon ground cumin
⅛ teaspoon garlic powder
6 (10-inch) flour tortillas
 Vegetable cooking spray
6 cups shredded iceberg lettuce
1 cup fresh cilantro sprigs
1 cup chopped tomato
¾ cup canned dark red kidney beans, drained
¾ cup frozen whole-kernel corn, thawed
 Fresh cilantro sprigs (optional)
 Jalapeño pepper slices (optional)

Trim fat from steak. Combine 1 tablespoon chili powder and next 6 ingredients; rub evenly over both sides of steak. Cover steak, and marinate in refrigerator 30 minutes.

Combine sour cream and next 4 ingredients in a small bowl. Cover and chill.

Press 1 tortilla gently into a medium bowl. Microwave at HIGH 1½ minutes or until crisp. Repeat procedure with remaining tortillas.

Place steak on rack of a broiler pan coated with cooking spray. Broil 5½ inches from heat (with electric oven door partially opened) 5 minutes on each side or to desired degree of doneness.

Cut steak in half lengthwise. Slice each piece of steak diagonally across grain into thin strips.

Combine lettuce and 1 cup cilantro; place lettuce mixture evenly into tortilla bowls. Arrange tomato, beans, corn, and steak over lettuce mixture in each bowl. Spoon sour cream mixture evenly over each serving. If desired, garnish with cilantro sprigs and jalapeño slices. Yield: 6 servings (375 calories per serving).

Per Serving:		
Fat 13.4g	Carbohydrate 37.6g	Fiber 4.3g
saturated fat 4.9g	Cholesterol 62mg	Iron 4.9mg
Protein 26.5g	Sodium 341mg	Calcium 133mg

Citrus-Jicama Salad

5 large oranges, peeled and cut crosswise into ¼-inch-thick slices
⅔ cup peeled, diced jicama
¼ cup sliced green onions
½ cup unsweetened orange juice
2 tablespoons chopped fresh cilantro
2 tablespoons lime juice
½ teaspoon sugar
⅛ teaspoon ground red pepper

Combine first 3 ingredients. Combine orange juice and remaining ingredients; pour over orange mixture, and toss gently. Cover and chill at least 30 minutes. Serve with a slotted spoon. Yield: 6 servings (78 calories per ¾-cup serving).

Per Serving:		
Fat 0.2g	Carbohydrate 19.2g	Fiber 5.6g
saturated fat 0.0g	Cholesterol 0mg	Iron 0.4mg
Protein 1.6g	Sodium 2mg	Calcium 58mg

Chilled Mexican Coffee

4¼ cups brewed coffee, chilled
¼ cup chocolate syrup
½ teaspoon ground cinnamon
1½ cups fat-free vanilla ice cream

Combine first 3 ingredients. Pour into individual mugs. Top each serving with ¼ cup ice cream. Serve immediately. Yield: 4½ cups (81 calories per ¾-cup serving).

Per Serving:		
Fat 0.2g	Carbohydrate 17.7g	Fiber 0g
saturated fat 0.0g	Cholesterol 0mg	Iron 1.0mg
Protein 2.6g	Sodium 49mg	Calcium 68mg

Pork and Pepper Skillet, Broccoli with Lemon, and Garlic Mashed Potatoes

Fast, Fresh Family Supper

Pork and Pepper Skillet
Broccoli with Lemon
Garlic Mashed Potatoes
Chocolate-Mocha Pudding

Serves 4
TOTAL CALORIES PER SERVING: 616
(Calories from Fat: 23%)

The flavors in this menu will remind you of a time when supper menus revolved around vegetables fresh from the garden. The only difference is that these easy recipes are designed for the way we cook today—in a hurry. Make the pudding first, and let it set up during supper. To save time, sauté the pork and peppers while you cook the potatoes and steam the broccoli. For a special touch, garnish the plates with fresh thyme.

Pork and Pepper Skillet

8 (2-ounce) boneless center-cut pork loin chops
½ teaspoon chopped fresh thyme
¼ teaspoon freshly ground pepper
⅛ teaspoon salt
   Vegetable cooking spray
1 teaspoon olive oil
½ medium onion, sliced lengthwise
3 medium-size sweet red peppers, seeded and sliced into thin strips
1 clove garlic, crushed
1 tablespoon red wine vinegar

Rub both sides of pork chops with fresh thyme, ground pepper, and salt. Coat a large nonstick skillet with cooking spray. Place over medium-high heat until hot. Add pork chops, and cook 2 to 3 minutes on each side or until pork chops are lightly browned. Remove pork chops from skillet; set aside, and keep warm.

Add oil to skillet. Place over medium-high heat until hot. Add onion and red pepper; sauté 5 minutes or until crisp-tender. Add garlic and pork; cover, reduce heat, and cook 10 minutes or until vegetables are tender and pork is done. Drizzle with vinegar. Yield: 4 servings (230 calories per serving).

Per Serving:

Fat 9.9g	Carbohydrate 8.3g	Fiber 2.2g
saturated fat 2.4g	Cholesterol 71mg	Iron 2.4mg
Protein 26.2g	Sodium 149mg	Calcium 20mg

Broccoli with Lemon

1   pound fresh broccoli
3   tablespoons canned low-sodium chicken
       broth, undiluted
1   tablespoon lemon juice
1½ teaspoons olive oil
¼   teaspoon salt
⅛   teaspoon freshly ground pepper
      Lemon wedges (optional)

Trim off large leaves of broccoli; remove tough ends of lower stalks. Wash broccoli, and cut into small spears. Arrange in a vegetable steamer over boiling water. Cover and steam 5 to 8 minutes or until crisp-tender. Drain; set aside.

Combine broth and next 4 ingredients. Add broccoli; toss. Serve with lemon wedges, if desired. Yield: 4 servings (44 calories per 1-cup serving).

Per Serving:

Fat 2.1g	Carbohydrate 5.3g	Fiber 2.5g
saturated fat 0.3g	Cholesterol 0mg	Iron 0.9mg
Protein 3.0g	Sodium 175mg	Calcium 45mg

Garlic Mashed Potatoes

4½ cups peeled, cubed baking potato
4   cloves garlic
1   bay leaf
¾   cup plain low-fat yogurt
½   cup skim milk
¼   teaspoon salt

Place potato, garlic, and bay leaf in a medium saucepan; add water to cover. Bring to a boil;

cover, reduce heat, and simmer 15 minutes or until potato is tender.

Drain potato; remove garlic and bay leaf. Mash garlic into a paste; discard bay leaf. Mash potato. Add garlic, yogurt, milk, and salt to mashed potato, and stir well. Serve immediately. Yield: 4 servings (143 calories per 1-cup serving).

Per Serving:

Fat 0.9g	Carbohydrate 27.0g	Fiber 3.1g
saturated fat 0.5g	Cholesterol 3mg	Iron 5.7mg
Protein 7.9g	Sodium 210mg	Calcium 174mg

Chocolate-Mocha Pudding

½   cup sugar
⅓   cup unsweetened cocoa
2   tablespoons plus 2 teaspoons cornstarch
1½ cups 1% low-fat milk
½   cup brewed coffee
1   teaspoon vanilla extract
¼   cup frozen reduced-calorie whipped
      topping, thawed
      Chocolate coffee beans (optional)

Combine first 3 ingredients in a medium saucepan. Gradually stir in milk and coffee. Bring to a boil over medium heat, stirring constantly. Cook, stirring constantly, 1 minute or until thickened. Stir in vanilla.

To serve, spoon chocolate mixture evenly into 4 (6-ounce) custard cups; top each serving with 1 tablespoon whipped topping. Garnish with chocolate coffee beans, if desired. Yield: 4 servings (199 calories per serving).

Per Serving:

Fat 2.5g	Carbohydrate 38.9g	Fiber 0g
saturated fat 1.2g	Cholesterol 4mg	Iron 1.4mg
Protein 5.2g	Sodium 53mg	Calcium 128mg

Chickpea and Tomato Soup

Soup's On—Vegetarian Style

Chickpea and Tomato Soup
Mushroom Crostini on Greens
Poached Dried Fruit

Serves 6
TOTAL CALORIES PER SERVING: 579
(Calories from Fat: 14%)

For a quick vegetarian meal, put on a pot of soup and toss a salad. You can simmer the soup while you toss the crisp greens for the salad, and sauté the mushrooms for the crostini. Sautéing the mushrooms with garlic and olive oil brings out their rich, earthy, almost meat-like flavor. Round out the menu with a medley of poached dried fruits that you can prepare a day or more ahead. For a finishing touch, garnish the soup bowl with a fresh parsley sprig.

Chickpea and Tomato Soup

Vegetable cooking spray
2 teaspoons olive oil
¾ cup chopped onion
¾ cup sliced celery
1 clove garlic, crushed
1 cup water
3 (14½-ounce) cans no-salt-added whole
    tomatoes, undrained and chopped
1 (14½-ounce) can vegetable broth
1 bay leaf
3 cups torn fresh spinach
2½ cups canned garbanzo beans (chickpeas)
¼ cup finely chopped parsley
½ teaspoon freshly ground pepper
¼ cup grated Parmesan cheese

Coat a Dutch oven with cooking spray; add oil.
Place over medium-high heat until hot. Add
onion, celery, and garlic; sauté 8 to 10 minutes.

Add 1 cup water and next 3 ingredients. Bring
to a boil; cover, reduce heat, and simmer 20 minutes. Add spinach and next 3 ingredients. Cook
until heated. Sprinkle with cheese. Yield: 10½
cups (208 calories per 1¾-cup serving).

Per Serving:
Fat 4.8g	Carbohydrate 33.3g	Fiber 5.5g
saturated fat 1.1g	Cholesterol 3mg	Iron 3.8mg
Protein 10.5g	Sodium 496mg	Calcium 183mg

Mushroom Crostini on Greens

Vegetable cooking spray
2 teaspoons olive oil, divided
2 (8-ounce) packages sliced fresh mushrooms
1 tablespoon minced fresh parsley
1½ teaspoons chopped fresh thyme
¼ teaspoon salt
¼ teaspoon freshly ground pepper
1 clove garlic, crushed
1 clove garlic, halved
6 cups mixed baby salad greens
1½ tablespoons lemon juice
6 (½-inch-thick) slices farmers' bread, toasted

Coat a large nonstick skillet with cooking spray;
add 1 teaspoon oil. Place over medium-high heat
until hot. Add sliced mushrooms, and sauté 3
minutes. Add parsley and next 4 ingredients;
sauté 5 minutes. Set aside, and keep warm.

Rub the inside of a large bowl with cut sides of
halved garlic. Add remaining 1 teaspoon oil,
greens, and lemon juice to bowl; toss well.
Arrange greens on individual salad plates. Top
bread slices with mushroom mixture; place over
greens. Yield: 6 servings (135 calories per serving).

Per Serving:
Fat 2.8g	Carbohydrate 23.4g	Fiber 2.1g
saturated fat 0.3g	Cholesterol 0mg	Iron 2.3mg
Protein 5.5g	Sodium 316mg	Calcium 57mg

Poached Dried Fruit

2¾ cups unsweetened apple juice
1½ tablespoons lemon juice
6 whole cloves
2 (3-inch) sticks cinnamon
¾ cup pitted prunes
¾ cup dried apricots
1½ cups peeled, diced apple
1½ tablespoons orange zest
1 cup vanilla low-fat yogurt
1 tablespoon reduced-calorie maple syrup

Combine first 4 ingredients in a medium
saucepan; bring to a boil. Add prunes and apricots; cover, reduce heat, and simmer 15 minutes or
until fruit is tender. Add apple and orange zest;
simmer 5 minutes. Remove and discard cloves
and cinnamon sticks. Let cool. Cover and chill.

Combine yogurt and syrup, stirring well. Spoon
fruit mixture into individual serving bowls. Top
with yogurt mixture. Yield: 6 servings (236 calories
per serving).

Per Serving:
Fat 1.6g	Carbohydrate 57.1g	Fiber 3.5g
saturated fat 0.4g	Cholesterol 2mg	Iron 2.2mg
Protein 3.5g	Sodium 45mg	Calcium 100mg

Orange Slices with Grand Marnier

A Taste of Provence

Baked Halibut Provençal
Oven-Roasted Potato Slices
Green Beans with Basil
Orange Slices with
Grand Marnier

Serves 2
TOTAL CALORIES PER SERVING: 591
(Calories from Fat: 16%)

Travel to sun-drenched Provence without leaving your kitchen. This menu highlights some of the French region's fresh-tasting foods such as seafood, tomatoes, and oranges.

Make the orange dessert ahead so it can chill. Cook the green beans while the fish and potatoes roast in the oven. Since this meal can be prepared in a jiffy, spend the time you saved on cooking relaxing with a friend.

Baked Halibut Provençal

(pictured on page 35)

1 small onion, thinly sliced
1 teaspoon olive oil
½ teaspoon dried rosemary, divided
1 small clove garlic, thinly sliced
1 (1½-inch) piece orange peel
¾ cup canned no-salt-added whole tomatoes,
     undrained and chopped
1 teaspoon capers
2 teaspoons fresh orange juice
⅛ teaspoon freshly ground pepper
2 (4-ounce) halibut fillets
2 teaspoons chopped kalamata olives

Combine onion, olive oil, ¼ teaspoon rosemary, garlic, and orange peel in a 13- x 9- x 2-inch baking dish. Bake, uncovered, at 400° for 10 minutes or until onion begins to brown, stirring once. Stir in tomato and capers; bake 5 additional minutes or until mixture thickens. Stir in orange juice and pepper.

Add halibut to tomato mixture; sprinkle with remaining ¼ teaspoon rosemary. Spoon tomato mixture over halibut; bake, uncovered, 10 minutes or until fish flakes easily when tested with a fork. Remove and discard orange peel. Sprinkle with olives; serve immediately. Yield: 2 servings (194 calories per serving).

Per Serving:
Fat 5.4g	Carbohydrate 10.6g	Fiber 2.0g
saturated fat 0.8g	Cholesterol 53mg	Iron 1.7mg
Protein 32.4g	Sodium 216mg	Calcium 104mg

Oven-Roasted Potato Slices

(pictured on page 35)

¾   pound baking potatoes, cut into
      ¼-inch-thick slices
1   tablespoon balsamic vinegar
1   teaspoon olive oil
      Olive oil-flavored vegetable cooking spray
⅛   teaspoon salt
⅛   teaspoon freshly ground pepper

Combine potato, vinegar, and oil in a medium bowl, tossing well.

Arrange potato in a single layer on a baking sheet coated with cooking spray. Bake at 400° for 30 minutes or until tender, turning once. Sprinkle with salt and pepper. Yield: 2 servings (209 calories per serving).

Per Serving:
Fat 2.8g	Carbohydrate 43.1g	Fiber 3.1g
saturated fat 0.4g	Cholesterol 0mg	Iron 2.4mg
Protein 3.8g	Sodium 160mg	Calcium 19mg

Green Beans with Basil

(pictured on page 35)

½   pound fresh green beans, trimmed
1   clove garlic, halved
¼   cup chopped fresh basil
1   teaspoon olive oil
⅛   teaspoon salt
⅛   teaspoon freshly ground pepper

Cook beans in boiling water to cover 8 minutes or until crisp-tender; drain well.

Rub the surface of a large bowl with cut sides of garlic. Leave garlic in bowl. Add basil and olive oil to bowl. Add beans, and toss well. Sprinkle with salt and pepper; toss. Remove and discard garlic halves. Yield: 2 servings (54 calories per serving).

Per Serving:
Fat 2.4g	Carbohydrate 7.8g	Fiber 2.2g
saturated fat 0.3g	Cholesterol 0mg	Iron 1.1mg
Protein 2.1g	Sodium 153mg	Calcium 51mg

Orange Slices with Grand Marnier

2   large seedless oranges, peeled
2   teaspoons sugar
2   tablespoons Grand Marnier or other
      orange-flavored liqueur
⅛   teaspoon ground cinnamon
      Orange zest (optional)

Cut oranges into ¼-inch-thick slices. Place orange slices in individual bowls; sprinkle with sugar. Drizzle with Grand Marnier, and sprinkle with cinnamon. Cover and chill thoroughly. Garnish with orange zest, if desired. Yield: 2 servings (134 calories per ¾-cup serving).

Per Serving:
Fat 0.2g	Carbohydrate 26.0g	Fiber 6.5g
saturated fat 0.1g	Cholesterol 0mg	Iron 0.2mg
Protein 1.4g	Sodium 0mg	Calcium 61mg

In-Line Skating Safety

In-line skating is the high-tech update on roller skating (the skates' wheels are in a line instead of side by side). It improves muscle tone and burns calories without pounding your joints, and it's easy to learn. But before you skate, take note of these safety tips:

- Always wear protective gear—helmet, wrist guards, elbow pads, and knee pads.
- Master the basics—moving, stopping, turning—before hitting the road.
- Keep your equipment in safe condition.
- Obey all traffic regulations.

Warm Lentil Salad and Marinated Broiled Lamb Chops

New Flavors for Old Favorites

Marinated Broiled Lamb Chops
Warm Lentil Salad
Commercial French Bread
Honey-Baked Apples

Serves 4
TOTAL CALORIES PER SERVING: 605
(Calories from Fat: 20%)

Gone are the days when you fried the chops, simmered the vegetables until limp, and served the apples swimming in syrup. Today, the chops are likely to be seasoned with fresh herbs then broiled or grilled. The vegetables are teamed with legumes, such as lentils, and served in an herbed vinaigrette dressing as a salad. A 1-ounce slice of French bread replaces cornbread. And the apples are left whole and sweetened with raisins, honey, and ginger.

What an easy way to get all the flavor of your old-time favorites for a lot fewer calories!

Marinated Broiled Lamb Chops

1   tablespoon chopped fresh rosemary
½   teaspoon freshly ground pepper
¼   teaspoon salt
2   cloves garlic, crushed
4   (5-ounce) lean lamb loin chops
     Vegetable cooking spray
     Fresh rosemary sprigs (optional)

Mash rosemary, pepper, salt, and garlic to a paste. Trim fat from chops. Rub garlic mixture over both sides of chops; cover and chill 30 minutes.

Place chops on rack of a broiler pan coated with cooking spray. Broil 5½ inches from heat (with electric oven door partially opened) 5 to 6 minutes on each side or to desired degree of doneness. Garnish with fresh rosemary sprigs, if desired. Yield: 4 servings (189 calories per serving).

Per Serving:

Fat 8.5g	Carbohydrate 0.8g	Fiber 0.1g
saturated fat 3.0g	Cholesterol 81mg	Iron 1.9mg
Protein 25.6g	Sodium 218mg	Calcium 25mg

Warm Lentil Salad

½   cup dried lentils, uncooked
2½   cups water
½   medium onion
1   bay leaf
¼   cup canned low-sodium chicken broth
3   tablespoons red wine vinegar
¼   teaspoon salt
¼   teaspoon freshly ground pepper
1   clove garlic, crushed
1   cup frozen English peas, thawed
¼   cup sliced green onions
¼   cup chopped fresh parsley
¼   cup chopped fresh dillweed
2   tablespoons chopped fresh mint
2   medium tomatoes, cut into thin wedges

Combine first 4 ingredients in a large saucepan. Bring to a boil; reduce heat, and simmer, uncov-

ered, 30 minutes or until lentils are tender. Drain well. Remove and discard onion and bay leaf.

Combine chicken broth and next 4 ingredients in a large bowl, stirring well with a wire whisk. Add lentils, peas, and next 4 ingredients; stir well. To serve, place ½ cup lentil mixture on each individual serving plate. Arrange tomato wedges around lentil mixture. Yield: 4 servings (123 calories per serving).

Per Serving:

Fat 0.8g	Carbohydrate 22.1g	Fiber 5.2g
saturated fat 0.1g	Cholesterol 0mg	Iron 3.9mg
Protein 8.8g	Sodium 198mg	Calcium 61mg

Honey-Baked Apples

4   Granny Smith apples
2   tablespoons raisins
1   tablespoon minced crystallized ginger
1   tablespoon margarine, cut into 4 pieces
¼   cup honey

Core apples, cutting to, but not through, bottom; peel top third of each apple. Place apples in an 8-inch square baking dish. Combine raisins and ginger in a small bowl; spoon raisin mixture evenly into cavity of each apple. Top each apple with 1 piece of margarine; drizzle 1 tablespoon honey over each apple.

Bake apples, uncovered, at 350° for 45 minutes or until apples are tender; baste occasionally with cooking liquid. Serve warm. Yield: 4 servings (211 calories per serving).

Per Serving:

Fat 3.4g	Carbohydrate 48.9g	Fiber 5.0g
saturated fat 0.7g	Cholesterol 0mg	Iron 1.2mg
Protein 0.6g	Sodium 37mg	Calcium 24mg

Simply Elegant

Orange-Basil Chicken
Simple Rice Pilaf
Zucchini and Tomatoes
Strawberries and Yogurt

Serves 4
TOTAL CALORIES PER SERVING: 650
(Calories from Fat: 17%)

Who says easy can't be elegant? Start with chicken breasts. Add fresh orange juice, orange wedges, white wine, and a bit of fresh basil. Then slice some zucchini, and cook it with tomatoes and fresh oregano. Next, pull out the rice—an aromatic variety such as basmati is best. Sauté it with onion, and stir in walnuts, oregano leaves, and currants for flavor. Finally, for dessert—combine fresh strawberries, vanilla yogurt, and a little sugar. Bon Appetit!

Orange-Basil Chicken

Vegetable cooking spray
1   teaspoon olive oil
4   (4-ounce) skinned, boned chicken breast
    halves
¾   cup fresh orange juice
¼   cup dry white wine
1   tablespoon chopped fresh basil
¼   teaspoon salt
¼   teaspoon freshly ground pepper
12 (½-inch-thick) wedges fresh orange
1   clove garlic, minced
2   teaspoons cornstarch
1   tablespoon water
    Fresh basil sprigs (optional)

Coat a large nonstick skillet with cooking spray; add oil. Place over medium heat until hot. Add chicken; cook 2 minutes on each side or until browned. Add orange juice and next 6 ingredients; bring to a boil. Cover, reduce heat, and simmer 15 minutes or until chicken is done. Remove chicken and orange wedges from skillet, using a slotted spoon; set aside, and keep warm.

Bring orange juice mixture to a boil. Reduce heat, and simmer, uncovered, 10 minutes or until mixture reduces to ¾ cup. Combine cornstarch and water, stirring well. Add to juice mixture; cook over medium heat, stirring constantly, until mixture thickens.

Transfer chicken and orange wedges to individual serving plates. Spoon sauce over chicken. Garnish with basil sprigs, if desired. Yield: 4 servings (176 calories per serving).

Per Serving:

Fat 2.8g	Carbohydrate 9.7g	Fiber 1.2g
saturated fat 0.5g	Cholesterol 66mg	Iron 1.0mg
Protein 26.8g	Sodium 222mg	Calcium 32mg

Orange-Basil Chicken, Simple Rice Pilaf
(page 48), Zucchini and Tomatoes (page 48)

Simple Rice Pilaf

*Sautéing basmati rice until it browns brings
out its natural nutty flavor.*

    2   teaspoons reduced-calorie margarine
    ½   cup chopped onion
    ¾   cup basmati rice, uncooked
    1½ cups canned no-salt-added chicken broth,
          undiluted
    ½   cup currants
    ¼   teaspoon salt
    ¼   teaspoon pepper
    ¼   cup chopped walnuts, toasted
    1   tablespoon fresh oregano leaves

Melt margarine in a saucepan over medium-
high heat. Add onion, and sauté until tender.
Add rice, and sauté 3 to 5 minutes or until rice
is lightly browned.

Add broth and next 3 ingredients. Bring to a
boil. Cover, reduce heat, and simmer 25 minutes
or until rice is tender and liquid is absorbed. Add
walnuts and oregano; toss gently. Yield: 4 servings
(246 calories per ¾-cup serving).

Per Serving:

Fat 6.2g	Carbohydrate 43.6g	Fiber 1.4g
saturated fat 0.6g	Cholesterol 0mg	Iron 3.0mg
Protein 4.6g	Sodium 176mg	Calcium 64mg

Zucchini and Tomatoes

        Vegetable cooking spray
    1   teaspoon olive oil
    4   cups sliced zucchini
    ½   cup chopped onion
    1   clove garlic, crushed
    1   (14½-ounce) can no-salt-added whole
          tomatoes, undrained and chopped
    1   teaspoon chopped fresh oregano
    ¼   teaspoon salt
    ¼   teaspoon freshly ground pepper

Coat a large saucepan with cooking spray; add
oil. Place over medium-high heat until hot. Add
zucchini, onion, and garlic; sauté until onion is
tender.

Add tomato and remaining ingredients. Bring
to a boil; reduce heat, and simmer, uncovered, 35
minutes or until zucchini is tender and liquid is
absorbed. Yield: 4 servings (62 calories per 1-cup
serving).

Per Serving:

Fat 1.5g	Carbohydrate 11.3g	Fiber 1.9g
saturated fat 0.2g	Cholesterol 0mg	Iron 1.2mg
Protein 2.8g	Sodium 165mg	Calcium 65mg

Strawberries and Yogurt

    2   cups fresh strawberries, hulled and
          divided
    2   tablespoons sugar, divided
    2½ cups vanilla low-fat yogurt

Place 1 cup strawberries and 1 tablespoon
sugar in a bowl; mash. Stir in yogurt.

Slice remaining 1 cup berries, and toss with
remaining 1 tablespoon sugar. Fold in yogurt mixture; spoon strawberry mixture into individual
serving dishes. Yield: 4 cups (166 calories per
1-cup serving).

Per Serving:

Fat 2.0g	Carbohydrate 30.8g	Fiber 1.8g
saturated fat 1.2g	Cholesterol 7mg	Iron 0.4mg
Protein 7.4g	Sodium 94mg	Calcium 253mg

*Ragoût of Veal and Mixed Greens with
Balsamic Vinaigrette (Menu begins
on page 57.)*

That's
Entertaining

Kentucky Derby Day Luncheon

Mint Juleps
Roasted Chicken and Vegetable Salad
Whole Wheat Clover Rolls
Strawberry Crunch Parfaits

Serves 8
TOTAL CALORIES PER SERVING: 782
(Calories from Fat: 20%)

Since the first Kentucky Derby in 1875, this race of the country's best three-year-old fillies and colts has been synonymous with entertaining. Whether you're celebrating with friends at Churchill Downs or at home in front of the television, this luncheon is favored to win.

To get a head start with party preparations, make the granola for the parfaits several days in advance. Prepare the salad and rolls (menu calories reflect one per person) the morning of your party. You can even arrange suitably Southern table decorations earlier in the day. Use a pretty basket of luscious strawberries garnished with fresh mint sprigs and, of course, a traditional bouquet of roses.

Then when the starting gate opens, let the party begin with the traditional Derby drink—a mint julep.

Mint Juleps

1   cup sugar
1   cup water
1   cup tightly packed fresh mint
      sprigs
1   cup bourbon
    Crushed ice
    Fresh mint sprigs (optional)

Combine sugar and water in a saucepan; bring to a boil. Cook over high heat 5 minutes (do not stir); remove from heat. Add 1 cup mint sprigs; let cool completely. Transfer sugar mixture to a wide-mouth quart glass jar; cover with lid. Let stand at room temperature 24 hours.

Pour mint mixture through a wire-mesh strainer into a glass pitcher, discarding mint remaining in strainer. Add bourbon, and stir well. To serve, fill individual glasses with crushed ice; add bourbon mixture. Garnish with fresh mint sprigs, if desired. Yield: 8 servings (165 calories per ¼-cup serving).

Per Serving:		
Fat 0.0g	Carbohydrate 25.0g	Fiber 0g
saturated fat 0.0g	Cholesterol 0mg	Iron 0mg
Protein 0.0g	Sodium 1mg	Calcium 0mg

Roasted Chicken and Vegetable Salad (page 52), Mint Juleps, and Whole Wheat Clover Rolls (page 53)

Roasted Chicken and Vegetable Salad

1   pound fresh mushrooms
8   (4-ounce) skinned, boned chicken breast halves
2   large zucchini, cut into ¾-inch-thick slices
2   large yellow squash, cut into ¾-inch-thick slices
2   large sweet red peppers, cut into 1-inch pieces
2   large sweet yellow peppers, cut into 1-inch pieces
1   large purple onion, cut into thin wedges
    Olive oil-flavored vegetable cooking spray
½   cup canned no-salt-added chicken broth, undiluted
¼   cup plus 2 tablespoons balsamic vinegar
3   tablespoons olive oil
2   teaspoons dried rosemary, crushed
1   teaspoon salt
½   teaspoon freshly ground pepper
6   cloves garlic, minced
    Red leaf lettuce leaves (optional)

Remove and discard stems from mushrooms. Arrange mushroom caps, chicken, and next 5 ingredients in a shallow roasting pan coated with cooking spray. Combine chicken broth and next 6 ingredients in a small bowl, stirring well. Pour half of broth mixture over chicken and vegetables.

Bake chicken mixture, uncovered, at 425° for 15 minutes. Turn chicken and vegetables; pour remaining broth mixture over top. Bake 10 additional minutes or until chicken is done and vegetables are tender.

Remove chicken from roasting pan; cut into 1-inch pieces. Return chicken to pan, and toss with vegetables.

Arrange chicken and vegetable mixture on a lettuce-lined serving platter, if desired. Yield: 8 servings (234 calories per 1½-cup serving).

Per Serving:		
Fat 7.3g	Carbohydrate 13.3g	Fiber 3.3g
saturated fat 1.2g	Cholesterol 66mg	Iron 2.9mg
Protein 29.5g	Sodium 375mg	Calcium 50mg

Don't Weight to Age

No one is arguing that some weight gain is a natural part of aging. But don't let any guidelines lull you into a false sense of security. Maintaining a healthy weight is a lifetime occupation. The U.S. Dietary Guidelines (1990) make large allowances for weight gain after the age of 35—too large, say some health-care professionals.

In these guidelines, the starting range for a healthy weight in someone 5'6" jumps by 12 pounds once a person passed age 35. Twelve pounds!

However, new research, particularly from a Harvard University study, connects even modest amounts of weight gain among middle-aged women with an increased risk for heart disease. Another study finds that gaining as few as 11 to 17 pounds during early- and middle-adult years can have an adverse effect on blood pressure, blood sugar, and heart health in men and women.

Whole Wheat Clover Rolls

1   package active dry yeast
¼   cup warm water (105° to 115°)
2   cups all-purpose flour, divided
⅔   cup whole wheat flour
2   tablespoons sugar
½   teaspoon salt
¾   cup skim milk
2   tablespoons margarine, melted
1   tablespoon all-purpose flour
    Butter-flavored vegetable cooking spray
2   tablespoons regular oats, uncooked

Combine yeast and warm water in a 1-cup liquid measuring cup; let stand 5 minutes.

Combine yeast mixture, 1½ cups all-purpose flour, whole wheat flour, sugar, salt, milk, and margarine in a large mixing bowl. Beat at medium speed of an electric mixer until well blended. Gradually stir in enough of the remaining ½ cup all-purpose flour to make a soft dough.

Sprinkle 1 tablespoon all-purpose flour evenly over work surface. Turn dough out onto floured surface, and knead until smooth and elastic (about 10 minutes). Place dough in a large bowl coated with cooking spray, turning to coat top. Cover and let rise in a warm place (85°), free from drafts, 1 hour or until doubled in bulk.

Coat muffin pans with cooking spray. Punch dough down, and divide into 2 equal portions. Shape each portion into 18 balls. Place 3 balls in each muffin cup. Coat tops with cooking spray, and sprinkle with oats. Cover and let rise in a warm place, free from drafts, 40 minutes or until doubled in bulk. Bake at 425° for 15 minutes or until golden. Yield: 12 rolls (138 calories each).

Per Roll:

Fat 2.6g	Carbohydrate 24.8g	Fiber 1.7g
saturated fat 0.5g	Cholesterol 0mg	Iron 1.4mg
Protein 4.0g	Sodium 129mg	Calcium 26mg

Strawberry Crunch Parfaits

This oat mixture also tastes delicious stirred into vanilla low-fat yogurt or mixed into hot cooked cereal.

1¼   cups regular oats, uncooked
⅓   cup chopped pecans
2   tablespoons brown sugar
    Vegetable cooking spray
3   tablespoons honey
2   tablespoons margarine, melted
2   teaspoons vanilla extract
1   teaspoon ground cinnamon
4   cups vanilla nonfat frozen yogurt
2   cups sliced fresh strawberries
    Fresh mint sprigs (optional)

Combine oats, pecans, and brown sugar; place mixture in a 13- x 9- x 2-inch pan coated with cooking spray. Combine honey and next 3 ingredients in a small bowl, stirring well. Drizzle honey mixture over oat mixture in pan; stir well. Bake at 350° for 20 minutes or until golden, stirring occasionally. Spoon oat mixture onto aluminum foil; let cool.

Spoon ¼ cup frozen yogurt into each of 8 (8-ounce) parfait glasses. Top each serving with 2 tablespoons strawberries and 2 tablespoons oat mixture; repeat layers with remaining yogurt, strawberries, and oat mixture. Garnish with mint sprigs, if desired. Yield: 8 servings (245 calories per serving).

Per Serving:

Fat 7.2g	Carbohydrate 40.7g	Fiber 2.9g
saturated fat 1.0g	Cholesterol 0mg	Iron 1.1mg
Protein 6.5g	Sodium 94mg	Calcium 148mg

Hearty Three-Bean Chili and Confetti Corn Muffins (page 56)

Classmates' Reunion

Sassy Snack Mix
Hearty Three-Bean Chili
Creamy Coleslaw
Confetti Corn Muffins
Sparkling Water

Serves 8
TOTAL CALORIES PER SERVING: 706
(Calories from Fat: 16%)

Why wait 10 or 20 years for a formal class reunion to visit with old school chums? Invite them to relive those bright years and to enjoy this make-ahead menu soon.

The snack mix (½-cup serving per person) and Confetti Corn Muffins (one per person) can be made in advance and stored in airtight containers. The chili and coleslaw can be refrigerated for a day.

Sassy Snack Mix

You can substitute raisins or chopped dried apricots or peaches for dried cherries.

2   cups crispy corn cereal squares
2   cups crispy whole wheat cereal squares
2   cups small fat-free pretzels
1½ cups oyster crackers
3   tablespoons margarine, melted
1   tablespoon low-sodium Worcestershire sauce
½   teaspoon Creole seasoning
1   cup dried cherries

Combine first 4 ingredients in a large bowl. Combine margarine, Worcestershire sauce, and Creole seasoning; drizzle over cereal mixture, tossing well.

Spread cereal mixture in a 15- x 10- x 1-inch jellyroll pan. Bake at 325° for 15 to 18 minutes or until golden, stirring once. Cool completely. Transfer to a serving bowl. Add cherries; toss gently. Yield: 7 cups (89 calories per ¼-cup serving).

Per Serving:

Fat 1.8g	Carbohydrate 17.3g	Fiber 1.0g
saturated fat 0.3g	Cholesterol 0mg	Iron 1.6mg
Protein 1.7g	Sodium 205mg	Calcium 4mg

Target Heart Smarts

Everyone says the same thing: For cardiovascular fitness, you need to exercise for 15 to 20 minutes, three times a week, at your target heart rate (number of beats per minute). How do you compute that mysterious target? It's easy:
  1. Subtract your age from the number 220. That's your maximum heart rate.
  2. Multiply your maximum by 50 percent. That's the low end of your target heart rate.
  3. Multiply your maximum by 75 percent. That's the high end of your target heart rate.

Now, the next time you're exercising, take a break, and check your pulse. You can count for a whole minute; or just count for ten seconds, and multiply by six. That number should fall in your target range. Is your pulse lower than the target? Turn up the intensity a little bit. Is it too high? Slow down. It's as simple as that.

Hearty Three-Bean Chili

1   teaspoon vegetable oil
2   cups chopped onion
3   cloves garlic, minced
2   tablespoons chili powder
1½   tablespoons ground cumin
½   teaspoon salt
2   (14½-ounce) cans no-salt-added stewed tomatoes, undrained
2   (15-ounce) cans black beans, drained
1   (16-ounce) can kidney beans, drained
1   (15-ounce) can pinto beans, drained
1   (14¼-ounce) can no-salt-added beef broth
½   cup water
1   large green pepper, cut into 1-inch pieces
1   large sweet red pepper, cut into 1-inch pieces
½   cup nonfat sour cream
⅓   cup diced green pepper
⅓   cup diced sweet red pepper

Heat oil in a large Dutch oven over medium-high heat until hot. Add onion and garlic; sauté 5 minutes or until onion is tender. Stir in chili powder, cumin, and salt; sauté 1 minute. Add tomato and next 7 ingredients. Bring to a boil; cover, reduce heat, and simmer 30 minutes, stirring occasionally.

Ladle chili into individual bowls, and top each serving with 1 tablespoon sour cream. Sprinkle diced pepper evenly over each serving. Yield: 12 cups (276 calories per 1½-cup serving).

Per Serving:

Fat 3.9g	Carbohydrate 48.3g	Fiber 8.1g
saturated fat 1.5g	Cholesterol 6mg	Iron 5.7mg
Protein 14.7g	Sodium 535mg	Calcium 120mg

Creamy Coleslaw

Save time by using a food processor to chop the cabbage and shred the carrot.

6¾ cups chopped cabbage (about 1 medium)
1½ cups shredded carrot
1 cup reduced-fat mayonnaise
1 cup nonfat sour cream
¼ cup sugar
¼ cup prepared horseradish
1½ tablespoons fresh lemon juice
½ teaspoon dry mustard
¼ teaspoon salt
¼ teaspoon celery seeds
¼ teaspoon garlic powder
⅛ teaspoon ground white pepper
⅛ teaspoon ground red pepper

Combine cabbage and carrot in a large bowl. Set aside.

Position knife blade in food processor bowl; add mayonnaise and remaining ingredients. Process 15 seconds or until smooth. Pour mayonnaise mixture over cabbage mixture; toss gently. Cover and chill at least 8 hours. Toss gently before serving. Yield: 6 cups (133 calories per ¾-cup serving).

Per Serving:		
Fat 2.3g	Carbohydrate 25.0g	Fiber 3.2g
saturated fat 0.0g	Cholesterol 0mg	Iron 0.8mg
Protein 3.6g	Sodium 407mg	Calcium 91mg

Confetti Corn Muffins

1¼ cups all-purpose flour
¾ cup yellow cornmeal
2 teaspoons baking powder
¼ teaspoon salt
1 tablespoon sugar
¼ teaspoon ground red pepper
1 cup nonfat buttermilk
2 tablespoons margarine, melted
1 egg, beaten
½ cup diced sweet red pepper
⅓ cup thinly sliced green onions
1 tablespoon seeded, minced jalapeño pepper
Vegetable cooking spray

Combine first 6 ingredients in a medium bowl, and make a well in center of mixture. Combine buttermilk, margarine, and egg; add to dry ingredients, stirring just until dry ingredients are moistened. Fold in diced red pepper, green onions, and jalapeño pepper.

Spoon batter into muffin pans coated with cooking spray, filling two-thirds full. Bake at 400° for 28 to 30 minutes or until golden. Remove from pans immediately. Yield: 12 muffins (119 calories each).

Per Muffin:		
Fat 2.9g	Carbohydrate 19.6g	Fiber 1.0g
saturated fat 0.6g	Cholesterol 19mg	Iron 1.2mg
Protein 3.5g	Sodium 99mg	Calcium 77mg

Cinnamon-Pear Tart (page 59) and Irish Coffee (page 59)

A Winter Celebration

Ragoût of Veal
Mixed Greens with Balsamic Vinaigrette
Cinnamon-Pear Tart
Irish Coffee

Serves 8
TOTAL CALORIES PER SERVING: 779
(Calories from Fat: 18%)

Chase away the midwinter blues with this hearty menu. The mellow, wine-laced ragoût atop fettuccine noodles pairs deliciously with the sweet yet tangy salad. After dinner, savor dessert and coffee beside a fire. For fun, ask friends to come prepared to share a poem by their favorite poet. Then enjoy the poetry reading as you relax with dessert.

Ragoût of Veal

(pictured on page 49)

2½   pounds lean boneless veal sirloin tip roast
1½   teaspoons paprika
½   teaspoon freshly ground pepper
     Vegetable cooking spray
1   tablespoon olive oil, divided
2½   cups sliced leeks (about 3 large leeks)
3   cloves garlic, minced
⅓   cup all-purpose flour
1½   cups dry vermouth
2   (14¼-ounce) cans no-salt-added
     chicken broth
2   teaspoons dried thyme
2   bay leaves
1   pound carrots, scraped and cut into
     2-inch-long strips
½   teaspoon salt
8   cups cooked fettuccine (cooked without
     salt or fat)
2   tablespoons chopped fresh thyme
     Fresh thyme sprigs (optional)

Trim fat from veal; cut veal into 1-inch cubes. Sprinkle paprika and pepper over veal.

Coat an ovenproof Dutch oven with cooking spray, and add 1 teaspoon oil. Place over medium-high heat until hot. Add half of veal mixture, and cook until browned on all sides, stirring frequently. Transfer to a bowl, and set aside. Repeat procedure with 1 teaspoon oil and remaining veal mixture. Wipe drippings from Dutch oven with a paper towel.

Add remaining 1 teaspoon oil to Dutch oven. Place over medium-high heat until hot. Add leeks and garlic; sauté 3 to 4 minutes. Return veal to Dutch oven; sprinkle with flour. Cook 1 minute, stirring constantly. Stir in vermouth and next 3 ingredients. Bring to a boil; cover and bake at 350° for 30 minutes.

Add carrot and salt to veal mixture, stirring well; bake, uncovered, 35 to 45 minutes or until veal and carrots are tender. Remove and discard bay leaves. Serve over pasta; sprinkle with chopped thyme. Garnish with thyme sprigs, if desired. Yield: 8 servings (439 calories per serving).

Per Serving:

Fat 7.2g	Carbohydrate 54.3g	Fiber 4.0g
saturated fat 1.8g	Cholesterol 120mg	Iron 5.2mg
Protein 36.1g	Sodium 325mg	Calcium 92mg

Mixed Greens with Balsamic Vinaigrette

(pictured on page 49)

½   cup canned no-salt-added chicken broth,
     undiluted
¼   cup balsamic vinegar
1½   tablespoons olive oil
1   tablespoon honey
2   teaspoons coarse-grained mustard
¼   teaspoon salt
1   large clove garlic, minced
1   (6-ounce) package mixed salad greens
7   cups torn Bibb lettuce (2 large heads)
½   teaspoon freshly ground pepper

Combine first 7 ingredients. Cover and chill.

Combine mixed greens and Bibb lettuce in a large bowl. Add dressing; toss. Arrange evenly on individual salad plates, and sprinkle with pepper. Yield: 8 servings (43 calories per 1½-cup serving).

Per Serving:

Fat 2.7g	Carbohydrate 4.0g	Fiber 0.6g
saturated fat 0.4g	Cholesterol 0mg	Iron 0.4mg
Protein 0.9g	Sodium 95mg	Calcium 14mg

It's Always Flex Time

Don't underestimate the benefits of stretching. This simple activity promotes flexibility, prevents injuries, and makes you feel good. The International Association of Fitness Professionals offers these tips on proper stretching:
- Try to stretch every day.
- Warm up your muscles with some simple fluid movements before you start to stretch.
- Concentrate on all major muscle groups.
- Hold each stretch for 15 to 60 seconds.

Cinnamon-Pear Tart

1   cup sifted cake flour
½   cup plus 1 tablespoon sugar, divided
1½   teaspoons ground cinnamon, divided
½   teaspoon baking powder
3   tablespoons margarine, cut into small
      pieces and chilled
2   to 3 tablespoons ice water
¼   cup all-purpose flour
5   medium pears (about 2 pounds), peeled,
      cored, and thinly sliced
2   cups vanilla nonfat frozen yogurt
      Ground cinnamon (optional)

Combine cake flour, 1 tablespoon sugar, ½ teaspoon cinnamon, and baking powder in a medium bowl; cut in margarine with a pastry blender until mixture resembles coarse meal and is pale yellow (about 3½ minutes). Sprinkle ice water, 1 tablespoon at a time, over surface; toss with a fork until dry ingredients are moistened and mixture is crumbly. (Do not form a ball.)

Gently press mixture into a 4-inch circle on heavy-duty plastic wrap. Cover with additional heavy-duty plastic wrap, and chill at least 15 minutes. Roll dough, still covered, into an 11-inch circle. Place dough in freezer 5 minutes or until plastic wrap can easily be removed.

Remove top sheet of plastic wrap. Invert and fit dough into an ungreased 9-inch tart pan; remove remaining sheet of plastic wrap. Prick bottom of pastry with a fork. Chill 15 minutes. Bake at 400° for 10 minutes or until lightly browned; let cool completely on a wire rack.

Combine remaining ½ cup sugar, remaining 1 teaspoon cinnamon, and ¼ cup all-purpose flour in a large bowl. Add pears; toss gently to coat. Let stand at room temperature 15 minutes. Arrange pears in prepared crust. Pour any remaining juices over pears. Bake at 350° for 30 minutes or until pears are tender. Let cool completely on a wire rack. Serve with frozen yogurt. Sprinkle with ground cinnamon, if desired. Yield: 8 servings (232 calories per serving).

Per Serving:		
Fat 4.7g	Carbohydrate 45.8g	Fiber 2.1g
saturated fat 0.9g	Cholesterol 0mg	Iron 1.5mg
Protein 3.5g	Sodium 80mg	Calcium 96mg

Irish Coffee

6   cups strong brewed coffee
½   cup Irish whiskey
2   tablespoons plus 2 teaspoons sugar
1   cup frozen reduced-calorie whipped
      topping, thawed

Pour ¾ cup brewed coffee into each mug. Add 1 tablespoon Irish whiskey and 1 teaspoon sugar to each mug, stirring until sugar dissolves. Top each serving with 2 tablespoons reduced-calorie whipped topping. Serve immediately. Yield: 8 servings (65 calories per ¾-cup serving).

Per Serving:		
Fat 1.1g	Carbohydrate 8.3g	Fiber 0g
saturated fat 0.7g	Cholesterol 0mg	Iron 0.7mg
Protein 0.5g	Sodium 10mg	Calcium 10mg

Skewered Shrimp and Sausage and Orange-Lemon Tea (page 62)

Beach Bash

Skewered Shrimp and Sausage
Spicy Slaw
Watermelon Wedges
Commercial French Bread
Caramel-Brownie Chunk Ice Cream
Orange-Lemon Tea

Serves 10
TOTAL CALORIES PER SERVING: 726
(Calories from Fat: 15%)

It's summertime! Bring the beach to your own front door with this great-tasting menu and a few simple props like beach balls, lounge chairs, and splashy beach music.

To get a head start, prepare the brownies for the ice cream, the slaw, and the tea a day ahead.

Slice the watermelon, marinate the shrimp and potatoes, and prepare the ice cream a few hours before the party. Just before guests arrive, assemble the kabobs, and fire up the grill. (Menu calories reflect 1 small watermelon wedge, 1 (1-ounce) slice bread, and ½ cup ice cream per person.)

Skewered Shrimp and Sausage

2   pounds unpeeled large fresh shrimp
⅔   cup canned no-salt-added chicken broth, undiluted
½   cup lemon juice
2   tablespoons chopped fresh parsley
1½ tablespoons minced onion
1½ tablespoons white wine Worcestershire sauce
1   tablespoon olive oil
1½ teaspoons sugar
½   teaspoon hot sauce
5   small round red potatoes, each cut into 4 pieces
5   ears fresh corn, each cut into 4 pieces
1   pound smoked turkey sausage, cut into 1½-inch pieces
    Vegetable cooking spray

Peel and devein shrimp, leaving tails intact. Set shrimp aside.

Combine chicken broth and next 7 ingredients in a small bowl, stirring well; set aside half of chicken broth mixture. Pour remaining half of chicken broth mixture into a large heavy-duty, zip-top plastic bag. Add shrimp and potato wedges; seal bag, and shake until shrimp and potato wedges are well coated. Marinate in refrigerator 2 to 3 hours, turning bag occasionally.

Remove shrimp and potato from marinade, discarding marinade. Thread shrimp on 4 (14-inch) skewers. Thread potato, corn, and sausage separately on 6 (14-inch) skewers.

Coat grill rack with cooking spray; place on grill over medium-hot coals (350° to 400°). Place potato kabobs on rack, and grill, covered, 10 minutes. Place corn and sausage kabobs on rack; grill, covered, 10 minutes or until potato and corn are tender and sausage is thoroughly heated, turning and basting occasionally with reserved chicken broth mixture. Remove potato, corn, and sausage kabobs from grill. Place shrimp on rack, and grill 3 to 4 minutes on each side or until shrimp turn pink, basting frequently with reserved broth mixture.

Remove vegetables, sausage, and shrimp from skewers, and place on a large serving platter. Yield: 10 servings (245 calories per serving).

Per Serving:		
Fat 8.7g	Carbohydrate 22.1g	Fiber 2.5g
saturated fat 2.5g	Cholesterol 130mg	Iron 3.2mg
Protein 20.8g	Sodium 528mg	Calcium 40mg

Spicy Slaw

As a time-saver, chop the vegetables in the food processor or substitute preshredded coleslaw mix for the green and red cabbage.

4   cups shredded green cabbage
4   cups shredded red cabbage
1   cup chopped green pepper
1   cup shredded carrot
⅔   cup chopped onion
⅔   cup low-sodium light and tangy vegetable juice
¼   cup white vinegar
1   tablespoon sugar
1   tablespoon vegetable oil
1   teaspoon chili powder
½   teaspoon salt
2   jalapeño peppers, seeded and minced
5   medium-size ripe tomatoes, thinly sliced

Combine first 5 ingredients in a large bowl, and set aside.

Combine vegetable juice and next 6 ingredients in a small bowl, stirring well. Pour juice mixture over cabbage mixture, and toss well. Cover and marinate in refrigerator at least 2 hours, tossing occasionally.

To serve, line a large platter with tomato slices. Spoon cabbage mixture evenly over tomato slices, using a slotted spoon. Yield: 10 servings (64 calories per serving).

Per Serving:		
Fat 1.9g	Carbohydrate 11.7g	Fiber 3.1g
saturated fat 0.3g	Cholesterol 0mg	Iron 1.0mg
Protein 1.9g	Sodium 142mg	Calcium 45mg

Caramel-Brownie Chunk Ice Cream

½ (20½-ounce) package light fudge brownie
     mix (about 2 cups)
¼ cup water
 1 egg white, lightly beaten
     Vegetable cooking spray
 1 (14-ounce) can low-fat sweetened
     condensed milk
¼ cup sugar
¼ cup all-purpose flour
 3 cups 1% low-fat milk
 2 (12-ounce) cans evaporated skimmed milk
 2 egg yolks, lightly beaten

Combine one-half package brownie mix, water, and egg white in a bowl, stirring well. Reserve remaining brownie mix for another use. Spread mixture into an 8-inch square pan coated with cooking spray. Bake at 350° for 20 to 22 minutes or just until done (do not overbake). Let cool on a wire rack.

Place sweetened condensed milk in a 9-inch pieplate. Cover pieplate with aluminum foil. Place pieplate in a larger shallow pan. Add hot water to pan to depth of ¼ inch. Bake at 425° for 1 hour and 20 minutes or until sweet-

ened condensed milk is thick and caramel colored. (Add hot water to pan as needed.) Remove aluminum foil, and let caramelized milk cool.

Combine sugar and flour in a large saucepan, stirring well. Gradually add low-fat and evaporated milks, stirring until smooth. Cook over medium heat, stirring constantly, until thickened (about 15 minutes). Gradually stir one-fourth of hot mixture into beaten egg yolks; add to remaining hot mixture, stirring constantly. Cook over medium heat 1 minute, stirring constantly. Remove from heat, and stir in caramelized milk. Let cool. Chill thoroughly.

Pour caramelized milk mixture into freezer can of a 1-gallon hand-turned or electric freezer. Freeze according to manufacturer's instructions. Cut cooled brownie into ½-inch cubes. Stir brownie cubes into ice cream. Pack freezer with additional ice and rock salt; let stand 1 hour before serving. Yield: 9 cups (203 calories per ½-cup serving).

Per Serving:

Fat 3.2g	Carbohydrate 36.2g	Fiber 0.5g
saturated fat 1.3g	Cholesterol 30mg	Iron 0.6mg
Protein 7.5g	Sodium 145mg	Calcium 207mg

Orange-Lemon Tea

 6 regular-size tea bags
 3 cups boiling water
½ cup sugar
1½ quarts cold water
 1 (6-ounce) can frozen orange juice
     concentrate, thawed and undiluted
½ (6-ounce) can frozen lemonade concentrate,
     thawed and undiluted
     Lemon slices (optional)
     Orange slices (optional)

Combine tea bags and boiling water. Cover and let steep 5 minutes. Remove and discard tea bags.

Combine tea, sugar, cold water, orange juice concentrate, and lemonade concentrate, stirring well; cover and chill. Serve over ice. If desired, garnish with lemon and orange slices. Yield: 2½ quarts (82 calories per 1-cup serving).

Per Serving:

Fat 0.1g	Carbohydrate 20.7g	Fiber 0.2g
saturated fat 0.0g	Cholesterol 0mg	Iron 0.1mg
Protein 0.4g	Sodium 3mg	Calcium 6mg

Italian Opera Dinner Party

Caponata Canapés
Lemon Chicken and Potatoes
Italian Green Beans
Small Commercial Hard Rolls
Blushing Poached Pears
Espresso

Serves 6
TOTAL CALORIES PER SERVING: 780
(Calories from Fat: 15%)

Dining with a few close friends is a delicious way for opera-lovers to celebrate the opera season. Set the stage for this menu of Italian classics while the voice of Domingo or Pavarotti fills the air.

To continue the Italian theme, you can use colorful green, red, and white serving pieces to showcase Italy's healthful fare. (Menu calories include 3 canapés, 1 (1-ounce) roll, and 1 cup of espresso.)

Blushing Poached Pears (page 64)

Caponata Canapés

1 tablespoon vegetable oil, divided
2 cups peeled, chopped eggplant
1 cup chopped onion
2 cloves garlic, minced
1 cup no-salt-added stewed tomatoes
¼ cup picante sauce
2 tablespoons balsamic vinegar
1 tablespoon capers
3 tablespoons chopped fresh basil
18 (½-inch-thick) slices French baguette, toasted

Heat 1½ teaspoons oil in a nonstick skillet over medium heat until hot. Add eggplant; cook 5 minutes, stirring occasionally. Transfer eggplant to a bowl. Add remaining 1½ teaspoons oil to skillet. Place over medium-high heat until hot. Add onion and garlic; sauté 4 minutes. Stir in tomato; bring to a boil. Cover, reduce heat, and simmer 5 minutes. Stir in eggplant, picante sauce, vinegar, and capers. Bring to a boil; cover, reduce heat, and simmer 20 minutes. Stir in basil.

Remove from heat, and spoon 2 heaping tablespoonfuls of eggplant mixture onto each baguette slice. Yield: 1½ dozen (54 calories each).

Per Appetizer:

Fat 1.0g	Carbohydrate 9.4g	Fiber 0.7g
saturated fat 0.2g	Cholesterol 0mg	Iron 0.5mg
Protein 1.6g	Sodium 183mg	Calcium 18mg

Lemon Chicken and Potatoes

Vegetable cooking spray
3 large baking potatoes, peeled and cut
    crosswise into ½-inch-thick slices
1 cup canned no-salt-added chicken broth
½ cup dry white wine
¼ cup fresh lemon juice
8 cloves garlic, minced
6 (6-ounce) skinned chicken breast halves
1 tablespoon olive oil
½ teaspoon salt
½ teaspoon freshly ground pepper
12 thin slices lemon

Coat a 13- x 9- x 2-inch pan with cooking spray. Arrange potato in pan. Combine broth and next 3 ingredients; pour half of broth mixture over potato. Bake, uncovered, at 375° for 15 minutes.

Add chicken to pan. Pour remaining broth mixture over chicken and potato. Brush chicken with oil. Sprinkle with salt and pepper. Top each chicken breast with 2 lemon slices. Bake, uncovered, 45 additional minutes or until chicken is done and potato is tender, basting frequently with pan juices. Yield: 6 servings (297 calories per serving).

Per Serving:
Fat 4.0g	Carbohydrate 34.3g	Fiber 2.9g
saturated fat 0.7g	Cholesterol 66mg	Iron 2.3mg
Protein 30.2g	Sodium 283mg	Calcium 36mg

Italian Green Beans

1½ pounds fresh green beans, trimmed
1 (14½-ounce) can no-salt-added stewed
    tomatoes, undrained
¼ cup water
1 teaspoon dried Italian seasoning
½ teaspoon dried rosemary, crushed
⅛ to ¼ teaspoon dried crushed red pepper
3 tablespoons chopped fresh basil
3 tablespoons grated Parmesan cheese

Combine beans, tomato, and next 4 ingredients in a large saucepan. Bring mixture to a boil; cover, reduce heat, and simmer 10 minutes.

Uncover and simmer 7 to 8 minutes or until beans are tender and tomato mixture is slightly thickened. Remove from heat; stir in basil, and sprinkle with cheese. Yield: 6 servings (65 calories per serving).

Per Serving:
Fat 0.9g	Carbohydrate 12.6g	Fiber 2.6g
saturated fat 0.5g	Cholesterol 2mg	Iron 1.8mg
Protein 3.8g	Sodium 64mg	Calcium 104mg

Blushing Poached Pears

6 firm ripe Bosc pears
2 cups port wine
1 cup water
⅓ cup sugar
2 (2-inch) strips orange rind
1 (2-inch) stick cinnamon
3 tablespoons crumbled Gorgonzola cheese
3 tablespoons chopped walnuts, toasted
    Fresh mint sprigs (optional)

Peel pears, leaving stems attached. Core from the bottom, cutting to, but not through, stem end.

Combine wine and next 4 ingredients in a Dutch oven; bring to a boil. Reduce heat; simmer, uncovered, 5 minutes. Add pears; cover and simmer 12 to 15 minutes or just until tender. Remove from heat; uncover and cool 20 minutes.

Remove pears from liquid; set aside. Remove and discard orange rind and cinnamon stick. Bring liquid to a boil; cook over high heat 10 minutes or until liquid mixture is slightly syrupy. Let syrup cool. (Liquid will thicken as it cools.)

Arrange pears on individual serving plates; drizzle syrup over pears. Sprinkle with cheese and walnuts. Garnish with mint sprigs, if desired. Yield: 6 servings (174 calories per serving).

Per Serving:
Fat 4.3g	Carbohydrate 34.4g	Fiber 4.0g
saturated fat 1.3g	Cholesterol 4mg	Iron 0.8mg
Protein 2.8g	Sodium 89mg	Calcium 56mg

Parmesan Chicken with Tomato Cream Sauce and Asparagus with Blue Cheese and Almonds (Menu begins on page 70.)

Holiday
Celebrations

Chinese New Year's Dinner Party

Shrimp Toast
Gingered Beef and Peppers
Orange and Onion Salad
Almond Moons
Jasmine or Green Tea

Serves 6
TOTAL CALORIES PER SERVING: 634
(Calories from Fat: 18%)

Chinese New Year is the second new moon after the beginning of winter. This year join in the fun and plan a dinner party celebrating light, healthful food, and a year of good fortune is surely ahead.

Set the scene with inexpensive chopsticks at each place setting (but have forks, too). If sprigs of orchids are available, use the delicate flowers as an attractive table decoration.

Start the meal with Shrimp Toast (4 per person). Then serve the gingered beef stir-fry and tangy salad. For lively after-dinner conversation, write creative fortunes on note cards. Fold them and place in a pretty dish. Then let guests draw and read their fortunes aloud as they sip on warm tea (½ cup per person) and munch on Almond Moons (2 per person), a sweet treat reminiscent of fortune cookies.

Shrimp Toast

1½ cups water
 ½ pound unpeeled medium-size fresh
       shrimp
  2 tablespoons finely chopped green onions
  2 tablespoons finely chopped sweet red
       pepper
  1 tablespoon chopped fresh cilantro
  2 tablespoons low-sodium soy sauce
  1 teaspoon dark sesame oil
  1 egg white
  6 (1-ounce) slices whole wheat bread,
       lightly toasted

Bring water to a boil; add shrimp, and cook 3 to 5 minutes or until shrimp turn pink. Drain well; rinse with cold water. Peel and devein shrimp.

Position knife blade in food processor bowl; add shrimp. Process until shrimp are finely chopped.

Combine shrimp, green onions, and next 4 ingredients in a medium bowl. Add egg white, stirring well.

Trim crusts from bread slices, and cut each slice into 4 triangles. Spread shrimp mixture evenly over bread triangles; place triangles on a large baking sheet.

Bake at 350° for 8 minutes or until thoroughly heated and lightly browned. Yield: 24 appetizers (25 calories each).

Per Appetizer:		
Fat 0.5g	Carbohydrate 3.5g	Fiber 0.3g
saturated fat 0.1g	Cholesterol 9mg	Iron 0.3mg
Protein 1.9g	Sodium 83mg	Calcium 10mg

Gingered Beef and Peppers (page 68)

Gingered Beef and Peppers

1 pound lean boneless top sirloin steak

¼ cup plus 2 tablespoons low-sodium soy sauce

1½ tablespoons peeled, minced fresh gingerroot

¼ teaspoon dried crushed red pepper

4 cloves garlic, minced

1½ cups canned no-salt-added beef broth, undiluted

2 tablespoons plus 2 teaspoons cornstarch
Vegetable cooking spray

2 teaspoons peanut oil, divided

1 cup julienne-sliced sweet red pepper

1 cup julienne-sliced sweet yellow pepper

1½ cups snow pea pods, trimmed

3 green onions, diagonally sliced into ½-inch pieces

6 cups cooked long-grain rice (cooked without salt or fat)
Green onion curls (optional)

Trim fat from steak; slice steak diagonally across grain into ⅛-inch-wide strips. Cut strips crosswise into 1½-inch-long pieces. Combine soy sauce and next 3 ingredients in a heavy-duty, zip-top plastic bag. Add steak; seal bag, and shake until steak is well coated. Marinate in refrigerator at least 8 hours, turning bag occasionally. Drain steak, reserving marinade. Set steak aside.

Combine marinade, beef broth, and cornstarch; set aside.

Coat a wok or large nonstick skillet with cooking spray; drizzle 1 teaspoon oil around top of wok, coating sides. Heat at medium-high (375°) until hot. Add sweet red pepper, sweet yellow pepper, and snow peas; stir-fry until vegetables are crisp-tender. Remove pepper mixture from wok; set aside.

Add remaining 1 teaspoon oil to wok. Add steak and sliced green onions; stir-fry 5 minutes or to desired degree of doneness. Add pepper mixture, and toss well. Stir marinade mixture with a wire whisk; add to steak mixture. Stir-fry 1 minute or until mixture comes to a boil. Stir-fry 1 additional minute. Serve over rice. Garnish with green onion curls, if desired. Yield: 6 servings (384 calories per serving).

Per Serving:

Fat 6.0g	Carbohydrate 56.9g	Fiber 2.4g
saturated fat 1.7g	Cholesterol 46mg	Iron 4.9mg
Protein 21.3g	Sodium 440mg	Calcium 46mg

Lick the Salt Habit

If you have high blood pressure, a small reduction in your salt intake may do more than lower the pressure. It may keep your heart at a healthier size, further reducing your risk of a heart attack.

New research from Finland suggests that a low-sodium diet—no more than 1600 mg per day (about ¾ teaspoon of salt)—helps reduce the volume of blood that the heart has to pump. When the heart doesn't have to work so hard, it stays at a healthier size and is less susceptible to damage.

If you want to consume less sodium, here are some great sodium switches you can make.

Eat . . .	(sodium mg)	Instead of . . .	(sodium mg)
½ cup fresh or frozen corn	14	½ cup canned corn	286
½ cup regular pudding mix	115	½ cup instant pudding	470
2 tablespoons oil and vinegar	0	2 tablespoons commercial Italian dressing	344
3 ounces cooked turkey breast	44	3 ounces deli-style turkey breast	864
3 ounces lean loin pork chop	59	3 ounces baked ham	1,215
¼ cup unsalted, dry-roasted peanuts	2	¼ cup salted, dry-roasted peanuts	297
½ cup cooked brown rice	5	½ cup seasoned rice mix	315

Orange and Onion Salad

Dark sesame oil adds an intense nutty flavor—a little goes a long way.

2   tablespoons rice wine vinegar
2   tablespoons low-sodium soy sauce
2   teaspoons dark sesame oil
¼   teaspoon grated orange rind
2   large oranges, peeled, seeded, and
     sliced
1   small purple onion, thinly sliced
3   cups torn red leaf lettuce

Combine first 4 ingredients in a small bowl, stirring with a wire whisk. Arrange orange and onion in a 13- x 9- x 2-inch dish. Pour vinegar mixture over orange and onion. Cover and chill at least 30 minutes.

Place lettuce evenly on individual salad plates. Arrange orange and onion over lettuce, using a slotted spoon. Drizzle vinegar mixture evenly over salads. Yield: 6 servings (42 calories per serving).

Per Serving:

Fat 1.6g	Carbohydrate 6.1g	Fiber 2.1g
saturated fat 0.2g	Cholesterol 0mg	Iron 0.3mg
Protein 0.7g	Sodium 132mg	Calcium 29mg

Almond Moons

The flavor of Almond Moons is similar to fortune cookies, but these cookies are softer and moister.

2   tablespoons margarine, softened
1   tablespoon almond paste
¼   cup sugar
2   tablespoons frozen egg substitute, thawed
⅛   teaspoon almond extract
¾   cup all-purpose flour
¼   teaspoon baking soda
     Dash of salt
2   teaspoons sugar
     Vegetable cooking spray

Beat margarine and almond paste at medium speed of an electric mixer until creamy; gradually add ¼ cup sugar, beating well. Add egg substitute and almond extract; beat well.

Combine flour, baking soda, and salt in a small bowl. Gradually add flour mixture to almond mixture, stirring well. Shape dough into a ball; cover and chill 1 hour.

Divide chilled dough into ten equal portions. Shape each portion into a 1-inch ball. Roll balls in 2 teaspoons sugar. Place balls, 4 inches apart, on a cookie sheet coated with cooking spray. Bake at 350° for 9 minutes or until golden. Remove from oven; cut cookies in half. Remove from cookie sheets, and let cool completely on a wire rack. Yield: 20 cookies (53 calories each).

Per Cookie:

Fat 1.4g	Carbohydrate 6.9g	Fiber 0.2g
saturated fat 0.2g	Cholesterol 0mg	Iron 0.2mg
Protein 0.7g	Sodium 39mg	Calcium 2mg

Raspberry-Cheese Crêpes (page 72) and Chocolate-Hazelnut Coffee (page 72)

Valentine's Day Dinner

Parmesan Chicken with Tomato Cream Sauce
Asparagus with Blue Cheese and Almonds
Raspberry-Cheese Crêpes
Chocolate-Hazelnut Coffee

Serves 6
TOTAL CALORIES PER SERVING: 660
(Calories from Fat: 15%)

Show your closest friends and family what a big heart you have with this dressed-up dinner menu designed for a Valentine's Day celebration. The menu features chicken smothered with a blushing rose-colored sauce on a bed of linguine,

and asparagus with blue cheese and almonds as an elegant side dish.

Finally, express the full measure of your devotion with an indulgent dessert of Raspberry-Cheese Crêpes and a cup of hazelnut-flavored coffee.

Parmesan Chicken with Tomato Cream Sauce

(pictured on page 65)

¼ cup 1% low-fat milk
1 tablespoon Dijon mustard
½ cup fine, dry breadcrumbs
¼ cup grated Parmesan cheese, divided
½ teaspoon dried Italian seasoning
⅛ teaspoon garlic powder
⅛ teaspoon pepper
6 (4-ounce) skinned, boned chicken breast halves
   Vegetable cooking spray
1 teaspoon olive oil
3 cloves garlic, minced
2 (14½-ounce) cans no-salt-added whole tomatoes, crushed
1 tablespoon chopped fresh basil
1 tablespoon chopped fresh oregano
2 teaspoons chopped fresh parsley
¼ teaspoon sugar
¼ teaspoon salt
1 cup 1% low-fat milk
1 tablespoon all-purpose flour
8 ounces linguine, uncooked
   Fresh basil sprigs (optional)

Combine ¼ cup milk and mustard, stirring with a wire whisk. Combine breadcrumbs, 2 tablespoons Parmesan cheese, Italian seasoning, garlic powder, and pepper in a small bowl. Dip chicken in milk mixture, and dredge in breadcrumb mixture. Place chicken on a baking sheet coated with cooking spray. Bake at 375° for 30 minutes or until golden.

Heat oil in a medium saucepan over medium-high heat until hot; add garlic, and sauté until tender. Add tomato and next 5 ingredients; bring to a boil. Reduce heat, and simmer, uncovered, 20 minutes, stirring occasionally.

Combine 1 cup milk and flour in a small bowl, stirring well with a wire whisk. Gradually add milk mixture to tomato mixture, stirring constantly. Cook, stirring constantly, 5 minutes or until slightly thickened. Stir in remaining 2 tablespoons Parmesan cheese; set aside, and keep warm.

Cook pasta according to package directions, omitting salt and fat; drain. Place 1 cup linguine on each serving plate; top linguine with chicken breasts. Spoon tomato sauce evenly over chicken. Garnish with fresh basil sprigs, if desired. Yield: 6 servings (387 calories per serving).

Per Serving:		
Fat 5.3g	Carbohydrate 45.8g	Fiber 1.4g
saturated fat 1.8g	Cholesterol 71mg	Iron 3.8mg
Protein 37.0g	Sodium 446mg	Calcium 218mg

Asparagus with Blue Cheese and Almonds

(pictured on page 65)

1½ pounds fresh asparagus spears
¾   cup canned no-salt-added chicken broth, undiluted
¼   cup sliced green onions
1   teaspoon dried tarragon
12 Bibb lettuce leaves
2   tablespoons crumbled blue cheese
1½ tablespoons sliced almonds, toasted

Snap off tough ends of asparagus. Remove scales from stalks with a knife or vegetable peeler, if desired.

Place broth in a large skillet. Bring to a boil over medium-high heat. Add asparagus, green onions, and tarragon. Reduce heat, and simmer, uncovered, 6 to 8 minutes or until asparagus is crisp-tender. Remove asparagus from skillet, using a slotted spoon; discard broth remaining in skillet.

Arrange asparagus on individual lettuce-lined salad plates. Sprinkle with blue cheese and almonds. Serve warm or chilled. Yield: 6 servings (44 calories per serving).

Per Serving:		
Fat 1.7g	Carbohydrate 5.3g	Fiber 2.1g
saturated fat 0.6g	Cholesterol 2mg	Iron 1.1mg
Protein 3.1g	Sodium 37mg	Calcium 36mg

Raspberry-Cheese Crêpes

½ cup 1% low-fat cottage cheese
½ cup light process cream cheese
3 tablespoons sugar
3 tablespoons nonfat sour cream
1 teaspoon grated lemon rind
1 teaspoon vanilla extract
¼ cup low-sugar seedless raspberry jam
1 tablespoon fresh lemon juice
2 teaspoons Chambord or other raspberry-flavored liqueur
1 cup fresh or frozen unsweetened raspberries, thawed
  Crêpes
  Lemon zest (optional)
  Lemon rind hearts (optional)

Position knife blade in food processor bowl; add first 6 ingredients. Process until smooth. Transfer cheese mixture to a small bowl; cover and chill.

Combine raspberry jam, lemon juice, and Chambord in a small saucepan; place over medium heat. Cook, stirring constantly, until jam melts. Remove from heat; cool. Stir in raspberries; set aside.

Spoon 3 tablespoons cheese mixture down center of each crêpe. Fold right and left sides of each crêpe over filling.

To serve, place a filled crêpe, seam side down, on each individual serving plate. Spoon raspberry mixture evenly over crêpes. If desired, garnish with lemon zest and lemon rind hearts. Yield: 6 servings (150 calories per serving).

Crêpes

¼ cup all-purpose flour
½ cup skim milk
⅛ teaspoon salt
2 egg whites
  Vegetable cooking spray

Combine first 4 ingredients in container of an electric blender or food processor. Cover and process 1 minute, scraping sides of container once. Transfer batter to a small bowl; cover and chill at least 1 hour.

Coat a 6-inch crêpe pan or nonstick skillet with cooking spray; place over medium heat until hot.

Pour 2 tablespoons batter into pan, and quickly tilt pan in all directions so batter covers pan in a thin film. Cook 1 minute or until crêpe can be shaken loose from pan. Flip crêpe, and cook about 30 seconds.

Place crêpe on a towel to cool. Repeat procedure until all batter is used. Stack crêpes between layers of wax paper to prevent sticking. Yield: 6 (6-inch) crêpes.

Per Serving:		
Fat 3.9g	Carbohydrate 21.1g	Fiber 1.4g
saturated fat 2.2g	Cholesterol 12mg	Iron 0.4mg
Protein 7.4g	Sodium 276mg	Calcium 77mg

Chocolate-Hazelnut Coffee

¼ cup plus 2 tablespoons powdered fat-free nondairy coffee creamer
¼ cup superfine sugar
¼ cup hazelnut-flavored instant coffee granules
2 tablespoons unsweetened cocoa
4½ cups hot water

Combine first 4 ingredients in a medium bowl, stirring well. Place 2 tablespoons plus 2 teaspoons coffee mixture into each individual mug. Pour ¾ cup hot water into each mug; stir until coffee mixture dissolves. Yield: 6 servings (79 calories per serving).

Per Serving:		
Fat 0.3g	Carbohydrate 15.2g	Fiber 0.1g
saturated fat 0.2g	Cholesterol 0mg	Iron 0.5mg
Protein 1.0g	Sodium 2mg	Calcium 8mg

Herb-Grilled Swordfish (page 74), Zesty Corn Salad (page 74), and Tangy Marinated Tomatoes (page 75)

Fourth of July Barbecue

Herb-Grilled Swordfish

Zesty Corn Salad

Tangy Marinated Tomatoes

Watermelon Sorbet

Serves 6
TOTAL CALORIES PER SERVING: 453
(Calories from Fat: 29%)

Most people get fired up for a traditional outdoor Fourth of July celebration. It's also the best time of year to showcase summer's juiciest fruits and garden-fresh vegetables, especially succulent tomatoes.

This menu allows you to join in the fireworks fun because you can do most of the preparation ahead. Set the corn salad in the refrigerator to marinate the day before. On the morning of the party, marinate the tomatoes, and make the sorbet (½ cup per person). People love to participate in party preparations, so once the guests arrive, ask one of them to grill the swordfish steaks while you set the table for a delicious spread.

Herb-Grilled Swordfish

¼ cup unsweetened orange juice
3 tablespoons minced onion
1 tablespoon chopped fresh thyme
1 tablespoon chopped fresh basil
2 tablespoons low-sodium soy sauce
1½ tablespoons fresh lemon juice
1 tablespoon olive oil
½ teaspoon sugar
⅛ teaspoon salt
⅛ teaspoon pepper
1 clove garlic, minced
6 (4-ounce) swordfish steaks (½ inch thick)
   Vegetable cooking spray
   Fresh basil sprigs (optional)

Combine first 11 ingredients in a large heavy-duty, zip-top plastic bag. Add swordfish steaks; seal bag, and shake until steaks are well coated. Marinate in refrigerator 2 hours, turning bag occasionally.

Remove steaks from marinade, reserving marinade. Place marinade in a small saucepan. Bring to a boil; boil 1 minute.

Coat grill rack with cooking spray. Place on grill over medium-hot coals (350° to 400°). Place swordfish steaks on rack; grill, covered, 3 to 4 minutes on each side or until fish flakes easily when tested with a fork, basting occasionally with marinade. Garnish swordfish steaks with fresh basil sprigs, if desired. Yield: 6 servings (165 calories per serving).

Per Serving:

Fat 6.8g	Carbohydrate 2.5g	Fiber 0.1g
saturated fat 1.5g	Cholesterol 43mg	Iron 1.2mg
Protein 21.8g	Sodium 277mg	Calcium 14mg

Zesty Corn Salad

4 cups fresh corn cut from cob (about 8 ears)
1 cup water
1⅓ cups chopped sweet red pepper
1 cup sliced celery
½ cup sliced green onions
½ cup chopped fresh parsley
½ cup chopped fresh basil
½ cup raspberry wine vinegar
¼ cup sugar
1 tablespoon vegetable oil
½ teaspoon salt
¼ teaspoon pepper

Combine corn kernels and water in a medium saucepan, and bring to a boil. Reduce heat, and simmer, uncovered, 15 minutes or until corn is tender. Drain well.

Combine cooked corn, sweet red pepper, celery, green onions, chopped parsley, and chopped basil in a medium bowl.

Combine raspberry wine vinegar, sugar, oil, salt, and pepper in a small bowl, stirring well. Pour vinegar mixture over corn mixture, and toss well. Cover and chill at least 8 hours, stirring occasionally. Toss gently before serving. Yield: 6 cups (165 calories per 1-cup serving).

Per Serving:

Fat 4.8g	Carbohydrate 31.4g	Fiber 4.2g
saturated fat 0.8g	Cholesterol 0mg	Iron 1.3mg
Protein 3.8g	Sodium 230mg	Calcium 26mg

Tangy Marinated Tomatoes

3　large tomatoes, cut into ¼-inch-thick slices
2　tablespoons sliced green onions
1　tablespoon chopped fresh parsley
1　tablespoon chopped fresh basil
¼　cup plus 2 tablespoons red wine vinegar
1　tablespoon olive oil
½　teaspoon salt
¼　teaspoon sugar
¼　teaspoon pepper
1　clove garlic, minced
　　Lettuce leaves (optional)

Place tomato slices in a large shallow dish. Combine green onions and next 8 ingredients in a small jar; cover tightly, and shake vigorously. Pour over tomato slices. Cover and marinate in refrigerator at least 2 hours. Transfer to a lettuce-lined serving platter, if desired. Yield: 6 servings (55 calories per serving).

Per Serving:

Fat 2.8g	Carbohydrate 7.8g	Fiber 2.0g
saturated fat 0.4g	Cholesterol 0mg	Iron 0.8mg
Protein 1.3g	Sodium 209mg	Calcium 12mg

Watermelon Sorbet

10　cups seeded, cubed watermelon
⅔　cup sugar
1½　cups unsweetened apple juice
½　cup lemon juice
　　Fresh mint sprigs (optional)

Position knife blade in food processor bowl; add watermelon. Process until smooth. Transfer to a large bowl; add sugar, apple juice, and lemon juice, stirring well.

Pour watermelon mixture into freezer can of a 4-quart hand-turned or electric freezer. Freeze according to manufacturer's instructions. Pack freezer with additional ice and rock salt, and let stand 1 hour before serving.

Scoop sorbet into individual dessert bowls. Garnish with fresh mint sprigs, if desired. Serve immediately. Yield: 2½ quarts (68 calories per ½-cup serving).

Per Serving:

Fat 0.4g	Carbohydrate 16.4g	Fiber 0.6g
saturated fat 0.2g	Cholesterol 0mg	Iron 0.2mg
Protein 0.6g	Sodium 3mg	Calcium 10mg

The Latest from the Fitness Front

Put away the word "aerobics."

According to Kathi Davis, the executive director of the International Association of Fitness Professionals, the more general term "fitness" is de rigueur at health clubs and Ys around the country. And with that broader definition comes an exciting variety of classes for the fitness-minded like "Show Tunes for Beginners" and "Urban Funk."

More trends from the ever-widening world of fitness include the following:

•**Circuit Training.** Classes combine cardiovascular workouts with toning exercises, and often include equipment such as weights, balls, and barres.

•**Step Aerobics Updated.** Instructors have turned up the intensity with taller steps, and they've gotten more creative with country, oldies, or funk music.

•**Water Fitness.** Clubs are putting any and all exercise into the pool for a low-stress, resistance-intensive workout, from in-the-water aerobics to pool walking. (Some clubs even have underwater treadmills!)

•**Box Aerobics.** These classes feature boxing or punching drills—great tension relievers—as the major workout, often along with high-intensity interval training.

White Bean and Tomato Soup, Pear and Watercress Salad, and Rosemary Focaccia with Garlic and Cheese Spread (page 78)

Columbus Day Dinner

White Bean and Tomato Soup
Pear and Watercress Salad
Rosemary Focaccia with Garlic and Cheese Spread
Cornmeal and Prune Streusel Cake

Serves 8
TOTAL CALORIES PER SERVING: 677
(Calories from Fat: 18%)

Gather a few friends to celebrate Columbus Day (October 12) and discover the flavors of fall. This menu sails into the crisp, colorful fall months with the season's best flavors—a hearty bean soup, a tangy pear salad, a robust flat bread topped with an herbed cheese spread, and a moist prune cake. You can make the bread and cake the day before and keep tightly covered until serving time. (Our menu calories reflect 1 slice of bread and 1 slice of cake per person.)

White Bean and Tomato Soup

If you forget to soak the beans overnight, don't fret. Simply cover the beans with water,
and bring to a boil; cover, remove from heat, and let stand 1 hour.

1   pound dried Great Northern beans
    Vegetable cooking spray
1   cup diced celery
½   cup chopped onion
6   cloves garlic, coarsely chopped
4   cups canned low-sodium chicken broth,
       undiluted
3   (14½-ounce) cans no-salt-added whole
       tomatoes, undrained
2   tablespoons chopped fresh basil
¾   teaspoon salt
½   teaspoon pepper
¼   cup nonfat sour cream
¼   cup freshly grated Romano cheese
    Fresh basil sprigs (optional)

Sort and wash beans; place beans in a large Dutch oven. Cover with water to depth of 2 inches above beans; let soak 8 hours. Drain beans; remove from Dutch oven, and set aside.

Coat Dutch oven with cooking spray; place over medium-high heat until hot. Add celery, onion, and garlic; sauté until tender.

Add beans and broth; bring to a boil. Cover, reduce heat, and simmer 40 minutes or until beans are tender.

Place 2 cups of bean mixture and 1 can of tomatoes in container of an electric blender; cover and process until smooth. Drain remaining 2 cans tomatoes; chop tomatoes. Add pureed mixture, chopped tomato, chopped basil, salt, and pepper to bean mixture in Dutch oven. Cook over medium heat until thoroughly heated.

Ladle soup into individual bowls; top evenly with sour cream, and sprinkle with cheese. Garnish with fresh basil sprigs, if desired. Yield: 12 cups (258 calories per 1½-cup serving).

Per Serving:

Fat 2.5g	Carbohydrate 44.2g	Fiber 23.9g
saturated fat 1.0g	Cholesterol 4mg	Iron 5.1mg
Protein 16.5g	Sodium 344mg	Calcium 197mg

Pear and Watercress Salad

Balsamic vinegar and walnut oil add a robust flavor to this salad without adding a lot of extra fat.

¼   cup balsamic vinegar
1   tablespoon water
1   tablespoon Dijon mustard
2   teaspoons walnut oil
¼   teaspoon garlic powder
¼   teaspoon dried oregano
3½ cups torn green leaf lettuce
3½ cups torn red leaf lettuce
1   cup watercress leaves
2   small ripe pears, cored and thinly
       sliced
2½ tablespoons chopped walnuts, toasted

Combine first 6 ingredients in a small jar; cover tightly, and shake vigorously.

Combine lettuces and watercress in a large serving bowl; toss well.

Pour vinegar mixture over lettuce mixture; toss gently. Place lettuce mixture on individual salad plates. Arrange pear slices over lettuce mixture; sprinkle with walnuts. Serve immediately. Yield: 8 servings (47 calories per serving).

Per Serving:

Fat 2.5g	Carbohydrate 6.2g	Fiber 1.4g
saturated fat 0.2g	Cholesterol 0mg	Iron 0.6mg
Protein 1.0g	Sodium 59mg	Calcium 25mg

Rosemary Focaccia with Garlic and Cheese Spread

3 cups bread flour, divided
¼ cup sugar
1½ tablespoons instant nonfat dry milk
    powder
½ teaspoon salt
1 package active dry yeast
1 cup hot water (120° to 130°)
1 cup frozen mashed potatoes, thawed
1 tablespoon margarine, melted
1 tablespoon bread flour
    Olive oil-flavored vegetable cooking spray
1 tablespoon dried rosemary
¼ teaspoon freshly ground pepper
    Garlic and Cheese Spread
    Fresh rosemary sprigs (optional)

Combine 1½ cups bread flour and next 4 ingredients in a large mixing bowl, stirring well. Gradually add hot water to flour mixture, beating well at low speed of an electric mixer. Beat 2 additional minutes at medium speed. Add mashed potato and margarine; beat well. Gradually stir in enough of the remaining 1½ cups bread flour to make a soft dough.

Sprinkle 1 tablespoon bread flour evenly over work surface. Turn dough out onto floured surface, and knead until smooth and elastic (about 10 minutes). Place dough in a large bowl coated with cooking spray, turning to coat top. Cover and let rise in a warm place (85°), free from drafts, 45 minutes or until doubled in bulk.

Punch dough down; turn out onto work surface, and knead lightly 4 or 5 times. Press dough onto a 14-inch pizza pan coated with cooking spray. Cover and let rise in a warm place, free from drafts, 30 minutes or until doubled in bulk. Coat with cooking spray, and sprinkle with 1 tablespoon rosemary and pepper; press lightly.

Bake at 400° for 20 minutes or until golden. Leave focaccia in pan; let cool slightly. Cut into 16 wedges.

Spread Garlic and Cheese Spread evenly over wedges. Broil 5½ inches from heat (with electric oven door partially opened) 1 to 2 minutes or until spread melts. Garnish with rosemary sprigs, if desired. Serve immediately. Yield: 16 servings (148 calories per serving).

Garlic and Cheese Spread

½ cup nonfat cream cheese
3 tablespoons low-fat sour cream
1 tablespoon nonfat mayonnaise
3 tablespoons freshly grated Parmesan
    cheese
3 tablespoons freshly grated Romano cheese
1½ tablespoons chopped fresh basil
1½ teaspoons minced fresh chives
⅛ teaspoon pepper

Combine first 3 ingredients in a medium bowl; beat at low speed of an electric mixer until smooth. Add Parmesan cheese and remaining ingredients; stir well. Yield: 1 cup.

Per Serving:		
Fat 2.5g	Carbohydrate 25.0g	Fiber 0.9g
saturated fat 1.0g	Cholesterol 5mg	Iron 1.4mg
Protein 5.6g	Sodium 190mg	Calcium 70mg

Cornmeal and Prune Streusel Cake

⅔ cup pitted prunes, chopped
2 tablespoons cognac
¾ cup sugar
3 tablespoons vegetable oil
1 egg
1 egg white
1½ cups all-purpose flour
⅓ cup yellow cornmeal
1½ teaspoons baking powder
¼ teaspoon salt
½ cup lemon nonfat yogurt
 Vegetable cooking spray
¼ cup sugar
2 tablespoons all-purpose flour
1 tablespoon grated lemon rind
½ teaspoon ground cinnamon
1 tablespoon margarine

Combine chopped prunes and cognac in a small bowl, stirring well; let stand 10 minutes. (Do not drain.)

Combine ¾ cup sugar and oil in a mixing bowl; beat at medium speed of an electric mixer until blended. Add egg and egg white, beating well.

Combine 1½ cups flour and next 3 ingredients, stirring well. Add to egg mixture alternately with yogurt, beginning and ending with flour mixture. Mix after each addition. Gently fold in prune mixture. Spoon batter into a 9-inch round cakepan coated with cooking spray.

Combine ¼ cup sugar, 2 tablespoons flour, lemon rind, and cinnamon. Cut in margarine with a pastry blender until mixture resembles coarse meal. Sprinkle over batter.

Bake at 350° for 45 minutes or until a wooden pick inserted in center comes out clean. Cool in pan on a wire rack 10 minutes. Remove from pan, and let cool completely on wire rack. Yield: 12 servings (224 calories per serving).

Per Serving:		
Fat 5.8g	Carbohydrate 40.3g	Fiber 0.8g
saturated fat 1.2g	Cholesterol 19mg	Iron 1.4mg
Protein 3.7g	Sodium 85mg	Calcium 65mg

Cracking the Case on Eggs and Cholesterol

The latest research news in the cholesterol-egg debate reveals that the effect of dietary cholesterol on blood cholesterol levels is a purely individual thing. In other words, some people can somehow compensate for an increase in dietary cholesterol, while others may be very sensitive to it.

Although it might be nice to know your body's response to dietary cholesterol so you can eat accordingly, it's difficult to tell without a number of tests. Experts say that one risk factor is a family history of high cholesterol and heart disease. On the other hand, if you can munch on foods that are high in cholesterol, yet blood tests taken soon thereafter reveal no change in your blood cholesterol level, you may have nothing to worry about.

This news means that eggs, which have been considered a cholesterol pariah (they contain about 213 mg per whole egg), may be back on your grocery list. Regardless, say the experts, you're still better off with a diet low in fat that contains no more than 300 mg of cholesterol per day, and no more than four egg yolks a week (the whites are okay). If you're an egg lover, and this amount seems like a penance, try substituting two egg whites for each whole egg in a recipe. Or use an egg substitute. And keep an eye out for more studies on this hot subject.

Cranberry-Walnut Scones, Creamy Amaretto Cocoa (page 82), and Spiced Fruit Compote (page 82)

Christmas Morning

Cranberry-Walnut Scones
Christmas Frittata
Spiced Fruit Compote
Creamy Amaretto Cocoa

Serves 4
TOTAL CALORIES PER SERVING: 607
(Calories from Fat: 12%)

Whatever your Christmas morning tradition, this menu lets you and your family enjoy it to the fullest because most of the preparation can be done the night before or earlier.

The dough for the Cranberry-Walnut Scones and the Spiced Fruit Compote will keep in the refrigerator up to 3 days. (Menu calories reflect 1 scone per person.) Chop the vegetables and combine the egg substitute mixture for the frittata the day before. With this advance work, your Christmas morning preparations are a breeze.

Cranberry-Walnut Scones

For variety, try dried apricots or currants in place of the cranberries, and pecans or hazelnuts instead of walnuts.

2	cups all-purpose flour
1	tablespoon baking powder
¼	teaspoon baking soda
⅓	cup sugar
2	tablespoons margarine
⅓	cup dried cranberries
1	cup nonfat buttermilk
1	tablespoon vanilla extract
	Vegetable cooking spray
3	tablespoons chopped walnuts
1½	teaspoons sugar

Combine first 4 ingredients in a medium bowl; cut in margarine with a pastry blender until mixture resembles coarse meal. Stir in cranberries. Add buttermilk and vanilla, stirring with a fork until dry ingredients are moistened.

Drop dough by 2 heaping tablespoonfuls, 2 inches apart, onto baking sheets coated with cooking spray. Sprinkle evenly with walnuts and 1½ teaspoons sugar. Bake at 400° for 15 to 17 minutes or until golden. Yield: 1 dozen (153 calories each).

Per Scone:

Fat 3.6g	Carbohydrate 26.3g	Fiber 0.9g
saturated fat 0.6g	Cholesterol 1mg	Iron 1.2mg
Protein 3.5g	Sodium 71mg	Calcium 98mg

Christmas Frittata

	Olive oil-flavored vegetable cooking spray
1	tablespoon sliced green onions
2	cloves garlic, minced
1	cup sliced fresh mushrooms
½	cup diced sweet red pepper
¼	cup chopped fresh broccoli flowerets
1½	cups frozen egg substitute, thawed
2	tablespoons grated Parmesan cheese
½	teaspoon dried basil
¼	teaspoon dried oregano
¼	teaspoon pepper
¼	teaspoon salt
⅛	teaspoon dried crushed red pepper
3	tablespoons crumbled feta cheese

Coat a medium-size nonstick skillet with cooking spray; place over medium-high heat until hot. Add onions and garlic; sauté 2 minutes. Add mushrooms, sweet red pepper, and broccoli; sauté 3 additional minutes.

Combine egg substitute and next 6 ingredients in a small bowl, stirring well. Pour egg substitute mixture over vegetable mixture. Cover and cook over medium heat 10 minutes or until egg substitute mixture is set. Sprinkle with feta cheese, and serve immediately. Yield: 4 servings (89 calories per serving).

Per Serving:

Fat 2.4g	Carbohydrate 4.9g	Fiber 0.9g
saturated fat 1.4g	Cholesterol 7mg	Iron 2.4mg
Protein 11.9g	Sodium 401mg	Calcium 113mg

It's Time to Cross Over to Cross Training

Although it may sound like the province of elite athletes, cross training is an ideal way for anyone to round out a workout. The notion is simple: instead of practicing one sport or activity over and over, you mix it up. If tennis is your game, alternate upper-body exercises and endurance training with those serves and cross-court forehands. Everything works together toward a better tennis game, and boredom is banished from center court.

A personal trainer or club pro could help design your cross-training program. Here are a few ideas to get you started:
- **Skiers**—Try climbing stairs, jumping rope, even playing ping-pong.
- **Walkers**—Try swimming, calisthenics, social dancing.
- **Golfers**—Try stationary cycling, volleyball, strength training.

Spiced Fruit Compote

1 (20-ounce) can pineapple tidbits in juice, undrained
1 (16-ounce) can apricot halves in juice, undrained
1 (16-ounce) can sliced peaches in water, undrained
1 (16-ounce) can pear halves in extra light syrup, undrained
¼ cup firmly packed brown sugar
¼ cup unsweetened orange juice
1 tablespoon cornstarch
1 tablespoon fresh lemon juice
4 whole cloves
1 (3-inch) stick cinnamon
⅛ teaspoon ground mace
   Cinnamon sticks (optional)

Drain canned fruit, reserving ¼ cup liquid from each can. Discard remaining liquid. Cut pear halves in half lengthwise. Combine pears, pineapple tidbits, apricot halves, and peaches in a 13- x 9- x 2-inch baking dish.

Combine reserved liquid, brown sugar, orange juice, cornstarch, lemon juice, cloves, 1 cinnamon stick, and mace in a medium saucepan, stirring well. Bring to a boil over medium heat; reduce heat, and simmer, uncovered, 2 minutes. Pour juice mixture over fruit.

Cover and chill at least 8 hours. Bake at 350° for 40 minutes or until fruit mixture is thoroughly heated. Remove and discard cloves and cinnamon stick from fruit mixture.

Spoon fruit mixture into a serving bowl. Garnish with cinnamon sticks, if desired. Serve warm. Yield: 5 cups (190 calories per 1-cup serving).

Per Serving:		
Fat 0.5g	Carbohydrate 48.4g	Fiber 4.4g
saturated fat 0.0g	Cholesterol 0mg	Iron 1.6mg
Protein 1.7g	Sodium 21mg	Calcium 33mg

Creamy Amaretto Cocoa

For a nonalcoholic version, substitute ½ teaspoon almond extract for the amaretto.

¼ cup plus 2 tablespoons sugar
3 tablespoons unsweetened cocoa
⅛ teaspoon salt
1⅔ cups water
1 cup evaporated skimmed milk
1 cup 1% low-fat milk
1 tablespoon amaretto

Combine first 3 ingredients in a saucepan. Gradually stir in water. Bring to a boil; add milks and amaretto. Cook until thoroughly heated. Yield: 4 cups (175 calories per 1-cup serving).

Per Serving:		
Fat 1.9g	Carbohydrate 31.7g	Fiber 0g
saturated fat 1.2g	Cholesterol 5mg	Iron 0.9mg
Protein 8.1g	Sodium 183mg	Calcium 268mg

Roasted Pepper Dip (page 84) and Orange-Lime Margaritas (page 93)

Appetizers
& Beverages

Smoked Trout Spread

4 ounces skinned, boned smoked trout, flaked
1 tablespoon finely chopped sweet red pepper
2 tablespoons nonfat mayonnaise
2 teaspoons finely chopped purple onion
2 teaspoons minced capers
2 teaspoons fresh lemon juice
1½ teaspoons prepared horseradish
   Paprika (optional)

Combine first 7 ingredients in a medium bowl, stirring well. Cover and chill. Sprinkle with paprika just before serving, if desired. Serve with melba toast, unsalted crackers, or toasted French baguette slices. Yield: ¾ cup (15 calories per tablespoon).

Per Tablespoon:

Fat 0.7g	Carbohydrate 0.8g	Fiber 0g
saturated fat 0.2g	Cholesterol 0mg	Iron 0.1mg
Protein 2.0g	Sodium 164mg	Calcium 1mg

Southwestern Two-Bean Salsa

1 (15-ounce) can black-eyed peas, drained
1 (15-ounce) can red beans, drained
1 cup seeded, chopped tomato
⅔ cup no-salt-added salsa
½ cup thinly sliced green onions
⅓ cup chopped fresh cilantro
3 tablespoons fresh lime juice
½ teaspoon ground cumin
2 cloves garlic, minced
1 jalapeño pepper, seeded and chopped

Combine all ingredients in a large bowl, stirring well. Cover and chill at least 2 hours. Serve with no-oil baked tortilla chips. Yield: 4 cups (13 calories per tablespoon).

Per Tablespoon:

Fat 0.1g	Carbohydrate 2.3g	Fiber 0.3g
saturated fat 0.0g	Cholesterol 0mg	Iron 0.3mg
Protein 0.9g	Sodium 22mg	Calcium 5mg

Roasted Pepper Dip

3 large sweet red peppers
8 sun-dried tomatoes (packed without oil)
¾ cup boiling water
2 tablespoons chopped fresh parsley
1 tablespoon lemon juice
¼ teaspoon salt
¼ teaspoon pepper
1 clove garlic, minced
4 ounces Neufchâtel cheese, cubed and softened
½ cup nonfat sour cream

Cut peppers in half lengthwise; remove and discard seeds and membrane. Place peppers, skin side up, on a baking sheet; flatten with palm of hand. Broil peppers 5½ inches from heat (with electric oven door partially opened) 15 to 20 minutes or until charred. Place peppers in ice water until cool. Remove peppers from water; peel and discard skins. Coarsely chop peppers.

Combine tomatoes and boiling water in a small bowl; let stand 5 minutes. Drain.

Position knife blade in food processor bowl; add chopped peppers, tomatoes, parsley, and next 4 ingredients. Process until smooth, stopping once to scrape down sides. Add cheese and sour cream; process until smooth, stopping once to scrape down sides. Transfer pepper mixture to a serving bowl. Serve with crisp breadsticks or fresh raw vegetables. Yield: 2½ cups (14 calories per tablespoon).

Per Tablespoon:

Fat 0.7g	Carbohydrate 1.2g	Fiber 0.3g
saturated fat 0.4g	Cholesterol 2mg	Iron 0.2mg
Protein 0.6g	Sodium 36mg	Calcium 7mg

Spiced Shrimp with Creamy Honey-Mustard Sauce

Cooking in wine and spices adds a delicate flavor to the shrimp without adding fat.

12 unpeeled large fresh shrimp (about ½ pound)
1 cup water
½ cup dry white wine
8 whole peppercorns
4 whole cloves
4 whole allspice
⅓ cup nonfat mayonnaise
2 teaspoons honey
2 teaspoons Chinese hot mustard

Peel and devein shrimp, leaving tails intact.

Combine water, wine, peppercorns, cloves, and allspice in a medium saucepan; bring to a boil. Add shrimp, and cook 3 to 5 minutes or until shrimp turn pink. Drain well; rinse with cold water, and drain again. Cover and chill thoroughly.

Combine mayonnaise, honey, and mustard, stirring well.

To serve, place mayonnaise mixture in a small bowl. Arrange shrimp around bowl. Yield: 12 appetizer servings (20 calories per shrimp and 1½ teaspoons sauce).

Per Serving:
Fat 0.2g
   saturated fat 0.0g
Protein 2.3g
Carbohydrate 2.4g
Cholesterol 21mg
Sodium 116mg
Fiber 0g
Iron 0.3mg
Calcium 11mg

Chilled Shrimp with Santa Fe Dip

To save time, call ahead and ask your grocer to peel, devein, and steam the shrimp.

40 unpeeled large fresh shrimp (about 1⅓ pounds)
4½ cups water
⅓ cup no-salt-added chunky salsa
¼ cup nonfat mayonnaise
¼ cup nonfat cream cheese, softened
2 tablespoons finely chopped purple onion
2 tablespoons chopped fresh cilantro
¼ teaspoon ground cumin
¼ teaspoon hot sauce
   Fresh cilantro sprigs (optional)

Peel and devein shrimp, leaving tails intact.

Bring water to a boil in a large saucepan; add shrimp, and cook 3 to 5 minutes or until shrimp turn pink. Drain well; rinse with cold water, and drain again. Cover and chill thoroughly.

Combine salsa, mayonnaise, and cream cheese, stirring well. Add onion and next 3 ingredients; stir well. Cover and chill.

Arrange shrimp on a serving platter, and serve with salsa mixture. Garnish with cilantro sprigs, if desired. Yield: 40 appetizer servings (16 calories per shrimp and 1 teaspoon dip).

Per Serving:
Fat 0.1g
   saturated fat 0.0g
Protein 2.8g
Carbohydrate 0.6g
Cholesterol 23mg
Sodium 67mg
Fiber 0g
Iron 0.4mg
Calcium 14mg

Burn the Fat—It's as Easy as That

How's this for incentive: Stick to your half-hour run three times a week for a year, and you'll lose 12 pounds of fat. That's without changing your eating habits. Here's how other sports stack up:

Swimming	**12 pounds**
Aerobics	**9 pounds**
Walking	**9 pounds**
Weight lifting	**5 pounds**

Salmon with Fresh Asparagus

16 fresh asparagus spears
1   (8-ounce) package nonfat cream cheese, softened
1   tablespoon skim milk
1   tablespoon chopped fresh dillweed
1   tablespoon capers
16 (⅛-inch-thick) slices smoked salmon (about 12 ounces)
    Fresh dillweed sprigs (optional)

Snap off tough ends of asparagus. Remove scales from stalks with a knife or vegetable peeler, if desired. Cut asparagus in half crosswise. Reserve asparagus bottoms for another use. Arrange asparagus in a vegetable steamer over boiling water. Cover and steam 1 minute or until crisp-tender. Rinse with cold water; drain well, and set aside.

Combine cream cheese and milk, stirring until smooth. Stir in chopped dillweed and capers. Spread cream cheese mixture evenly over one side of each salmon slice. Place 1 asparagus piece across narrow end of each slice. Roll up slices, jellyroll fashion.

Place salmon rolls on a serving platter. Cover and chill thoroughly. Garnish with dillweed sprigs, if desired. Yield: 16 appetizers (39 calories each).

Per Appetizer:

Fat 0.9g	Carbohydrate 0.9g	Fiber 0.1g
saturated fat 0.2g	Cholesterol 7mg	Iron 0.2mg
Protein 6.1g	Sodium 309mg	Calcium 45mg

Louisiana Crab Cakes

These crab cakes can be served with fat-free tartar sauce or low-sodium cocktail sauce.

1   pound fresh lump crabmeat, drained
1½ cups soft breadcrumbs
3   tablespoons finely chopped green onions
2   tablespoons fresh lemon juice
2   tablespoons nonfat mayonnaise
½   teaspoon paprika
⅛   teaspoon salt
1   egg white, beaten
1   jalapeño pepper, seeded and finely chopped
    Vegetable cooking spray
2   teaspoons vegetable oil, divided
    Lemon wedges (optional)
    Fresh chives (optional)

Combine first 9 ingredients in a medium bowl, stirring well. Shape mixture into 8 (½-inch-thick) patties.

Coat a large nonstick skillet with cooking spray; add 1 teaspoon oil. Place over medium heat until hot. Place 4 patties in skillet, and cook 3 minutes on each side or until golden. Repeat procedure with remaining 1 teaspoon oil and 4 patties. If desired, garnish with lemon wedges and chives. Yield: 8 appetizers (94 calories each).

Per Appetizer:

Fat 2.4g	Carbohydrate 5.6g	Fiber 0.3g
saturated fat 0.4g	Cholesterol 53mg	Iron 0.8mg
Protein 11.9g	Sodium 279mg	Calcium 68mg

Mussels in Tomato-Wine Sauce

Mussels in Tomato-Wine Sauce

1   pound fresh mussels
2   teaspoons olive oil
1   cup chopped onion
3   cloves garlic, minced
2   (14½-ounce) cans no-salt-added whole
      tomatoes, drained and chopped
½   cup dry white wine
⅓   cup chopped fresh basil
¼   teaspoon freshly ground pepper
12 (½-inch-thick) slices French baguette,
      toasted
      Fresh basil sprigs (optional)

Remove beards on mussels, and scrub shells with a brush. Discard open, cracked, or heavy mussels (they're filled with sand). Set aside remaining mussels.

Heat oil in a large saucepan over medium-high heat until hot. Add onion and garlic; sauté 4 minutes or until tender. Add tomato and wine; bring to a boil. Add mussels, basil, and pepper. Cover, reduce heat to medium-low, and simmer 3 to 5 minutes or until mussels open. Discard unopened mussels. Spoon mussels and tomato mixture into individual serving bowls. Serve with baguette slices. Garnish with basil sprigs, if desired. Yield: 6 appetizer servings (121 calories per serving).

Per Serving:		
Fat 2.4g	Carbohydrate 18.5g	Fiber 1.8g
saturated fat 0.4g	Cholesterol 9mg	Iron 2.3mg
Protein 6.9g	Sodium 196mg	Calcium 80mg

Curried Chicken Kabobs

1   pound skinned, boned chicken breast halves, cut into 1-inch pieces
¼   cup commercial mango chutney
1   tablespoon spicy brown mustard
½   teaspoon curry powder
⅛   teaspoon ground red pepper
1   medium-size sweet red pepper, seeded and cut into 1-inch pieces
4   green onions, sliced diagonally into 1-inch pieces
    Vegetable cooking spray
    Lime wedges
    Chopped fresh cilantro (optional)

Place chicken in a shallow dish. Combine chutney and next 3 ingredients, stirring well. Spoon chutney mixture over chicken, stirring to coat.

Cover and marinate chicken in refrigerator 1 hour, stirring once.

Soak 12 (6-inch) wooden skewers in water for at least 30 minutes. Remove chicken from marinade, reserving marinade. Thread chicken, sweet red pepper, and green onions alternately onto skewers. Brush kabobs with marinade.

Coat grill rack with cooking spray; place on grill over medium-hot coals (350° to 400°). Place kabobs on rack; grill, covered, 4 minutes on each side or until chicken is done and vegetables are tender. Serve with lime wedges. Garnish with cilantro, if desired. Yield: 12 appetizers (72 calories each).

Per Appetizer:

Fat 1.2g	Carbohydrate 5.6g	Fiber 0.3g
saturated fat 0.3g	Cholesterol 24mg	Iron 0.6mg
Protein 9.0g	Sodium 95mg	Calcium 10mg

Teriyaki Chicken Drummettes with Pineapple Sauce

24   chicken drummettes, skinned
⅓   cup sugar
⅓   cup water
⅓   cup low-sodium soy sauce
¼   cup unsweetened pineapple juice
1   tablespoon vegetable oil
1   teaspoon peeled, grated gingerroot
1   clove garlic, pressed
    Vegetable cooking spray
    Pineapple Sauce

Place chicken in a heavy-duty, zip-top plastic bag. Combine sugar and next 6 ingredients; stir well. Pour soy sauce mixture over chicken. Seal bag, and shake until chicken is coated. Marinate in refrigerator 8 hours, turning bag occasionally. Remove chicken from marinade; reserve marinade.

Place marinade in a small saucepan; bring to a boil, and cook 1 minute. Remove from heat.

Place chicken on rack of a broiler pan coated with cooking spray. Bake chicken at 350° for 50 minutes or until done, turning and basting occasionally with marinade. Serve with Pineapple Sauce. Yield: 24 appetizer servings (70 calories per drummette and 1 tablespoon sauce).

Pineapple Sauce

1   (8-ounce) can crushed pineapple in juice
¼   cup firmly packed brown sugar
¼   cup cider vinegar
2   tablespoons ketchup
2   teaspoons cornstarch

Combine all ingredients in a small saucepan. Cook over medium heat, stirring constantly, until mixture is thickened. Yield: 1½ cups.

Per Serving:

Fat 1.7g	Carbohydrate 7.6g	Fiber 0.1g
saturated fat 0.4g	Cholesterol 18mg	Iron 0.3mg
Protein 5.6g	Sodium 120mg	Calcium 7mg

Turkey-Spinach Pinwheels

Seed the tomato in this recipe to keep the pinwheels from getting soggy.

½   cup nonfat cream cheese, softened
1   tablespoon commercial pesto
2   teaspoons Dijon mustard
4   (8-inch) fat-free flour tortillas
1   medium tomato, very thinly sliced
     and seeded
12   (½-ounce) slices fat-free turkey breast
16   large spinach leaves, stems removed

Combine first 3 ingredients in a small bowl, stirring well. Spread cream cheese mixture evenly over one side of tortillas. Arrange tomato slices evenly over cream cheese mixture; top evenly with turkey and spinach leaves.

Roll up tortillas, jellyroll fashion. Wrap each roll in plastic wrap, and chill at least 1 hour. Remove plastic wrap, and cut each roll into 8 slices. Yield: 32 appetizers (25 calories each).

To seed tomato slices, use a spoon to scoop or press out seeds.

To seed tomatoes for chopping, cut tomatoes in half, and scoop out seeds with a spoon.

Per Appetizer:

Fat 0.3g	Carbohydrate 3.7g	Fiber 0.3g
saturated fat 0.1g	Cholesterol 2mg	Iron 0.2mg
Protein 1.8g	Sodium 108mg	Calcium 13mg

Baked Zucchini Wedges

For an excellent low-fat dip for these crispy vegetable wedges, try commercial marinara sauce.

½   cup fine, dry breadcrumbs
3   tablespoons grated Parmesan cheese
½   teaspoon dried Italian seasoning
¼   teaspoon salt
⅛   teaspoon ground red pepper
⅛   teaspoon garlic powder
3   small zucchini
½   cup frozen egg substitute, thawed
3   tablespoons all-purpose flour
     Olive oil-flavored vegetable cooking spray

Combine first 6 ingredients in a small bowl, and set aside.

Cut each zucchini lengthwise into 6 wedges. Dip zucchini wedges in egg substitute, and dredge in flour.

Dip wedges in egg substitute again; dredge in breadcrumb mixture. Place wedges in a single layer on a baking sheet coated with cooking spray.

Bake at 400° for 15 to 20 minutes or until golden. Serve warm or at room temperature. Yield: 18 appetizers (26 calories each).

Per Appetizer:

Fat 0.5g	Carbohydrate 3.9g	Fiber 0.3g
saturated fat 0.2g	Cholesterol 1mg	Iron 0.4mg
Protein 1.5g	Sodium 81mg	Calcium 24mg

Italian Appetizer Skewers

1 large sweet red pepper
1 large sweet yellow pepper
24 small mushroom caps
3 ounces part-skim mozzarella cheese, cut into 12 cubes
¼ cup canned low-sodium chicken broth, undiluted
1½ tablespoons white wine vinegar
1 teaspoon olive oil
½ teaspoon freshly ground pepper
¼ teaspoon salt
2 cloves garlic, minced
36 small fresh basil leaves

Cut peppers in half lengthwise; remove and discard seeds and membrane. Place peppers, skin side up, on a baking sheet, and flatten with palm of hand. Broil 5½ inches from heat (with electric oven door partially opened) 15 to 20 minutes or until charred. Place in ice water until cool. Remove peppers from water; peel and discard skins. Cut peppers into 1-inch pieces.

Place pepper pieces, mushroom caps, and cheese in a heavy-duty, zip-top plastic bag. Combine broth and next 5 ingredients; pour over pepper mixture in bag. Seal bag; shake gently until pepper mixture is coated. Marinate in refrigerator at least 1 hour, turning bag occasionally.

Remove pepper mixture from marinade, discarding marinade. Thread pepper pieces, mushroom caps, cheese, and basil leaves alternately onto 12 (8-inch) wooden skewers. Yield: 12 appetizers (33 calories each).

Per Appetizer:		
Fat 1.5g	Carbohydrate 2.8g	Fiber 0.7g
saturated fat 0.8g	Cholesterol 4mg	Iron 0.6mg
Protein 2.4g	Sodium 84mg	Calcium 53mg

Chinese Stuffed Mushrooms

24 large fresh mushrooms
Vegetable cooking spray
½ pound freshly ground raw turkey
2 cloves garlic, minced
¼ cup fine, dry breadcrumbs
¼ cup chopped fresh cilantro
2 tablespoons low-sodium soy sauce
1 teaspoon peeled, minced gingerroot
⅛ teaspoon ground red pepper
1 egg white, lightly beaten
1 tablespoon low-sodium soy sauce

Clean mushrooms with damp paper towels. Remove stems. Set mushroom caps aside. Finely chop stems, and set aside.

Coat a large nonstick skillet with cooking spray; place over medium-high heat until hot. Add mushroom caps; sauté 5 minutes. Remove mushroom caps from skillet, and drain on paper towels.

Coat skillet with cooking spray; place over medium heat until hot. Add chopped mushroom stems, turkey, and garlic; cook until turkey is browned, stirring until it crumbles. Remove from heat. Stir in breadcrumbs and next 5 ingredients; set aside.

Brush mushroom caps with 1 tablespoon soy sauce. Spoon turkey mixture evenly into mushroom caps. Place stuffed mushrooms in a 13- x 9- x 2-inch baking dish coated with cooking spray. Bake at 350° for 10 to 15 minutes or until thoroughly heated. Yield: 24 appetizers (26 calories each).

Per Appetizer:		
Fat 0.5g	Carbohydrate 2.4g	Fiber 0.5g
saturated fat 0.1g	Cholesterol 6mg	Iron 0.6mg
Protein 3.0g	Sodium 69mg	Calcium 7mg

Greek Mushrooms

1   tablespoon olive oil
3   cloves garlic, minced
½   cup no-salt-added chicken broth
¼   cup fresh lemon juice
1   tablespoon coriander seeds
½   teaspoon dried rosemary
¼   teaspoon salt
¼   teaspoon freshly ground pepper
1½   pounds medium-size fresh mushrooms
6   cups mixed baby salad greens

Heat oil in a nonstick skillet over medium-high heat until hot. Add garlic; sauté until tender. Add broth and next 5 ingredients; bring to a boil. Add mushrooms. Cover, reduce heat to medium, and cook 15 minutes, stirring occasionally.

Transfer mushroom mixture to a bowl; let cool. Cover and chill at least 8 hours.

To serve, place ½ cup salad greens on each individual serving plate. Spoon mushrooms evenly over salad greens, using a slotted spoon. Drizzle 2 teaspoons mushroom liquid over each serving; discard remaining liquid. Yield: 12 appetizer servings (25 calories per serving).

Per Serving:		
Fat 1.1g	Carbohydrate 3.6g	Fiber 1.0g
saturated fat 0.1g	Cholesterol 0mg	Iron 0.9mg
Protein 1.4g	Sodium 30mg	Calcium 13mg

Crispy Oriental Chips

17   fresh or frozen wonton skins, thawed
1   tablespoon low-sodium soy sauce
½   teaspoon sugar
½   teaspoon peeled, minced gingerroot
½   teaspoon dark sesame oil
1   clove garlic, minced
     Dash of hot sauce
     Vegetable cooking spray

Cut wonton skins in half diagonally; set aside. Combine soy sauce and next 5 ingredients in a small bowl. Brush both sides of wonton skins lightly with soy sauce mixture.

Arrange wonton skins in a single layer on a baking sheet coated with cooking spray. Bake at 375° for 7 minutes or until wonton skins are lightly browned and crisp; let cool completely. Store in an airtight container. Yield: 34 appetizers (12 calories per chip).

Per Appetizer:		
Fat 0.1g	Carbohydrate 2.1g	Fiber 0g
saturated fat 0.0g	Cholesterol 0mg	Iron 0.1mg
Protein 0.4g	Sodium 32mg	Calcium 2mg

Peppy Pizza Wedges

4   (6-inch) pita bread rounds
½   cup commercial fat-free spaghetti sauce
4   plum tomatoes, thinly sliced
½   teaspoon dried basil
¼   teaspoon dried thyme
1   sweet yellow pepper, seeded and cut into
        thin strips
4   thin slices purple onion, separated
        into rings
1   cup (4 ounces) shredded part-skim
        mozzarella cheese
2   tablespoons grated Romano cheese

Arrange pita bread rounds on an ungreased baking sheet. Broil 5½ inches from heat (with electric oven door partially opened) 2 minutes on each side.

Spread 2 tablespoons spaghetti sauce over one side of each pita round, leaving a ½-inch border; top rounds evenly with tomato. Sprinkle basil and thyme over tomato. Arrange yellow pepper and onion over tomato. Sprinkle cheeses evenly over pita rounds. Broil 5½ inches from heat (with electric oven door partially opened) 3 to 4 minutes or until cheese melts and pita rounds are thoroughly heated. Cut each round into 4 wedges. Yield: 16 appetizers (72 calories each).

Per Appetizer:		
Fat 1.7g	Carbohydrate 10.5g	Fiber 2.1g
saturated fat 0.9g	Cholesterol 5mg	Iron 0.8mg
Protein 3.1g	Sodium 155mg	Calcium 70mg

Black Currant and Raspberry Cooler

4½ cups apple-raspberry fruit juice blend, divided
14 fresh raspberries
14 fresh mint leaves
2½ cups water
4   black currant-flavored tea bags

Pour 1 cup fruit juice into an ice cube tray; place 1 raspberry and 1 mint leaf in each section of ice cube tray. Freeze until firm.

Bring water to a boil in a medium saucepan. Add tea bags; remove from heat. Cover and steep 10 minutes. Remove and discard tea bags.

Combine tea and remaining 3½ cups juice in a large pitcher. Cover and chill. Place frozen juice cubes in glasses; pour tea mixture over cubes. Yield: 6 cups (72 calories per 1-cup serving).

Per Serving:

Fat 0.0g	Carbohydrate 18.4g	Fiber 0.5g
saturated fat 0.0g	Cholesterol 0mg	Iron 0.6mg
Protein 0.1g	Sodium 18mg	Calcium 4mg

Pink Passion Cooler

3   cups unsweetened pink grapefruit juice
2½ cups passion fruit juice blend
1½ cups guava nectar
2   tablespoons grenadine syrup
2   cups lime-flavored sparkling water, chilled

Combine first 4 ingredients in a large pitcher. Cover and chill. Just before serving, stir in sparkling water. Yield: 9 cups (96 calories per 1-cup serving).

Per Serving:

Fat 0.1g	Carbohydrate 23.3g	Fiber 0.2g
saturated fat 0.0g	Cholesterol 0mg	Iron 1.7mg
Protein 0.4g	Sodium 22mg	Calcium 6mg

Black Currant and Raspberry Cooler

Orange-Lime Margarita

This refreshing beverage can be doubled to serve a large crowd.

1   cup unsweetened orange juice
1   (6-ounce) can frozen limeade concentrate, undiluted
¼   cup plus 2 tablespoons tequila
¼   cup Triple Sec or other orange-flavored liqueur
2   tablespoons fresh lime juice
4¼ cups crushed ice
    Lime slices (optional)
    Orange slices (optional)

Combine first 5 ingredients, stirring until limeade concentrate dissolves.

Pour orange mixture into container of an electric blender. Add crushed ice; cover and process 5 seconds. Pour into glasses. If desired, garnish with lime and orange slices. Yield: 5 cups (166 calories per 1-cup serving).

Per Serving:

Fat 0.1g	Carbohydrate 26.1g	Fiber 0.1g
saturated fat 0.0g	Cholesterol 0mg	Iron 0.2mg
Protein 0.4g	Sodium 1mg	Calcium 7mg

Gingered Tropical Smoothie

2   cups vanilla nonfat frozen yogurt
1   ripe papaya, peeled, seeded, and diced
1   (7-ounce) can papaya nectar
1   tablespoon chopped crystallized ginger
    Freshly grated nutmeg (optional)

Combine yogurt, diced papaya, nectar, and ginger in container of an electric blender; cover and process until smooth. Pour into chilled glasses. Sprinkle with nutmeg, if desired. Serve immediately. Yield: 4 cups (146 calories per 1-cup serving).

Per Serving:

Fat 0.1g	Carbohydrate 34.3g	Fiber 1.3g
saturated fat 0.0g	Cholesterol 0mg	Iron 0.8mg
Protein 3.7g	Sodium 62mg	Calcium 147mg

Mocha Milk Shake

You can substitute vanilla fat-free ice cream for vanilla fudge swirl.

1   cup hot water
2   teaspoons espresso powder
2   cups vanilla fudge swirl fat-free ice cream
½   cup skim milk
½   cup ice cubes
3   tablespoons chocolate syrup

Combine water and espresso powder, stirring until combined. Cover and chill.

Combine chilled espresso, ice cream, and remaining ingredients in container of an electric blender; cover and process until smooth, stopping once to scrape down sides. Serve immediately. Yield: 4 cups (150 calories per 1-cup serving).

Per Serving:
Fat 0.2g   Carbohydrate 32.7g   Fiber 1.0g
   saturated fat 0.0g   Cholesterol 1mg   Iron 0.3mg
Protein 4.6g   Sodium 101mg   Calcium 89mg

Piña Colada Freeze

Vanilla low-fat yogurt makes a good substitute for piña colada-flavored yogurt.

3¼   cups unsweetened pineapple juice
1   (8-ounce) carton piña colada low-fat yogurt
½   cup light rum
½   teaspoon coconut extract

Place juice in a shallow container, and freeze until firm. Break frozen juice into chunks. Combine frozen juice, yogurt, rum, and coconut extract in container of an electric blender; cover and process until smooth. Pour into chilled glasses. Serve immediately. Yield: 5¼ cups (140 calories per ¾-cup serving).

Per Serving:
Fat 0.7g   Carbohydrate 22.2g   Fiber 0.1g
   saturated fat 0.0g   Cholesterol 2mg   Iron 0.3mg
Protein 2.0g   Sodium 22mg   Calcium 67mg

Milking Fat Out of Your Diet

If you're trying to cut back on fat, don't forget milk. Consider that whole milk, which may be labeled as containing only 3.5 to 3.7 percent fat by weight, actually gets more than 50 percent of its calories from fat. (In fact, whole milk ranks as the second largest contributor of saturated fat to the American diet—the hamburger is number one.)

Think 2 percent milk is the lean alternative? Wrong. This milk still contains about five grams of fat per eight-ounce serving. Part of the problem is that manufacturers homogenize, or blend, the cream back into the whole and low-fat milks. Only skim (nonfat) milk is free from this added fat. For a low-fat diet, choose at least 1 percent low-fat milk or, preferably, skim milk.

Garlic-Rosemary Focaccia and variations (page 106)

Breads

Cranberry Silver Dollar Biscuits

1 package active dry yeast
¼ cup warm water (105° to 115°)
2 cups all-purpose flour
1 teaspoon baking powder
½ teaspoon baking soda
¼ teaspoon salt
¼ cup sugar
3 tablespoons margarine
¼ cup dried cranberries
¾ cup nonfat buttermilk
3 tablespoons all-purpose flour
   Vegetable cooking spray

Combine yeast and warm water in a 1-cup liquid measuring cup; let stand 5 minutes.

Combine 2 cups flour and next 4 ingredients in a medium bowl; cut in margarine with a pastry blender until mixture resembles coarse meal. Stir in cranberries. Add yeast mixture and buttermilk to flour mixture; stir with a fork just until dry ingredients are moistened.

Sprinkle 3 tablespoons flour evenly over work surface. Turn dough out onto floured surface, and knead 4 or 5 times. Pat dough to ½-inch thickness; cut into rounds with a 1½-inch biscuit cutter. Place rounds on a baking sheet coated with cooking spray. Bake at 400° for 10 minutes or until biscuits are golden. Yield: 1½ dozen (94 calories each).

Per Biscuit:		
Fat 2.1g	Carbohydrate 16.6g	Fiber 0.7g
saturated fat 0.4g	Cholesterol 0mg	Iron 0.8mg
Protein 2.2g	Sodium 101mg	Calcium 32mg

Nutty Sweet Potato Biscuits

The sweet potato adds flavor and moistness to these biscuits without adding extra fat.

2¾ cups all-purpose flour
1   tablespoon plus 1 teaspoon baking powder
½   teaspoon salt
⅔   cup sugar
½   teaspoon ground cinnamon
½   teaspoon ground nutmeg
¼   cup chopped walnuts
2   cups cooked, mashed sweet potato
3   tablespoons margarine, melted
1   teaspoon vanilla extract
2   tablespoons all-purpose flour
    Vegetable cooking spray

Combine first 6 ingredients in a large bowl. Add nuts; stir well.

Combine sweet potato, margarine, and vanilla in a medium bowl; add to flour mixture, stirring just until dry ingredients are moistened.

Sprinkle 2 tablespoons flour evenly over work surface. Turn dough out onto floured surface, and knead 10 to 12 times. Roll dough to ½-inch thickness; cut into rounds with a 2-inch biscuit cutter. Place rounds on a baking sheet coated with cooking spray. Bake at 450° for 12 to 15 minutes or until biscuits are golden. Yield: 22 biscuits (143 calories each).

Per Biscuit:		
Fat 3.0g	Carbohydrate 26.5g	Fiber 1.5g
saturated fat 0.4g	Cholesterol 0mg	Iron 1.1mg
Protein 2.7g	Sodium 76mg	Calcium 61mg

Date-Walnut Bread

Storing this sweet bread in foil before serving makes it moister.

1 cup pitted, chopped whole dates
⅓ cup chopped walnuts
1 cup boiling water
1 tablespoon margarine, softened
¾ cup sugar
1 egg
1½ cups all-purpose flour
1 teaspoon baking soda
¼ teaspoon salt
1 teaspoon vanilla extract
  Vegetable cooking spray

Combine first 3 ingredients in a small bowl. Cover and let stand 30 minutes.

Beat margarine at medium speed of an electric mixer until creamy; gradually add sugar, beating well. Add egg; beat well.

Combine flour, baking soda, and salt; add to sugar mixture, beating well. (Mixture will be crumbly.) Add date mixture and vanilla to batter, stirring well.

Pour batter into an 8½- x 4½- x 3-inch loafpan coated with cooking spray. Bake at 350° for 1 hour or until a wooden pick inserted in center comes out clean. Cool in pan 15 minutes.

Remove bread from pan, and let cool completely on a wire rack. Wrap bread in aluminum foil, and let stand at least 8 hours. Yield: 16 servings (128 calories per ½-inch slice).

Per Slice:

Fat 2.5g	Carbohydrate 24.8g	Fiber 1.2g
saturated fat 0.4g	Cholesterol 14mg	Iron 0.8mg
Protein 2.3g	Sodium 128mg	Calcium 8mg

Rosemary Sweet Bread

Fresh rosemary adds a pleasant, out-of-the-ordinary flavor to this quick bread. Serve a wedge for breakfast or with a cup of tea for an afternoon snack.

  Vegetable cooking spray
1½ teaspoons all-purpose flour
1 cup skim milk
½ cup golden raisins
¼ cup unsweetened applesauce
1 tablespoon finely chopped fresh rosemary
2 eggs
⅔ cup sugar
1 tablespoon margarine, melted
2 cups all-purpose flour
1½ teaspoons baking powder
½ teaspoon salt

Coat a 9-inch round cakepan with cooking spray; dust pan with 1½ teaspoons flour. Set pan aside.

Combine milk, raisins, applesauce, and chopped fresh rosemary in a small saucepan,

and bring to a simmer over medium heat. (Do not boil.) Remove from heat; cover and set aside.

Beat eggs at medium speed of an electric mixer until foamy. Add sugar and margarine, beating well. Combine 2 cups flour, baking powder, and salt; add to egg mixture, beating until smooth. Add milk mixture; beat until smooth. (Batter will be thin.)

Pour batter into prepared pan. Bake at 350° for 35 minutes or until a wooden pick inserted in center comes out clean. Cool in pan on a wire rack 10 minutes. Remove from pan, and let cool completely on a wire rack. Yield: 16 servings (129 calories per wedge).

Per Wedge:

Fat 1.6g	Carbohydrate 26.0g	Fiber 0.8g
saturated fat 0.4g	Cholesterol 28mg	Iron 1.0mg
Protein 3.2g	Sodium 99mg	Calcium 54mg

Blueberry Muffins

Blueberry Muffins

2 cups all-purpose flour
1 tablespoon baking powder
¼ teaspoon baking soda
½ teaspoon salt
½ cup sugar, divided
1 cup plain nonfat yogurt
2 tablespoons skim milk
1 tablespoon margarine, melted
1 egg, lightly beaten
1 teaspoon vanilla extract
1¼ cups fresh or frozen blueberries, thawed
Vegetable cooking spray

Combine flour, baking powder, soda, salt, and ¼ cup plus 3 tablespoons sugar in a medium bowl, and make a well in center of mixture. Combine yogurt and next 4 ingredients in a small bowl. Add to dry ingredients, stirring just until dry ingredients are moistened. (Batter will be thick.) Gently fold in blueberries.

Spoon batter into muffin pans coated with cooking spray, filling two-thirds full. Sprinkle evenly with remaining 1 tablespoon sugar. Bake at 400° for 23 to 25 minutes or until golden. Remove from pans immediately. Yield: 1 dozen (147 calories each).

Per Muffin:

Fat 1.9g	Carbohydrate 28.6g	Fiber 1.3g
saturated fat 0.4g	Cholesterol 19mg	Iron 1.2mg
Protein 4.0g	Sodium 158mg	Calcium 116mg

Oatmeal-Raisin Muffins

Since currants are smaller than raisins, substitute 1/3 cup currants for raisins
if you'd like a morsel of fruit in every bite.

1 cup quick-cooking oats, uncooked
1 cup nonfat buttermilk
1/4 cup plus 2 tablespoons firmly packed
    brown sugar
1/4 cup unsweetened applesauce
1/4 cup frozen egg substitute, thawed
3 tablespoons vegetable oil
1 cup all-purpose flour
1 teaspoon baking powder
3/4 teaspoon baking soda
1/4 teaspoon salt
1/3 cup raisins
    Vegetable cooking spray

Combine oats and buttermilk; let stand 1 hour. Add brown sugar and next 3 ingredients to oat mixture, stirring well.

Combine flour, baking powder, soda, and salt; add to oat mixture, stirring just until dry ingredients are moistened. Fold in raisins.

Spoon batter into muffin pans coated with cooking spray, filling three-fourths full. Bake at 400° for 15 minutes or until golden. Yield: 1 dozen (148 calories each).

Per Muffin:

Fat 4.3g	Carbohydrate 24.4g	Fiber 1.3g
saturated fat 0.8g	Cholesterol 1mg	Iron 1.1mg
Protein 3.6g	Sodium 82mg	Calcium 63mg

Basic Breadsticks

1 package active dry yeast
1 cup plus 2 tablespoons warm water
    (105° to 115°)
2¾ cups bread flour, divided
1/4 cup instant nonfat dry milk
    powder
1 teaspoon sugar
2 teaspoons olive oil
1/2 teaspoon salt
1 tablespoon bread flour
    Vegetable cooking spray
1 egg white
1 tablespoon water

Combine yeast and warm water in a 2-cup liquid measuring cup; let stand 5 minutes.

Combine yeast mixture, 2 cups flour, milk powder, and next 3 ingredients in a large mixing bowl; beat at medium speed of an electric mixer until blended. Gradually stir in enough of the remaining ¾ cup flour to make a soft dough.

Sprinkle 1 tablespoon flour evenly over work surface. Turn dough out onto floured surface, and knead until smooth and elastic (about 5 minutes). Place dough in a large bowl coated with cooking spray, turning to coat top. Cover and let rise in a warm place (85°), free from drafts, 30 minutes or until doubled in bulk.

Punch dough down. Divide dough into 20 equal portions. Roll each portion of dough into a 14-inch rope.

Place ropes, 2 inches apart, on baking sheets coated with cooking spray. Cover and let rise in a warm place, free from drafts, 20 minutes.

Combine egg white and 1 tablespoon water in a small bowl; brush egg white mixture evenly over breadsticks. Bake at 400° for 15 minutes or until breadsticks are golden. Yield: 20 breadsticks (82 calories each).

Per Breadstick:

Fat 0.9g	Carbohydrate 15.1g	Fiber 0.6g
saturated fat 0.1g	Cholesterol 0mg	Iron 0.9mg
Protein 3.2g	Sodium 70mg	Calcium 22mg

Sweet Anise Breadsticks

3 cups bread flour, divided
2 tablespoons sugar
½ teaspoon salt
1 package rapid-rise yeast
1 cup plus 2 tablespoons hot water
   (120° to 130°)
1 tablespoon plus 1 teaspoon anise seeds
1 tablespoon brandy
1 tablespoon olive oil
½ teaspoon vanilla extract
¼ cup bread flour, divided
   Vegetable cooking spray
2 teaspoons sugar

Combine 2 cups flour, 2 tablespoons sugar, salt, and yeast in a large mixing bowl, stirring well. Gradually add water to flour mixture, beating well at low speed of an electric mixer. Beat 2 additional minutes at medium speed. Add anise seeds, brandy, olive oil, and vanilla, beating well.

Gradually stir in enough of the remaining 1 cup flour to make a soft dough.

Sprinkle 3 tablespoons flour evenly over work surface. Turn dough out onto floured surface, and knead until smooth and elastic (about 5 minutes). Cover dough; let rest 10 minutes.

Sprinkle remaining 1 tablespoon flour evenly over work surface. Roll dough into a 24- x 9-inch rectangle. Cut dough into 24 (1-inch-wide) strips. Place strips, 2 inches apart, on baking sheets coated with cooking spray. Cover and let rise in a warm place (85°), free from drafts, 15 minutes.

Lightly coat breadsticks with cooking spray; sprinkle evenly with 2 teaspoons sugar. Bake at 400° for 12 minutes or until golden. Yield: 2 dozen (80 calories each).

Per Breadstick:

Fat 1.0g	Carbohydrate 15.2g	Fiber 0.7g
saturated fat 0.1g	Cholesterol 0mg	Iron 1.0mg
Protein 2.4g	Sodium 49mg	Calcium 6mg

Shaping Breadsticks

The variety of breadstick shapes is endless. They can be long or short, straight or twisted, plump or thin. Here are three different ways to shape breadsticks.

Ropes: *Divide dough into small equal portions. Roll each portion into a 12- to 14-inch-long rope. Let rise, and bake according to recipe directions. (See Basic Breadsticks on page 99.)*

Strips: *Roll dough into a rectangle (about ⅛ inch thick), and cut into 1-inch-wide strips. Let rise, and bake according to recipe directions. (See Sweet Anise Breadsticks on this page.)*

Twists: *Gently twist strips or ropes of dough, before or after rising. Let rise (if needed), and bake according to recipe directions. (See Sesame-Poppy Breadsticks on page 101.)*

Sesame-Poppy Breadsticks

1   package active dry yeast
1   cup plus 2 tablespoons warm water
     (105° to 115°)
1¾ cups whole wheat flour
1   cup bread flour
¼   teaspoon salt
1   tablespoon olive oil
1   tablespoon honey
1   tablespoon bread flour
     Vegetable cooking spray
1½ tablespoons sesame seeds
1   tablespoon poppy seeds
1   egg white, lightly beaten

Combine yeast and warm water in a 2-cup liquid measuring cup; let stand 5 minutes. Combine yeast mixture, whole wheat flour, and next 4 ingredients in a large mixing bowl; beat at medium speed of an electric mixer until well blended.

Sprinkle 1 tablespoon bread flour evenly over work surface. Turn dough out onto floured surface, and knead until smooth and elastic (about 5 minutes). Place dough in a large bowl coated with cooking spray, turning to coat top. Cover and let rise in a warm place (85°), free from drafts, 45 minutes or until doubled in bulk.

Punch dough down; turn dough out onto work surface, and roll into a 10- x 6-inch rectangle. Cut dough into 10 (1-inch-wide) strips. Place strips, 2 inches apart, on a large baking sheet coated with cooking spray. Cover and let rise in a warm place, free from drafts, 25 minutes or until doubled in bulk.

Combine sesame and poppy seeds; place on a sheet of wax paper. Brush egg white evenly over breadsticks. Pull each breadstick to a 12-inch length; roll in seed mixture. Twist breadsticks gently 3 or 4 times. Place breadsticks, 2 inches apart, on a large baking sheet coated with cooking spray. Bake at 375° for 18 to 20 minutes. Yield: 10 breadsticks (155 calories each).

Per Breadstick:

Fat 2.9g	Carbohydrate 28.2g	Fiber 3.3g
saturated fat 0.4g	Cholesterol 0mg	Iron 1.8mg
Protein 5.5g	Sodium 65mg	Calcium 31mg

Potato Pan Rolls

1   cup nonfat buttermilk
1   cup water
¼   cup margarine
4½ cups all-purpose flour, divided
1   cup instant potato flakes
2   tablespoons sugar
½   teaspoon salt
1   package active dry yeast
1   egg
¼   cup all-purpose flour
     Vegetable cooking spray
1   tablespoon margarine, melted

Combine first 3 ingredients in a medium saucepan; cook over medium heat until margarine melts, stirring occasionally. Cool to 120° to 130°.

Combine 2 cups flour, potato flakes, and next 3 ingredients in a large mixing bowl, stirring well.

Gradually add liquid mixture to flour mixture, beating well at low speed of an electric mixer. Beat 2 additional minutes at medium speed. Add egg; beat well. Gradually stir in enough of the remaining 2½ cups flour to make a soft dough.

Sprinkle ¼ cup flour evenly over work surface. Turn dough out onto floured surface, and knead until smooth and elastic (about 10 minutes). Place dough in a large bowl coated with cooking spray, turning to coat top. Cover and let rise in a warm place (85°), free from drafts, 1 hour or until doubled in bulk.

Punch dough down, and divide into 24 equal portions. Shape each portion into a ball, and place balls in two 9-inch round cakepans coated with cooking spray. Cover and let rise in a warm place, free from drafts, 30 minutes or until doubled in bulk.

Bake at 400° for 15 minutes or until golden. Brush rolls evenly with 1 tablespoon melted margarine. Serve warm. Yield: 2 dozen (133 calories each).

Per Roll:

Fat 2.9g	Carbohydrate 22.9g	Fiber 0.8g
saturated fat 0.6g	Cholesterol 10mg	Iron 1.3mg
Protein 3.6g	Sodium 94mg	Calcium 20mg

Russian Black Bread

This hearty bread gets its dark, rich color and robust flavor from coffee granules and unsweetened cocoa.

    2   packages active dry yeast
 1½   cups warm water (105° to 115°), divided
    1   tablespoon plus 1 teaspoon instant coffee
          granules
    1   tablespoon honey
    2   teaspoons margarine, melted
 2½   cups plus 1 tablespoon bread flour
 2½   tablespoons unsweetened cocoa
    1   tablespoon anise seeds
 1½   teaspoons caraway seeds
   ¾   teaspoon salt
    1   cup plus 1 tablespoon rye flour
    1   tablespoon bread flour
          Vegetable cooking spray
    2   teaspoons cornmeal
    1   egg white
    1   tablespoon water

Combine yeast and 1 cup warm water in a 2-cup liquid measuring cup; let stand five minutes.

Combine coffee granules and remaining ½ cup warm water, stirring until granules dissolve. Stir in honey and margarine.

Combine yeast mixture, coffee mixture, 2½ cups plus 1 tablespoon bread flour, and next 4 ingredients in a large mixing bowl; beat at medium speed of an electric mixer until well blended. Gradually stir in enough of the rye flour to make a soft dough.

Sprinkle 1 tablespoon bread flour evenly over work surface. Turn dough out onto floured surface, and knead until smooth and elastic (about 5 minutes). Place dough in a large bowl coated with cooking spray, turning to coat top. Cover and let rise in a warm place (85°), free from drafts, 35 minutes or until doubled in bulk.

Sprinkle cornmeal evenly over a large baking sheet; set aside.

Punch dough down, and shape into a 6-inch round loaf. Place loaf on prepared baking sheet. Cover and let rise in a warm place, free from drafts, 30 minutes or until doubled in bulk. Using a sharp knife, score 2 (½-inch-deep) slits in top of loaf, forming an X. Combine egg white and 1 tablespoon water; brush over loaf. Bake at 375° for 25 minutes or until loaf sounds hollow when tapped. Remove loaf from baking sheet; cool on a wire rack. Cut into 18 wedges. Yield: 18 servings (112 calories per wedge).

Per Wedge:

Fat 1.1g	Carbohydrate 21.4g	Fiber 1.7g
saturated fat 0.2g	Cholesterol 0mg	Iron 1.4mg
Protein 3.7g	Sodium 107mg	Calcium 11mg

Russian Black Bread

Hearty Grain Bread

1   tablespoon plus 1 teaspoon sesame seeds
1   tablespoon plus 1 teaspoon pearl barley
1   tablespoon plus 1 teaspoon polenta
1   tablespoon caraway seeds
⅓   cup boiling water
¾   cup plus 1 teaspoon water, divided
2   tablespoons honey
1⅔ cups plus 2 tablespoons bread flour
3   tablespoons yellow cornmeal
2   tablespoons rye flour
1¾ teaspoons rapid-rise yeast
½   teaspoon salt
⅔   cup whole wheat flour
1   tablespoon bread flour
    Vegetable cooking spray
1   egg white
1   tablespoon quick-cooking oats, uncooked

Combine first 5 ingredients; let stand 15 minutes.

Combine ¾ cup water and honey in a saucepan; cook over medium heat until warm (120° to 130°).

Combine 1⅔ cups plus 2 tablespoons bread flour and next 4 ingredients. Gradually add honey mixture to flour mixture, beating well at low speed of an electric mixer. Beat 2 minutes at medium speed. Gradually add seed mixture, beating 2 minutes at medium speed. Stir in enough of the whole wheat flour to make a soft dough.

Sprinkle 1 tablespoon bread flour evenly over work surface. Turn dough out onto floured surface; knead until smooth and elastic (10 minutes). Let rest 10 minutes.

Shape dough into an 8-inch round loaf. Place loaf on a baking sheet coated with cooking spray.

Cover and let rise in a warm place (85°), free from drafts, 1 hour or until doubled in bulk. Combine egg white and 1 teaspoon water; brush over loaf. Sprinkle loaf with oats. Bake at 400° for 22 minutes or until loaf sounds hollow when tapped. Remove loaf from baking sheet; cool on a wire rack. Yield: 24 servings (73 calories per wedge).

Per Wedge:

Fat 0.7g	Carbohydrate 14.5g	Fiber 1.1g
saturated fat 0.1g	Cholesterol 0mg	Iron 0.9mg
Protein 2.5g	Sodium 52mg	Calcium 14mg

Whole-Grain-Goodness Bread

1   package active dry yeast
½   cup warm water (105° to 115°)
2   cups bread flour
¼   teaspoon salt
¾   cup nonfat buttermilk
2   tablespoons honey
½   teaspoon ground cinnamon
¼   cup regular oats, uncooked
¼   cup chopped walnuts, lightly toasted
¼   cup raisins
1   cup whole wheat flour
2   teaspoons bread flour
    Vegetable cooking spray

Combine yeast and warm water in a 1-cup liquid measuring cup; let stand 5 minutes.

Combine yeast mixture, 2 cups bread flour, and next 4 ingredients in a large mixing bowl, beating at medium speed of an electric mixer until well blended. Stir in oats, nuts, raisins, and enough of the whole wheat flour to make a soft dough.

Sprinkle 2 teaspoons bread flour evenly over work surface. Turn dough out onto floured surface, and knead until smooth and elastic (about 5 minutes). Place dough in a large bowl coated with cooking spray, turning to coat top. Cover and let rise in a warm place (85°), free from drafts, 35 minutes or until doubled in bulk.

Punch dough down. Turn dough out onto work surface, and knead lightly 4 or 5 times. Roll dough into a 14- x 7-inch rectangle. Roll up dough, starting at short side, pressing firmly to eliminate air pockets; pinch ends to seal. Place dough, seam side down, in a 9- x 5- x 3-inch loafpan coated with cooking spray.

Cover and let rise in a warm place, free from drafts, 35 minutes or until doubled in bulk. Bake at 375° for 25 minutes or until loaf sounds hollow when tapped. Remove from pan immediately; cool on a wire rack. Yield: 18 servings (114 calories per ½-inch slice).

Per Slice:

Fat 1.5g	Carbohydrate 21.9g	Fiber 1.7g
saturated fat 0.2g	Cholesterol 0mg	Iron 1.2mg
Protein 4.0g	Sodium 45mg	Calcium 21mg

Chocolate Bread

1¼ teaspoons active dry yeast
¾ cup plus 1 tablespoon warm water
 (105° to 115°)
2¼ cups bread flour, divided
¼ cup sugar
3 tablespoons Dutch process unsweetened
 cocoa
½ teaspoon salt
1½ teaspoons margarine, softened
1 egg yolk
¼ cup semisweet chocolate morsels
 Vegetable cooking spray

Combine yeast and warm water in a 1-cup
liquid measuring cup; let stand 5 minutes.
Combine yeast mixture, 1¼ cups bread flour,
sugar, and next 3 ingredients in a large mixing
bowl; beat at medium speed of an electric mixer
until well blended. Add egg yolk; beat well.
Gradually stir in enough of the remaining 1 cup
flour to make a soft dough.

Turn dough out onto work surface, and knead
until smooth and elastic (about 10 minutes).
Knead in chocolate morsels during last 2 minutes.
Place dough in a large bowl coated with cooking
spray, turning to coat top. Cover; let rise in a warm
place (85°), free from drafts, 1 hour or until doubled in bulk.

Punch dough down. Turn dough out onto work
surface, and knead lightly 4 or 5 times. Roll
dough into a 14- x 7-inch rectangle. Roll up dough,
starting at short side, pressing firmly to eliminate
air pockets; pinch ends to seal. Place dough, seam
side down, in a 9- x 5- x 3-inch loafpan coated
with cooking spray.

Cover and let rise in a warm place, free from
drafts, 45 minutes or until doubled in bulk. Bake
at 350° for 35 minutes or until loaf sounds hollow
when tapped. Remove from pan immediately;
cool on a wire rack. Yield: 18 servings (96 calories
per ½-inch slice).

Per Slice:
Fat 1.9g   Carbohydrate 17.1g   Fiber 0.5g
 saturated fat 0.7g Cholesterol 12mg   Iron 1.1mg
Protein 2.7g   Sodium 70mg   Calcium 7mg

Italian-Style Flat Breads

1 package active dry yeast
1 cup warm water (105° to 115°)
1 cup whole wheat flour
2 tablespoons brown sugar
¼ cup skim milk
2 teaspoons margarine, melted
1 teaspoon vegetable oil
3 cups thinly sliced onion
1 teaspoon sugar
¾ teaspoon salt, divided
2¼ cups plus 3 tablespoons bread flour,
 divided
 Vegetable cooking spray

Combine yeast and warm water in a 2-cup
liquid measuring cup; let stand 5 minutes. Combine yeast mixture, whole wheat flour, and next
3 ingredients in a large bowl, stirring until mixture is smooth. Cover and chill overnight.

Heat oil in a large nonstick skillet over medium
heat until hot. Add onion; sprinkle with 1 teaspoon sugar and ¼ teaspoon salt. Cook 10 to 12
minutes or until golden, stirring frequently. Set
aside, and let cool.

Combine yeast mixture, remaining ½ teaspoon
salt, and 2¼ cups bread flour; stir until blended.
Sprinkle 1 tablespoon bread flour evenly over
work surface; turn dough out onto floured surface, and knead until smooth and elastic (about
10 minutes). Sprinkle remaining 2 tablespoons
bread flour over work surface. Spoon onion mixture over dough. Knead gently to incorporate
onion mixture into dough. (Dough will be sticky.)

Divide dough into 14 equal portions. Press each
portion into a 4½-inch round. Place rounds on
baking sheets coated with cooking spray. Poke
holes in rounds at 1-inch intervals with handle of
a wooden spoon. Let rise, uncovered, in a warm
place (85°), free from drafts, 20 minutes. Bake at
375° for 20 minutes or until golden. Serve warm.
Yield: 14 flat breads (145 calories each).

Per Flat Bread:
Fat 1.6g   Carbohydrate 28.3g   Fiber 2.4g
 saturated fat 0.3g Cholesterol 0mg   Iron 1.6mg
Protein 4.8g   Sodium 137mg   Calcium 21mg

Garlic-Rosemary Focaccia

Because each variation adds a unique flavor twist to the flat bread, we couldn't decide on just one recipe. So we printed them all!

¾ cup plus 2 tablespoons water
2   tablespoons olive oil
2¼ cups bread flour, divided
1   teaspoon salt
1   package rapid-rise yeast
1   tablespoon bread flour
    Olive oil-flavored vegetable cooking spray
1   tablespoon cornmeal
1½ tablespoons commercial minced garlic
2   teaspoons chopped fresh rosemary

Combine water and oil in a saucepan; heat to 120° to 130°. Combine 1 cup bread flour, salt, and yeast in a large mixing bowl, stirring well. Gradually add liquid mixture to flour mixture, beating well at low speed of an electric mixer. Beat 2 additional minutes at medium speed. Gradually add ¾ cup flour; beat 2 minutes at medium speed. Gradually stir in enough of the remaining ½ cup flour to make a soft dough.

Sprinkle 1 tablespoon flour evenly over work surface. Turn dough out onto floured surface, and knead until smooth and elastic (about 10 minutes). Cover dough; let rest 10 minutes.

Coat a 14-inch round pizza pan with cooking spray; sprinkle pan with cornmeal. Set aside.

Punch dough down; turn out onto work surface, and knead lightly 4 or 5 times. Roll dough into a 14-inch circle. Place dough in prepared pan. Poke holes in dough at 1-inch intervals with handle of a wooden spoon.

Cover and let rise in a warm place (85°), free from drafts, 30 minutes or until doubled in bulk. Coat top of dough with cooking spray. Sprinkle garlic and rosemary evenly over dough. Bake at 375° for 25 to 30 minutes or until golden. Cut into

14 wedges. Yield: 14 servings (106 calories per wedge).

Per Wedge:

Fat 2.4g	Carbohydrate 17.6g	Fiber 0.7g
saturated fat 0.3g	Cholesterol 0mg	Iron 1.2mg
Protein 3.1g	Sodium 168mg	Calcium 8mg

Mozzarella and Sun-Dried Tomato Focaccia:

Combine 1 cup sun-dried tomatoes (packed without oil) and 1 cup hot water in a small bowl; cover and let stand 15 minutes. Drain; chop tomatoes, and set aside.

Prepare dough as directed, omitting garlic and rosemary.

After second rising, bake at 375° for 10 minutes. Remove bread from oven, and coat with cooking spray. Sprinkle tomato over dough. Return to oven, and bake 10 minutes. Sprinkle with ¼ cup plus 2 tablespoons (1½ ounces) shredded part-skim mozzarella cheese and ¼ cup shredded fresh basil. Bake 5 additional minutes or until cheese melts and bread is golden. Yield: 14 servings (120 calories per wedge).

Per Wedge:

Fat 3.0g	Carbohydrate 19.2g	Fiber 1.3g
saturated fat 0.6g	Cholesterol 2mg	Iron 1.3mg
Protein 4.2g	Sodium 256mg	Calcium 29mg

Onion Focaccia:

Coat a large nonstick skillet with cooking spray; add 1 teaspoon olive oil. Place over medium-high heat until hot. Add 1 cup sliced sweet onion and 1 cup sliced purple onion, separated into rings; sauté until tender. Set sautéed onion rings aside.

Prepare dough as directed, omitting garlic and rosemary.

After second rising, coat dough with cooking spray. Arrange sautéed onion rings over dough. Bake as directed. Yield: 14 servings (114 calories per wedge).

Per Wedge:

Fat 2.8g	Carbohydrate 18.8g	Fiber 1.1g
saturated fat 0.4g	Cholesterol 0mg	Iron 1.2mg
Protein 3.2g	Sodium 168mg	Calcium 9mg

Poached Salmon with Yellow Tomato Salsa (page 110)

Fish & Shellfish

South-of-the-Border Bass

Want a quick and easy low-fat meal? Just serve yellow rice (see page 148 for cooking method) and steamed broccoli with the spicy fillets.

Olive oil-flavored vegetable cooking spray
1 teaspoon olive oil
1 cup finely chopped onion
1 tablespoon chili powder
2 teaspoons minced garlic
¼ teaspoon ground cumin
¼ teaspoon ground coriander
1 (14½-ounce) can no-salt-added whole tomatoes, undrained and chopped
¼ cup finely chopped ripe olives
¼ cup fresh lemon juice
1 tablespoon honey
½ teaspoon coarsely ground pepper
6 (4-ounce) sea bass fillets
½ cup chopped fresh parsley

Coat a large nonstick skillet with cooking spray; add oil. Place over medium-high heat until hot. Add onion and next 4 ingredients; sauté 3 minutes or until onion is tender. Add tomato and next 4 ingredients. Bring to a boil; cover, reduce heat, and simmer 15 minutes, stirring occasionally.

Place fillets in an 11- x 7- x 1½-inch baking dish coated with cooking spray; spoon tomato mixture over fillets. Cover and bake at 350° for 20 to 25 minutes or until fish flakes easily when tested with a fork. Sprinkle with parsley. Yield: 6 servings (190 calories per serving).

Per Serving:
Fat 6.2g
    saturated fat 1.2g
Protein 22.7g
Carbohydrate 11.1g
Cholesterol 77mg
Sodium 166mg
Fiber 1.8g
Iron 2.8mg
Calcium 137mg

Easy Parmesan Flounder

4 (4-ounce) flounder fillets
   Vegetable cooking spray
1 tablespoon lemon juice
¼ cup nonfat mayonnaise
3 tablespoons grated Parmesan cheese
1 tablespoon thinly sliced green onions
1 tablespoon reduced-calorie margarine, softened
⅛ teaspoon hot sauce

Place fillets on rack of a broiler pan coated with cooking spray; brush fillets with lemon juice. Broil 5½ inches from heat (with electric oven door partially opened) 5 to 6 minutes or until fish flakes easily when tested with a fork.

Combine mayonnaise and remaining ingredients, stirring well. Spread mayonnaise mixture evenly over fillets. Broil 1 additional minute or until lightly browned and bubbly. Yield: 4 servings (146 calories per serving).

Per Serving:
Fat 4.4g
    saturated fat 1.3g
Protein 22.1g
Carbohydrate 3.5g
Cholesterol 61mg
Sodium 378mg
Fiber 0g
Iron 0.3mg
Calcium 84mg

Grilled Mahimahi with Pineapple

3 tablespoons brown sugar
3 tablespoons minced green onions
2 teaspoons peeled, minced gingerroot
1½ teaspoons minced garlic
½ teaspoon dried crushed red pepper
1½ cups unsweetened pineapple juice
¼ cup plus 2 tablespoons low-sodium soy sauce
1 tablespoon dark sesame oil
4 (4-ounce) mahimahi fillets
8 (½-inch-thick) slices fresh pineapple
   Vegetable cooking spray
   Fresh spinach leaves (optional)
   Green onion curls (optional)

Grilled Mahimahi with Pineapple

Combine sugar, minced onions, gingerroot, garlic, pepper, pineapple juice, soy sauce, and oil. Place fillets and pineapple slices in a large shallow baking dish. Pour half of pineapple juice mixture over fillets and pineapple. Cover and marinate in refrigerator 2 hours, turning fillets and pineapple occasionally. Divide remaining pineapple juice mixture in half; set aside.

Remove fillets and pineapple from marinade; discard marinade.

Coat grill rack with cooking spray; place on grill over medium-hot coals (350° to 400°). Place fillets and pineapple on rack; grill, covered, 5 to 6 minutes on each side or until fish flakes easily when tested with a fork and pineapple is tender, basting frequently with half of reserved pineapple juice mixture.

Pour remaining half of reserved pineapple juice mixture through a wire-mesh strainer into a small saucepan, discarding solids remaining in strainer. Bring to a boil over medium heat. Remove from heat; set aside, and keep warm.

Transfer fillets and pineapple to a serving platter. Drizzle with warm pineapple juice mixture. If desired, garnish with spinach leaves and green onion curls. Yield: 4 servings (248 calories per serving).

Per Serving:

Fat 3.9g	Carbohydrate 32.1g	Fiber 2.4g
saturated fat 0.6g	Cholesterol 80mg	Iron 2.1mg
Protein 21.1g	Sodium 491mg	Calcium 28mg

Orange Roughy in Chunky Tomato Sauce

2 tablespoons lemon juice
6 (4-ounce) orange roughy fillets
   Olive oil-flavored vegetable cooking spray
2 teaspoons olive oil, divided
1 cup chopped purple onion
⅓ cup chopped sweet yellow pepper
⅓ cup chopped green pepper
1 tablespoon chopped garlic
2¼ cups sliced fresh mushrooms
2 cups peeled, seeded, and chopped tomato
½ cup dry white wine
½ cup water
2 tablespoons no-salt-added tomato paste
1 teaspoon dried basil
½ teaspoon dried oregano
¼ teaspoon salt
¼ teaspoon ground red pepper
2 tablespoons chopped fresh parsley

Pour lemon juice into a large shallow dish. Place fillets in a single layer in dish, turning to coat. Cover and marinate in refrigerator 30 minutes, turning fillets once.

Remove fish from marinade, discarding marinade. Coat a large nonstick skillet with cooking spray; add 1 teaspoon oil. Place over medium-high heat until hot. Add fillets; cook 2 minutes on each side or until lightly browned. Remove fish from skillet, and set aside.

Wipe skillet dry with a paper towel. Coat skillet with cooking spray; add remaining 1 teaspoon oil. Place over medium-high heat until hot. Add onion and chopped peppers; sauté 3 minutes. Add garlic, and sauté 1 minute.

Add mushrooms and next 8 ingredients; stir well. Bring to a boil; cover, reduce heat, and simmer 5 minutes. Stir in parsley. Add fillets; cover and simmer 10 minutes or until fish flakes easily when tested with a fork. Yield: 6 servings (133 calories per serving).

Per Serving:

Fat 2.9g	Carbohydrate 8.4g	Fiber 2.0g
saturated fat 0.3g	Cholesterol 23mg	Iron 1.5mg
Protein 18.6g	Sodium 180mg	Calcium 25mg

Poached Salmon with Yellow Tomato Salsa

(pictured on page 107)

½ cup water
⅓ cup dry white wine
1 tablespoon coarsely chopped onion
½ teaspoon freshly ground pepper
4 (4-ounce) salmon fillets
1 cup peeled, seeded, and chopped yellow tomato
½ cup plus 2 tablespoons peeled, seeded, and chopped cucumber
⅓ cup chopped sweet red pepper
¼ cup chopped green onions
2 tablespoons chopped fresh parsley
3 tablespoons lime juice
1 teaspoon minced garlic
½ teaspoon hot sauce
¼ teaspoon salt
   Fresh watercress sprigs (optional)
   Lemon wedges (optional)

Combine first 4 ingredients in a large nonstick skillet. Bring to a boil over medium heat. Reduce heat; add salmon fillets, skin side down. Cover and simmer 5 to 7 minutes or until fish flakes easily when tested with a fork. Transfer fillets and cooking liquid to a shallow baking dish. Cover and chill thoroughly.

Combine tomato and next 8 ingredients, stirring well. Cover and chill at least 1 hour.

Remove fillets from liquid; discard liquid. Place fillets on individual watercress-lined serving plates, if desired. Spoon tomato mixture evenly over fillets. Garnish with lemon wedges, if desired. Yield: 4 servings (209 calories per serving).

Per Serving:

Fat 9.6g	Carbohydrate 6.0g	Fiber 1.3g
saturated fat 1.7g	Cholesterol 74mg	Iron 1.2mg
Protein 24.2g	Sodium 215mg	Calcium 23mg

Vegetable-Filled Sole with Lemon Cream Sauce

Butter-flavored vegetable cooking spray
1 teaspoon reduced-calorie margarine
1½ cups chopped fresh mushrooms
3 tablespoons finely chopped green onions
3 tablespoons finely chopped sweet red pepper
¾ cup shredded fresh spinach
1 tablespoon finely chopped kalamata olives
18 small sole fillets (about 24 ounces)
2 tablespoons dry white wine
2 tablespoons water
⅓ cup light process cream cheese
1 tablespoon water
1 tablespoon fresh lemon juice
Chopped fresh parsley (optional)
Paprika (optional)

Coat a large nonstick skillet with cooking spray; add margarine. Place over medium-high heat until margarine melts. Add mushrooms, green onions, and red pepper; sauté 3 minutes. Add spinach; sauté 1 minute or until spinach wilts. Remove from heat, and stir in olives.

Place 3 fillets side by side, overlapping edges slightly. Spoon about 2½ tablespoons vegetable mixture down center portion of fish; roll up, jellyroll fashion, beginning at narrow end. Secure with a wooden pick. Repeat procedure 5 times with remaining fillets and vegetable mixture. Place rolls, seam side down, in an 11- x 7- x 1½-inch baking dish coated with cooking spray. Pour wine and 2 tablespoons water around rolls. Cover and bake at 375° for 30 minutes or until fish flakes easily when tested with a fork.

Place cream cheese in a small glass bowl. Cover with heavy-duty plastic wrap, and vent. Microwave at HIGH 10 to 15 seconds or until cheese is softened. Add 1 tablespoon water and lemon juice, stirring until smooth.

Transfer rolls to individual serving plates; remove picks. Spoon cream cheese sauce evenly over rolls. If desired, sprinkle with parsley and paprika. Yield: 6 servings (154 calories per serving).

Per Serving:

Fat 4.8g	Carbohydrate 3.4g	Fiber 0.8g
saturated fat 1.7g	Cholesterol 62mg	Iron 1.1mg
Protein 23.5g	Sodium 220mg	Calcium 49mg

1. Place 3 fillets side by side, overlapping edges slightly to form a wide base for vegetable filling.

2. Spoon about 2½ tablespoons vegetable mixture down center portion of fish.

3. Roll up fillets, jellyroll fashion, beginning at narrow end. Secure with a wooden pick.

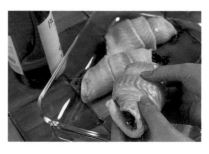

4. Place rolls, seam side down, in an 11- x 7- x 1½-inch baking dish coated with cooking spray.

Tilapia in Corn Husks

Tilapia in Corn Husks

6   large ears fresh corn with husks
½   cup water
¼   cup chopped onion
1   (4½-ounce) can chopped green chiles, drained
1   (2-ounce) jar diced pimiento, drained
1   tablespoon fresh lime juice
¼   teaspoon salt
¼   teaspoon ground cumin
¼   teaspoon pepper
6   (4-ounce) tilapia fillets
    Vegetable cooking spray
    Lime wedges (optional)

Carefully peel back husks from corn, leaving husks attached to stem. Remove corn cobs; set aside. Remove and discard silks. Cut 6 (8-inch) pieces of string. Place husks and string in a large bowl; add water to cover. Set aside.

Cut enough corn from cobs to measure ¾ cup. Reserve remaining corn for another use. Combine corn and ½ cup water in a saucepan. Bring to a boil; cover, reduce heat, and simmer 10 minutes or until corn is tender; drain. Combine corn, onion, and next 6 ingredients, stirring well; set aside.

Drain husks and string; pat dry with paper towels. Place 1 fillet in each husk near the stem.

Top each fillet with ¼ cup corn mixture. Return husks to original position, and tie tips with string.

Coat grill rack with cooking spray; place on grill over medium-hot coals (350° to 400°). Place husk packets on rack; grill, covered, 10 minutes on each side or until fish flakes easily when tested with a fork. Remove string; place husk packets on serving plates. Garnish with lime wedges, if desired. Yield: 6 servings (140 calories per serving).

NOTE: To bake fish without corn husks, place fillets in a 13- x 9- x 2-inch baking dish coated with cooking spray. Top with corn mixture. Bake, uncovered, at 350° for 15 minutes or until fish flakes easily when tested with a fork.

Per Serving:		
Fat 3.1g	Carbohydrate 6.3g	Fiber 1.0g
saturated fat 0.6g	Cholesterol 80mg	Iron 1.4mg
Protein 22.0g	Sodium 235mg	Calcium 74mg

Why Weight?

Strength training promises more than just sinewy biceps. This workout, which isolates specific muscles and pushes them to exhaustion, not only increases strength but decreases risk of certain diseases. Here are four reasons to pick up those dumbbells.

1. You'll lose inches quickly. Many women who do strength training drop a dress size or two without dropping a pound. Muscle weighs more than fat, so even though your scale won't show it, you'll look slimmer within a mere six to 10 weeks.

2. You'll be able to get fit and eat your cake, too. A strength-training routine naturally raises your body's metabolic rate. That's because muscles require more energy to sustain themselves than fat does. And basically that's what you're doing—creating more muscle mass.

3. You'll fight disease. Strength training increases bone density, a good hedge against osteoporosis. Strength training also decreases the risk of developing diabetes because the greater the muscle mass, the less insulin is needed to get its work done throughout the body.

4. You don't need a lot of time or money to do it. You only need two or three 30- to 40-minute workouts a week (but not on successive days; muscles need time to recover). Dumbbells for arms and strap-on ankle weights for legs are inexpensive and available at most sporting goods stores.

Tuna with Roasted Tomato, Onion, and White Beans

1	cup coarsely chopped plum tomato
½	cup coarsely chopped onion
2	teaspoons olive oil
2	cloves garlic, slivered
1	(15-ounce) can cannellini beans, drained
¼	cup chopped parsley
1	teaspoon chopped fresh oregano
1	teaspoon red wine vinegar
½	teaspoon chopped fresh thyme
¼	teaspoon freshly ground pepper
⅛	teaspoon salt
1	tablespoon red wine vinegar
2	teaspoons olive oil
⅛	teaspoon freshly ground pepper
4	(4-ounce) tuna steaks
	Vegetable cooking spray
	Fresh oregano sprigs (optional)
	Fresh thyme sprigs (optional)

Combine first 4 ingredients in a small bowl; spoon tomato mixture into an 11- x 7- x 1½-inch baking dish. Bake, uncovered, at 425° for 25 minutes or until tomato liquid evaporates and onion is tender. Add beans and next 6 ingredients; cover and bake 10 additional minutes or until thoroughly heated. Remove bean mixture from oven. Set aside, and keep warm.

Combine 1 tablespoon red wine vinegar, 2 teaspoons olive oil, and ⅛ teaspoon pepper in a small bowl, stirring well. Brush vinegar mixture evenly over both sides of tuna steaks.

Place steaks on rack of a broiler pan coated with cooking spray. Broil 5½ inches from heat (with electric oven door partially opened) 5 minutes on each side or until fish flakes easily when tested with a fork.

Transfer tuna steaks to a serving platter; spoon bean mixture evenly over steaks. If desired, garnish with oregano and thyme sprigs. Yield: 4 servings (312 calories per serving).

Per Serving:		
Fat 10.5g	Carbohydrate 22.0g	Fiber 4.0g
saturated fat 2.1g	Cholesterol 42mg	Iron 4.0mg
Protein 32.6g	Sodium 244mg	Calcium 41mg

Whole Whitefish with Cranberry-Pine Nut Dressing

Whole fish with the insides, head, fins, and scales removed are referred to as "dressed" fish. The tail may or may not be removed.

    Butter-flavored vegetable cooking spray
⅓ cup chopped shallots
3   tablespoons chopped celery
¾ cup chopped fresh mushrooms
¾ cup plus 2 tablespoons low-sodium
        chicken broth, divided
1   cup soft breadcrumbs
3   tablespoons chopped fresh parsley
1½ tablespoons pine nuts, lightly toasted
1   tablespoon dried cranberries, chopped
¼ teaspoon dried thyme
¼ teaspoon freshly ground pepper
1   (2-pound) dressed whitefish
⅓ cup dry white wine
    Lemon slices (optional)

Coat a nonstick skillet with cooking spray. Place over medium-high heat until hot. Add shallots and celery; sauté 2 minutes. Add mushrooms; sauté 2 minutes. Remove from heat; add 2 tablespoons chicken broth and next 6 ingredients. Set aside.

Remove any visible bones from whitefish cavity. Spoon breadcrumb mixture into cavity; secure opening with small metal skewers. Using a sharp knife, cut 2 diagonal slashes on top of fish.

Line a 15- x 10- x 1-inch jellyroll pan with heavy-duty aluminum foil; coat foil with cooking spray. Place fish in prepared pan; coat with cooking spray. Pour remaining ¾ cup chicken broth and wine over fish. Bake, uncovered, at 500° for 10 minutes. Reduce oven temperature to 400°; bake 20 additional minutes or until fish flakes easily when tested with a fork, basting frequently with pan juices. Garnish with lemon slices, if desired. Yield: 4 servings (246 calories per serving).

Per Serving:

Fat 10.4g	Carbohydrate 10.7g	Fiber 1.5g
saturated fat 1.6g	Cholesterol 77mg	Iron 1.9mg
Protein 27.2g	Sodium 142mg	Calcium 21mg

Seasoned Crab Cakes with Lemon Sauce

1½ cups soft breadcrumbs
2   tablespoons minced green onions
2   tablespoons minced sweet red pepper
2   tablespoons nonfat mayonnaise
1   tablespoon finely chopped fresh parsley
½ teaspoon dry mustard
¼ teaspoon ground red pepper
1   egg white
1   pound fresh crabmeat, drained
    Butter-flavored vegetable cooking spray
1   teaspoon vegetable oil
    Lemon Sauce
    Fresh parsley sprigs (optional)
    Lemon wedges (optional)

Combine first 8 ingredients; stir well. Add crabmeat, stirring gently. Shape mixture into 5 patties.

Coat a large nonstick skillet with cooking spray; add oil. Place over medium heat until hot. Add patties; cook 5 minutes on each side or until golden. Serve with Lemon Sauce. If desired, garnish with parsley sprigs and lemon wedges. Yield: 5 servings (227 calories per serving).

Lemon Sauce

    Vegetable cooking spray
1   tablespoon margarine
¼ cup finely chopped shallots
1   clove garlic, minced
½ cup canned no-salt-added chicken broth,
        undiluted
¼ cup dry white wine
¼ teaspoon grated lemon rind
3   tablespoons fresh lemon juice
¼ teaspoon pepper
⅛ teaspoon salt
2   teaspoons cornstarch
3   tablespoons evaporated skimmed milk

Coat a small saucepan with cooking spray; add margarine. Place over medium-high heat until margarine melts. Add shallots and garlic;

sauté until tender. Add chicken broth and next 5 ingredients; bring to a boil, stirring frequently.

Combine cornstarch and milk, stirring until smooth. Add to broth mixture, stirring constantly. Cook, stirring constantly, until mixture thickens. Yield: ¾ cup.

Per Serving:		
Fat 6.0g	Carbohydrate 20.7g	Fiber 0.8g
saturated fat 1.0g	Cholesterol 86mg	Iron 1.8mg
Protein 21.5g	Sodium 567mg	Calcium 154mg

Lobster Tails with Lemon Cream

*Lobster may be pricey, but it's definitely low fat.
This succulent recipe contains less than
1 gram of fat per serving.*

8   (8-ounce) fresh or frozen lobster tails,
      thawed
¾   cup plain nonfat yogurt
¼   cup chopped fresh parsley,
      divided
1   tablespoon fresh dillweed
1   tablespoon lemon juice
1   tablespoon water
2   teaspoons chopped capers
1   teaspoon minced garlic
1   teaspoon Dijon mustard
8   (⅛-inch-thick) slices cucumber,
      cut in half
16   (⅛-inch-thick) slices radish
      Fresh dillweed sprigs (optional)
      Lemon wedges (optional)

Cook lobster tails in boiling water 6 to 8 minutes or until done; drain. Rinse with cold water. Split lobster shells lengthwise, cutting through upper hard shell with an electric knife. Remove lobster meat through split shell, leaving meat intact. Set shells aside.

Score lobster meat at 2-inch intervals. Place lobster in a large heavy-duty, zip-top plastic bag. Combine yogurt, 1 tablespoon parsley, and next 6 ingredients; pour over lobster. Seal bag, and shake gently until lobster is well coated. Marinate in refrigerator 3 hours, turning occasionally.

Remove lobster from marinade, reserving marinade. Place reserved shells on individual serving plates. Place lobster meat on shells. Spoon remaining marinade over lobster. Dip cucumber slices in remaining 3 tablespoons parsley. Place a cucumber slice and a radish slice in each score on lobster. If desired, garnish with dillweed sprigs and lemon wedges. Yield: 8 servings (133 calories per serving).

Per Serving:		
Fat 0.8g	Carbohydrate 4.3g	Fiber 0.2g
saturated fat 0.2g	Cholesterol 85mg	Iron 0.7mg
Protein 25.7g	Sodium 597mg	Calcium 123mg

A Vacation That's Fit to be Tried

No longer solely havens for beauty and diet, spas are now places to get in shape. Every major spa in the country has a substantial fitness program, including one-on-one fitness consultations, sessions with personal trainers, lectures on healthy lifestyles, and even personalized fitness plans (with videos!) to pack up and take home.

Spas are usually on the cutting edge when it comes to fitness trends, so you can try a wide variety of new activities. And as a bonus, many spas are tucked away in beautiful secluded areas where you can unwind or rev up with daily strides on country roads and wooded trails. With more and more spas offering short-stay, fitness/revitalizer programs, this is just the jump-start any fitness regimen needs. For details on specific spas, contact Spa-Finders (800/255-7727) or Spa-Trek (800/272-3480).

Southwestern Grilled Shrimp

1½ pounds unpeeled large fresh shrimp
2 tablespoons fresh lime juice, divided
1 tablespoon water
1 tablespoon low-sodium soy sauce
1 teaspoon minced garlic
1 teaspoon olive oil
1 jalapeño pepper, seeded and halved
3 tomatillos, husked
¼ cup plus 2 tablespoons cubed avocado
¼ teaspoon sugar
⅛ teaspoon salt
⅛ teaspoon freshly ground pepper
   Vegetable cooking spray

Peel and devein shrimp; place in a heavy-duty, zip-top plastic bag. Combine 1 tablespoon lime juice and next 4 ingredients, and pour over shrimp. Seal bag; shake gently. Marinate in refrigerator 2 hours.

Place pepper, skin side up, on a baking sheet; flatten with palm of hand. Broil 5½ inches from heat (with electric oven door partially opened) 10 minutes or until charred. Place in ice water until cool. Remove from water; peel and discard skin. Coarsely chop pepper; place in container of an electric blender. Coarsely chop tomatillos. Add tomatillos, remaining lime juice, avocado, and next 3 ingredients to blender; cover and process until smooth. Chill.

Remove shrimp from marinade; discard marinade. Thread shrimp onto four 8-inch skewers. Coat grill rack with cooking spray; place on grill over medium-hot coals (350° to 400°). Place shrimp on rack; grill, covered, 3 to 4 minutes on each side or until done. Remove shrimp from skewers, and place on serving plates. Serve with tomatillo mixture. Yield: 4 servings (138 calories per serving).

Per Serving:		
Fat 4.6g	Carbohydrate 3.7g	Fiber 0.6g
saturated fat 0.8g	Cholesterol 180mg	Iron 3.1mg
Protein 19.9g	Sodium 379mg	Calcium 42mg

Southwestern Grilled Shrimp with red pepper and cilantro garnish and mixed greens.

Scallops in Shells with Vegetable-Cream Sauce

   Olive oil-flavored vegetable cooking spray
2 tablespoons chopped shallots
2 teaspoons minced garlic
2⅓ cups sliced fresh mushrooms
⅓ cup skim milk
2 ounces Neufchâtel cheese
¼ teaspoon salt
½ teaspoon olive oil
18 ounces sea scallops, cut in half
1½ tablespoons all-purpose flour
⅓ cup dry vermouth
2 tablespoons clam juice
1½ cups thinly sliced fresh spinach
1 teaspoon fresh lemon juice
¼ teaspoon ground white pepper
¼ cup plus 2 tablespoons (1½ ounces)
   shredded Gruyère cheese

Coat a medium-size nonstick skillet with cooking spray. Place over medium-high heat until hot. Add shallots and garlic, and sauté 1 minute. Add mushrooms; sauté 2 minutes. Add milk, Neufchâtel cheese, and salt; cook, stirring constantly, until cheese melts. Remove from heat; set aside.

Coat a large nonstick skillet with cooking spray; add oil. Place over medium-high heat until hot. Add scallops; cook 3 to 4 minutes or until scallops are lightly browned, turning to brown all sides. Combine flour, vermouth, and clam juice, stirring until smooth. Add vermouth mixture, mushroom mixture, and spinach to scallops. Bring to a boil; reduce heat, and simmer, uncovered, 4 minutes. Remove from heat; stir in lemon juice and pepper.

Spoon scallop mixture evenly into six scalloped baking shells; sprinkle evenly with Gruyère. Broil 5½ inches from heat (with electric oven door partially opened) 3 to 4 minutes or until lightly browned. Yield: 6 servings (167 calories per serving).

Per Serving:		
Fat 6.2g	Carbohydrate 8.3g	Fiber 0.9g
saturated fat 2.9g	Cholesterol 43mg	Iron 1.2mg
Protein 19.2g	Sodium 323mg	Calcium 131mg

Scallop, Mushroom, and Asparagus Rolls

6   ounces fresh asparagus
     Butter-flavored vegetable cooking spray
2⅔ cups chopped fresh mushrooms
¼   cup chopped shallots
8   ounces bay scallops
½   cup light process cream cheese
1   teaspoon freshly ground pepper
4   sheets commercial frozen phyllo pastry, thawed
2   tablespoons plus 2 teaspoons fine, dry breadcrumbs
1   teaspoon reduced-calorie margarine, melted

Snap off tough ends of asparagus. Remove scales from stalks with a knife or vegetable peeler, if desired. Coarsely chop asparagus. Arrange asparagus in a vegetable steamer over boiling water. Cover and steam 3 minutes or until crisp-tender. Drain and set aside.

Coat a large nonstick skillet with cooking spray. Place over medium-high heat until hot. Add mushrooms and shallots; sauté 4 minutes. Add scallops, and cook, stirring constantly, 2 minutes. Stir in asparagus, cream cheese, and pepper; cook, stirring constantly, 5 to 6 minutes or until mixture thickens. Remove from heat, and set aside.

Place 1 sheet of phyllo on a damp towel (keep remaining phyllo covered). Lightly coat phyllo with cooking spray; sprinkle with 2 teaspoons breadcrumbs. Repeat layers with 1 sheet of phyllo and 2 teaspoons breadcrumbs. Fold phyllo in half crosswise.

Spoon half of scallop mixture along one lengthwise edge of phyllo, leaving a 1-inch border on short edges. Fold short edges in about 1 inch, and roll up, jellyroll fashion, starting with long side containing scallop mixture.

Place roll, seam side down, on a baking sheet coated with cooking spray. Lightly coat top of pastry with cooking spray. Repeat procedure with remaining phyllo, breadcrumbs, and scallop mixture. Brush melted margarine evenly over rolls.

Bake at 400° for 15 minutes or until crisp and golden. Remove from oven, and cut each roll into fourths. Serve immediately. Yield: 4 servings (234 calories per serving).

Per Serving:

Fat 8.3g	Carbohydrate 23.5g	Fiber 1.4g
saturated fat 3.2g	Cholesterol 35mg	Iron 2.4mg
Protein 16.8g	Sodium 410mg	Calcium 77mg

Orecchiette with Fresh Vegetables and Herbs (page 127)

Grains
& Pastas

Barley-Vegetable Sauté

You can get about one-third of the daily recommendation for fiber (20 to 35 grams) from one serving of this fiber-rich side dish.

1¼ cups quick-cooking barley
2 tablespoons reduced-calorie margarine
1 cup diced carrot
½ cup chopped onion
¼ cup finely chopped fresh parsley
2 teaspoons dried oregano
1 teaspoon garlic powder
¼ teaspoon salt
¼ teaspoon pepper
1 cup diced zucchini
¾ cup fresh asparagus tips

Cook barley according to package directions, omitting salt and fat; set aside, and keep warm.

Melt margarine in a large nonstick skillet over medium-high heat. Add carrot and onion; sauté until tender. Add parsley and next 4 ingredients; stir well. Add zucchini and asparagus; sauté until tender. Stir in barley; cook over medium-high heat, stirring constantly, until thoroughly heated. Yield: 5 servings (202 calories per 1-cup serving).

Per Serving:

Fat 3.6g	Carbohydrate 39.4g	Fiber 8.0g
saturated fat 0.7g	Cholesterol 0mg	Iron 2.0mg
Protein 5.6g	Sodium 195mg	Calcium 50mg

Polenta with Sun-Dried Tomatoes

This soft polenta is similar to cooked grits. Serve it instead of mashed potatoes for a hearty side dish.

1 cup sun-dried tomatoes (packed without oil)
1 cup hot water
   Olive oil-flavored vegetable cooking spray
1 teaspoon olive oil
⅓ cup plus 1½ tablespoons finely chopped shallots
2 cloves garlic, crushed
2 (14¼-ounce) cans no-salt-added chicken broth
1½ cups water
½ teaspoon salt
½ teaspoon cracked pepper
1⅓ cups instant polenta
½ cup grated Asiago cheese

Combine tomatoes and hot water in a small bowl. Cover and let stand 15 minutes; drain. Coarsely chop tomatoes; set aside.

Coat a large saucepan with cooking spray; add oil. Place over medium-high heat until hot. Add shallots and garlic; sauté until tender.

Add chicken broth and next 3 ingredients to saucepan; bring to a boil. Add polenta in a slow, steady stream, stirring constantly. Reduce heat to medium, and cook, stirring constantly, 3 to 5 minutes or until thickened. Remove from heat. Stir in chopped tomato and cheese. Serve warm. Yield: 11 servings (100 calories per ½-cup serving).

Per Serving:

Fat 1.9g	Carbohydrate 16.7g	Fiber 0.9g
saturated fat 0.7g	Cholesterol 3mg	Iron 0.7mg
Protein 3.7g	Sodium 279mg	Calcium 56mg

Roasted Garlic and Onion Risotto

Arborio rice is a must in classic risotto. It absorbs a lot of water and creates the distinctive texture of risotto—creamy with a slight bite.

1 small head garlic, unpeeled
    Vegetable cooking spray
1 teaspoon margarine
¾ cup chopped onion
1 tablespoon sugar
1 tablespoon water
2 (14¼-ounce) cans no-salt-added chicken
    broth
1 cup water
1 cup Arborio rice, uncooked
2 teaspoons chopped fresh oregano
¼ teaspoon salt
¼ teaspoon pepper
½ cup frozen English peas, thawed
2 tablespoons freshly grated Parmesan
    cheese

Gently peel outer skin from garlic; cut off and discard top one-fourth of head. Place garlic, cut side up, in center of a piece of heavy-duty aluminum foil, coat garlic with cooking spray. Fold foil over garlic, sealing tightly. Bake at 350° for 1 hour or until garlic is soft. Remove from oven, and let cool. Remove and discard papery skin from garlic. Using a spoon, scoop out soft garlic; set pulp aside.

Coat a nonstick skillet with cooking spray; add margarine. Place over medium-high heat until margarine melts. Add onion, and sauté 4 minutes or until tender. Reduce heat to medium-low. Sprinkle onion with sugar and 1 tablespoon water. Cook 15 minutes or until onion is golden, stirring frequently. Set onion aside.

Combine chicken broth and 1 cup water in a saucepan; place over medium heat. Cover and bring to a simmer; reduce heat to low, and keep warm. (Do not boil.)

Combine rice and next 3 ingredients in a saucepan. Add 1 cup of simmering broth mixture to rice mixture. Cook over medium heat, stirring constantly, 5 minutes or until most of liquid is absorbed. Add remaining broth, ½ cup at a time, cooking and stirring constantly until each ½ cup addition is absorbed (about 30 minutes). (Rice will be tender and have a creamy consistency.) Stir in roasted garlic, onions, and peas. Sprinkle with cheese, and serve immediately. Yield: 4 servings (253 calories per 1-cup serving).

Per Serving:		
Fat 2.2g	Carbohydrate 48.4g	Fiber 2.1g
saturated fat 0.7g	Cholesterol 2mg	Iron 2.6mg
Protein 6.2g	Sodium 232mg	Calcium 63mg

Fiber Options

Fiber lowers cholesterol levels, helps you lose weight, and may even prevent cancer. The catch is that you need to consume a lot of it—20 to 35 grams daily—an amount that sounds like you might have to take the Quaker Oats man hostage to make your goal.

Have no fear. There's plenty of soluble and insoluble fiber in the foods you love. **Soluble fiber** (found in fruits, vegetables, legumes, oats, barley, brown rice, and seeds) is the cholesterol-lowering hero that absorbs liquid and swells to form a sticky gel that can trap cholesterol and remove it from the body. **Insoluble fiber** is the part of fruits, vegetables, and whole grains that isn't digested and moves everything through the digestive tract, reducing the risk of colorectal cancer.

One word of caution: Build up your fiber intake gradually, or you may end up with intestinal problems. Add about five grams of fiber each week until you reach at least 20 grams. Drink eight to 10 glasses of water daily as you increase your fiber intake to help move it through your system.

Mexican Rice Cakes

Mexican Rice Cakes

1   (4½-ounce) can chopped green chiles
2   cups cooked long-grain rice (cooked
      without salt or fat), chilled
1½ cups soft breadcrumbs
½   cup finely chopped tomato
2   egg whites, lightly beaten
2   tablespoons chopped fresh cilantro
1   teaspoon onion powder
1   teaspoon ground cumin
1   teaspoon chili powder
½   teaspoon garlic powder
½   teaspoon pepper
¼   teaspoon salt
      Vegetable cooking spray
      Fresh cilantro sprig (optional)
      No-salt-added salsa (optional)

Drain chopped green chiles, and press firmly between paper towels to remove excess moisture. Combine chiles, rice, and next 10 ingredients in a medium bowl, stirring well. Shape rice mixture into 6 patties.

Coat a large nonstick skillet with cooking spray; place over medium heat until hot. Add patties, and cook 5 minutes on each side or until lightly browned.

Transfer patties to a serving platter. If desired, garnish with a cilantro sprig, and serve with no-salt-added salsa. Yield: 6 servings (130 calories per serving).

Per Serving:

Fat 0.9g	Carbohydrate 26.2g	Fiber 1.3g
saturated fat 0.1g	Cholesterol 0mg	Iron 1.5mg
Protein 4.2g	Sodium 268mg	Calcium 28mg

Zucchini-Parmesan Rice

Basmati rice is an aromatic long-grain rice traditionally used in Indian cuisine.
It's interchangeable with regular long-grain rice.

1½ teaspoons reduced-calorie margarine
  1 cup chopped onion
  1 tablespoon dried parsley flakes
 ½ teaspoon dried basil
  1 clove garlic, minced
  2 cups canned no-salt-added chicken broth, undiluted
  1 cup basmati rice, uncooked
    Vegetable cooking spray
  3 cups julienne-sliced zucchini
 ½ teaspoon salt
 ¼ teaspoon pepper
 ¼ cup freshly grated Parmesan cheese

Melt margarine in a large Dutch oven over medium-high heat, and add chopped onion, parsley flakes, basil, and minced garlic. Sauté until onion is tender. Add chicken broth; bring to a boil.

Stir in rice; cover, reduce heat, and simmer 20 minutes or until rice is tender and liquid is absorbed. Set aside, and keep warm.

Coat a large nonstick skillet with cooking spray; place over medium-high heat until hot. Add zucchini, salt, and pepper; sauté until tender. Add rice mixture to skillet, stirring gently; cook until thoroughly heated. Remove from heat, and sprinkle with cheese. Yield: 7 servings (148 calories per 1-cup serving).

Per Serving:

Fat 2.0g	Carbohydrate 27.1g	Fiber 1.0g
saturated fat 0.7g	Cholesterol 3mg	Iron 1.7mg
Protein 4.7g	Sodium 246mg	Calcium 73mg

Mediterranean Rice Pilaf

    Vegetable cooking spray
1½ teaspoons reduced-calorie margarine
 ½ cup chopped onion
  1 cup long-grain brown rice, uncooked
2½ cups canned no-salt-added chicken broth, undiluted
  1 teaspoon ground coriander
 ¼ teaspoon salt
 ¼ teaspoon ground red pepper
 ¼ teaspoon ground turmeric
 ½ cup finely chopped fresh cilantro

Coat a large nonstick skillet with cooking spray; add margarine. Place over medium-high heat until margarine melts. Add onion; sauté 3 to 4 minutes or until tender. Add rice; cook, stirring constantly, 4 minutes or until rice is lightly browned.

Add chicken broth, coriander, salt, red pepper, and turmeric to rice in saucepan. Bring to a boil; cover, reduce heat, and simmer 40 minutes or until rice is tender and liquid is absorbed. Remove from heat, and stir in cilantro. Yield: 4 servings (204 calories per ¾-cup serving).

Per Serving:

Fat 2.6g	Carbohydrate 39.0g	Fiber 2.3g
saturated fat 0.4g	Cholesterol 0mg	Iron 1.4mg
Protein 4.5g	Sodium 172mg	Calcium 29mg

Autumn Grains

Wild rice, brown rice, and barley merge for a tasty mix of textures in this side dish.

1¾   cups canned no-salt-added chicken broth, undiluted
1   cup unsweetened orange juice
1½   cups peeled, seeded, and cubed butternut squash
½   cup chopped onion
⅓   cup wild rice, uncooked
⅓   cup long-grain brown rice, uncooked
¼   teaspoon salt
¼   teaspoon ground cinnamon
¼   teaspoon curry powder
⅛   teaspoon ground cardamom
⅛   teaspoon ground ginger
½   cup raisins
⅓   cup pearl barley, uncooked
¼   cup chopped pecans, toasted

Combine chicken broth and orange juice in a large saucepan; bring to a boil. Add squash and next 8 ingredients. Cover; reduce heat, and simmer 20 minutes. Add raisins and barley. Cover and cook 35 to 40 additional minutes or until grains are tender and liquid is absorbed.

Stir in pecans. Serve immediately. Yield: 5 servings (249 calories per ¾-cup serving).

Per Serving:

Fat 4.5g	Carbohydrate 49.0g	Fiber 4.8g
saturated fat 0.5g	Cholesterol 0mg	Iron 1.5mg
Protein 5.4g	Sodium 126mg	Calcium 49mg

Three-Pepper Pasta Toss

1   medium-size sweet red pepper
1   medium-size sweet yellow pepper
1   medium-size green pepper
      Olive oil-flavored vegetable cooking spray
2   teaspoons olive oil
1¾   cups coarsely chopped onion
3   cloves garlic, minced
1   (14½-ounce) can no-salt-added stewed tomatoes, undrained
1   (6-ounce) can no-salt-added tomato paste
1   teaspoon dried basil
1   teaspoon dried thyme
½   teaspoon dried crushed red pepper
10   ounces capellini, uncooked
½   cup grated Parmesan cheese

Cut peppers into 1-inch pieces. Coat a large nonstick skillet with cooking spray; add olive oil. Place over medium-high heat until hot. Add pepper pieces, onion, and garlic; sauté 7 minutes or until vegetables are tender. Add stewed tomatoes and next 4 ingredients. Reduce heat, and simmer, uncovered, 10 minutes, stirring occasionally.

Cook pasta according to package directions, omitting salt and fat; drain well. Place pasta in a serving bowl. Add pepper mixture, and toss well. Sprinkle with cheese. Serve immediately. Yield: 8 servings (235 calories per 1-cup serving).

Per Serving:

Fat 4.3g	Carbohydrate 40.4g	Fiber 3.8g
saturated fat 1.6g	Cholesterol 6mg	Iron 3.2mg
Protein 9.8g	Sodium 156mg	Calcium 143mg

Bookend Fitness: What to do Before and After Your Workout

Before your workout: Take five to 10 minutes to warm up your body with movements that mirror the real workout to come. Running? Gently swing your legs. Golfing? Lightly move through your stroke.

After your workout: During the last five minutes of your workout, slowly decrease the intensity of your activity. Power walkers should cut the speed, and stroll for a while. Ditto for runners and swimmers. It may look funny to keep playing squash in slow motion, so just keep walking around, moving your arms through their range of motion. Then add a few leg, back, and arm stretches to keep muscles from tightening up.

Roasted Vegetables with Gemelli

Gemelli, a rope-shaped pasta, adds a special twist to this dish. If it's not available, substitute fusilli.

1   large zucchini
1   large yellow squash
1   large sweet red pepper
1   (8-ounce) package fresh mushrooms
1   large onion, cut into thin wedges
2   tablespoons balsamic vinegar
2   teaspoons olive oil
½   teaspoon dried rosemary
½   teaspoon sugar
¼   teaspoon salt
¼   teaspoon freshly ground pepper
2   large tomatoes, coarsely chopped
10   ounces gemelli, uncooked
2   ounces goat cheese, crumbled
¼   cup shredded fresh basil
   Freshly ground pepper (optional)

Line a 15- x 10- x 1-inch jellyroll pan with aluminum foil; set aside. Cut zucchini, squash, and red pepper into 1-inch pieces. Place on prepared pan; add mushrooms and onion.

Combine vinegar and next 5 ingredients in a small bowl, stirring well. Brush evenly over vegetables. Bake at 425° for 15 minutes. Stir vegetables, and add tomato. Bake 10 additional minutes or until vegetables are tender and golden.

Cook pasta according to package directions, omitting salt and fat; drain. Place pasta in a serving bowl. Add roasted vegetables; toss well. Top with goat cheese and basil. Sprinkle with freshly ground pepper, if desired. Yield: 10 servings (160 calories per 1-cup serving).

Per Serving:

Fat 2.9g	Carbohydrate 28.3g	Fiber 2.4g
saturated fat 1.1g	Cholesterol 5mg	Iron 2.0mg
Protein 6.1g	Sodium 130mg	Calcium 51mg

Linguine with Exotic Mushrooms

The robust flavors of the mushrooms in this pasta dish pair well with beef tenderloin or pork loin.

½   ounce dried porcini mushrooms
½   cup boiling water
4   ounces fresh shiitake mushrooms
   Olive oil-flavored vegetable cooking spray
2   teaspoons olive oil
4   ounces fresh oyster mushrooms
⅓   cup finely chopped shallots
2   cloves garlic, minced
1½   tablespoons all-purpose flour
1   (14¼-ounce) can no-salt-added beef broth
3   tablespoons chopped fresh thyme
¼   teaspoon salt
12   ounces linguine, uncooked
⅓   cup grated Asiago cheese
   Freshly ground pepper (optional)

Rinse porcini mushrooms thoroughly. Combine porcini mushrooms and boiling water in a small bowl; cover and let stand 30 minutes. Drain mushrooms, reserving liquid. Chop mushrooms.

Remove and discard shiitake mushroom stems. Coat a large nonstick skillet with cooking spray; add oil. Place over medium-high heat until hot. Add porcini, shiitake, and oyster mushrooms, shallots, and garlic. Sauté 3 to 4 minutes or until mushrooms are tender.

Sprinkle flour over mushroom mixture; cook, stirring constantly, 30 seconds. Add reserved mushroom liquid, beef broth, thyme, and salt. Bring to a boil; reduce heat, and simmer, uncovered, 10 minutes.

Cook pasta according to package directions, omitting salt and fat; drain well. Place pasta in a serving bowl; add mushroom mixture, and toss gently. Sprinkle pasta with cheese. Sprinkle with freshly ground pepper, if desired. Yield: 8 servings (218 calories per ¾-cup serving).

Per Serving:

Fat 3.2g	Carbohydrate 38.4g	Fiber 1.9g
saturated fat 0.4g	Cholesterol 3mg	Iron 2.3mg
Protein 8.1g	Sodium 150mg	Calcium 72mg

Mostaccioli with Fresh Tomatoes and Goat Cheese

Olive oil-flavored vegetable cooking spray
½ teaspoon olive oil
1 clove garlic, minced
1 large tomato, seeded and chopped
3 ounces goat cheese, crumbled
1 tablespoon chopped fresh basil
1½ teaspoons balsamic vinegar
¼ teaspoon sugar
¼ teaspoon dried crushed red pepper
6 ounces mostaccioli, uncooked

Coat a medium saucepan with cooking spray; add olive oil. Place over medium-high heat until hot. Add garlic; sauté 30 seconds. Add tomato; cook 8 to 10 minutes or until slightly thickened, stirring occasionally. Reduce heat to low; add goat cheese. Cook 2 minutes or until cheese melts, stirring frequently. Stir in basil and next 3 ingredients; cook until thoroughly heated. Remove from heat; set aside, and keep warm.

Cook pasta according to package directions, omitting salt and fat; drain. Place pasta in a serving bowl. Add tomato mixture; toss gently. Serve immediately. Yield: 4 servings (242 calories per 1-cup serving).

Per Serving:
Fat 6.2g
  saturated fat 3.4g
Protein 9.3g
Carbohydrate 37.3g
Cholesterol 19mg
Sodium 249mg
Fiber 2.2g
Iron 2.2mg
Calcium 124mg

Baked Vegetable Macaroni and Cheese

Macaroni and cheese without the guilt! Fresh vegetables boost the nutrient content, flavor, and color, and leave each serving with only 16% fat.

9 ounces elbow macaroni, uncooked
Vegetable cooking spray
1 teaspoon vegetable oil
¾ cup chopped onion
2 cloves garlic, minced
2 cups small broccoli flowerets
1 cup seeded, coarsely chopped tomato
¼ cup chopped fresh basil
¼ cup chopped fresh parsley
⅓ cup all-purpose flour
½ teaspoon salt
⅛ teaspoon pepper
2½ cups skim milk
½ cup (2 ounces) shredded reduced-fat Cheddar cheese
½ cup (2 ounces) shredded reduced-fat Swiss cheese

Cook macaroni according to package directions, omitting salt and fat; drain and set aside.

Coat a large nonstick skillet with cooking spray; add oil. Place skillet over medium-high heat until hot. Add chopped onion and minced garlic; sauté 3 minutes. Add broccoli flowerets, and sauté 1 minute or until vegetables are crisp-tender. Stir in tomato, basil, and parsley; set vegetable mixture aside.

Combine flour, salt, and pepper in a medium saucepan. Gradually add milk, stirring until smooth. Cook over medium heat, stirring constantly, until mixture is thickened and bubbly.

Add cheeses, stirring until smooth. Stir in cooked macaroni and vegetable mixture. Spoon macaroni mixture into a 2-quart baking dish coated with vegetable cooking spray. Bake at 350° for 30 minutes. Yield: 8 servings (230 calories per serving).

Per Serving:
Fat 4.2g
  saturated fat 1.8g
Protein 12.8g
Carbohydrate 35.4g
Cholesterol 10mg
Sodium 261mg
Fiber 2.2g
Iron 2.0mg
Calcium 262mg

Orecchiette with Fresh Vegetables and Herbs

Orecchiette is a small bowl-shaped pasta.
(pictured on page 119)

10	ounces fresh asparagus
1	(14½-ounce) can vegetable broth
1½	cups julienne-sliced sweet yellow pepper
1	cup diagonally sliced carrot
2	cups Sugar Snap peas, trimmed
1	cup frozen English peas
¼	cup chopped fresh chives
2	tablespoons chopped fresh basil
1	tablespoon chopped fresh thyme
⅛	teaspoon salt
12	ounces orecchiette, uncooked
¾	cup grated Romano cheese
	Freshly ground pepper (optional)

Snap off tough ends of asparagus. Remove scales from stalks with a knife or vegetable peeler, if desired. Cut asparagus into 1-inch pieces, and set aside.

Bring vegetable broth to a boil in a large saucepan. Add asparagus, yellow pepper, and carrot. Reduce heat; simmer, uncovered, 4 minutes. Add Sugar Snap peas and English peas; cook 3 additional minutes or until vegetables are crisp-tender. Add chives, basil, thyme, and salt.

Cook pasta according to package directions, omitting salt and fat; drain well. Place pasta in a serving bowl. Add vegetable mixture; toss well. Add ½ cup cheese to pasta mixture; toss well. Sprinkle with remaining ¼ cup cheese. Sprinkle with freshly ground pepper, if desired. Yield: 8 servings (241 calories per ¾-cup serving).

Per Serving:		
Fat 3.9g	Carbohydrate 40.6g	Fiber 3.8g
saturated fat 1.9g	Cholesterol 11mg	Iron 3.0mg
Protein 11.2g	Sodium 350mg	Calcium 143mg

Spinach and Cheese Manicotti

1	(10-ounce) package frozen chopped spinach
	Olive oil-flavored vegetable cooking spray
2	teaspoons olive oil
⅔	cup finely chopped onion
2	cloves garlic, minced
1	(15-ounce) carton light ricotta cheese
½	cup freshly grated Parmesan cheese, divided
2	egg whites
¼	teaspoon dried crushed red pepper
⅛	teaspoon ground nutmeg
8	manicotti shells, uncooked
2	cups commercial fat-free spaghetti sauce

Cook spinach according to package directions, omitting salt. Drain spinach, and press gently between paper towels to remove excess moisture. Set spinach aside.

Coat a medium saucepan with cooking spray; add oil. Place over medium-high heat until hot. Add onion and garlic; sauté 8 minutes. Transfer onion mixture to a bowl. Add spinach, ricotta cheese, ¼ cup Parmesan cheese, egg whites, crushed red pepper, and nutmeg; stir well.

Cook manicotti shells according to package directions, omitting salt and fat; drain well. Stuff spinach mixture evenly into cooked shells.

Spread ½ cup spaghetti sauce over bottom of a 13- x 9- x 2-inch baking dish. Place filled shells over sauce. Pour remaining spaghetti sauce over shells.

Cover and bake at 375° for 30 minutes or until thoroughly heated. Sprinkle with remaining ¼ cup Parmesan cheese. Yield: 4 servings (369 calories per serving).

Per Serving:		
Fat 10.3g	Carbohydrate 47.9g	Fiber 6.9g
saturated fat 4.8g	Cholesterol 23mg	Iron 5.2mg
Protein 25.7g	Sodium 705mg	Calcium 396mg

Roasted Vegetable Lasagna

1 large sweet red pepper
1 large sweet yellow pepper
  Olive oil-flavored vegetable cooking spray
2 medium zucchini
2 medium-size yellow squash
1 small eggplant
1 tablespoon olive oil
3 cloves garlic, minced
½ teaspoon freshly ground pepper
1 (25½-ounce) jar fat-free spaghetti sauce
6 cooked lasagna noodles (cooked without salt or fat)
1 (15-ounce) carton light ricotta cheese
¼ cup chopped fresh basil
1 cup (4 ounces) shredded part-skim mozzarella cheese

Cut red and yellow peppers in half lengthwise; remove and discard seeds and membrane. Place peppers, skin side up, in a shallow roasting pan coated with cooking spray, and flatten with palm of hand.

Cut zucchini and yellow squash in half lengthwise. Cut eggplant crosswise into ½-inch-thick slices. Arrange vegetables in a single layer in roasting pan with peppers.

Combine oil and garlic; brush evenly over vegetables. Sprinkle with ½ teaspoon pepper. Bake at 425° for 30 minutes, turning vegetables once. Cut roasted peppers and squash crosswise into ½-inch-thick slices. Cut eggplant slices into quarters.

Spread ½ cup spaghetti sauce over bottom of a 13- x 9- x 2-inch baking dish coated with cooking spray. Place 3 lasagna noodles over sauce; top evenly with half of vegetables. Combine ricotta cheese and basil; spoon half of cheese mixture evenly over vegetables. Spoon 1 cup spaghetti sauce over cheese mixture. Repeat layers with remaining noodles, vegetables, cheese mixture, and spaghetti sauce.

Cover and bake at 375° for 45 minutes. Uncover and sprinkle with mozzarella cheese. Bake, uncovered, 5 additional minutes or until cheese melts. Let lasagna stand 10 minutes

before serving. Yield: 8 servings (267 calories per serving).

Per Serving:

Fat 8.9g	Carbohydrate 33.2g	Fiber 2.7g
saturated fat 4.4g	Cholesterol 25mg	Iron 3.2mg
Protein 14.7g	Sodium 414mg	Calcium 291mg

Mexicali Pasta and Beans

Tripolini (very small bow tie-shaped pasta) is attractive in this recipe, but you can use macaroni or any small shaped pasta instead.

  Vegetable cooking spray
2 teaspoons vegetable oil
1⅓ cups chopped onion
2 cloves garlic, minced
1 (14½-ounce) can no-salt-added stewed tomatoes, undrained
¾ cup no-salt-added salsa
1 teaspoon chili powder
1 teaspoon ground cumin
½ teaspoon dried oregano
1 (16-ounce) can pinto beans, drained
6 ounces tripolini, uncooked
½ cup (2 ounces) shredded reduced-fat Cheddar cheese
2 tablespoons chopped fresh cilantro

Coat a large saucepan with cooking spray; add oil. Place over medium-high heat until hot. Add onion and garlic; sauté 5 minutes. Add tomato and next 4 ingredients; bring to a boil. Stir in beans. Cover, reduce heat, and simmer 15 minutes.

Cook pasta according to package directions, omitting salt and fat; drain. Stir pasta into bean mixture. Cook, stirring constantly, until mixture is thoroughly heated. Sprinkle with cheese and cilantro. Serve immediately. Yield: 7 servings (217 calories per 1-cup serving).

Per Serving:

Fat 3.7g	Carbohydrate 36.4g	Fiber 3.2g
saturated fat 1.3g	Cholesterol 5mg	Iron 2.9mg
Protein 10.1g	Sodium 229mg	Calcium 131mg

Greek Beef and Pasta

¾ pound lean boneless top round steak
  Olive oil-flavored vegetable cooking spray
2 teaspoons olive oil
½ cup chopped onion
½ cup chopped green pepper
2 cloves garlic, minced
1 cup frozen artichoke hearts, thawed and
  cut in half lengthwise
1 (14½-ounce) can no-salt-added whole
  tomatoes, undrained and chopped
½ cup water
1 tablespoon red wine vinegar
1 teaspoon low-sodium Worcestershire sauce
½ teaspoon beef-flavored bouillon granules
1 tablespoon chopped fresh oregano
¼ teaspoon salt
12 ounces fettuccine, uncooked
¼ cup crumbled feta cheese
2 tablespoons sliced ripe olives

Trim fat from steak, and cut steak into thin strips. Coat a large nonstick skillet with cooking spray; add oil. Place over medium-high heat until hot. Add steak, onion, green pepper, and garlic. Cook until meat is browned on all sides, stirring frequently.

Add artichoke hearts and next 5 ingredients to meat mixture in skillet. Bring to a boil; cover, reduce heat, and simmer 35 minutes or until steak is tender. Stir in oregano and salt. Cook, uncovered, 15 additional minutes or until slightly thickened.

Cook pasta according to package directions, omitting salt and fat; drain. Place pasta on a serving platter; top with steak mixture, and sprinkle with cheese and olives. Yield: 6 servings (229 calories per serving).

Per Serving:

Fat 6.6g	Carbohydrate 24.1g	Fiber 2.2g
saturated fat 2.3g	Cholesterol 39mg	Iron 2.9mg
Protein 18.2g	Sodium 354mg	Calcium 82mg

Chicken and Vegetable Lo Mein

Bok choy is a Chinese vegetable with white stalks and dark green leaves. Store it in an airtight container in the refrigerator up to four days.

6 ounces vermicelli, uncooked
2 (4-ounce) skinned, boned chicken breast
  halves, cut into thin strips
½ teaspoon dried crushed red pepper
2 cloves garlic, minced
  Vegetable cooking spray
2 teaspoons dark sesame oil, divided
3 cups sliced bok choy
¾ cup canned low-sodium chicken broth,
  undiluted
2 tablespoons low-sodium soy sauce
1 tablespoon oyster sauce
½ cup coarsely shredded carrot
⅓ cup diagonally sliced green onions
2 teaspoons sesame seeds, toasted

Cook pasta according to package directions, omitting salt and fat; drain and set aside.

Combine chicken, red pepper, and garlic, tossing well.

Coat a wok or large nonstick skillet with cooking spray; drizzle 1 teaspoon sesame oil around top of wok, coating sides. Heat at medium-high (375°) until hot. Add chicken mixture; stir-fry 2 minutes. Add bok choy; stir-fry 2 minutes. Add chicken broth, soy sauce, and oyster sauce to wok; stir-fry 1 minute. Add carrot and green onions; stir-fry 1 minute.

Add cooked pasta and remaining 1 teaspoon sesame oil to wok; toss gently until thoroughly heated. Sprinkle with sesame seeds. Serve immediately. Yield: 4 servings (282 calories per 1¼-cup serving).

Per Serving:

Fat 5.2g	Carbohydrate 36.7g	Fiber 2.3g
saturated fat 0.8g	Cholesterol 33mg	Iron 3.1mg
Protein 20.8g	Sodium 439mg	Calcium 84mg

Moroccan Chicken and Orzo

Moroccan Chicken and Orzo

1 teaspoon paprika
½ teaspoon ground cumin
¼ teaspoon salt
¼ teaspoon saffron threads
⅛ teaspoon ground cinnamon
1 clove garlic, minced
4 (4-ounce) skinned, boned chicken breast
    halves, cut into 1-inch pieces
   Vegetable cooking spray
2 teaspoons vegetable oil
1¼ cups chopped onion
1 cup canned low-sodium chicken broth,
    undiluted
¼ cup golden raisins
1 cup orzo, uncooked
¼ cup chopped fresh cilantro
   Fresh cilantro leaves (optional)

Combine first 6 ingredients in a medium bowl. Add chicken, tossing to coat. Set aside.

Coat a nonstick skillet with cooking spray; add oil. Place over medium-high heat until hot. Add onion; sauté 4 minutes. Add chicken mixture, and cook 6 minutes or until chicken is browned, stirring frequently. Add broth and raisins; reduce heat to medium, and cook 5 minutes.

Cook pasta according to package directions, omitting salt and fat; drain. Add pasta to skillet, stirring until heated. Spoon mixture into individual serving bowls. Sprinkle with chopped cilantro. Garnish with cilantro leaves, if desired. Yield: 5 servings (327 calories per 1-cup serving).

Per Serving:

Fat 4.3g	Carbohydrate 43.4g	Fiber 2.4g
saturated fat 0.8g	Cholesterol 53mg	Iron 3.2mg
Protein 27.8g	Sodium 199mg	Calcium 39mg

Cavatappi with Turkey and Basil-Cilantro Pesto

Traditional pesto is high in fat. But by using chicken broth to replace most of the olive oil,
we trimmed the fat considerably.

1   **(7-ounce) jar roasted red peppers in water**
¾   **cup tightly packed fresh basil leaves**
¼   **cup tightly packed fresh cilantro leaves**
¼   **cup grated Parmesan cheese**
3   **tablespoons canned no-salt-added chicken broth, undiluted**
1   **tablespoon olive oil**
1   **clove garlic, halved**
1   **tablespoon all-purpose flour**
1   **cup evaporated skimmed milk**
¼   **cup dry white wine**
¼   **teaspoon salt**
10   **ounces cavatappi (corkscrew-shaped pasta), uncooked**
3   **cups cubed cooked turkey breast**
2   **tablespoons pine nuts, toasted**

Drain roasted peppers, reserving liquid. Chop enough peppers to measure ¼ cup; set aside.

Reserve remaining roasted peppers in liquid for another use.

Position knife blade in food processor bowl; add basil and next 5 ingredients. Process 1 minute, scraping sides of processor bowl once; set aside.

Place flour in a medium saucepan. Gradually add milk, stirring until smooth. Add wine and salt. Cook over medium heat, stirring constantly, until mixture is slightly thickened. Stir in basil mixture.

Cook pasta according to package directions, omitting salt and fat; drain. Combine pasta and basil mixture in a serving bowl; toss gently. Add chopped red pepper, turkey, and pine nuts; toss gently. Serve immediately. Yield: 8 servings (362 calories per 1-cup serving).

Per Serving:

Fat 8.6g	Carbohydrate 32.2g	Fiber 1.0g
saturated fat 2.8g	Cholesterol 66mg	Iron 3.2mg
Protein 36.2g	Sodium 320mg	Calcium 229mg

The Calorie-Burner Index

It's not a good idea to get too hung up on calories; remember, the types of food you eat will have a major impact on your overall health. But if you're making decisions about exercising, it's always nice to know how much calorie-burning benefit you're getting for your efforts. Here's a guide to an hour's worth of:

Body Weight/Calories Burned				
Activity (one hour)	**120 lbs.**	**150 lbs.**	**180 lbs.**	**220 lbs.**
Walking 3 mph	198	246	294	360
Running 5½ mph	480	600	702	888
Cycling 6 mph	192	240	282	360
Cross-country skiing 4 mph	468	474	714	870
Swimming 1 mph	312	396	480	585

Szechuan Noodles with Shrimp

1 pound unpeeled medium-size fresh
    shrimp
½ cup reduced-calorie ketchup
¼ cup sugar
¼ cup canned no-salt-added chicken broth,
    undiluted
2 tablespoons Chinese chili puree with
    garlic
1 tablespoon red wine vinegar
1 tablespoon low-sodium soy sauce
1 teaspoon peeled, minced gingerroot
1½ teaspoons dark sesame oil
⅛ teaspoon pepper
2 cloves garlic, minced
6 ounces Chinese egg noodles,
    uncooked
4 ounces fresh shiitake mushrooms
    Vegetable cooking spray
1 teaspoon hot chile oil
1 teaspoon vegetable oil
2 cups julienne-sliced snow pea pods
1 cup diced sweet red pepper

Peel and devein shrimp; set aside.

Combine ketchup and next 9 ingredients in a bowl, stirring well. Add shrimp. Cover and marinate in refrigerator 30 minutes.

Cook noodles according to package directions, omitting salt and fat. Set aside, and keep warm.

Remove and discard mushroom stems; slice mushroom caps.

Coat a wok or large nonstick skillet with cooking spray; drizzle chile and vegetable oils around top of wok, coating sides. Heat at medium-high (375°) until hot. Add mushrooms, snow peas, and red pepper; stir-fry 2 to 3 minutes or until crisp-tender.

Add shrimp and marinade to wok; stir-fry 3 to 4 minutes or until shrimp turn pink. Add noodles, and stir-fry 1 minute or until thoroughly heated. Serve immediately. Yield: 4 servings (405 calories per 1½-cup serving).

Per Serving:

Fat 7.8g	Carbohydrate 56.9g	Fiber 3.4g
saturated fat 1.4g	Cholesterol 170mg	Iron 5.8mg
Protein 25.6g	Sodium 593mg	Calcium 83mg

*Eggplant Parmesan Soufflé with
Tomato Sauce (page 134)*

Meatless
Main Dishes

Eggplant Parmesan Soufflé with Tomato Sauce

You'll need large eggplant slices for this recipe, so buy an eggplant that's large in diameter. (pictured on page 133)

Vegetable cooking spray
½   cup finely chopped onion
⅓   cup finely chopped sweet red pepper
1   clove garlic, minced
2   (8-ounce) cans no-salt-added tomato sauce
1   tablespoon minced fresh basil
¼   teaspoon pepper
⅛   teaspoon salt
3   tablespoons freshly grated Parmesan cheese
2   tablespoons Italian-seasoned breadcrumbs
4   (¾-inch-thick) slices eggplant
2   teaspoons reduced-calorie margarine
2   small cloves garlic, minced
2   teaspoons all-purpose flour
⅔   cup 1% low-fat milk
2   tablespoons light process cream cheese
½   cup freshly grated Parmesan cheese
2   egg whites
1   teaspoon sugar
Fresh basil sprigs (optional)

Coat a large saucepan with cooking spray. Place over medium-high heat until hot. Add onion, sweet red pepper, and 1 clove minced garlic; sauté until tender. Stir in tomato sauce, minced basil, pepper, and salt. Cook until thoroughly heated, stirring frequently. Set aside, and keep warm.

Combine 3 tablespoons Parmesan cheese and breadcrumbs. Set aside.

Coat a large baking sheet with cooking spray. Coat both sides of eggplant slices with cooking spray; place on baking sheet. Broil 3 inches from heat (with electric oven door partially opened) 4 minutes on each side or until lightly browned. Sprinkle breadcrumb mixture evenly over top of eggplant slices. Broil 1½ to 2 additional minutes or until golden; set aside.

Melt margarine in a saucepan over medium heat; add 2 cloves minced garlic, and sauté 30 seconds. Add flour; cook 1 minute, stirring constantly with a wire whisk. Gradually stir in milk. Cook, stirring constantly, 5 minutes or until thickened and bubbly. Remove from heat; add cream cheese, stirring until cheese melts. Stir in ½ cup Parmesan cheese; set aside.

Beat egg whites at high speed of an electric mixer until soft peaks form. Add sugar, beating until stiff peaks form. Gently fold about ½ cup egg white mixture into cream cheese mixture. Gently fold remaining egg white mixture into cheese mixture.

Spoon cheese mixture evenly over top of eggplant slices. Bake at 375° for 15 to 20 minutes or until golden. To serve, spoon tomato sauce mixture onto individual serving plates; top each with an eggplant slice. Garnish with basil sprigs, if desired. Yield: 4 servings (199 calories per serving).

Per Serving:

Fat 6.4g	Carbohydrate 25.7g	Fiber 3.8g
saturated fat 3.0g	Cholesterol 14mg	Iron 2.0mg
Protein 11.3g	Sodium 498mg	Calcium 266mg

Fiber-Filled Foods For Your Family

Cereals and Grains	Legumes	Vegetables	Fruits
Oat and wheat bran cereals	Kidney beans	Broccoli	Apples
Oatmeal	Lentils	Brussels sprouts	Bananas
Brown rice	Lima beans	Carrots	Berries
Popcorn	Pinto beans	Sweet potatoes	Oranges
	White beans	Turnips	Pears

Mushroom Popover Squares

Vegetable cooking spray
1 teaspoon olive oil
2 cups peeled, cubed eggplant
½ cup chopped onion
3 tablespoons chopped fresh parsley
2 (8-ounce) packages sliced fresh
    mushrooms
2 tablespoons spaghetti sauce seasoning mix
1 (14½-ounce) can no-salt-added whole
    tomatoes, undrained and chopped
½ cup plus 2 tablespoons grated Parmesan
    cheese, divided
¾ cup all-purpose flour
1½ teaspoons sugar
⅛ teaspoon salt
¾ cup skim milk
1 egg
1 egg white

Coat a large nonstick skillet with cooking spray; add oil. Place over medium-high heat until hot. Add eggplant, onion, parsley, and mushrooms; sauté 10 minutes or until vegetables are tender. Add spaghetti sauce mix and tomato; cook, uncovered, over medium heat 10 minutes, stirring occasionally.

Spoon vegetable mixture into an 8-inch square baking dish coated with cooking spray. Sprinkle with ½ cup Parmesan cheese.

Combine flour and next 5 ingredients in container of an electric blender; cover and process until smooth. Pour egg mixture over vegetable mixture; sprinkle with remaining 2 tablespoons Parmesan cheese. Bake at 400° for 25 to 30 minutes or until puffed and golden. Let stand 5 minutes before serving. Yield: 6 servings (182 calories per serving).

Per Serving:

Fat 4.8g	Carbohydrate 26.4g	Fiber 2.6g
saturated fat 2.1g	Cholesterol 44mg	Iron 2.4mg
Protein 10.4g	Sodium 567mg	Calcium 200mg

Potato-Stuffed Peppers

2 large baking potatoes (about 1⅔ pounds)
4 medium-size sweet red peppers (about
    1¾ pounds)
Olive oil-flavored vegetable cooking spray
1 teaspoon olive oil
1½ cups diced zucchini
¼ cup chopped onion
¼ cup dry white wine
½ teaspoon dried oregano
½ teaspoon dried basil
1 clove garlic, minced
½ cup freshly grated Parmesan cheese
½ cup frozen egg substitute, thawed
½ teaspoon salt

Scrub potatoes; prick each several times with a fork. Bake at 400° for 1 hour or until tender; let cool completely.

Cut red peppers in half lengthwise; remove and discard seeds and membrane. Cook pepper halves in boiling water 30 seconds; drain well, and set aside.

Coat a large nonstick skillet with cooking spray; add oil. Place over medium-high heat until hot. Add zucchini and onion; sauté until crisp-tender. Add wine, oregano, basil, and garlic. Bring to a boil; reduce heat, and simmer, uncovered, 2 minutes or until most of liquid evaporates. Set aside.

Peel and mash potatoes. Add mashed potato, Parmesan cheese, egg substitute, and salt to zucchini mixture; stir well. Spoon potato mixture evenly into pepper halves; place stuffed peppers in a 13- x 9- x 2-inch baking dish coated with cooking spray. Bake, uncovered, at 350° for 20 to 25 minutes or until golden. Yield: 4 servings (174 calories per serving).

Per Serving:

Fat 4.4g	Carbohydrate 24.9g	Fiber 4.7g
saturated fat 1.7g	Cholesterol 6mg	Iron 6.4mg
Protein 11.0g	Sodium 498mg	Calcium 177mg

Potato-Cheese Tart

This potato-cheese entrée is reminiscent of a savory cheesecake. For a low-fat meal, add steamed asparagus and a fresh fruit salad.

2   medium baking potatoes (about
      1¼ pounds)
      Vegetable cooking spray
¼   cup melba toast crumbs (about 6 rounds)
3   cups sliced fresh mushrooms
½   cup chopped shallots
½   cup minced green onions
¾   cup Marsala wine
2   tablespoons minced fresh thyme
2   cups nonfat ricotta cheese
2   (8-ounce) packages light process cream
      cheese, softened
½   cup frozen egg substitute, thawed
½   cup grated Asiago cheese
¼   teaspoon salt
¼   teaspoon pepper
⅛   teaspoon ground red pepper
2   egg whites
¼   teaspoon cream of tartar

Scrub potatoes; prick each several times with a fork. Bake potatoes at 400° for 1 hour or until tender; let potatoes cool.

Coat a 9-inch springform pan with cooking spray. Sprinkle melba toast crumbs evenly over bottom of pan; set aside.

Coat a large nonstick skillet with cooking spray. Place over medium-high heat until hot. Add mushrooms, shallots, and green onions; sauté until tender. Add Marsala and thyme; bring to a boil. Reduce heat, and simmer, uncovered, 3 minutes or until most of liquid evaporates; set aside.

Combine ricotta cheese and cream cheese in a medium bowl; beat at medium speed of an electric mixer until well blended. Add egg substitute, beating well. Stir in Asiago cheese and next 3 ingredients; set aside.

Beat egg whites and cream of tartar at high speed of an electric mixer until stiff peaks form.

Gently fold egg white mixture into cream cheese mixture.

Peel potatoes, and cut into ¼-inch-thick slices. Arrange half of potato slices over crumbs, overlapping slices slightly. Top with half of mushroom mixture and half of cheese mixture. Repeat procedure with remaining potato slices, mushroom mixture, and cheese mixture.

Bake at 325° for 1 hour or until set; let cool slightly on a wire rack. Yield: 8 servings (266 calories per serving).

Per Serving:		
Fat 11.5g	Carbohydrate 25.4g	Fiber 2.2g
saturated fat 6.7g	Cholesterol 39mg	Iron 2.2mg
Protein 17.3g	Sodium 573mg	Calcium 220mg

Wilted Spinach with Cheese Pot Stickers

      Vegetable cooking spray
1   teaspoon sesame oil
2   cloves garlic, minced
1¼ cups thinly sliced sweet red pepper
⅓   cup thinly sliced green onions
4   ounces fresh shiitake mushroom caps,
      cut in half
6   cups loosely packed fresh spinach leaves
      Cheese Pot Stickers
3   tablespoons water
2   tablespoons low-sodium soy sauce
1   teaspoon sesame seeds

Coat a large nonstick skillet with cooking spray; add oil. Place over medium-high heat until hot. Add garlic; sauté 30 seconds. Add sweet red pepper and green onions; sauté 2 minutes. Add mushroom caps; sauté until tender. Add spinach; toss gently. Cover and steam 1 to 2 minutes or just until spinach wilts. Transfer spinach mixture to a bowl; set aside, and keep warm.

Arrange Cheese Pot Stickers in a single layer in skillet. Combine 3 tablespoons water and soy sauce. Pour soy sauce mixture over pot stickers.

Wilted Spinach with Cheese Pot Stickers

Bring to a boil over high heat; reduce heat to medium-high. Cook, uncovered, 2 to 3 minutes or until liquid evaporates. To serve, spoon spinach mixture onto individual serving plates. Top each serving with 3 pot stickers; sprinkle with sesame seeds. Serve immediately. Yield: 4 servings (245 calories per serving).

Cheese Pot Stickers

24   **wonton wrappers**
12   **(½-inch) cubes Asiago cheese**
2   **quarts water**

Place 1 wonton wrapper on work surface. Place a second wrapper (at a one-quarter turn) on top of first wrapper, creating a star design. Place 1 cheese cube in center of wonton wrappers.

Moisten edges of wrappers with water; fold in half, bringing edges together, and pressing firmly. Crimp and pleat edges to form a ruffled design. Repeat procedure with remaining wrappers and cheese.

Bring 2 quarts water to a boil in a large saucepan over high heat. Add half of pot stickers; boil, uncovered, 1 minute. Remove from water, using a slotted spoon; cover and set aside. Repeat procedure with remaining pot stickers. Yield: 1 dozen.

Per Serving:

Fat 6.4g	Carbohydrate 35.5g	Fiber 3.3g
saturated fat 2.2g	Cholesterol 14.0mg	Iron 3.7mg
Protein 12.1g	Sodium 729mg	Calcium 256mg

Corn Cakes with Creamy Vegetable Topping

To avoid last-minute work, you can make the corn cakes up to two days ahead of time; store them, well wrapped, in the refrigerator. Or freeze them up to one month. To reheat, bake at 350° for 10 to 12 minutes.

Butter-flavored vegetable cooking spray
1 teaspoon reduced-calorie margarine
¾ cup peeled, diced red potato
¾ cup diced carrot
½ cup chopped onion
½ cup chopped celery
½ cup chopped green pepper
1 (14½-ounce) can vegetable broth
½ cup all-purpose flour
¼ teaspoon pepper
⅛ teaspoon salt
1½ cups 1% low-fat milk
¾ cup frozen English peas, thawed
1 tablespoon plus 2 teaspoons chopped fresh parsley, divided
1 teaspoon white wine Worcestershire sauce
Corn Cakes

Coat a large nonstick skillet with cooking spray; add margarine. Place over medium-high heat until margarine melts. Add potato and next 4 ingredients; sauté until vegetables are crisp-tender. Add vegetable broth; bring to a boil. Cover, reduce heat, and simmer 10 minutes or until vegetables are tender. Drain vegetables, reserving ½ cup liquid. Set aside reserved liquid and vegetables.

Combine flour, pepper, and salt in a large saucepan. Gradually stir in milk and reserved liquid. Cook over medium heat, stirring constantly, until mixture thickens. Add cooked vegetables, peas, 1 tablespoon parsley, and Worcestershire sauce. Cook until thoroughly heated, stirring frequently.

To serve, place 2 Corn Cakes on each individual serving plate. Spoon vegetable mixture over Corn Cakes. Sprinkle with remaining 2 teaspoons parsley. Yield: 6 servings (332 calories per serving).

Corn Cakes

1¾ cups yellow cornmeal
2 teaspoons baking powder
¼ teaspoon salt
1 tablespoon sugar
1½ cups nonfat buttermilk
¼ cup frozen egg substitute, thawed
1 tablespoon reduced-calorie margarine, melted
Butter-flavored vegetable cooking spray
3 teaspoons vegetable oil, divided

Combine first 4 ingredients in a medium bowl; make a well in center of mixture.

Combine buttermilk, egg substitute, and margarine; add to dry ingredients, stirring just until dry ingredients are moistened.

Coat a large nonstick skillet with cooking spray; add 1 teaspoon oil. Heat over medium-high heat until hot. Cook 4 corn cakes at a time, pouring ¼ cup batter into skillet for each corn cake. Cook corn cakes until tops are covered with bubbles and edges look cooked; turn corn cakes, and cook other side. Repeat procedure twice with remaining oil and batter. Yield: 12 corn cakes.

Per Serving:		
Fat 5.9g	Carbohydrate 57.3g	Fiber 4.1g
saturated fat 1.4g	Cholesterol 5mg	Iron 3.2mg
Protein 11.4g	Sodium 405mg	Calcium 265mg

Garden Vegetable Lasagna

One serving of this lasagna is a good source of calcium. It gives you one-third the recommended daily amount (800 milligrams).

Vegetable cooking spray
1 teaspoon olive oil
2 cups thinly sliced fresh mushrooms
½ cup chopped onion
2 cloves garlic, minced
1 (10-ounce) package frozen chopped spinach, thawed
¾ cup finely shredded carrot
1 cup light ricotta cheese
¼ cup grated Parmesan cheese
2 egg whites
1 (25½-ounce) jar commercial fat-free spaghetti sauce
9 cooked lasagna noodles (cooked without salt or fat)
1½ cups (6 ounces) shredded part-skim mozzarella cheese

Coat a nonstick skillet with cooking spray; add oil. Place over medium-high heat until hot. Add mushrooms, onion, and garlic; sauté until vegetables are tender and liquid evaporates.

Drain spinach, and press gently between paper towels to remove excess moisture. Add spinach and carrot to mushroom mixture; stir well.

Combine ricotta cheese, Parmesan cheese, and egg whites in a small bowl, stirring well.

Spread ⅔ cup spaghetti sauce over bottom of a 13- x 9- x 2-inch baking dish coated with cooking spray. Place 3 lasagna noodles over sauce; spoon half of ricotta cheese mixture over noodles. Top with half of vegetable mixture; spoon ⅔ cup spaghetti sauce over vegetable mixture. Repeat procedure with 3 noodles, remaining cheese mixture, remaining vegetable mixture, and ⅔ cup spaghetti sauce. Top with remaining 3 lasagna noodles and remaining spaghetti sauce. Cover and bake at 350° for 40 minutes.

Uncover and sprinkle with mozzarella cheese. Bake, uncovered, 5 additional minutes or until cheese melts. Let stand 15 minutes before serving. Yield: 8 servings (231 calories per serving).

Per Serving:

Fat 6.4g	Carbohydrate 29.7g	Fiber 2.5g
saturated fat 3.4g	Cholesterol 19mg	Iron 2.9mg
Protein 15.5g	Sodium 498mg	Calcium 272mg

Long and Strong for Total Fitness

It's a two-part equation: aerobic exercise and weight training are the building blocks of true fitness. Here's why: Although strength training can enhance just about every muscle group, it doesn't do the job on the heart, the muscle which is responsible for pumping blood throughout the body. Aerobic workouts take care of the heart, but they lack important muscular and bone-building benefits.

Recently, the American College of Sports Medicine revised its official position on exercise to include both weight training and aerobic exercise. Previously, in the College's 1978 report, frequent aerobic exercise was thought to be sufficient to maintain overall fitness.

This two-tier approach to fitness doesn't have to mean twice as much time, however. Many health clubs are designing programs that incorporate both types of exercise in one workout. One popular program is circuit training, which alternates aerobic activities with weight training. At the Sears Tower Club in Chicago, the circuit-training class, called "PT55" for "Personally Trained in 55 Minutes," alternates strength training with jumping jacks and military marches and is always packed.

You can work toward total fitness at home, too. Combine weekday walks with weight lifting, and add tennis or rowing on the weekend.

Grilled Vegetables with Pasta and Black Beans

Grilled Vegetables with Pasta and Black Beans

2   medium-size yellow squash
1   medium zucchini
1   medium-size sweet red pepper
1   medium-size sweet yellow pepper
½   cup white balsamic vinegar
⅓   cup canned vegetable broth, undiluted
1   tablespoon shredded fresh basil
1   tablespoon Dijon mustard
1   tablespoon olive oil
2   cloves garlic, minced
    Vegetable cooking spray
2   cups cooked rotini pasta (cooked without
      salt or fat)
1   (15-ounce) can no-salt-added black beans,
      drained
    Fresh basil sprigs (optional)

Cut squash, zucchini, and peppers in half lengthwise. Remove and discard seeds and membrane from peppers. Set aside prepared vegetables.

Combine vinegar and next 5 ingredients. Divide vinegar mixture in half; set aside half of mixture. Pour remaining half of mixture into a large heavy-duty, zip-top plastic bag; add vegetables. Seal bag, and shake until vegetables are well coated. Let stand at least 30 minutes, turning once. Remove vegetables from marinade, reserving marinade.

Coat grill rack with cooking spray; place on grill over medium-hot coals (350° to 400°). Place vegetables on rack; grill, covered, 12 to 14 minutes or until vegetables are tender, turning and basting frequently with reserved marinade.

Cut vegetables into bite-size pieces. Combine vegetables, cooked rotini, and beans in a bowl. Add reserved half of vinegar mixture; toss gently.

To serve, spoon into individual serving bowls. Garnish with fresh basil sprigs, if desired. Yield: 4 servings (286 calories per 1½-cup serving).

Per Serving:

Fat 5.2g	Carbohydrate 44.0g	Fiber 6.4g
saturated fat 0.7g	Cholesterol 0mg	Iron 4.0mg
Protein 11.1g	Sodium 186mg	Calcium 51mg

Polenta with Spicy Black Beans

3½	cups water
½	teaspoon salt
1	(6.6-ounce) package instant polenta
1	cup frozen whole-kernel corn, thawed
½	cup (2 ounces) shredded reduced-fat sharp Cheddar cheese
½	cup minced green onions
	Vegetable cooking spray
1	teaspoon vegetable oil
1	cup chopped onion
1	cup chopped green pepper
1	cup chopped celery
2	cloves garlic, minced
1	(15-ounce) can no-salt-added black beans, drained
1	(14½-ounce) can no-salt-added stewed tomatoes
¾	cup canned vegetable broth, undiluted
2	tablespoons seeded, minced jalapeño pepper
2	tablespoons chili powder
1	teaspoon ground cumin

Combine water and salt in a large saucepan; bring to a boil. Add polenta in a slow, steady stream, stirring constantly. Reduce heat to low; cook 2 to 3 minutes or until thickened, stirring frequently. Remove from heat. Add corn, cheese, and green onions, stirring until cheese melts.

Spoon polenta mixture into a 13- x 9- x 2-inch pan coated with cooking spray, pressing to smooth top. Let cool completely.

Coat a large nonstick skillet with cooking spray; add oil. Place over medium-high heat until hot. Add chopped onion and next 3 ingredients; sauté until vegetables are tender. Add black beans and remaining ingredients; bring to a boil. Reduce heat, and simmer, uncovered, 25 minutes or until liquid evaporates.

Turn polenta out onto a cutting board, and cut into 6 squares. Cut each square in half diagonally. Place polenta triangles on a large baking sheet coated with vegetable cooking spray. Broil 3 inches from heat (with electric oven door partially opened) 5 to 7 minutes on each side or until polenta is crusty and golden.

To serve, place 2 polenta triangles on each individual serving plate. Top evenly with black bean mixture. Yield: 6 servings (286 calories per serving).

Per Serving:

Fat 4.4g	Carbohydrate 52.2g	Fiber 6.9g
saturated fat 1.4g	Cholesterol 6mg	Iron 4.0mg
Protein 12.3g	Sodium 484mg	Calcium 155mg

Ancient Exercise is the Newest Thing

What's old is new again. Exercises from the past, such as yoga and tai chi chuan, are gaining widespread appeal today, largely because these "ancient" exercises benefit both the body and the mind.

Yoga is becoming a popular workout for increasing strength and flexibility while reducing stress. Tai chi chuan is a nonviolent form of Chinese martial arts that combines slow and gentle movement with deep breathing to enhance physical and emotional strength and energy. Many forms of yoga and tai chi chuan instruction are now offered at fitness centers, spas, and even YMCAs.

Lentil Shepherd's Pie

Vegetable cooking spray
1   teaspoon vegetable oil
½   cup chopped onion
2   cloves garlic, minced
1   cup dried lentils, uncooked
3   cups water
1   bay leaf
1   cup thinly sliced carrot
1   (8-ounce) can no-salt-added tomato sauce
2   teaspoons low-sodium Worcestershire
      sauce
½   teaspoon dried basil
¼   teaspoon salt
¼   teaspoon fennel seeds, crushed
1   tablespoon all-purpose flour
1   tablespoon water
5   cups peeled, cubed baking potato
⅓   cup 1% low-fat milk
2   tablespoons reduced-calorie margarine
¼   teaspoon salt

Coat a saucepan with cooking spray; add oil. Place over medium-high heat until hot. Add onion and garlic; sauté until crisp-tender. Add lentils, 3 cups water, and bay leaf; bring to a boil. Cover, reduce heat, and simmer 30 minutes. Add carrot; cook 20 minutes or until lentils are tender.

Remove and discard bay leaf; stir in tomato sauce and next 4 ingredients. Combine flour and 1 tablespoon water. Add flour mixture to lentil mixture. Cook, stirring constantly, until mixture is thickened. Spoon mixture into an 11- x 7- x 1½-inch baking dish coated with cooking spray.

Cook potato in boiling water to cover 15 minutes or until tender. Drain potato; mash. Add milk, margarine, and ¼ teaspoon salt; beat at medium speed of an electric mixer until smooth. Spoon or pipe potato mixture over lentil mixture. Bake at 350° for 40 to 45 minutes or until potato is golden. Yield: 6 servings (274 calories per serving).

Per Serving:

Fat 4.0g	Carbohydrate 49.1g	Fiber 7.2g
saturated fat 0.6g	Cholesterol 1mg	Iron 4.4mg
Protein 12.9g	Sodium 273mg	Calcium 61mg

Cajun Beans and Rice Casserole

1   (16-ounce) can red beans, drained
1   (15-ounce) can no-salt-added pinto beans,
      drained
1   (14½-ounce) can no-salt-added stewed
      tomatoes
Vegetable cooking spray
2   cups chopped onion
½   cup chopped celery
½   cup chopped green pepper
1   teaspoon dried thyme
½   teaspoon dried oregano
½   teaspoon pepper
¼   teaspoon salt
¼   teaspoon onion powder
⅛   teaspoon ground white pepper
3   cups cooked long-grain rice (cooked
      without salt or fat)
1   (8-ounce) carton low-fat sour cream
½   cup (2 ounces) shredded reduced-fat
      Cheddar cheese

Mash beans slightly with a fork. Combine beans and tomato in a medium saucepan; bring to a boil. Reduce heat; simmer, uncovered, 25 minutes or until most of liquid evaporates.

Coat a large nonstick skillet with cooking spray; place over medium-high heat until hot. Add onion, celery, and green pepper; sauté 4 minutes or until tender. Add thyme and next 5 ingredients; cook 5 minutes, stirring frequently. Stir half of onion mixture into bean mixture.

Combine remaining onion mixture, rice, and sour cream. Spoon half of rice mixture into an 11- x 7- x 1½-inch baking dish coated with cooking spray; top with half of bean mixture. Repeat layers with remaining rice and bean mixtures.

Cover and bake at 325° for 25 minutes. Uncover and sprinkle with cheese. Bake, uncovered, 5 additional minutes or until cheese melts. Let stand 5 minutes before serving. Yield: 6 servings (354 calories per serving).

Per Serving:

Fat 7.2g	Carbohydrate 58.9g	Fiber 7.6g
saturated fat 4.0g	Cholesterol 20mg	Iron 4.2mg
Protein 14.6g	Sodium 345mg	Calcium 211mg

Spinach Gnocchi with Roasted Peppers

Gnocchi are small dumplings made from potatoes, flour, or farina. They are often served like pasta—topped with sauce and cheese.

1 medium-size red potato (about ½ pound)
2 large sweet red peppers (about 1 pound)
2 large sweet yellow peppers (about 1 pound)
   Olive oil-flavored vegetable cooking spray
¼ cup finely chopped onion
1 clove garlic, minced
1 egg, beaten
1 cup plus 2 tablespoons all-purpose flour, divided
¾ cup finely chopped fresh spinach
½ teaspoon salt
14 cups water
½ cup grated Asiago cheese
1½ tablespoons chopped fresh basil

Cook potato in boiling water to cover 25 minutes or until tender. Drain and let cool. Peel potato, and place in a large bowl; mash. Set aside.

Cut peppers in half lengthwise; remove and discard seeds and membrane. Place peppers, skin side up, on a baking sheet; flatten with palm of hand. Broil peppers 5½ inches from heat (with electric oven door partially opened) 15 to 20 minutes or until charred. Place peppers in ice water until cool. Remove peppers from water; peel and discard skins. Coarsely chop peppers. Set aside.

Coat a large nonstick skillet with cooking spray. Place over medium-high heat until hot. Add onion and garlic; sauté until tender. Add onion mixture and egg to potato; stir well. Stir in ¾ cup flour, spinach, and salt.

Sprinkle remaining ¼ cup plus 2 tablespoons flour evenly over work surface. Turn potato mixture out onto floured surface, and knead until flour is incorporated.

Divide potato mixture into thirds. Roll each portion into a 12-inch rope. Cut each rope into 12 (1-inch) pieces. Shape each piece into a ball.

Place balls on a baking sheet coated with cooking spray. Dip a fork in flour, and drag the tines through half of each ball, forming a concave shape.

Bring 14 cups water to a boil in a large Dutch oven. Add half of gnocchi, and cook 1½ minutes. (Do not overcook.) Remove gnocchi, using a slotted spoon; drain well. Repeat procedure with remaining half of gnocchi.

Place gnocchi in a 9-inch gratin or quiche dish coated with cooking spray. Sprinkle with roasted peppers and cheese. Broil 5½ inches from heat (with electric oven door partially opened) 1 to 1½ minutes or until cheese melts. Sprinkle with basil. Serve immediately. Yield: 4 servings (282 calories per serving).

Per Serving:

Fat 5.7g	Carbohydrate 46.9g	Fiber 4.8g
saturated fat 0.6g	Cholesterol 62mg	Iron 4.4mg
Protein 11.9g	Sodium 495mg	Calcium 167mg

1. Divide potato mixture into thirds. Roll each portion into a 12-inch rope. Cut each rope into 12 (1-inch) pieces. Shape each piece into a ball.

2. To make a traditional gnocchi shape, dip a fork into flour, and drag the tines through half of each ball.

3. To cook, add gnocchi to boiling water, and cook 1½ minutes. (Do not overcook.) Remove gnocchi from water, using a slotted spoon.

Pizza Primavera

Pizza Primavera

2 cups bread flour

½ teaspoon salt

1 package rapid-rise yeast

¾ cup plus 2 tablespoons hot water
    (120° to 130°)
    Vegetable cooking spray

1 tablespoon plus 2 teaspoons cornmeal

6 fresh asparagus spears

1 cup thinly sliced small round red potatoes

½ cup thinly sliced onion

½ cup thinly sliced sweet red pepper

1 tablespoon chopped fresh thyme

2 teaspoons olive oil

¼ teaspoon salt

¼ teaspoon dried crushed red pepper

⅛ teaspoon pepper

6 cloves garlic, thinly sliced

½ cup (2 ounces) shredded reduced-fat
    Cheddar cheese

¼ cup (1 ounce) part-skim mozzarella cheese

Position knife blade in food processor bowl; add flour, salt, and yeast. Pulse 3 times or until combined. Pour hot water through food chute with processor running. Process 30 seconds or until mixture pulls away from sides of processor bowl. Process 1 additional minute. Turn dough out onto work surface. Cover dough; let rest 10 minutes.

Coat a 14-inch pizza pan with cooking spray. Sprinkle with cornmeal. Roll dough into a 14-inch circle, and place in prepared pan. Cover and let rise in a warm place (85°), free from drafts, 30 minutes or until doubled in bulk.

Snap off tough ends of asparagus. Remove scales from stalks with a knife or vegetable peeler, if desired. Cut each spear in half lengthwise.

Combine asparagus, potato, and next 8 ingredients in a large bowl, tossing gently to coat. Arrange vegetable mixture over crust. Bake at 425° for 10 minutes. Sprinkle with cheeses, and bake 5 to 7 additional minutes or until crust is golden. Let stand 5 minutes before cutting. Yield: 4 servings (406 calories per serving).

Per Serving:

Fat 7.8g	Carbohydrate 66.8g	Fiber 2.7g
saturated fat 2.8g	Cholesterol 13mg	Iron 4.7mg
Protein 17.3g	Sodium 584mg	Calcium 204mg

Pizza Milanese

Buy a Boboli or another brand of Italian bread shell for this zesty pizza.

1   (9-ounce) package frozen artichoke hearts, thawed and coarsely chopped
3   tablespoons commercial oil-free Italian dressing
½   cup light ricotta cheese
⅓   cup crumbled feta cheese
2   tablespoons nonfat sour cream
⅛   teaspoon hot sauce
2   cloves garlic, minced
1   (16-ounce) Italian bread shell
2   plum tomatoes, thinly sliced
1   yellow tomato, thinly sliced
⅛   teaspoon paprika
¼   teaspoon cracked pepper

Combine artichokes and Italian dressing; toss gently. Cover and chill 1 hour; drain.

Combine artichokes, ricotta cheese, and next 4 ingredients, stirring well.

Spread artichoke mixture evenly over bread shell. Arrange tomato slices over artichoke mixture. Sprinkle with paprika and pepper. Bake at 450° for 15 to 18 minutes or until thoroughly heated. Yield: 6 servings (272 calories per serving).

Per Serving:

Fat 6.0g	Carbohydrate 41.2g	Fiber 1.8g
saturated fat 2.5g	Cholesterol 14mg	Iron 2.2mg
Protein 13.2g	Sodium 558mg	Calcium 122mg

Vegetable Pilaf

Using only half the seasoning packet from the rice mix reduces the sodium in this recipe without sacrificing the flavor.

1½   cups frozen whole-kernel corn, thawed
3   shallots, thinly sliced
2   teaspoons vegetable oil
     Vegetable cooking spray
1   (6-ounce) package long-grain and wild rice mix
½   cup dried apricots, cut into thin strips
2   tablespoons chopped fresh parsley
1   (15-ounce) can no-salt-added garbanzo beans, drained
2   tablespoons balsamic vinegar
2   tablespoons unsweetened orange juice
⅛   teaspoon pepper

Combine first 3 ingredients in a 2-quart casserole coated with cooking spray, tossing gently. Bake, uncovered, at 375° for 30 to 35 minutes or until vegetables are tender, stirring occasionally.

Cook rice according to package directions, omitting fat and half of contents of seasoning packet.

Add rice, apricots, parsley, and beans to corn mixture; stir well. Combine vinegar, orange juice, and pepper. Drizzle vinegar mixture over rice mixture; toss gently. Serve immediately. Yield: 4 servings (395 calories per 1½-cup serving).

Per Serving:

Fat 4.3g	Carbohydrate 78.9g	Fiber 8.3g
saturated fat 0.4g	Cholesterol 0mg	Iron 3.7mg
Protein 13.5g	Sodium 255mg	Calcium 66mg

Stacked Rice and Cheese Enchiladas

In some areas of New Mexico, enchiladas are served flat instead of rolled around a filling.

1   tablespoon fresh lime juice
8   (¼-inch-thick) slices tomato, halved
1½ teaspoons minced fresh cilantro
1   clove garlic
1   (15-ounce) can no-salt-added black beans,
     drained
½   cup canned vegetable broth, undiluted
¾   cup cooked long-grain rice (cooked
     without salt or fat)
¼   cup 1% low-fat cottage cheese
2   tablespoons nonfat sour cream
2   tablespoons finely chopped onion
2   ounces Monterey Jack cheese with peppers,
     cut into ¼-inch cubes
4   (10-inch) flour tortillas
     Vegetable cooking spray

Brush lime juice over tomato slices; sprinkle with cilantro. Cover and chill.

Position knife blade in food processor bowl. Drop garlic through food chute with processor running. Process 3 seconds or until garlic is minced. Add beans and vegetable broth; process until smooth, scraping sides of processor bowl once. Transfer bean mixture to a medium saucepan. Cook, uncovered, over low heat 5 minutes or until slightly thickened, stirring frequently. Set aside, and keep warm.

Combine rice, cottage cheese, sour cream, onion, and cubed cheese in a small bowl, stirring well. Set aside.

Place 2 tortillas on a large baking sheet. Coat tortillas with cooking spray. Broil 3 inches from heat (with electric oven door partially opened) 1 minute or until golden. Remove from oven; set aside, and keep warm. Repeat procedure with remaining tortillas.

Place 1 tortilla, browned side up, on a 12-inch round glass platter; top with about ⅓ cup rice mixture, spreading to edges. Repeat layers twice with 2 tortillas and ⅔ cup rice mixture. Top with remaining tortilla. Microwave at HIGH 2 minutes or until cheese melts, rotating platter once.

Remove from microwave, and cut into 4 wedges. Top each wedge with ⅓ cup bean mixture and 4 halved tomato slices. Serve immediately. Yield: 4 servings (315 calories per serving).

Per Serving:

Fat 8.1g	Carbohydrate 46.7g	Fiber 4.0g
saturated fat 3.3g	Cholesterol 12mg	Iron 3.0mg
Protein 14.0g	Sodium 437mg	Calcium 193mg

Brie-Filled Pork Chops with Apple Stuffing (page 159)

Meats

Jerk Meat Loaf

For a fiery version of this meat loaf, substitute two Scotch Bonnet peppers for the jalapeño peppers.

1   pound ground round
1   cup soft whole wheat breadcrumbs
½   cup finely chopped green onions
¼   cup frozen egg substitute, thawed
¼   cup skim milk
¼   cup reduced-calorie ketchup
2   tablespoons white vinegar
1   teaspoon dried thyme
½   teaspoon salt
½   teaspoon ground allspice
½   teaspoon coarsely ground pepper
⅛   teaspoon ground nutmeg
⅛   teaspoon ground cinnamon
2   jalapeño peppers, seeded and finely
      chopped
    Vegetable cooking spray

Combine first 14 ingredients in a medium bowl. Shape mixture into an 8- x 4-inch loaf; place on a rack in a roasting pan coated with cooking spray. Bake at 350° for 1 hour. Yield: 6 servings (151 calories per serving).

Per Serving:

Fat 3.6g	Carbohydrate 8.3g	Fiber 0.8g
saturated fat 1.2g	Cholesterol 44mg	Iron 2.6mg
Protein 19.8g	Sodium 314mg	Calcium 41mg

Talk Yourself Skinny

The best friend to healthy eating, the experts say, is a healthy attitude. Research has shown that negative moods or emotional stress can often lead to a loss of self-control over your diet.

How do you develop the right eating mind-set? To quote the old song, "accentuate the positive." Instead of badgering yourself about a small dietary indiscretion, focus on what you did accomplish. Praise yourself for choosing an apple over a candy bar at your afternoon break. Instead of feeling guilty about skipping a noontime workout, congratulate yourself for exercising three days this week. Before long you'll notice just how much you do that's worth a pat on the back.

Curried Beef Rolls

For a colorful plate, serve the beef rolls over yellow rice. Add ½ teaspoon ground saffron or ground turmeric to color the rice as it cooks.

    Vegetable cooking spray
½   cup shredded zucchini
¼   cup shredded carrot
¼   cup minced green pepper
½   teaspoon dried thyme
6   (4-ounce) beef cube steaks
1   (8-ounce) can no-salt-added tomato sauce
1   teaspoon curry powder
¼   teaspoon salt
¼   teaspoon pepper
6   cups cooked long-grain rice (cooked
      without salt or fat)
2   tablespoons chopped fresh parsley

Coat a large nonstick skillet with cooking spray; place over medium-high heat until hot. Add zucchini and next 3 ingredients; sauté until tender.

Spread vegetable mixture evenly over steaks, spreading to within ½ inch of sides. Carefully roll up steaks, jellyroll fashion; secure with wooden picks.

Coat skillet with cooking spray; place over medium-high heat until hot. Add steak rolls, and brown evenly on all sides. Remove steak rolls from skillet. Drain and pat dry with paper towels. Wipe drippings from skillet with a paper towel.

Return steak rolls to skillet. Combine tomato sauce and next 3 ingredients; pour over steak rolls. Bring to a boil; cover, reduce heat, and simmer 1 hour or until meat is tender.

To serve, spoon 1 cup rice onto each individual serving plate. Remove wooden picks from steak rolls. Place a steak roll over rice on each plate, using a slotted spoon. Stir chopped parsley into tomato sauce mixture. Spoon tomato sauce evenly over steak rolls. Yield: 6 servings (386 calories per serving).

Per Serving:

Fat 5.4g	Carbohydrate 52.3g	Fiber 2.0g
saturated fat 1.8g	Cholesterol 61mg	Iron 4.1mg
Protein 29.3g	Sodium 169mg	Calcium 40mg

Grilled Spicy Flank Steak

*Capellini, also called angel hair pasta, is long, extremely thin strands of pasta. It cooks in about
5 or 6 minutes, so be careful not to overcook it.*

¼ cup hoisin sauce
1 tablespoon molasses
1 teaspoon Chinese chili puree with garlic
½ teaspoon salt-free lemon-pepper
    seasoning
1 (1½-pound) lean flank steak
    Vegetable cooking spray
6 cups cooked capellini (cooked without
    salt or fat)
½ cup sliced green onions
2 tablespoons low-sodium soy sauce

Combine first 4 ingredients; set aside. Trim fat from steak.

Coat grill rack with cooking spray; place on grill over medium-hot coals (350° to 400°). Place steak on rack; grill, covered, 6 to 7 minutes on each side or to desired degree of doneness, basting frequently during the last 5 minutes with hoisin sauce mixture. Let steak stand 5 minutes. Cut diagonally across grain into thin slices. Set aside, and keep warm.

Combine pasta, onions, and soy sauce; toss gently. Place mixture on a serving platter. Top with steak slices. Yield: 6 servings (416 calories per serving).

Per Serving:

Fat 13.7g	Carbohydrate 42.5g	Fiber 2.2g
saturated fat 5.6g	Cholesterol 60mg	Iron 4.4mg
Protein 28.1g	Sodium 518mg	Calcium 30mg

Stir-Fried Beef and Greens

1 pound lean boneless top sirloin steak
¼ cup low-sodium soy sauce
¼ cup no-salt-added beef broth, undiluted
¼ cup molasses
2 teaspoons ground ginger
2 teaspoons dry mustard
1 pound fresh mustard greens
2 tablespoons cornstarch
    Vegetable cooking spray
1 teaspoon vegetable oil
1 medium-size sweet red pepper, seeded and
    cut into thin strips
¼ teaspoon dried crushed red pepper
¼ cup water

Partially freeze steak; trim fat from steak. Slice steak diagonally across grain into ¼-inch-wide strips. Combine soy sauce and next 4 ingredients in a heavy-duty, zip-top plastic bag. Add steak; seal bag, and shake until steak is well coated. Marinate in refrigerator at least 1 hour, turning bag occasionally.

Remove and discard stems from mustard greens; wash leaves thoroughly, and pat dry. Coarsely chop greens; set aside.

Remove steak from marinade, reserving marinade. Combine reserved marinade and cornstarch, stirring well; set aside.

Coat a wok or large nonstick skillet with cooking spray; drizzle oil around top of wok, coating sides. Heat at medium-high (375°) until hot. Add steak strips, and stir-fry 5 minutes. Remove steak strips from wok; drain and pat dry with paper towels.

Add sweet red pepper and crushed red pepper to wok. Stir-fry 1 minute. Add greens and water. Cover and cook 5 minutes or until greens are tender. Add steak strips and marinade mixture. Bring to a boil, and stir-fry 1 minute or until beef mixture is slightly thickened. Yield: 4 servings (300 calories per serving).

Per Serving:

Fat 8.6g	Carbohydrate 24.4g	Fiber 1.2g
saturated fat 2.7g	Cholesterol 79mg	Iron 5.8mg
Protein 29.8g	Sodium 479mg	Calcium 141mg

Steak with Ale and Crispy Onion Rings (page 215)

Steak with Ale

1 (1½-pound) lean boneless top sirloin
   steak
½ cup finely chopped onion
½ cup boiling water
½ cup flat pale ale
1 tablespoon brown sugar
1 tablespoon red wine vinegar
1 teaspoon dried thyme
1 teaspoon beef-flavored bouillon
   granules
   Vegetable cooking spray
   Freshly ground pepper (optional)
   Fresh thyme sprigs (optional)

Trim fat from steak, and place steak in a shallow dish; set aside.

Combine chopped onion and next 6 ingredients in container of an electric blender; cover and process until smooth, stopping once to scrape down sides. Reserve ½ cup ale mixture. Pour remaining ale mixture over steak; turn steak to coat. Cover and marinate in refrigerator at least 8 hours; turn steak occasionally.

Remove steak from marinade; discard marinade. Coat grill rack with cooking spray; place on grill over medium-hot coals (350° to 400°). Place steak on rack; grill, covered, 5 to 6 minutes on each side or to desired degree of doneness, basting frequently with reserved ½ cup ale mixture. Transfer steak to a serving platter. If desired, sprinkle with pepper, and garnish with fresh thyme sprigs. Yield: 6 servings (177 calories per serving).

Per Serving:

Fat 6.3g	Carbohydrate 2.3g	Fiber 0.2g
saturated fat 2.4g	Cholesterol 76mg	Iron 3.0mg
Protein 26.0g	Sodium 110mg	Calcium 14mg

Savory Beef Roast

1	**(4-pound) lean boneless rump roast**
	Vegetable cooking spray
½	**teaspoon garlic powder**
¼	**teaspoon salt**
1	**cup hot water**
2	**tablespoons low-sodium Worcestershire sauce**
1	**teaspoon beef-flavored bouillon granules**
2	**tablespoons all-purpose flour**
1	**teaspoon salt-free lemon-pepper seasoning**
¾	**cup skim milk**
¼	**cup plain nonfat yogurt**
1	**teaspoon Dijon mustard**
½	**teaspoon anchovy paste**
¼	**cup minced fresh parsley**
1	**tablespoon grated Parmesan cheese**

Trim fat from roast. Coat a Dutch oven with cooking spray; place over medium-high heat until hot. Add roast, and cook until browned on all sides.

Sprinkle roast with garlic powder and salt. Combine water, Worcestershire sauce, and bouillon granules, stirring well. Pour Worcestershire sauce mixture over roast. Bring to a boil; cover, reduce heat, and simmer 2 to 2½ hours or until roast is tender. Transfer roast to a serving platter; set aside, and keep warm.

Skim fat from pan juices in Dutch oven; reserve ¼ cup pan juices. Discard remaining pan juices. Return ¼ cup pan juices to Dutch oven.

Combine flour and lemon-pepper seasoning; add to pan juices in Dutch oven, stirring until smooth. Gradually add milk, stirring constantly. Cook over medium heat, stirring constantly, until thickened. Combine yogurt, mustard, and anchovy paste; add to milk mixture in Dutch oven, stirring just until blended.

Cut roast diagonally across grain into ¼-inch-thick slices. Spoon gravy over slices. Sprinkle with parsley and cheese. Yield: 16 servings (157 calories per serving).

Per Serving:

Fat 4.9g	Carbohydrate 2.0g	Fiber 0.1g
saturated fat 1.7g	Cholesterol 64mg	Iron 2.3mg
Protein 24.7g	Sodium 138mg	Calcium 32mg

Meat—Part of a Healthy Diet

Meat doesn't have to be the villain. It's rich in protein, iron, zinc, and B vitamins and, when wisely used, can be a valuable part of a low-fat, healthy diet. Here are some pointers for finding the leanest cuts.

• Cuts of beef with the words "loin" (sirloin, tenderloin) and "round" (eye-of-round, top round) have the least amount of fat.

• The leanest cuts of pork and lamb come from the "loin" and the "leg."

• All veal cuts are low in fat; however, veal is higher in cholesterol than other lean cuts of meat.

• For ground meat, choose ground chuck, or preferably ground round, or ultra-lean ground beef.

• In whole cuts, look for the cut with the least marbling, or white veins of fat, in it.

• If the beef carries a grade, look for "Select" and "Choice."

Cranberry Pot Roast with Roasted Acorn Squash

Using a pressure cooker is an ideal way to tenderize a lean cut of meat like a round tip roast.

1 (3-pound) lean boneless round tip roast
  Vegetable cooking spray
1 cup canned no-salt-added beef broth,
  undiluted
2 tablespoons brown sugar
2 tablespoons spicy brown mustard
¼ teaspoon ground ginger
¼ teaspoon pepper
1 (16-ounce) can whole-berry cranberry sauce
¾ teaspoon salt
¼ cup water
3 tablespoons cornstarch
  Roasted Acorn Squash

Trim fat from roast. Coat a 6-quart pressure cooker with cooking spray. Place over medium-high heat until hot. Add roast; cook until browned on all sides.

Combine broth and next 4 ingredients; pour over roast. Close pressure cooker lid securely. According to manufacturer's directions, bring cooker to high pressure over high heat (about 10 to 12 minutes). Reduce heat to medium or level needed to maintain high pressure; cook 25 minutes. Remove from heat; run cold water over cooker to reduce pressure rapidly. Remove lid so that steam escapes away from you.

Add cranberry sauce and salt to cooker. Close lid securely, and return to high pressure over high heat (about 5 minutes). Reduce heat to medium or level needed to maintain high pressure; cook 5 additional minutes. Remove from heat; run cold water over cooker to reduce pressure rapidly. Remove lid so that steam escapes away from you. Transfer roast to a serving platter. Set aside, and keep warm.

Skim fat from cranberry mixture; reserve 3 cups cranberry mixture. Discard remaining cranberry mixture. Return 3 cups cranberry mixture to cooker. Combine water and cornstarch, stirring until smooth. Add cornstarch mixture to cranberry mixture. Cook over medium heat, stirring constantly, until thickened.

Cut roast diagonally across grain into ¼-inch-thick slices. Serve with cranberry gravy and Roasted Acorn Squash. Yield: 12 servings (268 calories per 3 ounces cooked meat and 2 squash wedges).

Roasted Acorn Squash

3 small acorn squash (about 2½ pounds)
  Vegetable cooking spray
2 tablespoons reduced-calorie margarine,
  melted
2 teaspoons brown sugar
¼ teaspoon salt
⅛ teaspoon ground ginger
⅛ teaspoon ground cinnamon

Cut each squash in half crosswise; remove and discard seeds. Cut squash halves into quarters. Place squash, skin side down, in a 15- x 10- x 1-inch jellyroll pan coated with cooking spray.

Combine margarine and remaining ingredients. Brush evenly over cut sides of squash. Cover and bake at 350° for 30 minutes. Uncover and bake 30 additional minutes or until squash is tender. Yield: 12 servings.

Per Serving:		
Fat 7.2g	Carbohydrate 26.6g	Fiber 1.1g
saturated fat 2.1g	Cholesterol 61mg	Iron 2.9mg
Protein 22.4g	Sodium 311mg	Calcium 36mg

Saucy Veal Skillet

If you can't find ground veal, ask your butcher to grind some lean veal (like veal loin or shoulder) for you.

1	pound lean ground veal
2	tablespoons fine, dry breadcrumbs
2	tablespoons minced onion
1	tablespoon chopped fresh basil
2	teaspoons white wine Worcestershire sauce
¼	teaspoon pepper
⅛	teaspoon salt
	Vegetable cooking spray
1½	cups commercial fat-free chunky spaghetti sauce
⅓	cup (1.3 ounces) shredded part-skim mozzarella cheese

Combine first 7 ingredients, stirring well. Shape veal mixture into 4 (½-inch-thick) patties.

Coat a large nonstick skillet with cooking spray. Place over medium heat until hot. Add veal patties, and cook 4 minutes on each side or until done. Remove veal patties from skillet. Wipe drippings from skillet with a paper towel, if necessary.

Return veal patties to skillet. Pour spaghetti sauce over patties; sprinkle with cheese. Bring to a boil; cover, reduce heat, and simmer 5 minutes. Yield: 4 servings (219 calories per serving).

Per Serving:

Fat 8.3g	Carbohydrate 10.5g	Fiber 1.8g
saturated fat 3.6g	Cholesterol 93mg	Iron 2.0mg
Protein 24.3g	Sodium 502mg	Calcium 101mg

Veal Shanks with Red Wine

Be sure to serve some crusty French bread with this recipe for sopping up the extra sauce.

6	(5-ounce) veal shanks
2	tablespoons all-purpose flour
½	teaspoon paprika
	Vegetable cooking spray
2	teaspoons vegetable oil
2	large onions, sliced
½	cup dry red wine
1½	cups canned no-salt-added beef broth, undiluted
⅓	cup tawny port wine
1½	tablespoons minced fresh thyme, divided
2	tablespoons no-salt-added tomato paste
2	tablespoons balsamic vinegar

Trim fat from veal shanks. Combine flour and paprika; dredge veal shanks in flour mixture.

Coat a large Dutch oven with cooking spray; add oil. Place over medium heat until hot. Add veal, and cook 3 minutes on each side or until browned. Remove veal from Dutch oven. Wipe drippings from Dutch oven with a paper towel, if necessary.

Coat Dutch oven with cooking spray; place over medium-high heat until hot. Add onion; sauté until tender. Add red wine; cook 1 minute, stirring constantly. Add broth, port wine, 1 tablespoon thyme, tomato paste, and vinegar; stir well. Return veal to Dutch oven; cover, reduce heat, and simmer 1 hour or until veal is tender. Sprinkle remaining 1½ teaspoons thyme over veal mixture. Yield: 6 servings (197 calories per serving).

Per Serving:

Fat 5.2g	Carbohydrate 11.9g	Fiber 2.1g
saturated fat 1.3g	Cholesterol 98mg	Iron 1.7mg
Protein 24.2g	Sodium 114mg	Calcium 50mg

Grilled Veal Chops with Peach-Onion Relish

Grilled Veal Chops with Peach-Onion Relish

½ cup chopped onion
¼ cup firmly packed brown sugar
1 tablespoon peeled, minced gingerroot
2 teaspoons dry mustard
¾ cup water
2 tablespoons cider vinegar
2 tablespoons lemon juice
1 dried red chile pepper
2 cups peeled, chopped fresh peaches
6 (6-ounce) lean veal loin chops (¾ inch thick)
⅓ cup peach nectar
2 teaspoons vegetable oil
    Vegetable cooking spray
¼ cup minced fresh cilantro
    Fresh cilantro sprigs (optional)

Combine first 8 ingredients in a medium saucepan. Bring to a boil; reduce heat, and sim-mer, uncovered, 10 minutes. Add peaches, and cook 5 additional minutes. Remove and discard pepper.

Position knife blade in food processor bowl; add half of peach mixture, and process until smooth. Stir into remaining peach mixture in saucepan. Cook until thoroughly heated, stirring occasionally. Remove from heat; set aside, and keep warm.

Trim fat from chops. Combine peach nectar and oil, stirring well. Brush peach nectar mixture over both sides of veal chops; reserve remaining peach nectar mixture.

Coat grill rack with cooking spray; place on grill over medium-hot coals (350° to 400°). Place chops on rack; grill, uncovered, 5 minutes on each side or to desired degree of doneness, basting fre-quently with remaining nectar mixture.

Transfer chops to individual serving plates. Spoon warm peach mixture over chops; sprinkle with minced cilantro. Garnish with cilantro sprigs, if desired. Yield: 6 servings (239 calories per serving).

Per Serving:
Fat 7.9g Carbohydrate 18.8g Fiber 1.2g
  saturated fat 2.5g Cholesterol 90mg Iron 1.2mg
Protein 23.2g Sodium 89mg Calcium 37mg

roast diagonally across grain into thin slices; serve with mustard sauce. Garnish with fresh basil sprigs, if desired. Yield: 14 servings (187 calories per serving).

Per Serving:
Fat 6.0g Carbohydrate 2.0g Fiber 0g
  saturated fat 1.6g Cholesterol 100mg Iron 1.1mg
Protein 28.3g Sodium 251mg Calcium 31mg

Veal Roast with Mustard Cream Sauce

1   (3½-pound) boneless veal round roast
2   tablespoons minced fresh basil
¼   teaspoon garlic powder
¼   teaspoon pepper
    Vegetable cooking spray
¾   cup dry white wine
½   teaspoon beef-flavored bouillon granules
1   cup nonfat sour cream
¼   cup Dijon mustard
2   tablespoons reduced-calorie maple syrup
1   teaspoon peeled, minced gingerroot
    Fresh basil sprigs (optional)

Trim fat from roast. Combine minced basil, garlic powder, and pepper; sprinkle basil mixture over entire surface of roast.

Coat a large ovenproof Dutch oven with cooking spray; place over medium-high heat until hot. Add roast; cook until browned on all sides, turning occasionally.

Combine white wine and bouillon granules. Pour wine mixture over roast. Cover and bake at 325° for 1 hour and 30 minutes or until roast is tender, basting frequently with pan juices. Transfer roast to a serving platter; set aside, and keep warm.

Skim fat from pan juices. Reserve ¼ cup pan juices; discard remaining pan juices. Combine ¼ cup pan juices, sour cream, Dijon mustard, maple syrup, and gingerroot in Dutch oven; cook over medium heat, stirring constantly, until sour cream mixture is thoroughly heated. (Do not boil.) Cut

Hungarian Smothered Lamb

¼   cup all-purpose flour
½   teaspoon salt
¼   teaspoon pepper
1   pound lean boneless lamb, cut into 1-inch cubes
    Vegetable cooking spray
2   teaspoons vegetable oil
1   cup chopped onion
2   cloves garlic, minced
1½ cups canned no-salt-added beef broth, undiluted
1   tablespoon paprika
1   teaspoon instant coffee granules
½   teaspoon chili powder
¼   teaspoon cumin
4   prunes, coarsely chopped
4   cups cooked egg noodles (cooked without salt or fat)

Combine first 3 ingredients; place in a heavy-duty, zip-top plastic bag. Add lamb; seal bag, and shake until lamb is well coated.

Coat a nonstick skillet with cooking spray; add oil. Place over medium-high heat until hot. Add lamb; cook until browned, stirring frequently. Remove lamb from skillet; set aside. Add onion and garlic; sauté until tender. Add broth and next 5 ingredients; stir in lamb. Bring to a boil; cover, reduce heat, and simmer 1 hour or until lamb is tender and mixture is thickened, stirring occasionally. Serve over noodles. Yield: 4 servings (408 calories per serving).

Per Serving:
Fat 10.6g Carbohydrate 45.2g Fiber 4.4g
  saturated fat 3.0g Cholesterol 113mg Iron 5.1mg
Protein 30.7g Sodium 385mg Calcium 47mg

Grecian Lamb Kabobs

It's important to seed the cucumbers for the relish to keep it from becoming watery.

1   small eggplant (about ¾ pound)
1   pound lean boneless leg of lamb, cut into
      1-inch cubes
2   medium-size sweet red peppers, seeded
      and cut into 1-inch pieces
¼   cup no-salt-added tomato juice
¼   cup lemon juice
2   tablespoons minced onion
1   teaspoon minced fresh oregano
1   teaspoon minced fresh rosemary
2   teaspoons olive oil
¼   teaspoon salt
¼   teaspoon cracked pepper
2   cloves garlic, minced
      Vegetable cooking spray
      Cool Cucumber Relish

Cut eggplant into 1-inch cubes. Measure 3 cups cubes; reserve remaining cubes for another use. Place 3 cups cubed eggplant, lamb, and red pepper in a heavy-duty, zip-top plastic bag; set aside.

Combine tomato juice and next 8 ingredients in a small bowl, stirring well. Pour tomato juice mixture over lamb and vegetables in bag; seal bag, and shake until lamb and vegetables are well coated. Marinate in refrigerator 4 hours, turning bag occasionally.

Remove lamb and vegetables from marinade; reserve marinade. Place marinade in a small saucepan; bring to a boil. Remove from heat, and set aside. Thread lamb onto 2 (10-inch) skewers. Thread red pepper and eggplant alternately on 4 (10-inch) skewers.

Coat grill rack with cooking spray; place on grill over medium-hot coals (350° to 400°). Place lamb kabobs on rack; grill, covered, 15 minutes or to desired degree of doneness, turning and basting frequently with reserved marinade. Place vegetable kabobs on rack; grill, covered, 12 minutes or until tender, turning and basting frequently with reserved marinade. Remove meat and vegetables from skewers. Serve with Cool Cucumber Relish. Yield: 4 servings (253 calories per serving).

Cool Cucumber Relish

2   cups peeled, seeded, and diced cucumber
¼   cup chopped fresh parsley
¼   cup plain nonfat yogurt
2   tablespoons thinly sliced green onions
1   tablespoon white wine vinegar
¼   teaspoon cracked pepper
¼   teaspoon salt

Combine all ingredients in a bowl, stirring well. Cover and chill thoroughly. Yield: 2 cups.

Per Serving:		
Fat 9.8g	Carbohydrate 15.3g	Fiber 2.9g
saturated fat 2.8g	Cholesterol 76mg	Iron 4.4mg
Protein 27.2g	Sodium 376mg	Calcium 128mg

Lamb Chops with Cherry Sauce

4   (5-ounce) lean lamb loin chops (1 inch thick)
½   teaspoon cracked pepper
      Olive oil-flavored vegetable cooking spray
1   cup coarsely chopped onion
½   cup chopped celery
1   clove garlic, minced
1   cup dry red wine
1   cup canned no-salt-added beef broth,
      undiluted
2   tablespoons red currant jelly
1   teaspoon dried thyme
½   teaspoon pepper
¼   teaspoon salt
⅛   teaspoon ground cinnamon
3   teaspoons cornstarch
3   teaspoons water
2   cups frozen pitted sweet cherries, halved
      Fresh thyme sprigs (optional)

Trim fat from chops; sprinkle with cracked pepper. Coat a large nonstick skillet with cooking

Lamb Chops with Cherry Sauce

spray; place over medium heat until hot. Add chops; cover and cook 4 minutes on each side or until browned. Uncover and cook 5 minutes on each side or to desired degree of doneness. Remove chops from skillet. Set aside, and keep warm. Wipe drippings from skillet with a paper towel, if necessary.

Coat skillet with cooking spray; place over medium-high heat until hot. Add onion, celery, and garlic; sauté until crisp-tender. Add wine and broth; bring to a boil. Cook 5 minutes or until mixture is reduced by half. Pour wine mixture through a wire-mesh strainer into a bowl; discard vegetables remaining in strainer.

Return wine mixture to skillet; add jelly and next 4 ingredients. Cook over low heat until jelly melts, stirring occasionally.

Combine cornstarch and water in a small bowl. Add to wine mixture in skillet. Cook over medium heat, stirring constantly, until mixture is thickened and bubbly.

Add chops and cherries to wine mixture in skillet; cook until thoroughly heated. Garnish with thyme sprigs, if desired. Yield: 4 servings (304 calories per serving).

Per Serving:		
Fat 10.1g	Carbohydrate 21.5g	Fiber 1.4g
saturated fat 3.5g	Cholesterol 93mg	Iron 3.3mg
Protein 30.8g	Sodium 256mg	Calcium 59mg

Italian Lamb Chops

2 (5-ounce) lean lamb loin chops (¾ inch thick)
¼ teaspoon olive oil
2 teaspoons brown sugar
¼ teaspoon cracked pepper
  Olive oil-flavored vegetable cooking spray
½ medium-size sweet red pepper, seeded and cut into thin strips
½ medium onion, thinly sliced and halved
3 tablespoons commercial oil-free Italian dressing
2 teaspoons crumbled feta cheese

Trim fat from chops. Brush oil over both sides of chops. Combine brown sugar and cracked pepper; rub over both sides of chops.

Coat a large nonstick skillet with cooking spray; place over medium heat until hot. Add chops; cook 2 to 3 minutes on each side or until browned. Remove chops from skillet. Set aside, and keep warm. Wipe drippings from skillet with a paper towel, if necessary.

Coat skillet with cooking spray; place over medium-high heat until hot. Add sweet red pepper and onion; sauté until tender. Stir in Italian dressing. Return chops to skillet. Bring to a boil; reduce heat, and simmer, uncovered, 5 to 7 minutes or to desired degree of doneness. Transfer chops to a serving platter; top with pepper mixture. Sprinkle with feta cheese. Yield: 2 servings (241 calories per serving).

Per Serving:

Fat 9.4g	Carbohydrate 12.5g	Fiber 1.6g
saturated fat 3.6g	Cholesterol 81mg	Iron 2.9mg
Protein 25.7g	Sodium 402mg	Calcium 67mg

German Pork with Sauerkraut

Since this one-dish meal is high in sodium, serve it with a low-sodium side dish like fresh fruit.

  Vegetable cooking spray
1 pound lean boneless pork, cut into 1-inch cubes
1 cup water
¼ cup no-salt-added tomato paste
3 tablespoons brown sugar
2 tablespoons paprika
3 small carrots, scraped and cut into 1-inch pieces
1 medium Granny Smith apple, cut into thin wedges
1 medium onion, thinly sliced and separated into rings
1 (32-ounce) jar sauerkraut, drained
  Freshly ground pepper (optional)

Coat a large nonstick skillet with cooking spray, and place over medium heat until hot. Add pork, and cook until browned on all sides, stirring frequently. Drain, if necessary.

Combine water and next 3 ingredients in a small bowl, stirring well; pour over pork. Add carrot, apple, and onion; top with sauerkraut, spreading evenly. Bring to a boil. Cover, reduce heat, and simmer 1 hour or until pork is tender. Sprinkle with pepper, if desired. Yield: 6 servings (206 calories per serving).

Per Serving:

Fat 6.1g	Carbohydrate 19.1g	Fiber 3.5g
saturated fat 1.9g	Cholesterol 48mg	Iron 1.6mg
Protein 19.4g	Sodium 647mg	Calcium 27mg

Grilled Pork and Potatoes

Pair this flavorful meat-and-potatoes dish with a fresh spinach salad tossed with orange wedges and fat-free honey mustard dressing.

4   (8-ounce) baking potatoes
1   pound lean boneless pork loin
2   tablespoons ground thyme
3   tablespoons fresh lime juice
2   tablespoons jalapeño hot sauce
2   teaspoons minced fresh garlic
1   teaspoon onion powder
1   teaspoon chili powder
1   teaspoon paprika
½   teaspoon pepper
¼   teaspoon salt
¼   cup mango chutney
    Butter-flavored vegetable
      cooking spray

Scrub potatoes; prick each several times with a fork. Bake at 400° for 45 minutes or until done. Let cool slightly.

Soak 4 (10-inch) wooden skewers in water for at least 30 minutes.

Cut pork into 4- x ½-inch strips; set aside.

Combine thyme, lime juice, hot sauce, garlic, onion powder, chili powder, paprika, pepper, and salt, stirring well. Divide juice mixture in half. Stir chutney into half of juice mixture, and set aside. Combine pork and remaining juice mixture, tossing well. Thread pork onto skewers.

Cut each potato lengthwise into ½-inch-thick slices; coat slices with cooking spray.

Coat grill rack with cooking spray; place on grill over medium-hot coals (350° to 400°). Place pork skewers and potato slices on rack; grill, covered, 10 minutes or until pork and potato are done, turning occasionally. Serve warm with chutney mixture. Yield: 4 servings (445 calories per serving).

Per Serving:
Fat 9.9g
  saturated fat 3.3g
Protein 32.9g
Carbohydrate 55.9g
Cholesterol 83mg
Sodium 452mg
Fiber 4.5g
Iron 6.5mg
Calcium 91mg

Brie-Filled Pork Chops with Apple Stuffing

(pictured on page 147)

4   (4-ounce) boneless center-cut pork loin
      chops
2   ounces Brie cheese
2   tablespoons all-purpose flour
½   teaspoon pepper
½   teaspoon paprika
    Vegetable cooking spray
2   teaspoons vegetable oil
¾   cup canned no-salt-added chicken broth
¾   cup unsweetened apple cider
2   cloves garlic, halved
2   sprigs fresh rosemary
2   cups herb-seasoned stuffing mix
1⅓ cups chopped Red Delicious apple
    Apple wedges (optional)
    Fresh rosemary sprigs (optional)

Cut a pocket in one side of each chop, cutting to, but not through, remaining 3 sides. Cut cheese into 4 portions; place 1 portion of cheese into each pocket. Secure openings with wooden picks.

Combine flour, pepper, and paprika; dredge chops in flour mixture.

Coat a large oven-proof skillet with cooking spray, and add oil. Place over medium heat until hot. Add chops; cook 3 minutes on each side or until browned. Remove from skillet. Wipe drippings from skillet with a paper towel, if necessary.

Combine broth, cider, garlic, and 2 rosemary sprigs in skillet; bring to a boil. Boil 1 minute; remove and discard garlic and rosemary. Add stuffing mix and chopped apple, stirring well. Return chops to skillet. Cover and bake at 350° for 30 minutes or until chops are tender. If desired, garnish with apple wedges and fresh rosemary sprigs. Yield: 4 servings (420 calories per serving).

Per Serving:
Fat 15.6g
  saturated fat 8.9g
Protein 31.7g
Carbohydrate 36.0g
Cholesterol 86mg
Sodium 542mg
Fiber 3.5g
Iron 2.5mg
Calcium 60mg

Peppercorn-Crusted Pork Loin Roast

Peppercorn-Crusted Pork Loin Roast

1   (2½-pound) lean boneless pork loin roast
3   tablespoons Dijon mustard
1   tablespoon nonfat buttermilk
2   cups soft whole wheat breadcrumbs
2   tablespoons cracked pepper
2   teaspoons whole assorted peppercorns,
      crushed
2   teaspoons chopped fresh thyme
¼   teaspoon salt
     Vegetable cooking spray
     Creamy Peppercorn Sauce
     Fresh thyme sprigs (optional)

Trim fat from roast. Combine mustard and buttermilk. Spread mustard mixture over roast.

Combine breadcrumbs and next 4 ingredients; press breadcrumb mixture evenly onto roast. Place roast on a rack in a roasting pan coated with cooking spray. Insert meat thermometer into thickest part of roast, if desired. Bake at 325° for 2 hours or until meat thermometer registers 160°. Let roast stand 10 minutes before slicing. Serve with Creamy Peppercorn Sauce. Garnish with thyme sprigs, if desired. Yield: 10 servings (241 calories per serving).

Creamy Peppercorn Sauce

¾ cup nonfat buttermilk
⅓ cup nonfat sour cream
3 tablespoons grated Parmesan cheese
3 tablespoons reduced-fat mayonnaise
1½ tablespoons lemon juice
1½ teaspoons whole assorted peppercorns, crushed
¼ teaspoon salt

Combine all ingredients in a small bowl, stirring well. Yield: 1¼ cups plus 1 tablespoon.

Per Serving:

Fat 10.1g	Carbohydrate 10.0g	Fiber 0.8g
saturated fat 3.4g	Cholesterol 70mg	Iron 2.9mg
Protein 26.7g	Sodium 478mg	Calcium 80mg

Basil-Scented Pork Roast with Zucchini Pesto

1 (2½-pound) lean boneless double pork loin roast, tied
½ cup loosely packed fresh basil leaves
2 cloves garlic, thinly sliced
¼ teaspoon salt
¼ teaspoon freshly ground pepper
  Vegetable cooking spray
  Zucchini Pesto
5 cups cooked linguine (cooked without salt or fat)
  Fresh basil sprigs (optional)

Untie roast, and trim fat. Cut ½-inch-deep slits into middle of roast; place basil leaves and garlic slices in slits. Retie roast. Sprinkle roast with salt and pepper. Place roast on a rack in a roasting pan coated with cooking spray. Insert meat thermometer into thickest part of roast, if desired. Bake at 375° for 1 hour and 10 minutes or until meat thermometer registers 160°.

Let roast stand 10 minutes. Remove string; cut roast diagonally across grain into ¼-inch-thick slices. Toss Zucchini Pesto with linguine; serve with roast. Garnish with basil sprigs, if desired. Yield: 10 servings (338 calories per serving).

Zucchini Pesto

3¾ cups diced zucchini (about 3 medium)
¼ cup plus 2 tablespoons sliced carrot
1 large clove garlic
½ cup loosely packed fresh basil leaves
2 tablespoons fresh parsley leaves
2 tablespoons grated Parmesan cheese
¼ teaspoon salt
1½ teaspoons olive oil

Arrange zucchini and carrot in a vegetable steamer over boiling water. Cover and steam 10 to 12 minutes or until tender; drain well.

Position knife blade in food processor bowl. Drop garlic through food chute with processor running; process 3 seconds or until garlic is minced. Add steamed vegetables, basil, and next 3 ingredients. Process 15 seconds or until blended, scraping sides of processor bowl once. Slowly add oil through food chute with processor running, blending well. Yield: 1¾ cups.

Per Serving:

Fat 12.4g	Carbohydrate 26.6g	Fiber 1.8g
saturated fat 3.3g	Cholesterol 75mg	Iron 2.4mg
Protein 28.5g	Sodium 197mg	Calcium 41mg

Mesquite-Smoked Pork with Texas Caviar

This recipe doesn't require a smoker. You can prepare it on a gas or charcoal grill.

1	cup frozen black-eyed peas
1	cup water
⅓	cup seeded, chopped tomato
¼	cup chopped sweet yellow pepper
¼	cup chopped green pepper
¼	cup chopped onion
¼	cup commercial oil-free Italian dressing
1	tablespoon chopped fresh parsley
2	teaspoons seeded, minced jalapeño pepper
¼	teaspoon minced garlic
⅛	teaspoon pepper
⅛	teaspoon ground cumin
	Mesquite chips
	Vegetable cooking spray
1	(8-rib) center rib pork roast (about 4 pounds)
8	cloves garlic, minced
½	teaspoon salt
½	teaspoon coarsely ground pepper

Combine peas and 1 cup water. Bring to a boil. Cover, reduce heat, and simmer 35 minutes or until tender. Drain; let cool.

Combine peas, tomato, and next 9 ingredients in a medium bowl, stirring well. Cover and chill at least 2 hours.

Soak mesquite chips in water at least 30 minutes; drain. Wrap chips in heavy-duty aluminum foil, and make several holes in foil.

Light gas grill on one side; place foil-wrapped chips directly on hot lava rocks. Coat grill rack on opposite side of grill with cooking spray. Place rack over cool lava rocks; let grill preheat to medium-hot (350° to 400°) 10 to 15 minutes.

Trim fat from roast. Mash 8 cloves minced garlic, salt, and ½ teaspoon pepper to a paste. Rub surface of roast with garlic paste. Coat roast with cooking spray. Insert meat thermometer into thickest part of roast, if desired, making sure it does not touch bone or fat. Place roast on rack opposite hot lava rocks. Grill, covered, 1½ hours or until meat thermometer registers 150°. Remove roast from grill. Cover with aluminum foil; let stand 15 minutes or until thermometer registers 160°.

Carve roast into 8 chops, and serve with black-eyed pea mixture. Yield: 8 servings (263 calories per serving).

For a charcoal grill: Prepare black-eyed pea mixture as directed. Soak mesquite chips as directed. Pile charcoal on each side of grill, leaving center empty. Place a drip pan between coals. Prepare fire; let burn 10 to 15 minutes. Place chips directly on hot coals. Coat grill rack with cooking spray, and place over coals.

Trim fat from roast; coat with garlic paste and cooking spray as directed. Insert meat thermometer into thickest part of roast, if desired. Place roast on rack over drip pan. Grill, covered, 1½ hours or until meat thermometer registers 150°. Remove roast from grill. Cover with aluminum foil, and let stand 15 minutes or until thermometer registers 160°.

Per Serving:		
Fat 12.5g	Carbohydrate 7.6g	Fiber 0.7g
saturated fat 4.1g	Cholesterol 85mg	Iron 1.8mg
Protein 28.6g	Sodium 295mg	Calcium 21mg

Tropical Cornish Hens (page 172)

Poultry

Skillet Chicken Pizza

Cooking the pizza in a cast-iron skillet creates a crisp outer crust.

Olive oil-flavored vegetable cooking spray
1 teaspoon olive oil
1 cup sliced fresh mushrooms
½ cup chopped onion
1 clove garlic, minced
1 (9-ounce) package frozen artichoke hearts, thawed and chopped
¼ cup water
¼ cup dry white wine
¼ teaspoon chicken-flavored bouillon granules
2 cups chopped cooked chicken breast (skinned before cooking and cooked without salt)
¾ cup nonfat ricotta cheese
½ cup (2 ounces) shredded provolone cheese, divided
½ cup (2 ounces) shredded part-skim mozzarella cheese, divided
2 tablespoons grated Parmesan cheese
1½ tablespoons cornmeal
1 (10-ounce) can refrigerated pizza crust dough

Coat a nonstick skillet with cooking spray; add oil. Place over medium-high heat until hot. Add mushrooms, onion, and garlic; sauté until vegetables are tender. Add chopped artichoke, water, wine, and bouillon granules. Bring to a boil; reduce heat, and simmer, uncovered, 5 minutes. Add chicken; simmer 6 to 8 additional minutes or until liquid evaporates. Remove from heat, and set aside.

Combine ricotta cheese, ¼ cup provolone cheese, ¼ cup mozzarella cheese, and Parmesan cheese in a small bowl, stirring well; set aside.

Coat a 10-inch cast-iron skillet with vegetable cooking spray, and sprinkle with cornmeal. Press pizza dough in bottom and 1 inch up sides of skillet. Spread cheese mixture evenly over dough, leaving a ¼-inch border. Top with chicken mixture.

Bake at 425° for 15 minutes. Sprinkle remaining ¼ cup provolone cheese and ¼ cup mozzarella cheese over chicken mixture, and bake 5 additional minutes or until cheese melts and crust is golden. Yield: 6 servings (303 calories per serving).

Per Serving:		
Fat 9.0g	Carbohydrate 30.8g	Fiber 1.7g
saturated fat 3.8g	Cholesterol 48mg	Iron 2.0mg
Protein 25.4g	Sodium 512mg	Calcium 198mg

Online, In Shape

It won't raise your heart rate, but it will raise your consciousness. With a modem attached to your computer, you can team up with online services that provide an ever-growing supply of health and fitness information.

Browse through magazines such as *Bicycling* on America Online. Check out the Health and Fitness Forum on CompuServ which features discussions on exercise and family health. Post a note on a Prodigy "bulletin board" and see what responses you get. If you already subscribe to an online service, keep an eye out for health and fitness offerings. Or shop the services for the one that gives you the most fitness information for your dollar.

Thai Spring Rolls with Chicken

It's worth a trip to an Oriental market to collect the specialty ingredients for this flavor-packed entrée.

2 ounces Chinese rice noodles, uncooked
1 cup fresh bean sprouts
1 cup chopped fresh cilantro
¾ cup finely shredded cabbage
½ cup finely shredded carrot
⅓ cup diced celery
¼ cup reduced-fat peanut butter spread
1 tablespoon peeled, grated gingerroot
2 tablespoons rice wine vinegar
1 tablespoon low-sodium soy sauce
1 tablespoon sesame oil
1 tablespoon hoisin sauce
1 tablespoon fish sauce
1 teaspoon sugar
1 teaspoon Thai chili sauce
¼ teaspoon pepper
6 cloves garlic, minced
21 round rice papers
2 cups finely shredded cooked chicken
   (skinned before cooking and cooked
   without salt)
¼ cup rice wine vinegar
3 tablespoons low-sodium soy sauce
1 tablespoon sugar
1 teaspoon fish sauce

Soak rice noodles in boiling water to cover 5 minutes; drain.

Combine rice noodles, bean sprouts, and next 4 ingredients in a medium bowl. Combine peanut butter and next 10 ingredients, stirring well. Pour peanut butter mixture over noodle mixture; toss well. Cover and chill 30 minutes.

Separate rice papers, and place in a large shallow dish; add boiling water to cover. Let stand 3 minutes; drain. (Do not allow rice papers to stand in water longer than 3 minutes or they will be difficult to handle.)

Carefully place 1 rice paper on work surface. Spoon about 1½ tablespoons shredded chicken just below center of rice paper; top chicken with about 3 tablespoons noodle mixture. Fold over left and right sides of rice paper to partially enclose filling. Roll up rice paper, jellyroll fashion; place roll, seam side down, in a large shallow dish. Repeat procedure with remaining rice papers, shredded chicken, and noodle mixture. Cover and chill thoroughly.

Combine ¼ cup rice wine vinegar and remaining ingredients in a saucepan; cook over low heat until sugar dissolves, stirring occasionally.

To serve, place 3 spring rolls on each individual serving plate. Pour rice wine vinegar mixture evenly into 7 small bowls. Serve vinegar mixture as a dipping sauce with spring rolls. Yield: 7 servings (287 calories per serving).

Per Serving:		
Fat 9.5g	Carbohydrate 33.3g	Fiber 1.4g
saturated fat 1.7g	Cholesterol 36mg	Iron 2.9mg
Protein 17.5g	Sodium 625mg	Calcium 61mg

1. After placing chicken and noodle mixture on rice paper, fold over left and right sides of rice paper to partially enclose filling.

2. Roll up rice paper, jellyroll fashion; place roll, seam side down, in a large shallow dish.

Chicken Breast Dijon

For a super-quick supper, serve this entrée with steamed Sugar Snap peas (the frozen kind), instant brown rice, and orange wedges.

⅓ cup fine, dry breadcrumbs
1 tablespoon Parmesan cheese
1 teaspoon dried Italian seasoning
½ teaspoon dried thyme
¼ teaspoon salt
¼ teaspoon freshly ground pepper
4 (4-ounce) skinned, boned chicken breast halves
2 tablespoons Dijon mustard
1 teaspoon olive oil
1 teaspoon reduced-calorie margarine

Combine first 6 ingredients in a small bowl, stirring well. Brush both sides of each chicken breast half with mustard; dredge in breadcrumb mixture.

Heat olive oil and margarine in a nonstick skillet over medium-high heat until margarine melts. Add chicken breasts, and sauté 6 to 8 minutes on each side or until chicken is done. Yield: 4 servings (192 calories per serving).

Per Serving:

Fat 4.6g	Carbohydrate 7.5g	Fiber 0.5g
saturated fat 1.0g	Cholesterol 67mg	Iron 1.9mg
Protein 27.9g	Sodium 553mg	Calcium 64mg

Poached Ginger Chicken

4 (4-ounce) skinned, boned chicken breast halves
2 cups water
Vegetable cooking spray
1 teaspoon peanut oil
¾ cup chopped green onions
¼ cup peeled, grated gingerroot
2 tablespoons dark brown sugar
2 tablespoons dry sherry
2 tablespoons low-sodium soy sauce
Boston lettuce leaves (optional)
Green onions (optional)

Combine chicken and water in a large saucepan. Bring to a boil; cover, reduce heat, and simmer 20 minutes or until chicken is done. Remove chicken from broth; discard broth. Cut chicken into thin slices; place slices in a shallow baking dish.

Coat a small nonstick skillet with cooking spray; add oil. Place over medium-high heat until hot. Add chopped green onions and gingerroot; sauté 30 seconds. Remove from heat, and spoon over chicken.

Add sugar, sherry, and soy sauce to skillet; bring to a boil. Boil 1 minute. Pour soy sauce mixture over chicken. Cover and chill thoroughly. If desired, spoon chicken mixture evenly onto individual lettuce-lined salad plates, and garnish with green onions. Yield: 4 servings (187 calories per serving).

Per Serving:

Fat 4.4g	Carbohydrate 7.8g	Fiber 0.4g
saturated fat 1.1g	Cholesterol 72mg	Iron 1.2mg
Protein 26.9g	Sodium 264mg	Calcium 29mg

Poached Ginger Chicken

Country Chicken Pot Pie

Using low-fat biscuit and baking mix is convenient, but the mix isn't low in sodium.
If you're on a sodium-restricted diet, make the low-sodium topping variation.
It has 326 milligrams less sodium per serving.

2   pounds skinned chicken breast halves
4   sprigs fresh parsley
3   stalks celery, cut into 2-inch pieces
1   small onion, quartered
1   bay leaf
5   cups water
    Vegetable cooking spray
1   cup chopped onion
¾   cup diced celery
1½ cups peeled, cubed potato
1   (10-ounce) package frozen mixed
      vegetables
⅔   cup all-purpose flour
1   (12-ounce) can evaporated skimmed milk
½   teaspoon poultry seasoning
½   teaspoon salt
¼   teaspoon pepper
¼   teaspoon dried thyme
2   cups low-fat biscuit and baking mix
2   tablespoons chopped fresh parsley
¾   cup 1% low-fat milk

Combine first 6 ingredients in a large Dutch oven. Bring to a boil; cover, reduce heat, and simmer 1 hour. Remove chicken from broth, reserving broth. Let chicken cool. Bone chicken, and coarsely chop; set aside.

Pour broth through a wire-mesh strainer lined with a layer of cheesecloth into a bowl, discarding vegetables and herbs remaining in strainer. Skim fat from broth; set aside 4 cups broth. Reserve remaining broth for another use.

Coat Dutch oven with cooking spray; place over medium-high heat until hot. Add chopped onion and diced celery; sauté until vegetables are tender. Add reserved 4 cups broth, cubed potato, and frozen mixed vegetables; bring to a boil. Cover, reduce heat, and simmer 15 minutes or until vegetables are tender.

Combine flour and ¾ cup evaporated milk in a small bowl, stirring until smooth. Add milk mixture to vegetable mixture in Dutch oven, stirring constantly. Add remaining evaporated milk, and cook over medium heat, stirring constantly, until mixture is thickened and bubbly. Remove vegetable mixture from heat. Stir in chopped chicken, poultry seasoning, and next 3 ingredients. Spoon chicken mixture into a 13- x 9- x 2-inch baking dish coated with cooking spray.

Combine baking mix and chopped parsley in a medium bowl. Gradually add low-fat milk, stirring just until dry ingredients are moistened. Drop biscuit topping by heaping spoonfuls over chicken mixture, forming 8 biscuits. Bake at 350° for 35 minutes or until golden. Yield: 8 servings (384 calories per serving).

Note: For a lower-sodium biscuit topping, replace the low-fat biscuit and baking mix with 2 cups all-purpose flour, 2 teaspoons baking powder, and ½ teaspoon salt. Add 2 tablespoons chopped parsley. Add 1½ tablespoons melted margarine and ¾ cup low-fat milk to dry ingredients, stirring just until dry ingredients are moistened.

Per Serving:		
Fat 3.4g	Carbohydrate 64.6g	Fiber 3.2g
saturated fat 0.9g	Cholesterol 55mg	Iron 3.0mg
Protein 29.1g	Sodium 796mg	Calcium 191mg

Chicken and Saffron Rice Skillet

¾   cup sun-dried tomatoes (packed
         without oil)
1   cup boiling water
     Olive oil-flavored vegetable cooking spray
2   teaspoons olive oil
4   (6-ounce) skinned chicken breast halves
½   cup chopped onion
2   cloves garlic, minced
2½   cups water
1   teaspoon chicken-flavored bouillon
         granules
1   cup long-grain rice, uncooked
1   cup thinly sliced zucchini
1   medium-size green pepper, seeded and cut
         into thin strips
½   teaspoon dried oregano
¼   teaspoon salt
¼   teaspoon saffron threads
1   bay leaf
¼   cup frozen English peas, thawed
     Fresh oregano sprigs (optional)

Combine tomatoes and 1 cup boiling water in a
small bowl; let stand 5 minutes. Drain tomatoes,
and coarsely chop.

Coat a large nonstick skillet with cooking
spray; add oil. Place over medium-high heat until
hot; add chicken, and cook 2 minutes on each
side or until lightly browned. Remove chicken
from skillet; set aside.

Add onion and garlic to skillet; sauté until tender. Add chicken, 2½ cups water, and bouillon
granules to skillet. Bring to a boil; cover, reduce
heat, and simmer 5 minutes. Stir in chopped
tomato, rice, and next 6 ingredients. Cover and
simmer 25 minutes or until chicken is done, rice
is tender, and liquid is absorbed. Remove and
discard bay leaf. Stir in peas; cover and let stand
5 minutes before serving. Garnish with fresh
oregano sprigs, if desired. Yield: 4 servings (375
calories per serving).

Per Serving:

Fat 4.8g	Carbohydrate 49.3g	Fiber 4.4g
saturated fat 0.9g	Cholesterol 66mg	Iron 4.4mg
Protein 32.7g	Sodium 570mg	Calcium 56mg

Garlic-Ginger Chicken

*For an effortless meal, serve this chicken with baked
potatoes and steamed broccoli.*

1   teaspoon peeled, grated gingerroot
2   teaspoons rice wine vinegar
2   teaspoons ketchup
1   teaspoon water
¼   teaspoon salt
¼   teaspoon ground cinnamon
¼   teaspoon ground cardamom
¼   teaspoon ground red pepper
4   cloves garlic, minced
4   (6-ounce) skinned chicken breast halves
     Vegetable cooking spray

Combine first 9 ingredients in a small bowl,
stirring well.

Place chicken, skinned side up, on a rack in a
roasting pan coated with cooking spray. Brush
ketchup mixture over chicken. Bake at 375° for 45
minutes or until chicken is done, turning and
basting occasionally with ketchup mixture. Yield:
4 servings (152 calories per serving).

Per Serving:

Fat 3.2g	Carbohydrate 2.2g	Fiber 0.2g
saturated fat 0.9g	Cholesterol 72mg	Iron 1.0mg
Protein 26.7g	Sodium 240mg	Calcium 22mg

The Accidental Exerciser

Can't make it to the health club for a workout?
Not to worry. There are plenty of ways to exercise
around the house to burn off that piece of pie you
had for dessert.

Calories Burned (per 10 minutes)	Women (132 lbs)	Men (176 lbs)
Weeding	45	60
Moving furniture	60	80
Scrubbing floors	55	73
Shoveling snow	60	80
Cleaning gutters	50	67
Running up stairs	150	200

Chicken Breasts with Marmalade

Chicken Breasts with Marmalade

Vegetable cooking spray
1   teaspoon margarine
½   cup finely chopped onion
4   large fresh crimini mushrooms, sliced
⅛   teaspoon salt
⅛   teaspoon pepper
4   (6-ounce) skinned chicken breast halves
¼   cup water
¼   cup low-sodium teriyaki sauce
2   tablespoons low-sugar orange marmalade
2   cups cooked couscous (cooked without salt or fat)
    Orange slices (optional)
    Flat-leaf parsley sprigs (optional)

Coat a large nonstick skillet with cooking spray; add margarine. Place over medium-high heat until margarine melts. Add onion and mushrooms; sauté until tender. Transfer mushroom mixture to a small bowl. Stir in salt and pepper; set aside.

Coat skillet with cooking spray; place over medium-high heat until hot. Add chicken, and cook 2 minutes on each side or until browned. Combine water, teriyaki sauce, and orange marmalade; pour over chicken in skillet. Bring to a boil; cover, reduce heat, and simmer 20 minutes or until chicken is done, turning occasionally. Add mushroom mixture to skillet; bring to a boil. Reduce heat, and simmer, uncovered, 3 minutes.

To serve, place ½ cup couscous on each individual serving plate. Top with chicken breasts. Spoon mushroom mixture evenly over chicken. If desired, garnish with orange slices and parsley sprigs. Yield: 4 servings (258 calories per serving).

Per Serving:		
Fat 3.0g	Carbohydrate 25.6g	Fiber 1.5g
saturated fat 0.6g	Cholesterol 66mg	Iron 1.6mg
Protein 30.7g	Sodium 481mg	Calcium 21mg

Malaysian Chicken

¼   teaspoon salt
1½ pounds skinned, boned chicken thighs
1   teaspoon peanut oil
1   cup thinly sliced shallots
3   medium onions, thinly sliced
4   dried red chiles, seeded and minced
1   cup water
1   tablespoon sugar
2   tablespoons low-sodium soy sauce
¼   teaspoon salt
1   tablespoon cornstarch
2   tablespoons water
4½ cups cooked long-grain rice (cooked
      without salt or fat)
¼   cup unsalted dry roasted peanuts, chopped
3   tablespoons chopped fresh cilantro

Sprinkle ¼ teaspoon salt evenly over chicken;
set aside.

Heat peanut oil in a large nonstick skillet over
medium-high heat until hot. Add chicken thighs,
and cook 5 to 7 minutes on each side or until
chicken is lightly browned. Remove chicken from
skillet, and set aside. Add shallots, onion, and
chiles to skillet; sauté 5 minutes or until vegetables are tender.

Return chicken to skillet. Combine 1 cup water
and next 3 ingredients; pour over chicken and
vegetables. Bring to a boil; cover, reduce heat,
and simmer 15 to 20 minutes or until chicken is
done. Remove chicken from skillet; set aside, and
keep warm.

Combine cornstarch and 2 tablespoons water,
stirring well. Add cornstarch mixture to onion
mixture in skillet, stirring constantly. Bring to a
boil over medium heat, stirring constantly; boil 1
minute.

Spoon rice onto a serving platter. Top with
chicken thighs; pour sauce over chicken. Sprinkle
with peanuts and cilantro. Yield: 6 servings (396
calories per serving).

Per Serving:

Fat 8.4g	Carbohydrate 50.2g	Fiber 2.8g
saturated fat 1.7g	Cholesterol 94mg	Iron 3.1mg
Protein 28.3g	Sodium 429mg	Calcium 57mg

Chicken and Noodles

*A rich, flavorful vegetable puree helps thicken the
broth without adding fat.*

1   (3-pound) broiler-fryer, cut up and skinned
7   cups water
½   cup chopped fresh parsley
6   cloves garlic
2   medium carrots, scraped and cut into
      1-inch pieces
2   medium parsnips, scraped and cut into
      1-inch pieces
2   stalks celery, cut into 1-inch pieces
2   medium turnips, peeled and quartered
1   large onion, sliced
1   bay leaf
12 ounces medium egg noodles, uncooked
½   teaspoon salt
½   teaspoon pepper

Combine first 10 ingredients in a large Dutch
oven. Bring to a boil; cover, reduce heat, and simmer 2½ hours. Remove chicken, vegetables, and
bay leaf from broth, reserving broth; discard bay
leaf. Bone chicken, and coarsely chop; set chopped
chicken aside.

Position knife blade in food processor bowl;
add vegetable mixture. Process until smooth,
scraping sides of processor bowl once; set aside.

Skim fat from broth. Add chicken to broth in
Dutch oven; bring to a boil. Stir in noodles;
reduce heat, and simmer, uncovered, 8 minutes or
until noodles are tender. Stir in vegetable puree,
salt, and pepper. Cook until thoroughly heated.
Yield: 10 servings (277 calories per 1-cup serving).

Per Serving:

Fat 5.5g	Carbohydrate 32.7g	Fiber 2.5g
saturated fat 1.4g	Cholesterol 80mg	Iron 2.7mg
Protein 21.3g	Sodium 202mg	Calcium 48mg

Southeast Asian Chicken Curry

Vegetable cooking spray
2   teaspoons vegetable oil
1½ cups finely chopped onion
1   teaspoon peeled, minced gingerroot
2   cloves garlic, minced
1   (3-inch) stick cinnamon
3   tablespoons curry powder
2   cups water
1   (4-pound) broiler-fryer, cut up and skinned
4   small dried red chiles
4   large baking potatoes (about 2½ pounds), peeled and cut into wedges
¾   teaspoon salt
½   teaspoon freshly ground pepper
1   jalapeño pepper, seeded and cut into rings
6   cups cooked basmati rice (cooked without salt or fat)
¼   cup fresh cilantro leaves
6   green onions, diagonally sliced into ½-inch pieces

Coat a large Dutch oven with cooking spray; add oil. Place over medium-high heat until hot. Add chopped onion and next 3 ingredients; sauté until onion is tender. Add curry powder; cook 30 seconds. Add 2 cups water; bring to a boil. Add chicken and red chiles; cover, reduce heat, and simmer 30 minutes.

Add potato; cover and cook 25 minutes or until chicken is done and potato is tender. Stir in salt, pepper, and jalapeño pepper; cook 3 minutes. Remove and discard cinnamon stick and red chiles. To serve, spoon ¾ cup basmati rice onto each individual serving plate. Spoon chicken mixture evenly over each serving; sprinkle with cilantro and green onions. Yield: 8 servings (431 calories per serving).

Per Serving:
Fat 5.5g	Carbohydrate 62.3g	Fiber 4.3g
saturated fat 1.2g	Cholesterol 82mg	Iron 4.2mg
Protein 31.5g	Sodium 322mg	Calcium 67mg

Tropical Cornish Hens

1¾ cups water
½   cup wild rice, uncooked
⅔   cup long-grain rice, uncooked
2   (1-pound) Cornish hens, skinned
2   tablespoons curry powder
Vegetable cooking spray
½   cup commercial peach sauce
¼   cup fresh lime juice
4   kiwifruit, peeled and cut into ¼-inch-thick slices
2   starfruit, cut into ¼-inch-thick slices
1   ripe mango, peeled, seeded, and cut into 1-inch pieces
Lime rind curls (optional)

Combine water and wild rice in a saucepan. Bring to a boil. Cover, reduce heat, and simmer 30 minutes. Stir in long-grain rice; cover and simmer 20 minutes or until rice is tender and liquid is absorbed. Set aside, and keep warm.

Remove and discard giblets from hens. Rinse hens under cold water, and pat dry with paper towels. Split each hen in half lengthwise, using an electric knife. Sprinkle hens with curry powder.

Place hen halves, cut side down, on a rack in a roasting pan coated with cooking spray. Bake, uncovered, at 350° for 30 minutes.

Combine peach sauce and lime juice. Combine 1 tablespoon peach sauce mixture, kiwifruit, starfruit, and mango, tossing well; set aside.

Remove hens from oven; baste with remaining peach mixture. Bake 20 additional minutes, basting occasionally with peach mixture. Arrange fruit mixture around hen halves in roasting pan. Bake 10 to 12 minutes or until hens are done and fruit mixture is thoroughly heated.

To serve, spoon ¾ cup rice mixture onto each individual serving plate. Top with hen halves. Spoon fruit mixture evenly around hens. Garnish with lime rind curls, if desired. Yield: 4 servings (480 calories per serving).

Per Serving:
Fat 9.0g	Carbohydrate 64.5g	Fiber 7.8g
saturated fat 2.2g	Cholesterol 91mg	Iron 3.3mg
Protein 34.9g	Sodium 353mg	Calcium 63mg

Turkey Enchiladas

Turkey Enchiladas

1   pound freshly ground raw turkey breast
2   cups no-salt-added salsa, divided
1   (10-ounce) package frozen chopped
       spinach, thawed and drained
1   (8-ounce) package nonfat cream cheese,
       cubed
12 (6-inch) corn tortillas
       Vegetable cooking spray
1   (14½-ounce) can no-salt-added whole
       tomatoes, undrained and chopped
1   teaspoon ground cumin
¾   cup (3 ounces) shredded reduced-fat
       Cheddar cheese
3   cups shredded iceberg lettuce
¼   cup plus 2 tablespoons nonfat sour cream

Cook turkey in a large nonstick skillet over medium heat until browned, stirring until it crumbles. Add 1 cup salsa and next 2 ingredients. Cook until cheese melts, stirring frequently.

Remove turkey mixture from skillet; set aside. Wipe skillet dry with a paper towel; place over medium heat until hot. Coat both sides of tortillas with cooking spray. Place 1 tortilla in skillet. Cook 15 seconds on each side. Spoon about ⅓ cup turkey mixture across center of tortilla. Roll up; place seam side down in a 13- x 9- x 2-inch baking dish coated with cooking spray. Repeat procedure with remaining tortillas and turkey mixture.

Combine remaining salsa, tomato, and cumin; pour over tortillas. Bake, uncovered, at 350° for 25 to 30 minutes or until thoroughly heated. Sprinkle with shredded cheese, and let stand 2 minutes.

Place ½ cup lettuce on each individual serving plate. Arrange two enchiladas over lettuce on each plate. Top each serving with 1 tablespoon sour cream. Yield: 6 servings (349 calories per serving).

Per Serving:		
Fat 6.0g	Carbohydrate 39.7g	Fiber 5.1g
saturated fat 2.6g	Cholesterol 63mg	Iron 3.7mg
Protein 34.2g	Sodium 703mg	Calcium 474mg

Spicy Sausage and Bean Bake

Vegetable cooking spray
¾ pound smoked turkey sausage, sliced
½ cup chopped onion
½ cup chopped green pepper
½ cup chopped sweet red pepper
1 tablespoon minced garlic
2 (15-ounce) cans no-salt-added black beans, drained
1 (16-ounce) can chili hot beans
1 (10-ounce) package frozen whole-kernel corn, thawed
¾ cup reduced-calorie ketchup
1 tablespoon chili powder
¾ teaspoon cumin
½ cup (2 ounces) shredded reduced-fat Monterey Jack cheese
1 tablespoon chopped fresh cilantro
½ cup nonfat sour cream
Dried crushed red pepper (optional)

Coat a large nonstick skillet with cooking spray. Place over medium-high heat until hot. Add sausage and next 4 ingredients; sauté until tender. Add black beans and next 5 ingredients; stir well.

Spoon sausage mixture into a 13- x 9- x 2-inch baking dish coated with cooking spray. Cover and bake at 375° for 25 minutes or until thoroughly heated. Uncover and sprinkle with cheese. Bake, uncovered, 5 additional minutes or until cheese melts.

To serve, spoon bean mixture evenly into individual serving bowls. Sprinkle with cilantro. Top each serving with 1 tablespoon sour cream. Sprinkle with crushed red pepper, if desired. Yield: 8 servings (325 calories per serving).

Per Serving:		
Fat 11.1g	Carbohydrate 37.3g	Fiber 5.7g
saturated fat 3.0g	Cholesterol 56mg	Iron 3.5mg
Protein 19.9g	Sodium 594mg	Calcium 160mg

Sausage and Apple Risotto

Olive oil-flavored vegetable cooking spray
1 pound turkey breakfast sausage links
1 tablespoon water
1½ cups chopped onion
1 cup chopped sweet red pepper
1 cup chopped fresh crimini mushrooms
1 medium apple, peeled, cored, and chopped
1 cup Arborio rice, uncooked
1½ cups canned no-salt-added chicken broth, undiluted
¼ cup dry white wine
1 (14½-ounce) can no-salt-added whole tomatoes, undrained and chopped
1 teaspoon dried basil
½ teaspoon dried oregano
¼ teaspoon salt
¼ teaspoon pepper

Coat a large nonstick skillet with cooking spray; place over medium-high heat until hot. Add sausage and water. Cover and cook 2 minutes or until browned, turning frequently. Remove sausage from skillet; drain and pat dry with paper towels. Wipe skillet dry with a paper towel. Cut sausage into ½-inch-thick slices. Remove and discard sausage casings, if desired; set sausage aside.

Coat skillet with cooking spray; place over medium-high heat until hot. Add onion and next 3 ingredients; sauté 5 minutes or until tender. Add sausage, rice, and remaining ingredients to skillet. Bring to a boil; cover, reduce heat, and simmer 30 to 35 minutes or until rice is tender and liquid is absorbed. Yield: 7 servings (289 calories per serving).

Per Serving:		
Fat 9.7g	Carbohydrate 35.2g	Fiber 2.7g
saturated fat 2.4g	Cholesterol 41mg	Iron 2.2mg
Protein 12.5g	Sodium 438mg	Calcium 36mg

Warm Sesame Pork Salad (page 184)

Salads & Salad Dressings

Mandarin Orange Salad

This salad is a snap to prepare. Team it with Grilled Spicy Flank Steak (page 149) and steamed broccoli for an almost effortless meal.

6   cups torn romaine lettuce
½   cup diced purple onion
1   (11-ounce) can mandarin oranges in light syrup, drained
¼   cup unsweetened orange juice
1   teaspoon sugar
1   teaspoon peeled, grated gingerroot
1   teaspoon low-sodium soy sauce
1   teaspoon dark sesame oil

Combine lettuce, onion, and oranges in a large bowl, tossing gently.

Combine orange juice and remaining ingredients. Pour juice mixture over lettuce mixture, and toss gently. Serve immediately. Yield: 6 servings (44 calories per 1-cup serving).

Per Serving:		
Fat 0.8g	Carbohydrate 8.6g	Fiber 0.7g
saturated fat 0.1g	Cholesterol 0mg	Iron 0.4mg
Protein 0.7g	Sodium 26mg	Calcium 13mg

Chicory and Papaya Salad with Poppy Seed Dressing

Chicory is a bitter-tasting green with curly leaves. The sweet papaya chunks are a pleasing contrast to the bitter greens.

4   cups torn fresh chicory
1   papaya, peeled, seeded, and cut into 1-inch pieces
⅓   cup commercial fat-free Catalina dressing
1   kiwifruit, peeled and sliced
1   tablespoon lime juice
2   teaspoons poppy seeds

Combine chicory and papaya; place evenly on individual salad plates. Cover and chill.

Combine dressing, kiwifruit, lime juice, and poppy seeds in container of an electric blender. Cover and process until smooth, stopping once to scrape down sides. Drizzle dressing mixture evenly over salads. Yield: 4 servings (73 calories per 1¼-cup serving).

Per Serving:		
Fat 0.9g	Carbohydrate 16.0g	Fiber 1.8g
saturated fat 0.1g	Cholesterol 0mg	Iron 0.5mg
Protein 1.2g	Sodium 249mg	Calcium 60mg

Fruit and Cheese Platter

½   cup commercial fat-free honey-mustard dressing
⅓   cup plain nonfat yogurt
2   tablespoons raspberry vinegar
2   teaspoons sugar
24   (¼-inch-thick) slices cantaloupe (about 1½ medium)
3   cups fresh strawberries, halved
2¼   cups fresh blueberries
1½   cups seedless green grapes
1½   cups julienne-sliced jicama
1¼   cups (6 ounces) cubed nonfat Cheddar cheese
     Fresh strawberry halves (optional)
     Fresh mint sprigs (optional)

Combine first 4 ingredients. Cover and chill.

Place dressing mixture in a small bowl on a large serving platter. Arrange cantaloupe, 3 cups fresh strawberries, blueberries, grapes, jicama, and cheese on platter. If desired, garnish with strawberry halves and fresh mint sprigs. Yield: 8 servings (178 calories per serving).

Per Serving:		
Fat 1.0g	Carbohydrate 35.5g	Fiber 5.6g
saturated fat 0.3g	Cholesterol 4mg	Iron 0.8mg
Protein 9.9g	Sodium 308mg	Calcium 51mg

Fruit and Cheese Platter

Stuffed Pear Salad

½   cup nonfat ricotta cheese
2   tablespoons golden raisins
1   tablespoon honey
⅛   teaspoon ground nutmeg
2   firm ripe red pears
½   teaspoon lemon juice
2   cups torn watercress
    Piquant Dressing
1½ tablespoons pine nuts, toasted

Combine first 4 ingredients in a small bowl, stirring well. Set aside.

Core pears; cut each in half lengthwise. Brush cut sides of pears with lemon juice.

Place ½ cup watercress on each individual salad plate. Place one pear half on watercress on each salad plate. Spoon ricotta cheese mixture evenly onto pear halves. Drizzle Piquant Dressing over pears, and sprinkle with pine nuts. Serve immediately. Yield: 4 servings (136 calories per serving).

Piquant Dressing

¼   cup unsweetened applesauce
1   tablespoon white balsamic vinegar
1   teaspoon sugar
⅛   teaspoon salt
⅛   teaspoon pepper

Combine all ingredients in a small bowl, stirring well. Yield: ¼ cup plus 1 tablespoon.

Per Serving:

Fat 2.8g	Carbohydrate 26.7g	Fiber 3.0g
saturated fat 0.4g	Cholesterol 3mg	Iron 0.5mg
Protein 5.6g	Sodium 99mg	Calcium 82mg

Asian Cabbage Slaw

Bok choy and napa cabbage are types of Chinese cabbage. Bok choy has long white stalks and dark green leaves. Napa cabbage has cream-colored leaves with light green tips.

4   cups thinly sliced bok choy
4   cups thinly sliced napa cabbage
½   cup minced fresh cilantro
½   cup sliced green onions
1   (8-ounce) can sliced water chestnuts, drained
1   tablespoon sesame seeds, toasted
1   teaspoon peeled, grated gingerroot
⅛   teaspoon pepper
1   clove garlic, minced
¾   cup nonfat mayonnaise-type salad dressing
1   tablespoon fresh lime juice
1   tablespoon low-sodium soy sauce

Combine first 9 ingredients in a large bowl, tossing well. Combine salad dressing, lime juice, and soy sauce; pour over cabbage mixture, and toss well. Cover and chill at least 2 hours. Yield: 8 servings (56 calories per 1-cup serving).

Per Serving:

Fat 0.7g	Carbohydrate 11.4g	Fiber 1.0g
saturated fat 0.1g	Cholesterol 0mg	Iron 0.9mg
Protein 1.5g	Sodium 302mg	Calcium 96mg

Southwestern Corn and Pepper Salad

1¾ cups fresh corn cut from cob
1½ cups water
¾ cup diced green pepper
¾ cup diced sweet red pepper
¾ cup peeled, diced jicama
¼ cup diced purple onion
3 tablespoons sliced ripe olives
2 tablespoons minced fresh cilantro
2½ tablespoons balsamic vinegar
1 teaspoon sugar
1 teaspoon olive oil
½ teaspoon ground coriander
½ teaspoon ground cumin
¼ teaspoon salt
⅛ teaspoon pepper

Combine corn and water in a saucepan. Bring to a boil; cover, reduce heat, and simmer 20 minutes or until tender. Drain and let cool.

Combine corn, green pepper, and remaining ingredients in a large bowl, tossing well. Cover and chill at least 2 hours. Yield: 4 servings (104 calories per 1-cup serving).

Per Serving:
Fat 3.1g	Carbohydrate 19.3g	Fiber 3.3g
saturated fat 0.5g	Cholesterol 0mg	Iron 1.9mg
Protein 2.9g	Sodium 238mg	Calcium 24mg

Baked Potato Salad

This hearty side dish salad is virtually fat free. Each serving contains less than ½ gram of fat.

4 (8-ounce) baking potatoes
¾ cup nonfat mayonnaise-type salad dressing
⅓ cup minced onion
⅓ cup minced fresh parsley
¼ cup nonfat sour cream
1 tablespoon cider vinegar
¼ teaspoon salt
¼ teaspoon pepper
1 large clove garlic, minced
Fresh parsley sprigs (optional)

Scrub potatoes; prick each several times with a fork. Bake at 400° for 1 hour or until done. Let cool slightly; remove skin, if desired. Cut potato into ½-inch cubes.

Combine salad dressing and next 7 ingredients in a medium bowl; add cubed potato, and toss well. Cover and chill at least 2 hours. Garnish with parsley sprigs, if desired. Yield: 6 servings (199 calories per ¾-cup serving).

Per Serving:
Fat 0.2g	Carbohydrate 45.7g	Fiber 3.0g
saturated fat 0.1g	Cholesterol 0mg	Iron 2.2mg
Protein 4.1g	Sodium 398mg	Calcium 63mg

Water, Water Everywhere

Do you really need to drink eight glasses of water a day? Yes, and maybe even more if you're exercising. Consider that on an average day the body loses two to three quarts of fluid just from breathing, perspiring, and excreting. Add in any physical exertion, and the debit is even greater. Most people get about two cups of fluid back from the food they eat, leaving at least six to eight cups that have to be made up another way.

To see whether you're drinking enough fluids during exercise, try this: weigh yourself before working out and again afterward. If your weight doesn't change, you've stayed properly hydrated.

If you weigh less, sip more water the next time. You'll find the proper balance with a little experimentation.

Here are some good strategies to ensure that you drink more water.
- Drink before, during, and after exercise.
- Keep a glass of water at your desk, and sip while you work or study.
- Stop and take a drink whenever you pass a water fountain.
- Leave a glass of water at your bedside, and drink when you wake up during the night.
- Drink water with every meal.

Baby Greens with Toasted Sesame Croutons

If you can't find mixed baby salad greens, use 4 cups of your favorite salad greens instead.

12 (¼-inch-thick) slices French baguette
1½ teaspoons olive oil
1 tablespoon sesame seeds, toasted
  Vegetable cooking spray
1 medium carrot, scraped
4 cups mixed baby salad greens
⅓ cup nonfat mayonnaise
¼ cup plain nonfat yogurt
1 tablespoon grated Parmesan cheese
1 tablespoon skim milk
1 teaspoon cider vinegar
¼ teaspoon salt
¼ teaspoon freshly ground pepper
1 clove garlic, minced

Brush both sides of bread slices with olive oil; sprinkle one side of slices with sesame seeds. Place slices, seed side up, on a baking sheet coated with cooking spray. Bake at 400° for 10 minutes or until crisp and golden; let cool.

Slice carrot lengthwise into very thin slices to form ribbons, using a vegetable peeler and applying firm pressure. Reserve center core of carrot for another use. Combine carrot strips and salad greens in a large bowl, tossing gently.

Combine mayonnaise and remaining ingredients in a small bowl, stirring until smooth. Pour mayonnaise mixture over salad greens mixture; toss gently. Place 1 cup salad greens mixture on each individual serving plate. Top each serving with 2 sesame croutons, seed side up. Yield: 6 servings (107 calories per 1-cup serving).

Per Serving:

Fat 3.4g	Carbohydrate 15.6g	Fiber 0.8g
saturated fat 0.6g	Cholesterol 2mg	Iron 0.9mg
Protein 3.7g	Sodium 411mg	Calcium 69mg

Italian Green Salad

Regular crumbled feta cheese is a tasty substitute for basil-tomato feta cheese.

1 cup frozen artichoke hearts, thawed
¼ cup plus 2 tablespoons commercial oil-free Italian dressing
1 tablespoon red wine vinegar
¼ teaspoon dry mustard
2 cups torn red leaf lettuce
2 cups torn romaine lettuce
1 cup pear-shaped cherry tomatoes, halved
½ small purple onion, sliced and separated into rings
¼ cup crumbled basil- and tomato-flavored feta cheese

Place artichoke hearts in a heavy-duty, zip-top plastic bag. Combine Italian dressing, vinegar, and mustard, stirring well with a wire whisk. Spoon 2 tablespoons dressing mixture over artichokes. Seal bag, and shake until artichokes are well coated. Marinate in refrigerator 1 hour. Remove artichokes from marinade, discarding marinade.

Combine artichokes, lettuces, tomato, and onion. Add remaining dressing mixture, and toss well. Place 1¼ cups lettuce mixture on each individual salad plate. Sprinkle with feta cheese. Yield: 4 servings (75 calories per 1¼-cup serving).

Per Serving:

Fat 2.4g	Carbohydrate 11.2g	Fiber 1.7g
saturated fat 1.4g	Cholesterol 8mg	Iron 0.9mg
Protein 3.6g	Sodium 368mg	Calcium 75mg

Tabbouleh-Vegetable Salad

Tabbouleh-Vegetable Salad

1 cup bulgur (cracked wheat), uncooked
2 cups canned no-salt-added chicken broth
3 cloves garlic, minced and divided
1 (15-ounce) can whole baby corn, drained
1 (14-ounce) can artichoke hearts, drained
1¼ cups sliced green onions
½ cup minced fresh mint
½ cup minced fresh parsley
¼ cup sliced ripe olives
¼ cup commercial oil-free Italian dressing
3 tablespoons fresh lemon juice
5 sun-dried tomatoes (packed in oil), drained and cut into thin strips
2 ounces feta cheese, crumbled
Romaine lettuce leaves (optional)
Lemon slices (optional)

Combine bulgur, broth, and 1 minced clove garlic in a saucepan; bring to a boil. Cover, reduce heat, and simmer 15 minutes or until bulgur is tender and liquid is absorbed. Let cool.

Cut each ear of corn into thirds. Cut artichoke hearts into quarters. Combine corn, artichoke hearts, bulgur, remaining 2 minced cloves garlic, green onions, and next 7 ingredients in a large bowl; toss well. Cover and chill at least 2 hours.

If desired, spoon bulgur mixture into a lettuce-lined serving bowl, and garnish with lemon slices. Yield: 8 servings (143 calories per 1-cup serving).

Per Serving:

Fat 3.0g	Carbohydrate 25.1g	Fiber 5.8g
saturated fat 1.4g	Cholesterol 6mg	Iron 1.9mg
Protein 5.9g	Sodium 462mg	Calcium 87mg

Herbed Rice-Stuffed Tomatoes

This hearty grain salad contains only 8 percent calories from fat.

1   cup long-grain rice, uncooked
5   medium tomatoes
¾   cup minced fresh parsley
½   cup nonfat mayonnaise
¼   cup minced shallots
3   tablespoons lemon juice
1   teaspoon dried tarragon
2   teaspoons Dijon mustard
1   teaspoon olive oil
¼   teaspoon salt
¼   teaspoon pepper
1   clove garlic, minced
    Fresh parsley sprigs (optional)
    Fresh tarragon sprigs (optional)

Cook rice according to package directions, omitting salt and fat. Transfer rice to a large bowl; cover and chill 1 hour.

Cut top off each tomato. Scoop out pulp, leaving shells intact. Reserve pulp for another use. Invert tomato shells on paper towels; let stand 30 minutes.

Combine minced parsley and remaining ingredients. Add to rice; toss. Cover; chill 30 minutes.

To serve, spoon ½ cup rice mixture into each tomato shell. If desired, garnish with parsley and tarragon. Yield: 5 servings (199 calories per serving).

Per Serving:

Fat 1.7g	Carbohydrate 42.2g	Fiber 2.1g
saturated fat 0.2g	Cholesterol 0mg	Iron 2.8mg
Protein 4.1g	Sodium 497mg	Calcium 62mg

Exercising for Two

There is good news for pregnant women who want to stay in shape. New guidelines for exercise from the American College of Obstetricians and Gynecologists (ACOG) encourage you to exercise. And the benefits of regular exercise make it well worth your effort.

Guidelines:

• Work with your physician to tailor exercise goals to your particular fitness level and condition of pregnancy.
• If you were physically active prior to your pregnancy, you are no longer limited to a maximum heartrate of 140 beats per minute.
• If you were not active prior to your pregnancy, start out slowly with a low-intensity activity, such as walking, and add intensity over time.

Benefits:

• Strong, well-conditioned muscles, particularly in the back and abdomen, will help with control and pushing during labor. (They will not make it easier, however.) And recovery of muscle control and tone will come back much faster to strong abs and backs.
• Regular aerobic exercise, such as walking, will help regulate your digestion—a big help during pregnancy.
• Any endurance exercise will condition you for the rigors of labor. Again, it won't make labor any faster or easier, but if you're fit you'll endure the often lengthy ordeal a lot better.
• Any activity will improve your confidence and self-image.

Southwestern Bean and Pasta Salad

If you plan to serve this salad cold, chill the pasta mixture and dressing separately. Combine the two just before serving to keep the pasta from absorbing all the dressing.

8   ounces rotini pasta, uncooked
1   cup frozen whole-kernel corn, thawed
½   cup diced sweet red pepper
½   cup diced purple onion
½   cup minced fresh cilantro
1   (16-ounce) can dark red kidney beans, drained
1   (4½-ounce) can chopped green chiles
¾   cup nonfat mayonnaise
2   tablespoons cider vinegar
2   teaspoons chili powder
1   teaspoon ground cumin
¼   teaspoon salt
¼   teaspoon pepper
1   large clove garlic, minced

Cook pasta according to package directions, omitting salt and fat. Drain; rinse with cold water, and drain again. Place pasta in a large bowl. Add corn and next 5 ingredients; toss well.

Combine mayonnaise and remaining ingredients, stirring well. Pour mayonnaise mixture over pasta mixture; toss well. Yield: 8 servings (225 calories per 1-cup serving).

Per Serving:

Fat 0.9g	Carbohydrate 45.7g	Fiber 4.0g
saturated fat 0.1g	Cholesterol 0mg	Iron 3.4mg
Protein 9.7g	Sodium 537mg	Calcium 57mg

Tuna Pasta Salad

4   ounces tricolor fusilli pasta, uncooked
1   cup frozen English peas, thawed
½   cup diced celery
½   cup diced carrot
½   cup minced fresh parsley
¼   cup diced green pepper
¼   cup diced sweet red pepper
¼   cup minced onion
¼   cup sliced ripe olives
2   cloves garlic, minced
1   (6-ounce) can low-sodium tuna in water, drained
½   cup nonfat mayonnaise
½   cup nonfat sour cream
1   tablespoon lemon juice
2   teaspoons Dijon mustard
¼   teaspoon pepper

Cook pasta according to package directions, omitting salt and fat. Drain pasta; rinse under cold water, and drain again. Place pasta in a large bowl. Add peas and next 9 ingredients, tossing gently.

Combine mayonnaise and remaining ingredients in a small bowl, stirring well. Pour mayonnaise mixture over pasta mixture, and toss well. Cover and chill thoroughly. Toss gently before serving. Yield: 4 servings (266 calories per 1½-cup serving).

Per Serving:

Fat 5.5g	Carbohydrate 38.8g	Fiber 3.9g
saturated fat 2.6g	Cholesterol 21mg	Iron 3.0mg
Protein 15.3g	Sodium 609mg	Calcium 108mg

Warm Sesame Pork Salad

(pictured on page 175)

1 (1-pound) pork tenderloin
⅓ cup firmly packed brown sugar
½ cup low-sodium soy sauce
⅓ cup dry sherry
3 tablespoons rice wine vinegar
2 teaspoons dark sesame oil
1½ teaspoons peeled, grated gingerroot
¼ teaspoon pepper
¼ teaspoon ground red pepper
   Vegetable cooking spray
3 cups torn fresh spinach
1 cup torn arugula
1 cup torn watercress
½ cup fresh bean sprouts
½ cup sweet red pepper strips
2 tablespoons thinly sliced green onions
1 tablespoon sesame seeds
   Flowering chives (optional)

Trim fat from tenderloin. Place tenderloin in a large heavy-duty, zip-top plastic bag.

Combine brown sugar and next 7 ingredients. Pour half of soy mixture over tenderloin; reserve remaining soy mixture. Seal bag, and shake until tenderloin is well coated. Marinate in refrigerator at least 2 hours, turning once. Remove tenderloin from marinade; discard marinade.

Place tenderloin on a rack in a roasting pan coated with cooking spray. Insert meat thermometer into thickest part of tenderloin, if desired. Bake at 375° for 30 to 35 minutes or until meat thermometer registers 160°. Let stand 5 minutes; cut diagonally across grain into thin slices.

Combine spinach and next 4 ingredients; toss gently. Place 1 cup spinach mixture on each individual salad plate. Arrange pork slices evenly over spinach mixture on each plate.

Pour reserved soy sauce mixture into a small saucepan; place over medium heat. Cook just until thoroughly heated, stirring occasionally. Drizzle warm soy sauce mixture over tenderloin; sprinkle with green onions and sesame seeds.

Garnish with chives, if desired. Yield: 6 servings (154 calories per serving).

Per Serving:

Fat 4.9g	Carbohydrate 8.6g	Fiber 1.4g
saturated fat 1.2g	Cholesterol 53mg	Iron 2.0mg
Protein 17.8g	Sodium 317mg	Calcium 68mg

Curried Chicken Salad Platter

1 fennel bulb (about 1 pound)
1 pound skinned, boned chicken breasts
1 cup canned no-salt-added chicken broth, undiluted
¼ cup dry white wine
½ cup nonfat mayonnaise
¼ cup nonfat sour cream
¼ cup plain nonfat yogurt
1 tablespoon minced onion
1 teaspoon curry powder
⅛ teaspoon salt
1 clove garlic, minced
   Bibb lettuce leaves (optional)
1 cup peeled, sliced banana
1 cup peeled, sliced kiwifruit
1 cup sliced fresh strawberries
4 (1-inch-thick) slices cantaloupe

Trim tough stalks from fennel. Cut bulb in half lengthwise; remove core.

Combine fennel and next 3 ingredients in a Dutch oven; bring to a boil. Cover, reduce heat, and simmer 15 minutes or until chicken is done. Remove chicken from broth, discarding fennel and broth. Cut chicken into ½-inch cubes. Cover and chill.

Combine mayonnaise and next 6 ingredients, stirring well. Add chicken; stir well.

Spoon chicken mixture onto individual lettuce-lined salad plates, if desired. Arrange fruit evenly around chicken mixture. Yield: 4 servings (296 calories per serving).

Per Serving:

Fat 4.0g	Carbohydrate 34.9g	Fiber 5.1g
saturated fat 1.2g	Cholesterol 73mg	Iron 1.7mg
Protein 30.5g	Sodium 550mg	Calcium 125mg

Stone Crab Claws with Creamy Dijon Dressing

2   tablespoons nonfat mayonnaise
2   tablespoons nonfat sour cream
2   teaspoons dry white wine
2   teaspoons lemon juice
2   teaspoons Dijon mustard
1   teaspoon prepared horseradish
½   teaspoon prepared mustard
4   cups tightly packed watercress leaves
1   cup shredded iceberg lettuce
½   cup sliced radishes
2   tablespoons chopped pecans, toasted
3½   tablespoons commercial reduced-calorie
     Italian dressing
2   pounds cooked stone crab claws,
     chilled

Combine first 7 ingredients in a small bowl; cover and chill for at least 3 hours.

Combine watercress and next 4 ingredients in a medium bowl. Toss well, and set aside.

Crack all sections of crab claw shells with a hammer or nutcracker except the black-tipped claw portion. Remove the cracked shell, leaving meat attached to the intact claw.

To serve, place 1¼ cups watercress mixture on each individual serving plate. Top evenly with crab claws. Serve with mustard mixture. Yield: 4 servings (135 calories per serving).

Per Serving:

Fat 4.4g	Carbohydrate 5.1g	Fiber 1.0g
saturated fat 0.4g	Cholesterol 80mg	Iron 1.0mg
Protein 17.7g	Sodium 606mg	Calcium 134mg

Stone crab claws are very large black-tipped crab claws. These claws are marketed cooked because if they are frozen raw, the meat will stick to the shell.

To crack stone crab claws, use a hammer or seafood cracker to crack all sections of shell except the black-tipped portion. Remove cracked shell, leaving black-tipped portion intact.

For this recipe, place claws on watercress mixture and serve with mustard dressing.

Shrimp and Spinach Salad

Shrimp and Spinach Salad

½ cup plain nonfat yogurt
½ cup nonfat mayonnaise-type salad
    dressing
2 tablespoons grated orange rind
1 tablespoon crystallized ginger
2 tablespoons unsweetened orange
    juice
2 tablespoons lime juice
2 pounds unpeeled medium-size fresh
    shrimp
6 cups water
1 pound fresh spinach
1 cup julienne-sliced jicama
16 tear drop cherry tomatoes, halved
1 medium papaya, peeled, seeded, and
    sliced
    Lime zest (optional)
    Lemon zest (optional)

Combine first 6 ingredients in container of an electric blender; cover and process until smooth, stopping once to scrape down sides. Chill.

Peel and devein shrimp. Bring 6 cups water to a boil in a medium saucepan; add shrimp. Cook 3 to 5 minutes or until shrimp turn pink. Drain well; rinse with cold water. Cover and chill.

Remove and discard stems from spinach; wash leaves thoroughly, and pat dry. Tear spinach into bite-size pieces.

Place spinach evenly on individual salad plates. Arrange shrimp, jicama, cherry tomatoes, and papaya evenly over spinach. Top with yogurt mixture. If desired, garnish with lime and lemon zest. Yield: 4 servings (216 calories per serving).

Per Serving:		
Fat 1.7g	Carbohydrate 23.7g	Fiber 3.1g
saturated fat 0.4g	Cholesterol 222mg	Iron 5.8mg
Protein 27.5g	Sodium 596mg	Calcium 169mg

Orange-Grapefruit Dressing

1   cup orange-grapefruit juice, divided
3   tablespoons orange marmalade
3   tablespoons cider vinegar
1   teaspoon grated orange rind
2   teaspoons Dijon mustard
¼   teaspoon garlic powder
¼   teaspoon onion powder
2   teaspoons cornstarch

Combine ¾ cup orange-grapefruit juice and next 6 ingredients in a small saucepan. Combine remaining ¼ cup juice and cornstarch, stirring well.

Add cornstarch mixture to juice mixture, stirring constantly. Bring to a boil over medium heat, stirring constantly; cook 1 minute. Cover and chill thoroughly. Serve with salad greens. Yield: 1¼ cups plus 2 tablespoons (14 calories per tablespoon).

Per Tablespoon:		
Fat 0.0g	Carbohydrate 3.4g	Fiber 0g
saturated fat 0.0g	Cholesterol 0mg	Iron 0mg
Protein 0.1g	Sodium 15mg	Calcium 2mg

Creamy Poppy Seed Dressing

½   cup nonfat mayonnaise-type salad dressing
½   cup nonfat sour cream
½   cup unsweetened orange juice
1   tablespoon poppy seeds
1   teaspoon sugar
2   teaspoons lemon juice
⅛   teaspoon pepper

Combine all ingredients in a bowl, stirring with a wire whisk until smooth. Cover and chill thoroughly. Serve with fresh fruit or salad greens. Yield: 1½ cups (12 calories per tablespoon).

Per Tablespoon:		
Fat 0.2g	Carbohydrate 2.2g	Fiber 0g
saturated fat 0.0g	Cholesterol 0mg	Iron 0mg
Protein 0.4g	Sodium 50mg	Calcium 17mg

Dijon-Herb Dressing

⅓   cup nonfat mayonnaise
⅓   cup water
¼   cup minced fresh parsley
2   tablespoons rice wine vinegar
1   tablespoon Dijon mustard
½   teaspoon sugar
⅛   teaspoon freshly ground pepper
1   clove garlic, minced

Combine all ingredients in a small bowl, stirring well. Cover and chill thoroughly. Serve with salad greens or fresh raw vegetables. Yield: ¾ cup (9 calories per tablespoon).

Per Tablespoon:		
Fat 0.1g	Carbohydrate 1.7g	Fiber 0g
saturated fat 0.0g	Cholesterol 0mg	Iron 0mg
Protein 0.0g	Sodium 123mg	Calcium 8mg

Creamy Garlic Dressing

Nonfat cream cheese makes a velvety smooth base for this fat-free dressing.

1   (8-ounce) package nonfat cream cheese, softened
⅓   cup skim milk
1   tablespoon tarragon vinegar
½   cup minced shallots
1   teaspoon dried parsley flakes
¼   teaspoon salt
¼   teaspoon freshly ground pepper
2   large cloves garlic, minced

Beat cream cheese at medium speed of an electric mixer until creamy. Add milk and vinegar, beating until smooth. Stir in shallots and remaining ingredients. Cover and chill thoroughly. Serve with salad greens or potato salad. Yield: 1½ cups (11 calories per tablespoon).

Per Tablespoon:		
Fat 0.0g	Carbohydrate 1.0g	Fiber 0g
saturated fat 0.0g	Cholesterol 2mg	Iron 0.1mg
Protein 1.5g	Sodium 83mg	Calcium 32mg

Parmesan-Peppercorn Dressing

1 cup nonfat mayonnaise
¾ cup plus 2 tablespoons nonfat buttermilk
½ cup nonfat cream cheese, softened
¼ cup minced fresh parsley
2 tablespoons grated Parmesan cheese
2 tablespoons minced onion
1 teaspoon coarsely ground pepper
1 teaspoon salt-free lemon-pepper seasoning
1 teaspoon freeze-dried chives
½ teaspoon dried basil
½ teaspoon dried tarragon
1 clove garlic, minced

Combine first 3 ingredients in small bowl, stirring well. Add parsley and remaining ingredients; stir until smooth. Cover and chill thoroughly. Serve with salad greens. Yield: 2¼ cups plus 2 tablespoons (13 calories per tablespoon).

Per Tablespoon:

Fat 0.2g	Carbohydrate 1.9g	Fiber 0.1g
saturated fat 0.1g	Cholesterol 1mg	Iron 0.1mg
Protein 0.9g	Sodium 115mg	Calcium 32mg

Tarragon Dressing

Tarragon is an aromatic herb often used in French cuisine. It has a distinctive anise-like flavor.

½ cup chopped fresh tarragon
½ cup nonfat mayonnaise
½ cup nonfat buttermilk
2 tablespoons minced shallots
1 tablespoon tarragon vinegar
1 tablespoon dry white wine
1 teaspoon sugar
⅛ teaspoon salt
¼ teaspoon pepper
1 clove garlic, minced

Combine all ingredients in container of an electric blender; cover and process until smooth. Transfer to a small bowl. Cover and chill

thoroughly. Serve with salad greens. Yield: 1 cup plus 2 tablespoons (13 calories per tablespoon).

Per Tablespoon:

Fat 0.1g	Carbohydrate 2.7g	Fiber 0.1g
saturated fat 0.0g	Cholesterol 0mg	Iron 0.3mg
Protein 0.5g	Sodium 109mg	Calcium 26mg

Creamy Pesto Dressing

½ cup loosely packed fresh basil leaves
½ cup nonfat mayonnaise
¼ cup nonfat sour cream
2 tablespoons pine nuts
2 tablespoons skim milk
2 tablespoons white wine vinegar
⅛ teaspoon pepper
2 large cloves garlic, minced

Combine all ingredients in container of an electric blender; cover and process until smooth, stopping once to scrape down sides. Transfer mixture to a small bowl. Cover and chill thoroughly. Serve with salad greens, pasta salad, or grain salad. Yield: 1 cup plus 2 tablespoons (18 calories per tablespoon).

Per Tablespoon:

Fat 1.0g	Carbohydrate 2.1g	Fiber 0.1g
saturated fat 0.2g	Cholesterol 0mg	Iron 0.1mg
Protein 0.5g	Sodium 89mg	Calcium 15mg

Ham and Apple Sandwiches (page 193)

Sandwiches & Snacks

Peppery Vegetable Confetti on Dark Rye

Here's a vegetarian sandwich that will fill you up. The filling is hearty, and the flavor is intense.

      Butter-flavored vegetable cooking spray
1½ teaspoons reduced-calorie margarine
 ½ cup chopped zucchini
 ½ cup shredded carrot
 ½ cup sliced fresh mushrooms
 ¼ cup chopped sweet red pepper
 ¼ cup chopped onion
 ½ teaspoon pepper
 ½ teaspoon hot sauce
 1 clove garlic, minced
 4 slices dark rye bread
 2 ounces reduced-fat Swiss cheese, sliced

Coat a large nonstick skillet with cooking spray; add margarine. Place over medium-high heat until margarine melts. Add zucchini and next 7 ingredients; sauté until vegetables are tender and liquid evaporates. Transfer to a bowl; set aside, and keep warm.

Coat skillet with cooking spray. Place bread slices in skillet. Place cheese slices over 2 slices of bread. Cook over low heat until cheese melts and bread is lightly browned. Transfer to individual serving plates. Spoon vegetable mixture evenly over cheese. Top with remaining 2 bread slices. Serve immediately. Yield: 2 servings (346 calories per serving).

Per Serving:

Fat 8.6g	Carbohydrate 52.1g	Fiber 5.7g
saturated fat 3.1g	Cholesterol 18mg	Iron 2.4mg
Protein 18.8g	Sodium 552mg	Calcium 420mg

Grilled Spinach and Cheese Sandwiches

      Vegetable cooking spray
 1 cup chopped onion
 ¼ teaspoon ground oregano
 1 clove garlic, minced
 1 (10-ounce) package frozen chopped spinach, thawed
 ⅓ cup nonfat sour cream
 2 tablespoons prepared horseradish
12 slices whole wheat bread
1¼ cups (5 ounces) shredded reduced-fat Monterey Jack cheese
 2 tablespoons reduced-calorie margarine, melted

Coat a nonstick skillet with cooking spray. Place over medium-high heat until hot. Add onion, oregano, and garlic; sauté until onion is tender. Add spinach, and cook until liquid evaporates, stirring frequently. Remove from heat; set aside, and keep warm.

Combine sour cream and horseradish, stirring well. Spread sour cream mixture over 6 bread slices. Spoon spinach mixture over sour cream mixture. Sprinkle cheese evenly over spinach mixture; top with remaining bread slices.

Brush one side of 2 sandwiches with 1 teaspoon margarine. Coat a large nonstick skillet with cooking spray. Place over medium heat until hot. Place 2 sandwiches, margarine side down, in skillet; cook until bread is lightly browned. Brush tops of sandwiches in skillet with 1 teaspoon margarine. Turn sandwiches, and cook until bread is lightly browned and cheese melts. Repeat procedure twice with remaining sandwiches and margarine. Serve immediately. Yield: 6 servings (247 calories per serving).

Per Serving:

Fat 9.0g	Carbohydrate 29.7g	Fiber 3.8g
saturated fat 3.6g	Cholesterol 17mg	Iron 2.2mg
Protein 14.8g	Sodium 500mg	Calcium 315mg

Inside Out Pizza

A pizza sandwich? Kids will love it! You can toss a salad and slice some apples for quick side dishes.

1   cup plus 1 tablespoon bread flour, divided
½   cup whole wheat flour
½   teaspoon sugar
¼   teaspoon salt
1   package active dry yeast
⅔   cup hot water (120° to 130°)
½   teaspoon olive oil
     Vegetable cooking spray
4   ounces ultra-lean ground beef
1   cup chopped onion
1   clove garlic, minced
1   cup commercial fat-free spaghetti sauce
⅛   teaspoon salt
½   cup (2 ounces) shredded part-skim
     mozzarella cheese

Combine 1 cup bread flour and next 4 ingredients in a large mixing bowl.

Gradually add water and oil to flour mixture, beating well at low speed of an electric mixer. Beat 2 additional minutes at medium speed.

Sprinkle remaining 1 tablespoon bread flour evenly over work surface. Turn dough out onto floured surface; knead until smooth and elastic (about 5 minutes). Place dough in a large bowl coated with cooking spray, turning to coat top. Cover and let rise in a warm place (85°), free from drafts, 1 hour or until doubled in bulk.

Punch dough down; turn out onto work surface, and knead lightly 4 or 5 times. Press dough onto a 12-inch pizza pan coated with cooking spray; set aside.

Coat a large nonstick skillet with cooking spray; place over medium-high heat until hot. Add ground beef, onion, and garlic, and cook until beef is browned, stirring until it crumbles; drain, if necessary. Add spaghetti sauce and salt. Bring to a boil. Cover, reduce heat, and simmer 10 minutes, stirring occasionally.

Spoon meat mixture over half of dough in pizza pan, leaving a ½-inch border; sprinkle cheese over meat mixture. Moisten edge of dough with water. Fold uncoated half of dough over meat mixture to form a half circle; seal edges of dough by firmly pressing with a fork dipped in flour. Bake at 375° for 20 minutes or until golden. Cut pizza into 4 wedges. Serve warm. Yield: 4 servings (306 calories per serving).

Per Serving:
Fat 5.8g	Carbohydrate 47.6g	Fiber 5.3g
saturated fat 2.4g	Cholesterol 26mg	Iron 3.2mg
Protein 16.8g	Sodium 523mg	Calcium 117mg

Barbecued Chicken Sandwiches

¾   cup chopped onion
⅔   cup no-salt-added tomato sauce
3   tablespoons sugar
2   tablespoons balsamic vinegar
2   teaspoons garlic powder
1   teaspoon celery seeds
1   teaspoon chili powder
2   teaspoons low-sodium Worcestershire
     sauce
¼   teaspoon salt
2   cups chopped cooked chicken breast
     (skinned before cooking and cooked
     without salt)
4   reduced-calorie whole wheat hamburger
     buns

Combine first 9 ingredients. Set aside ¼ cup tomato mixture.

Combine remaining tomato mixture and chicken in an 11- x 7- x 1½-inch baking dish, stirring well. Cover and bake at 350° for 30 minutes or until thoroughly heated.

Spoon ½ cup chicken mixture onto bottom half of each bun; drizzle reserved tomato mixture evenly over each serving. Top with remaining bun halves. Yield: 4 servings (268 calories per serving).

Per Serving:
Fat 3.8g	Carbohydrate 31.9g	Fiber 2.2g
saturated fat 1.3g	Cholesterol 60mg	Iron 2.9mg
Protein 25.1g	Sodium 446mg	Calcium 37mg

Chicken Caesar Sandwiches

Chicken Caesar Sandwiches

¼ cup lemon juice
1 tablespoon olive oil
1 teaspoon freshly ground pepper
2 teaspoons low-sodium Worcestershire sauce
1½ teaspoons anchovy paste
2 cloves garlic, minced
4 (4-ounce) skinned, boned chicken breast halves
8 (½-inch-thick) slices French bread
1 clove garlic, halved
 Butter-flavored vegetable cooking spray
1 cup shredded romaine lettuce
1½ teaspoons freshly grated Parmesan cheese

Combine first 6 ingredients in a small bowl. Pour half of lemon juice mixture into a heavy-duty, zip-top plastic bag. Set aside remaining lemon juice mixture. Add chicken to bag; seal bag, and shake until chicken is well coated. Marinate in refrigerator 2 hours, turning bag occasionally.

Rub bread slices evenly with halved garlic; coat bread with cooking spray.

Remove chicken from marinade, reserving marinade. Place marinade in a small microwave-safe bowl. Microwave at HIGH 45 seconds or until marinade comes to a boil.

Coat grill rack with cooking spray; place on grill over medium-hot coals (350° to 400°). Place chicken and bread slices on rack; grill, covered, 4 minutes on each side or until chicken is done and bread slices are toasted; baste chicken frequently with reserved marinade.

Combine lettuce and cheese; drizzle with remaining half of lemon juice mixture, and toss.

Arrange lettuce mixture over 4 slices of bread. Place chicken over lettuce mixture. Top with remaining bread slices. Serve immediately. Yield: 4 servings (296 calories per serving).

Per Serving:

Fat 8.0g	Carbohydrate 22.7g	Fiber 1.2g
saturated fat 1.7g	Cholesterol 74mg	Iron 2.0mg
Protein 30.8g	Sodium 551mg	Calcium 49mg

Oven-Fried Catfish Sandwiches

4 (4-ounce) farm-raised catfish fillets
½ teaspoon coarsely ground pepper
⅔ cup corn flake crumbs
1 teaspoon paprika
4 egg whites, lightly beaten
 Vegetable cooking spray
¼ cup commercial fat-free Thousand Island
  dressing
¼ cup nonfat sour cream
¼ teaspoon ground red pepper
4 reduced-calorie whole wheat hamburger
  buns
4 green leaf lettuce leaves
4 tomato slices

Sprinkle catfish with ½ teaspoon pepper.
 Combine corn flake crumbs and paprika in a small bowl, stirring well. Dip fillets in egg whites; dredge in cereal mixture. Place fillets on a baking sheet coated with cooking spray. Bake at 400° for 25 to 30 minutes or until fish flakes easily when tested with a fork.
 Combine salad dressing, sour cream, and red pepper in a small bowl, stirring well. Spread salad dressing mixture evenly over top half of each bun. Place a lettuce leaf and a tomato slice on bottom half of each bun; top each with a fish fillet. Place remaining bun halves, coated side down, over fillets. Yield: 4 servings (321 calories per serving).

Per Serving:

Fat 6.2g	Carbohydrate 33.7g	Fiber 1.7g
saturated fat 1.7g	Cholesterol 66mg	Iron 3.8mg
Protein 29.6g	Sodium 600mg	Calcium 57mg

Ham and Apple Sandwiches

(pictured on page 189)

½ cup apple butter
2 teaspoons grated onion
½ teaspoon dry mustard
8 (1-ounce) slices raisin bread, toasted
¼ pound thinly sliced reduced-fat,
  low-salt ham
2 ounces Edam cheese, thinly sliced
1 small Red Delicious apple, cored and
  sliced crosswise into rings
 Small apple wedges (optional)

Combine apple butter, onion, and mustard in a small bowl, stirring well. Spread apple butter mixture evenly over one side of bread slices.
 Place ham, cheese, and apple rings evenly over apple butter mixture on 4 bread slices. Top with remaining bread slices, coated side down. Garnish with apple wedges, if desired. Yield: 4 servings (322 calories per serving).

Per Serving:

Fat 7.2g	Carbohydrate 53.7g	Fiber 3.3g
saturated fat 3.4g	Cholesterol 28mg	Iron 0.9mg
Protein 12.6g	Sodium 564mg	Calcium 151mg

Virtual Cycling Hits the Road

Stationary bicycling may be the most popular form of exercise in the country, according to the National Sporting Goods Association, but it certainly isn't the most exciting. However, the high-tech world of virtual reality is introducing some stimulating changes.

New "interactive" stationary bicycles allow you to sit and pedal in front of a screen showing, for example, the European countryside, while a breeze ruffles your hair and you feel "bumps" in the road under your tires. Just think, in the dead of a snowy winter, you can spin through England's Lake District in May. Look for virtual reality bikes at your local health club soon.

Roasted Pork Sandwiches with Peach-Onion Chutney

Skip the mayo, and top the pork slices with chutney for extra flavor and less fat.

1   cup peeled, chopped fresh peaches
¾   cup chopped onion
⅓   cup raisins
¼   cup firmly packed brown sugar
½   cup white vinegar
1   teaspoon mustard seeds
½   teaspoon ground cinnamon
½   teaspoon peeled, grated gingerroot
¼   teaspoon salt
¼   teaspoon ground cloves
¼   teaspoon ground red pepper
1   small clove garlic, minced
1   (1-pound) pork tenderloin
    Vegetable cooking spray
2   tablespoons spicy brown mustard
6   onion rolls, split and toasted

Combine first 12 ingredients in a small bowl. Cover and let stand at room temperature 8 hours.

Transfer peach mixture to a large saucepan. Bring to a boil; reduce heat, and simmer, uncovered, 1 hour or until peach mixture is thickened, stirring frequently.

Trim fat from tenderloin. Place tenderloin on a rack in a roasting pan coated with cooking spray. Brush mustard evenly over tenderloin. Insert meat thermometer into thickest part of tenderloin, if desired. Bake at 350° for 50 to 55 minutes or until meat thermometer registers 160°. Let pork stand 5 minutes. Slice pork diagonally across grain into thin slices. Arrange pork slices evenly over bottom halves of rolls. Spoon warm peach mixture over pork. Top with remaining roll halves. Serve warm. Yield: 6 servings (348 calories per serving).

Per Serving:

Fat 6.5g	Carbohydrate 51.4g	Fiber 2.7g
saturated fat 2.5g	Cholesterol 53mg	Iron 2.8mg
Protein 22.7g	Sodium 480mg	Calcium 86mg

Should You Belly up to the Energy Bar?

Energy bars, those candy bar-like concoctions of carbohydrates, vitamins, minerals, fat, and protein, promise to deliver as much nutritional punch as a meal, without any fuss. Not surprisingly, these big-bang-in-a-few-bites bars are all the rage; soon we'll see energy bars created for specific sports. So what's keeping you from packing an energy bar in your brown bag every day? Common sense, one hopes.

The real story is that these energy bars don't do any more for the average active adult than a well-balanced diet would do (except eliminate those messy dishes). In many cases, energy bars don't deliver nutrients as well as real food does, and many types of energy bars on the market have fat grams in the double digits or more than 30 percent of calories from fat.

So, if you plan to go on a long hike, an energy bar might be the perfect midtrail snack—easy, unsquishable, and a good supply of carbohydrates—but for most days, just skip the energy bar. Spend your money on fresh pasta instead.

Cornbread-Turkey Sandwiches

Cornbread-Turkey Sandwiches

1 cup yellow cornmeal
1 cup all-purpose flour
2 teaspoons baking powder
½ teaspoon baking soda
½ teaspoon salt
1 cup chopped onion
1 tablespoon sugar
2 jalapeño peppers, seeded and chopped
1½ cups skim milk
½ cup frozen egg substitute, thawed
3 tablespoons vegetable oil
    Vegetable cooking spray
¾ cup commercial cranberry-orange relish
1 pound roasted turkey breast, thinly sliced
    Fresh sage sprigs (optional)

Combine first 8 ingredients in a bowl; make a well in center of mixture. Combine milk, egg substitute, and oil; add to dry ingredients, stirring just until dry ingredients are moistened.

Pour batter into a 9- x 5- x 3-inch loafpan coated with cooking spray. Bake at 400° for 35 minutes or until golden. Remove cornbread from pan, and cool completely on a wire rack.

Cut cornbread into 16 slices; place on an ungreased baking sheet. Broil 5½ inches from heat (with electric oven door partially opened) 2 to 3 minutes on each side or until lightly toasted.

Spread cranberry-orange relish over 1 side of 8 cornbread slices. Place 2 ounces sliced turkey over cranberry relish on each slice; top with remaining bread slices. Garnish with sage sprigs, if desired. Yield: 8 servings (321 calories per serving).

Per Serving:

Fat 7.9g	Carbohydrate 38.6g	Fiber 2.6g
saturated fat 1.7g	Cholesterol 40mg	Iron 2.5mg
Protein 23.1g	Sodium 317mg	Calcium 148mg

Tomato-Cheese Melts

By combining reduced-fat and regular cheeses, we created a hearty snack with an intense cheese flavor but without a lot of fat.

2   onion bagels, split
4   (¼-inch-thick) slices tomato
¼   cup (1 ounce) shredded reduced-fat
      Cheddar cheese
¼   cup crumbled feta cheese
      Ground red pepper (optional)

Place bagel halves on a large ungreased baking sheet; top each with a tomato slice. Sprinkle evenly with cheeses. Sprinkle with ground red pepper, if desired. Broil 3 inches from heat (with electric oven door partially opened) 3 minutes or until cheeses melt. Serve immediately. Yield: 4 servings (193 calories per serving).

Per Serving:

Fat 3.8g	Carbohydrate 30.5g	Fiber 1.6g
saturated fat 2.0g	Cholesterol 11mg	Iron 2.1mg
Protein 9.0g	Sodium 418mg	Calcium 132mg

Spicy Pizza Snacks

      Vegetable cooking spray
3   ounces freshly ground raw turkey
1   tablespoon finely chopped green pepper
1   teaspoon dried onion flakes
1   teaspoon low-sodium Worcestershire sauce
½   teaspoon pepper
¼   teaspoon rubbed sage
¼   cup commercial fat-free spaghetti sauce
6   miniature English muffins, split
6   ounces part-skim mozzarella cheese,
      cut into 24 slices

Coat a nonstick skillet with cooking spray; place over medium-high heat until hot. Add turkey and next 5 ingredients. Cook until turkey is browned, stirring until it crumbles; drain, if necessary. Add spaghetti sauce; cook until heated.

Place English muffin halves on an ungreased baking sheet; broil 5½ inches from heat (with electric oven door partially opened) until lightly toasted.

Spoon 1 tablespoon turkey mixture onto each muffin half; top each serving with 2 slices cheese. Broil 5½ inches from heat (with electric oven door partially opened) until cheese melts. Serve warm. Yield: 1 dozen (102 calories each).

Per Snack:

Fat 3.4g	Carbohydrate 11.2g	Fiber 0.8g
saturated fat 1.7g	Cholesterol 12mg	Iron 0.8mg
Protein 6.4g	Sodium 184mg	Calcium 124mg

Green Chile Dip

Serve this creamy dip with fresh raw vegetables or fat-free potato chips.

1   (4½-ounce) can chopped green chiles
1   cup nonfat sour cream
1   cup nonfat mayonnaise
¼   cup chopped fresh cilantro
1   teaspoon dried onion flakes
½   teaspoon garlic powder
1   pickled jalapeño pepper, seeded
      and minced

Drain chiles; press between paper towels until barely moist.

Combine chiles, sour cream, and remaining ingredients in a medium bowl, stirring well. Cover and chill thoroughly. Yield: 2½ cups (10 calories per tablespoon).

Per Tablespoon:

Fat 0.0g	Carbohydrate 1.8g	Fiber 0g
saturated fat 0.0g	Cholesterol 0mg	Iron 0mg
Protein 0.4g	Sodium 95mg	Calcium 13mg

Smoky Cheddar-Pimiento Spread

This spread is delicious as a light snack on crackers or as a flavorful filling for sandwiches.

½   cup nonfat cream cheese, softened
2   tablespoons reduced-fat mayonnaise
1   teaspoon sugar
2   teaspoons cider vinegar
⅓   cup (1.3 ounces) shredded reduced-fat
      sharp Cheddar cheese
¼   cup (1 ounce) shredded smoked Cheddar
      cheese
¼   cup (1 ounce) shredded nonfat process
      American cheese
1   (2-ounce) jar diced pimiento, drained

Combine first 4 ingredients in a medium bowl; beat at medium speed of an electric mixer until smooth. Stir in cheeses and pimiento. Serve at room temperature or chilled. Yield: 1 cup (29 calories per tablespoon).

Per Tablespoon:

Fat 1.4g	Carbohydrate 1.3g	Fiber 0g
saturated fat 0.7g	Cholesterol 5mg	Iron 0mg
Protein 2.6g	Sodium 118mg	Calcium 56mg

Chutney Spread

Spread this cheesy chutney mixture on bagels, English muffins, raisin bread, or apple slices.

⅓   cup plus 1 tablespoon light process cream
      cheese, softened
¼   cup mango chutney
2   tablespoons nonfat sour cream

Combine all ingredients in a small bowl, stirring until smooth. Yield: ¾ cup (38 calories per tablespoon).

Per Tablespoon:

Fat 1.2g	Carbohydrate 5.3g	Fiber 0g
saturated fat 0.7g	Cholesterol 4mg	Iron 0mg
Protein 0.9g	Sodium 100mg	Calcium 13mg

Crispy Potato Skin Snacks

These crispy, spicy, low-fat snacks will make you forget about high-fat potato chips.

4   (8-ounce) baking potatoes
1½ tablespoons chili powder
2   teaspoons paprika
1   teaspoon ground cumin
½   teaspoon garlic powder
½   teaspoon onion powder
½   teaspoon dried oregano
¼   teaspoon salt
¼   teaspoon ground red pepper
      Butter-flavored vegetable cooking spray
½   cup (2 ounces) finely shredded reduced-fat
      sharp Cheddar cheese

Scrub potatoes; prick each several times with a fork. Bake at 400° for 45 minutes or until done. Let potatoes cool.

Combine chili powder and next 7 ingredients, stirring well; set aside.

Cut potatoes in half lengthwise. Carefully scoop out pulp, leaving ¼-inch-thick shells. Reserve potato pulp for another use. Cut each potato shell into four wedges. Coat wedges with cooking spray; sprinkle evenly with chili powder mixture and cheese. Bake at 400° for 10 minutes or until crisp. Store in an airtight container. Yield: 32 snacks (21 calories each).

Per Snack:

Fat 0.5g	Carbohydrate 3.5g	Fiber 0.4g
saturated fat 0.2g	Cholesterol 1mg	Iron 0.3mg
Protein 0.9g	Sodium 36mg	Calcium 19mg

Peanut Butter Granola Squares

Once the granola cools, it tends to crumble when cut. So cut it into squares while it's warm.

2   cups regular oats, uncooked
1   cup crisp rice cereal
⅓   cup firmly packed brown sugar
¼   cup light corn syrup
2   tablespoons reduced-calorie margarine
¼   cup reduced-fat peanut butter spread
½   teaspoon vanilla extract
    Vegetable cooking spray

Combine oats and rice cereal in a medium bowl, stirring well; set aside.

Combine brown sugar, corn syrup, and margarine in a small saucepan. Cook over medium-high heat, stirring constantly, until margarine melts. Remove from heat; add peanut butter and vanilla, stirring until well blended. Pour peanut butter mixture over cereal mixture; stir well.

Press cereal mixture firmly into an 8-inch square pan coated with cooking spray. Bake at 250° for 45 minutes or until golden. Let cool 10 minutes; cut into 16 squares. Let cool completely in pan. Yield: 16 squares (87 calories each).

Per Square:

Fat 2.8g	Carbohydrate 14.4g	Fiber 0.7g
saturated fat 0.4g	Cholesterol 0mg	Iron 0.4mg
Protein 1.9g	Sodium 46mg	Calcium 7mg

Sugar and Spice Snack Mix

6   cups crispy corn cereal squares
2   cups miniature pretzels
1⅓ cups sugar
2   teaspoons ground cinnamon
1   teaspoon orange extract
3   egg whites, lightly beaten
     Vegetable cooking spray

Combine cereal and pretzels in a large bowl; set aside.

Combine sugar and next 3 ingredients in a medium bowl, stirring well with a wire whisk. Pour sugar mixture over cereal mixture; toss gently to coat.

Spread cereal mixture in a 15- x 10- x 1-inch jelly-roll pan coated with cooking spray. Bake at 275° for 50 minutes or until crisp, stirring every 15 minutes. Cool completely. Store cereal mixture in an airtight container. Yield: 9 cups (61 calories per ¼-cup serving).

Per Serving:

Fat 0.2g	Carbohydrate 13.8g	Fiber 0.1g
saturated fat 0.0g	Cholesterol 0mg	Iron 0.5mg
Protein 0.8g	Sodium 83mg	Calcium 4mg

Southwestern Cocktail Sauce (page 202)

Sauces &
Condiments

Caramel-Apple Sauce

It's hard to believe that this sinfully delicious sauce contains only 1 percent calories from fat.

½   cup low-fat sweetened condensed milk
½   cup coarsely chopped Rome apple
¼   cup unsweetened apple juice
3   tablespoons brown sugar
1   teaspoon vanilla extract

Pour sweetened condensed milk into a 1-quart casserole dish. Cover dish, and place in a large shallow pan. Add hot water to pan to depth of ¼ inch. Bake at 425° for 1 hour or until condensed milk is thick and caramel colored (add hot water to pan as needed). Remove caramelized milk from oven; uncover and let cool.

Combine chopped apple, apple juice, and brown sugar in a medium saucepan. Bring to a boil; cover, reduce heat, and simmer 2 minutes or until apple is tender. Add caramelized milk and vanilla to apple mixture; stir well. Cook, stirring constantly, until thoroughly heated.

Serve warm over fat-free pound cake or nonfat vanilla ice cream. Yield: 1 cup (44 calories per tablespoon).

Per Tablespoon:

Fat 0.4g	Carbohydrate 9.3g	Fiber 0.1g
saturated fat 0.3g	Cholesterol 1mg	Iron 0.1mg
Protein 0.8g	Sodium 11mg	Calcium 23mg

Vanilla Custard Sauce

¼   cup sugar
1½ tablespoons cornstarch
1   cup 1% low-fat milk
½   cup evaporated skimmed milk
1   (3-inch) vanilla bean, split lengthwise
1   egg yolk, beaten

Combine sugar and cornstarch in a medium saucepan. Gradually add low-fat milk and evaporated milk, stirring until smooth. Add vanilla

bean. Cook over medium heat, stirring constantly, until thickened.

Gradually stir about one-fourth of hot mixture into egg yolk; add to remaining hot mixture, stirring constantly. Remove from heat. Remove and discard vanilla bean. Serve warm with fat-free pound cake or fresh fruit. Yield 1½ cups (21 calories per tablespoon).

Per Tablespoon:

Fat 0.3g	Carbohydrate 3.6g	Fiber 0g
saturated fat 0.1g	Cholesterol 10mg	Iron 0mg
Protein 0.9g	Sodium 12mg	Calcium 29mg

Sherry Sauce

Leftover sauce is delicious served the next day, too. Just cover and store it in the refrigerator; then reheat it before serving.

¼   cup sugar
1   tablespoon cornstarch
1   cup evaporated skimmed milk
1   tablespoon margarine
2   tablespoons dry sherry

Combine sugar and cornstarch in a small saucepan. Gradually add evaporated milk, stirring until smooth. Add margarine; bring to a boil over medium heat, stirring constantly, until thickened. Remove from heat; stir in sherry. Serve warm over fat-free pound cake or nonfat ice cream. Yield: 1 cup (35 calories per tablespoon).

Per Tablespoon:

Fat 0.7g	Carbohydrate 5.4g	Fiber 0g
saturated fat 0.2g	Cholesterol 1mg	Iron 0.1mg
Protein 1.2g	Sodium 27mg	Calcium 47mg

White Chocolate-Irish Cream Sauce

White Chocolate-Irish Cream Sauce

⅓ cup sugar
1½ tablespoons cornstarch
⅛ teaspoon salt
1½ cups 1% low-fat milk
3 tablespoons Irish Cream liqueur
2 (1-ounce) squares white chocolate, chopped

Combine first 3 ingredients in a small saucepan. Gradually add milk, stirring until smooth. Cook over medium heat, stirring constantly, until thickened. Cook 1 additional minute, stirring constantly. Remove from heat. Add Irish Cream liqueur and white chocolate, stirring until chocolate melts.

Serve warm over fat-free chocolate pound cake, low-fat chocolate ice cream, or fresh berries. Yield: 1¾ cups plus 3 tablespoons (34 calories per tablespoon).

Per Tablespoon:		
Fat 1.4g	Carbohydrate 4.6g	Fiber 0g
saturated fat 0.8g	Cholesterol 1mg	Iron 0mg
Protein 0.6g	Sodium 20mg	Calcium 18mg

Southwestern Cocktail Sauce

We gave cocktail sauce a Southwestern twist by adding cilantro and jalapeño pepper.
(pictured on page 199)

1   (8-ounce) can no-salt-added tomato sauce
¼   cup chopped fresh cilantro
1   tablespoon finely chopped onion
1½ tablespoons lime juice
1   tablespoon prepared horseradish
1   jalapeño pepper, seeded and chopped
½   teaspoon garlic powder
½   teaspoon onion powder
½   teaspoon salt
⅛   teaspoon hot sauce
    Fresh jalapeño pepper (optional)

Combine first 10 ingredients in a bowl, stirring well. Cover and chill at least 3 hours. To serve, transfer to a serving bowl; garnish with jalapeño pepper, if desired. Serve with fish or shellfish. Yield: 1 cup (7 calories per tablespoon).

Per Tablespoon:

Fat 0.0g	Carbohydrate 1.6g	Fiber 0.3g
saturated fat 0.0g	Cholesterol 0mg	Iron 0.2mg
Protein 0.2g	Sodium 42mg	Calcium 5mg

Lemon-Ginger Sauce

¾   cup canned no-salt-added chicken broth, undiluted
¼   cup fresh lemon juice
1½ tablespoons brown sugar
1   tablespoon finely chopped crystallized ginger
¼   teaspoon salt
¼   teaspoon grated lemon rind
1   tablespoon cornstarch
2   tablespoons water

Combine first 6 ingredients in a small saucepan; bring to a boil, stirring frequently. Cover, reduce heat, and simmer 3 minutes.

Combine cornstarch and water, stirring well. Add cornstarch mixture to broth mixture, stirring constantly. Bring to a boil; cook, stirring constantly, until thickened. Serve warm with chicken, fish, or steamed vegetables. Yield: ¾ cup plus 2 tablespoons (13 calories per tablespoon).

Per Tablespoon:

Fat 0.0g	Carbohydrate 3.3g	Fiber 0g
saturated fat 0.0g	Cholesterol 0mg	Iron 0.2mg
Protein 0.0g	Sodium 43mg	Calcium 4mg

Vinaigrette Sauce

Broth, seasonings, and balsamic vinegar blend together to make a great-tasting sauce that has minimal calories and almost no fat!

¾   cup canned no-salt-added chicken broth, undiluted
2   tablespoons minced fresh parsley
3   tablespoons balsamic vinegar
1   teaspoon onion powder
1   teaspoon paprika
1   teaspoon olive oil
¼   teaspoon salt
1   clove garlic, minced
1   tablespoon cornstarch
1   tablespoon water

Combine first 8 ingredients in a small saucepan; set aside.

Combine cornstarch and water, stirring well. Add cornstarch mixture to broth mixture, stirring until smooth. Cook over medium heat, stirring constantly, until mixture comes to a boil; cook 1 additional minute. Serve with beef, pork, poultry, or steamed vegetables. Yield: 1 cup (7 calories per tablespoon).

Per Tablespoon:

Fat 0.3g	Carbohydrate 0.9g	Fiber 0.1g
saturated fat 0.0g	Cholesterol 0mg	Iron 0.1mg
Protein 0.1g	Sodium 37mg	Calcium 2mg

Creamy Apple-Wine Sauce

1   pound Granny Smith apples, peeled
       and cored
¼   cup water
¼   cup sugar
¼   cup nonfat sour cream
2   tablespoons dry white wine
1½   teaspoons all-purpose flour
½   teaspoon lemon juice
⅛   teaspoon ground cinnamon
       Dash of ground nutmeg

Combine apples and water in a saucepan.
Bring to a boil. Cover and cook 20 minutes or
until apples are tender; drain.

Position knife blade in food processor bowl;
add apples. Process until smooth. Add sugar and
remaining ingredients to apple; process until
combined. Serve warm or chilled with ham or
pork. Yield: 1½ cups (19 calories per tablespoon).

Per Tablespoon:

Fat 0.1g	Carbohydrate 4.5g	Fiber 0.4g
saturated fat 0.0g	Cholesterol 0mg	Iron 0mg
Protein 0.2g	Sodium 2mg	Calcium 4mg

Dillweed-Horseradish Sauce

*This sauce is thick, creamy, and fat free, thanks to
nonfat sour cream and nonfat buttermilk.*

½   cup nonfat sour cream
¼   cup nonfat buttermilk
2   tablespoons minced fresh chives
1   tablespoon chopped fresh
       dillweed
2   teaspoons prepared horseradish

Combine all ingredients in a small bowl, stirring well. Cover and chill at least 8 hours. Serve
with fish. Yield: 1 cup (7 calories per tablespoon).

Per Tablespoon:

Fat 0.0g	Carbohydrate 0.8g	Fiber 0g
saturated fat 0.0g	Cholesterol 0mg	Iron 0.1mg
Protein 0.7g	Sodium 10mg	Calcium 15mg

Tarragon-Onion Sauce

*We recommend using Vidalia, Texas Spring Sweet,
or another sweet onion when they're in season.*

1   tablespoon reduced-calorie margarine
2   cups chopped sweet onion
1   teaspoon dried tarragon
2   tablespoons all-purpose flour
1   tablespoon tarragon vinegar
½   teaspoon pepper
¼   teaspoon salt
1   cup canned no-salt-added chicken broth,
       undiluted
½   cup dry white wine

Melt margarine in a saucepan over medium-
high heat. Add onion and tarragon; sauté 5 minutes or until onion is tender. Stir in flour and next
3 ingredients. Gradually add broth and wine, stirring constantly. Cook over medium heat, stirring
constantly, until thickened. Serve warm with beef
or poultry. Yield: 1½ cups (11 calories per tablespoon).

Per Tablespoon:

Fat 0.3g	Carbohydrate 1.7g	Fiber 0.2g
saturated fat 0.0g	Cholesterol 0mg	Iron 0.1mg
Protein 0.2g	Sodium 30mg	Calcium 3mg

Can You Be Overactive?

Overtraining is not just a risk for advanced
athletes. Even beginners can suffer from being
too ambitious in their workouts. According to
exercise physiologists, the warning signs include
the following:

- **Fatigue.** Generally when you finish an exercise workout, you should be feeling ener-
getic. If you leave the gym feeling tired,
you're pushing yourself too hard.
- **Decline in performance.** If you can't keep
up the same pace as before, it's time for
a break.
- **Aches and pains.** You're doing too much if
your joints and muscles begin to ache and
you begin to injure easily. Time to cut back.

Creamy Herb Sauce

Toss just enough sauce with the pasta to coat the noodles. We recommend ⅓ cup sauce to 1½ cups cooked noodles.

 2   cloves garlic
 2   cups tightly packed fresh parsley
 ¼   cup loosely packed fresh basil leaves
 ¼   cup loosely packed fresh oregano
 1   teaspoon dried marjoram
 ½   teaspoon pepper
 ¼   teaspoon salt
 1   teaspoon olive oil
 1   cup nonfat sour cream
 ½   cup grated Parmesan cheese
 ½   cup skim milk

Position knife blade in food processor bowl. Drop garlic through food chute with processor running; process 3 seconds or until garlic is minced. Add parsley and next 5 ingredients; process 20 seconds or until fresh herbs are minced.

Add olive oil through food chute with processor running; process until herbs are pureed, scraping sides of processor bowl once. Add sour cream, Parmesan cheese, and milk to processor; process 10 seconds or until herb mixture is smooth.

Transfer herb mixture to a small saucepan; cook over low heat, stirring constantly, until thoroughly heated. Serve over pasta. Yield: 1¾ cups plus 2 tablespoons (19 calories per tablespoon).

Per Tablespoon:

Fat 0.8g	Carbohydrate 1.2g	Fiber 0.2g
saturated fat 0.4g	Cholesterol 2mg	Iron 0.3mg
Protein 1.6g	Sodium 64mg	Calcium 48mg

Hearty Tomato Sauce

For a filling meatless entrée, spoon 1 cup sauce over 1½ cups cooked fettuccine (384 calories and 8% calories from fat).

      Olive oil-flavored vegetable cooking spray
 2   teaspoons olive oil
 1½ cups sliced fresh mushrooms
 1½ cups coarsely chopped zucchini
 1   cup coarsely chopped yellow squash
 ½   cup chopped onion
 ½   cup chopped green pepper
 1   tablespoon minced garlic
 4   cups peeled, seeded, and chopped plum tomato
 1¾ cups no-salt-added tomato juice
 1   (6-ounce) can no-salt-added tomato paste
 2   tablespoons chopped fresh basil
 1   tablespoon balsamic vinegar
 2   teaspoons chopped fresh oregano
 1   teaspoon sugar
 ¾   teaspoon salt
 ¼   teaspoon pepper

Coat a large Dutch oven with cooking spray; add oil. Place over medium-high heat until hot. Add mushrooms and next 5 ingredients; sauté 6 minutes or until vegetables are tender.

Stir in tomato and remaining ingredients. Bring to a boil; reduce heat, and simmer, uncovered, 40 minutes or until thickened, stirring occasionally. Serve over pasta. Yield: 7 cups (6 calories per tablespoon).

Per Tablespoon:

Fat 0.1g	Carbohydrate 1.1g	Fiber 0.2g
saturated fat 0.0g	Cholesterol 0mg	Iron 0.1mg
Protein 0.2g	Sodium 18mg	Calcium 2mg

Creamy Herb Sauce

Curried Fruit Chutney

Using canned instead of fresh fruit shortens preparation time without sacrificing flavor.

Vegetable cooking spray
½ cup finely chopped celery
¼ cup finely chopped onion
1 clove garlic, minced
1 (16-ounce) can sliced peaches in juice, drained and chopped
1 (14½-ounce) can pitted tart red cherries in water, drained
1 (8-ounce) can pineapple chunks in juice, drained
½ cup sugar
½ cup raisins
2 tablespoons cider vinegar
1 teaspoon curry powder
1 (3-inch) stick cinnamon
1 (3-inch) vanilla bean

Coat a medium saucepan with cooking spray; place over medium-high heat until hot. Add celery, onion, and garlic; sauté until tender. Add peaches and remaining ingredients. Bring to a boil; reduce heat, and simmer, uncovered, 1 hour or until thickened, stirring occasionally. Remove and discard cinnamon stick and vanilla bean.

Transfer fruit mixture to a bowl. Cover and chill thoroughly. Serve with beef, chicken, or pork. Yield: 2¾ cups (22 calories per tablespoon).

Per Tablespoon:

Fat 0.1g	Carbohydrate 5.5g	Fiber 0.2g
saturated fat 0.0g	Cholesterol 0mg	Iron 0.1mg
Protein 0.2g	Sodium 2mg	Calcium 3mg

Spicy Tomato-Corn Relish

Friends will relish a jar of garden-fresh flavor as a gift. To make a batch large enough to share, just double the recipe.

2 cups finely chopped tomato
1 cup canned whole baby corn, drained and chopped
1 cup finely chopped onion
½ cup chopped fresh parsley
2 jalapeño peppers, seeded and finely chopped
⅓ cup red wine vinegar
3 tablespoons lime juice
1 teaspoon ground cumin
1 teaspoon pepper
½ teaspoon salt
½ teaspoon celery seeds
¼ teaspoon mustard seeds

Combine all ingredients in a large saucepan, stirring well. Bring tomato mixture to a boil over high heat; cook, stirring constantly, 2 minutes. Remove from heat.

Spoon tomato mixture into hot sterilized jars, leaving ½-inch headspace; wipe jar rims. Cover at once with metal lids, and screw on bands. Process in boiling-water bath 10 minutes. Refrigerate after opening. Serve with chicken, fish, or pork. Yield: 3½ cups (4 calories per tablespoon).

Per Tablespoon:

Fat 0.0g	Carbohydrate 0.8g	Fiber 0.2g
saturated fat 0.0g	Cholesterol 0mg	Iron 0.1mg
Protein 0.1g	Sodium 23mg	Calcium 3mg

Mexican Meat Marinade

½ cup minced onion
½ cup no-salt-added vegetable juice
2 tablespoons red wine vinegar
2 teaspoons Dijon mustard
½ teaspoon garlic powder
½ teaspoon ground cumin
½ teaspoon chili powder
¼ teaspoon salt
¼ teaspoon pepper

Combine all ingredients in a small jar. Cover tightly, and shake vigorously.

Chill at least 8 hours. Use half to marinate beef, chicken, or fish before grilling and remainder to baste while grilling. Yield: 1 cup (5 calories per tablespoon).

Per Tablespoon:

Fat 0.1g	Carbohydrate 1.0g	Fiber 0.1g
saturated fat 0.0g	Cholesterol 0mg	Iron 0.1mg
Protein 0.2g	Sodium 58mg	Calcium 3mg

Blueberry-Mint Vinegar

(pictured on page 22)

1 cup loosely packed fresh mint leaves
¾ cup fresh blueberries
1 (3-inch) stick cinnamon
2 cups apple cider vinegar
Fresh mint sprigs (optional)
Cinnamon sticks (optional)
Fresh blueberries (optional)

Place first 3 ingredients in a wide-mouth quart glass jar. Pour vinegar over mint mixture in jar; cover with lid. Let stand at room temperature 2 weeks.

Pour mixture through a wire-mesh strainer lined with 2 layers of cheesecloth into a bowl; discard mint, berries, and cinnamon remaining in strainer. Pour strained vinegar into decorative bottles or jars. Add additional mint sprigs,

cinnamon sticks, and blueberries to bottles, if desired. Seal bottles with a cork or other airtight lid. Use in salad dressings or vinaigrettes. Yield: 1¾ cups (2 calories per tablespoon).

Per Tablespoon:

Fat 0.0g	Carbohydrate 1.0g	Fiber 0g
saturated fat 0.0g	Cholesterol 0mg	Iron 0.1mg
Protein 0.0g	Sodium 0mg	Calcium 1mg

Strawberry-Lemon Vinegar

(pictured on page 22)

2 cups fresh strawberries, hulled
2 teaspoons grated lemon rind
2 cups red wine vinegar
Fresh strawberries (optional)
Lemon rind strips (optional)

Place 2 cups strawberries and grated lemon rind in a wide-mouth quart glass jar. Pour vinegar over berries in jar; cover with lid. Let stand at room temperature 2 weeks.

Pour mixture through a wire-mesh strainer lined with 2 layers of cheesecloth into a bowl; discard strawberries and lemon rind remaining in strainer. Pour strained vinegar into decorative bottles or jars. Add additional strawberries and lemon rind strips to bottles, if desired. Seal bottles with a cork or other airtight lid. Use in salad dressings or vinaigrettes. Yield: 2 cups (2 calories per tablespoon).

Per Tablespoon:

Fat 0.0g	Carbohydrate 0.5g	Fiber 0g
saturated fat 0.0g	Cholesterol 0mg	Iron 0mg
Protein 0.0g	Sodium 0mg	Calcium 0mg

Bouquet Garni Vinegar

½ cup loosely packed fresh parsley sprigs
½ cup loosely packed fresh thyme sprigs
2 bay leaves
2 cups red wine vinegar
   Fresh parsley sprigs (optional)
   Fresh thyme sprigs (optional)

Place ½ cup parsley, ½ cup thyme, and bay leaves in a wide-mouth quart glass jar. Pour vinegar over herbs in jar; cover with lid. Let stand at room temperature 2 weeks.

Pour mixture through a wire-mesh strainer lined with 2 layers of cheesecloth into a bowl; discard herbs remaining in strainer. Pour strained vinegar into decorative bottles or jars. Add additional parsley and thyme sprigs to bottles, if desired. Seal bottles with a cork or other airtight lid. Use in salad dressings or vinaigrettes. Yield: 2 cups (2 calories per tablespoon).

Per Tablespoon:

Fat 0.0g	Carbohydrate 0.0g	Fiber 0g
saturated fat 0.0g	Cholesterol 0mg	Iron 0mg
Protein 0.0g	Sodium 1mg	Calcium 0mg

Peppercorn-Chive Vinegar

½ cup chopped fresh chives
¼ cup whole peppercorns
2 cups white wine vinegar
   Fresh chives (optional)
   Whole peppercorns (optional)

Place chopped chives and ¼ cup peppercorns in a wide-mouth quart glass jar. Pour vinegar over chives and peppercorns in jar; cover with lid. Let stand at room temperature 2 weeks.

Pour mixture through a wire-mesh strainer lined with 2 layers of cheesecloth into a bowl; discard chives and peppercorns remaining in strainer. Pour strained vinegar into decorative bottles or jars. Add additional fresh chives and peppercorns to bottles, if desired. Seal bottles with a cork or other airtight lid. Use in salad dressings or vinaigrettes. Yield: 1¾ cups (2 calories per tablespoon).

Per Tablespoon:

Fat 0.0g	Carbohydrate 0.0g	Fiber 0.3g
saturated fat 0.0g	Cholesterol 0mg	Iron 0mg
Protein 0.0g	Sodium 2mg	Calcium 0mg

Making Flavored Vinegars

Follow these simple steps for making flavored vinegars. For ideas for using flavored vinegars see page 22.

1. Wash jars or bottles in hot, soapy water; rinse and dry completely.

2. Fill jars or bottles with clean, dry herbs or fruit. Pour vinegar over herbs in container. Cover with lid, and let stand 2 weeks.

3. Pour aged vinegar through a wire-mesh strainer lined with 2 layers of cheesecloth into a bowl.

4. Pour strained vinegar into clean decorative bottles or jars. Add fresh herbs or fruit to jars, if desired. Seal bottles with a cork or lid.

Jicama, Corn, and Green Pepper Skillet (page 220)

Side
Dishes

Brandied Apples

Team this spirited side dish with Peppercorn-Crusted Pork Loin (page 160) and steamed fresh asparagus.

½ cup water
2 tablespoons sugar
2 tablespoons raisins
2 tablespoons brandy
½ teaspoon ground cinnamon
4 large Red Delicious apples, cored and sliced

Combine first 5 ingredients in a large saucepan. Bring to a boil over medium heat, stirring until sugar dissolves. Stir in apple. Cover, reduce heat, and simmer 10 minutes or until apple is tender. Yield: 6 servings (103 calories per ¾-cup serving).

Per Serving:

Fat 0.5g	Carbohydrate 26.8g	Fiber 4.1g
saturated fat 0.1g	Cholesterol 0mg	Iron 0.4mg
Protein 0.4g	Sodium 1mg	Calcium 13mg

Minted Grapefruit

4 medium grapefruit, peeled and sectioned
½ cup chopped fresh mint
1 cup unsweetened pineapple juice
3 tablespoons honey
Fresh mint sprigs (optional)

Combine grapefruit and chopped mint in a small bowl, tossing gently.

Combine pineapple juice and honey in a small bowl, stirring well with a wire whisk.

Pour pineapple juice mixture over grapefruit mixture, and toss gently. Garnish with mint sprigs, if desired. Yield: 4 servings (130 calories per 1-cup serving).

Per Serving:

Fat 0.2g	Carbohydrate 33.3g	Fiber 0.9g
saturated fat 0.0g	Cholesterol 0mg	Iron 0.5mg
Protein 1.2g	Sodium 1mg	Calcium 35mg

Spiced Peaches and Pineapple

3½ tablespoons firmly packed brown sugar
2 teaspoons cornstarch
⅛ teaspoon whole cloves
⅛ teaspoon ground cloves
1 (8-ounce) can pineapple tidbits in juice, undrained
3 cups sliced frozen peaches, thawed

Combine brown sugar, cornstarch, whole cloves, and ground cloves in a small saucepan. Stir in pineapple. Cook over medium heat, stirring constantly, until sugar dissolves; stir in peaches.

Bring to a boil; reduce heat, and simmer, uncovered, 5 minutes or until mixture thickens. Serve warm. Yield: 4 servings (126 calories per ½-cup serving).

Per Serving:

Fat 0.1g	Carbohydrate 32.5g	Fiber 2.0g
saturated fat 0.0g	Cholesterol 0mg	Iron 0.5mg
Protein 0.9g	Sodium 6mg	Calcium 23mg

Poached Pineapple

To make preparation a snap, buy peeled, cored fresh pineapple. You'll find it prepackaged in the produce section of the grocery store.

1 medium-size fresh pineapple, peeled and cored
1 cup unsweetened pineapple juice
2 tablespoons sugar
2 tablespoons lemon zest
¼ teaspoon whole cloves
1 (3-inch) stick cinnamon

Cut pineapple lengthwise into 12 spears, and set aside.

Combine pineapple juice and next 4 ingredients in a medium saucepan. Bring to a boil over medium-high heat; cook, stirring constantly, until sugar dissolves. Reduce heat, and simmer, uncovered, 10 minutes.

Add pineapple spears. Bring to a boil; reduce heat, and simmer, uncovered, 8 minutes. Remove and discard cloves and cinnamon stick. Serve warm or chilled. Yield: 4 servings (129 calories per serving).

Per Serving:

Fat 0.7g	Carbohydrate 32.7g	Fiber 2.2g
saturated fat 0.0g	Cholesterol 0mg	Iron 0.7mg
Protein 0.8g	Sodium 2mg	Calcium 23mg

Artichoke and Portabella Mushroom Mélange

1   cup chopped onion
½   cup minced fresh parsley
1   (14½-ounce) can no-salt-added whole tomatoes, undrained and finely chopped
1   (9-ounce) package frozen artichoke hearts, thawed and halved
1   (6-ounce) package sliced fresh portabella mushrooms
1   tablespoon no-salt-added tomato paste
1   teaspoon sugar
1   teaspoon dried basil
½   teaspoon dried thyme
¼   teaspoon salt
⅛   teaspoon pepper
2   cloves garlic, minced
1   tablespoon all-purpose flour
¼   cup dry white wine
¼   cup sliced pimiento-stuffed olives

Combine first 12 ingredients in a large skillet, stirring well. Bring to a boil; cover, reduce heat to medium, and cook 10 minutes or until artichokes are tender, stirring once.

Combine flour and wine, stirring until smooth. Add wine mixture and olives to vegetable mixture; cook, stirring constantly, until thickened. Yield: 4 servings (95 calories per serving).

Per Serving:

Fat 1.2g	Carbohydrate 19.7g	Fiber 2.3g
saturated fat 0.2g	Cholesterol 0mg	Iron 2.4mg
Protein 4.5g	Sodium 277mg	Calcium 84mg

Asparagus with Creamy Chive Sauce

Asparagus is low in calories and fat and is a source of beta carotene, an antioxidant that helps fight disease.

1   pound fresh asparagus spears
½   cup plain nonfat yogurt
2   tablespoons skim milk
4   ounces nonfat cream cheese
2   tablespoons freeze-dried chives
¼   teaspoon salt
⅛   teaspoon garlic powder
⅛   teaspoon pepper

Snap off tough ends of asparagus. Remove scales from stalks with a knife or vegetable peeler, if desired. Arrange asparagus in a vegetable steamer over boiling water. Cover and steam 7 minutes or until crisp-tender; drain. Transfer to a serving platter; set aside, and keep warm.

Combine yogurt, milk, and cream cheese in a small saucepan, stirring well with a wire whisk. Place over medium-high heat; cook, stirring constantly, 5 minutes or until cheese melts and mixture is thoroughly heated. Remove from heat; stir in chives and remaining ingredients. Pour yogurt mixture over asparagus. Yield: 6 servings (43 calories per serving).

Per Serving:

Fat 0.2g	Carbohydrate 5.0g	Fiber 0.6g
saturated fat 0.1g	Cholesterol 4mg	Iron 0.5mg
Protein 5.5g	Sodium 234mg	Calcium 110mg

Bok Choy with Ginger and Water Chestnuts

Follow these bok choy basics: pull off ragged or discolored leaves; then slice the leaves across the rib.

Vegetable cooking spray
1   teaspoon sesame oil
1¼ pounds bok choy, trimmed and thinly
      sliced
½   cup thinly sliced green onions
1   teaspoon peeled, grated gingerroot
2   cloves garlic, minced
1   (8-ounce) can sliced water chestnuts,
      drained
3   tablespoons low-sodium soy sauce

Coat a large nonstick skillet with cooking spray; add oil. Place over medium-high heat until hot. Add bok choy and next 3 ingredients; cover and cook 5 minutes, stirring once.

Add water chestnuts and soy sauce to skillet; cook 1 minute. Yield: 4 servings (59 calories per ¾-cup serving).

Per Serving:
Fat 1.6g	Carbohydrate 9.0g	Fiber 2.0g
saturated fat 0.2g	Cholesterol 0mg	Iron 1.7mg
Protein 2.8g	Sodium 390mg	Calcium 162mg

Sesame Broccoli

2   tablespoons plus 1 teaspoon low-sodium
      soy sauce
1   tablespoon rice wine vinegar
2¼ teaspoons sugar
2   teaspoons sesame oil
¾   teaspoon dried crushed red pepper
2   small cloves garlic, minced
6   cups broccoli flowerets
2   teaspoons sesame seeds, toasted

Combine first 6 ingredients in a nonstick skillet. Place over medium-high heat until hot. Add broccoli, and cook, uncovered, 8 to 10 minutes or until

crisp-tender, stirring occasionally. Sprinkle with sesame seeds. Yield: 4 servings (73 calories per 1-cup serving).

Per Serving:
Fat 3.4g	Carbohydrate 8.7g	Fiber 3.3g
saturated fat 0.5g	Cholesterol 0mg	Iron 1.2mg
Protein 3.4g	Sodium 257mg	Calcium 66mg

Foods for Life

You've known all your life that fruits and vegetables were good for you, and new research is uncovering even more compelling reasons to eat them. Special compounds in these foods may help ward off everything from cancer to heart disease. Here are five more reasons to head straight for the produce aisle.

1. **Apples.** Dutch scientists have found that people who consume large amounts of apples, onions, and tea suffer fewer heart attacks than people who consume very little of these foods. Researchers think that compounds called flavonoids may help curb the formation of the plaque that can clog arteries and precipitate a heart attack.

2. **Broccoli.** Researchers at Johns Hopkins University have identified a chemical in broccoli that can boost the effectiveness of sulforphane, an enzyme that inhibits cancer.

3. **Cranberry Juice.** According to a recent report from Harvard Medical School, drinking a 10-ounce glass of cranberry juice each day may help prevent urinary tract infections. The researchers think that substances in the juice help keep infection-causing bacteria at bay.

4. **Garlic.** After pooling the findings of five clinical trials, researchers from New York Medical College concluded that as little as one-half to one clove of garlic per day can be an effective cholesterol-lowering agent for people with elevated blood-cholesterol levels.

5. **Tomatoes.** Researchers at Cornell University have isolated two substances in tomatoes that could help block cancer. Both P-coumaric and chlorogenic acid indirectly block the formation of cancer-causing compounds called nitrosamines.

Glazed Brussels Sprouts and Baby Carrots

Glazed Brussels Sprouts and Baby Carrots

The sweetest brussels sprouts are small, bright green ones. Be sure to skip over any that look old because they'll taste bitter.

¾ **pound fresh brussels sprouts**
¾ **pound baby carrots, scraped**
2 **teaspoons grated orange rind**
⅓ **cup commercial honey-mustard barbecue sauce**
¼ **cup unsweetened orange juice**
Orange zest (optional)

Wash brussels sprouts thoroughly, and remove discolored leaves. Cut off stem ends, and cut a shallow X in bottom of each sprout.

Place brussels sprouts and carrots in a large saucepan; add water to cover. Bring to a boil; cook 15 minutes or until vegetables are tender. Drain; transfer to a medium bowl.

Combine orange rind, barbecue sauce, and orange juice; add to vegetables, tossing gently. Garnish with orange zest, if desired. Yield: 4 servings (112 calories per 1-cup serving).

Per Serving:		
Fat 0.4g	Carbohydrate 25.2g	Fiber 6.0g
saturated fat 0.1g	Cholesterol 0mg	Iron 1.4mg
Protein 3.3g	Sodium 272mg	Calcium 56mg

Cauliflower with Pimiento-Olive Vinaigrette

4½   cups cauliflower flowerets (about
     1 medium head)
½   cup no-salt-added chicken broth,
     undiluted
¼   cup sliced pimiento-stuffed olives
1   (2-ounce) jar diced pimiento, drained
1   tablespoon lemon juice
1   tablespoon white wine vinegar
2   teaspoons olive oil
½   teaspoon dried oregano
¼   teaspoon salt
¼   teaspoon pepper
1   clove garlic, crushed

Arrange cauliflower in a vegetable steamer over boiling water. Cover and steam 8 minutes or until crisp-tender. Transfer to a serving bowl; set aside, and keep warm.

Combine chicken broth and remaining ingredients in a small saucepan; bring to a boil. Pour over cauliflower; toss gently. Yield: 4 servings (62 calories per 1-cup serving).

Per Serving:

Fat 3.2g	Carbohydrate 7.3g	Fiber 2.9g
saturated fat 0.5g	Cholesterol 0mg	Iron 1.2mg
Protein 2.5g	Sodium 260mg	Calcium 47mg

Italian Eggplant and Rice

If you use regular instead of converted long-grain rice in this recipe, the cooking time may vary slightly.

   Vegetable cooking spray
1   teaspoon olive oil
3¾   cups cubed eggplant
2   cups chopped green pepper
1   cup diced onion
2   cloves garlic, minced
½   cup converted long-grain rice, uncooked
½   cup minced fresh parsley
1   cup water
1   cup no-salt-added tomato sauce
1   (4½-ounce) can chopped green chiles
1   (4-ounce) jar diced pimiento, drained
2   tablespoons capers
2   tablespoons no-salt-added tomato paste
1   tablespoon balsamic vinegar
1   teaspoon dried Italian seasoning
1   teaspoon sugar
¼   teaspoon dried crushed red pepper
1   tablespoon freshly grated Parmesan cheese

Coat a large Dutch oven with cooking spray; add oil. Place over medium-high heat until hot. Add eggplant and next 3 ingredients; sauté 8 to 10 minutes or until vegetables are tender. Reduce heat to low; cook, uncovered, 20 minutes, stirring frequently.

Add rice and next 11 ingredients; bring to a boil over medium-high heat. Cover, reduce heat, and simmer 20 minutes or until rice is tender, stirring occasionally. Sprinkle with Parmesan cheese. Yield: 5 servings (167 calories per 1-cup serving).

Per Serving:

Fat 1.9g	Carbohydrate 34.6g	Fiber 4.0g
saturated fat 0.4g	Cholesterol 0mg	Iron 3.4mg
Protein 4.7g	Sodium 466mg	Calcium 71mg

Roasted Green Beans and Onions

1   pound fresh green beans
1   small purple onion, sliced and separated
     into rings
4   large cloves garlic, cut in half lengthwise
     Olive oil-flavored vegetable cooking spray
½   teaspoon dried thyme
¼   teaspoon salt
¼   teaspoon freshly ground pepper

Wash beans; trim ends, and remove strings. Place beans, onion, and garlic in a 13- x 9- x 2-inch pan coated with cooking spray. Coat vegetables with cooking spray. Sprinkle thyme and salt over vegetables; toss well.

Bake at 450° for 15 minutes or until tender, stirring once. Sprinkle with pepper. Yield: 4 servings (54 calories per ¾-cup serving).

Per Serving:
Fat 0.5g	Carbohydrate 11.8g	Fiber 2.5g
saturated fat 0.0g	Cholesterol 0mg	Iron 1.5mg
Protein 2.5g	Sodium 156mg	Calcium 62mg

Hearty Lentil Potpourri

1   (14¼-ounce) can no-salt-added beef broth
1   cup chopped carrot
¾   cup chopped celery
¾   cup chopped onion
¾   cup frozen whole-kernel corn, thawed
½   cup dried lentils, uncooked
1   tablespoon low-sodium soy sauce
½   teaspoon ground coriander
¼   teaspoon dried basil
¼   teaspoon dried marjoram
¼   teaspoon dried thyme
⅛   teaspoon pepper
2   cloves garlic, minced
¼   teaspoon salt

Combine first 13 ingredients in a Dutch oven. Bring to a boil; cover, reduce heat, and simmer 40 minutes or until lentils and vegetables are tender. Stir in salt; serve immediately. Yield: 5 servings (78 calories per ¾-cup serving).

Per Serving:
Fat 0.4g	Carbohydrate 14.7g	Fiber 3.1g
saturated fat 0.1g	Cholesterol 0mg	Iron 1.3mg
Protein 3.9g	Sodium 225mg	Calcium 29mg

Crispy Onion Rings

(pictured on page 150)

2   large sweet onions (about 1¼ pounds)
6   cups whole wheat flake cereal, finely
     crushed
1   tablespoon chili powder
2   teaspoons sugar
1   teaspoon ground cumin
¼   teaspoon ground red pepper
1   cup frozen egg substitute, thawed
     Vegetable cooking spray

Cut each onion into 4 thick slices; separate into rings. Reserve small rings for another use. Set large rings aside.

Combine cereal and next 4 ingredients; divide mixture in half, and set aside.

Beat egg substitute at high speed of an electric mixer until soft peaks form. Dip half of onion rings in egg substitute; dredge in half of crumb mixture. Place in a single layer on baking sheets coated with cooking spray. Repeat procedure with remaining onion rings, egg substitute, and crumb mixture. Bake at 375° for 10 to 15 minutes or until crisp. Serve warm. Yield: 6 servings (171 calories per serving).

Per Serving:
Fat 1.2g	Carbohydrate 34.4g	Fiber 3.7g
saturated fat 0.1g	Cholesterol 0mg	Iron 6.8mg
Protein 8.0g	Sodium 517mg	Calcium 81mg

Four-Pepper Medley

Vegetable cooking spray
1   teaspoon olive oil
1½ cups thinly sliced Vidalia onion or other
    sweet onion
1   cup julienne-sliced green pepper
1   cup julienne-sliced sweet purple pepper
1   cup julienne-sliced sweet red pepper
1   cup julienne-sliced sweet yellow pepper
¼   teaspoon salt
¼   teaspoon freshly ground pepper
1   clove garlic, minced

Coat a large nonstick skillet with cooking
spray; add oil. Place over medium-high heat until
hot. Add onion and remaining ingredients; sauté
5 minutes or until vegetables are crisp-tender.
Serve immediately. Yield: 6 servings (32 calories
per ¾-cup serving).

Per Serving:

Fat 1.2g	Carbohydrate 5.2g	Fiber 1.5g
saturated fat 0.2g	Cholesterol 0mg	Iron 1.0mg
Protein 0.8g	Sodium 100mg	Calcium 9mg

Seasoned Potatoes and Beans

3   cups cubed Yukon Gold potato or other
    baking potato
1½ cups chopped onion
1   cup canned no-salt-added chicken broth,
    undiluted
¼   teaspoon poultry seasoning
¼   teaspoon salt
⅛   teaspoon pepper
1   clove garlic, minced
1   (15-ounce) can no-salt-added garbanzo
    beans, drained

Combine first 7 ingredients in a large saucepan,
stirring well. Bring to a boil over medium-high
heat; partially cover, reduce heat, and simmer 10
minutes or until potato is tender. Add garbanzo
beans; cook until thoroughly heated. Yield: 6 servings (188 calories per ¾-cup serving).

Per Serving:

Fat 1.3g	Carbohydrate 38.1g	Fiber 4.0g
saturated fat 0.2g	Cholesterol 0mg	Iron 1.8mg
Protein 6.7g	Sodium 199mg	Calcium 39mg

You Say Potato

There's a lot to love about potatoes: They're rich in vitamins and minerals, and they're virtually fat free. And now there are more varieties to choose from than ever before. Here's a sampling:

Yukon Gold: For mashing, baking, frying, or making hash browns, it's hard to beat this round, buttery-tasting potato with its distinctive yellow flesh.

Russet: Best known as the Idaho potato, the russet's mealy texture is good for baking, mashing, and for making scalloped or au gratin dishes.

Round White: This potato with a light tan skin is an excellent choice for salads, chips, and roasting.

Round Red: These waxy-textured, smooth-skinned potatoes are best boiled, roasted, or steamed.

Long White: These potatoes suit most any recipe, especially salads, chips, and casseroles.

Fingerling: These small oval potatoes are perfect for steaming or roasting, and are colorful, too. Look for pink, yellow, blue, or light tan ones.

Yellow Finn: When these tan-skinned potatoes with yellow flesh are steamed or roasted, their flavor may convince you that you don't need butter.

Rose Fir: This member of the round white family is generally small with a waxy texture and pink-to-red skin.

Purple Peruvian: This potato is a conversation piece. Its grayish blue skin and dark blue flesh will make it the most talked-about side dish you've ever served. And its delicate flavor makes it ideal for all preparations.

*For a mail-order source for specialty potatoes, see page 272.

Russet

Yellow Finn

Round Red

Round White

Purple Peruvian

Yukon Gold

Chili-Corn Mashed Potatoes

¾ cup frozen whole-kernel corn, thawed
2½ cups peeled, cubed baking potato
3 tablespoons nonfat sour cream
3 tablespoons skim milk
1 tablespoon reduced-calorie margarine
½ teaspoon chili powder
¼ teaspoon salt
⅛ teaspoon ground cumin

Cook corn according to package directions, omitting salt; drain and set aside.

Place potato in a medium saucepan; add water to cover. Bring to a boil; cover, reduce heat, and simmer 10 minutes or until tender. Drain potato; transfer to a large bowl. Beat at medium speed of an electric mixer 1 minute or until smooth. Add sour cream and next 5 ingredients, beating well. Stir in corn. Yield: 4 servings (139 calories per ¾-cup serving).

Per Serving:		
Fat 2.3g	Carbohydrate 26.8g	Fiber 2.7g
saturated fat 0.4g	Cholesterol 0mg	Iron 1.0mg
Protein 4.2g	Sodium 201mg	Calcium 31mg

Rutabaga and Pear Puree

5½ cups peeled, cubed rutabaga
2 medium-size ripe pears, peeled, cored, and cubed
½ cup unsweetened orange juice
1 tablespoon brown sugar
½ teaspoon onion powder
¼ teaspoon salt
⅛ teaspoon ground white pepper

Combine rutabaga and pear in a large saucepan; add water to cover. Bring to a boil; cover, reduce heat, and simmer 40 to 45 minutes or until tender; drain.

Position knife blade in food processor bowl; add rutabaga mixture, orange juice, and brown sugar. Process until smooth. Transfer puree to a serving bowl; stir in onion powder, salt, and pepper. Yield: 8 servings (68 calories per ½-cup serving).

Per Serving:		
Fat 0.3g	Carbohydrate 16.2g	Fiber 2.0g
saturated fat 0.0g	Cholesterol 0mg	Iron 0.7mg
Protein 1.5g	Sodium 94mg	Calcium 55mg

Cheddar-Stuffed Squash

6 medium-size yellow squash (about 1¾ pounds)
Butter-flavored vegetable cooking spray
½ cup minced onion
½ cup minced green pepper
1 cup soft whole wheat breadcrumbs
⅔ cup (2.6 ounces) shredded reduced-fat sharp Cheddar cheese
1 tablespoon chopped fresh parsley
¼ teaspoon salt
⅛ teaspoon ground red pepper

Cook squash in a large saucepan in boiling water to cover 6 to 8 minutes or until tender; drain. Cut a lengthwise strip from top of each squash; scoop out pulp, leaving ¼-inch-thick shells. Chop pulp and tops; set aside. Invert shells onto paper towels; let drain 30 minutes.

Coat a nonstick skillet with cooking spray; place over medium-high heat until hot. Add onion and green pepper; sauté until tender. Stir in chopped squash, breadcrumbs, and remaining ingredients.

Place squash shells in an 11- x 7- x 1½-inch baking dish coated with cooking spray. Spoon squash mixture into shells. Broil 5½ inches from heat (with electric oven door partially opened) 3 to 5 minutes or until golden. Yield: 6 servings (95 calories per serving).

Per Serving:		
Fat 3.2g	Carbohydrate 12.1g	Fiber 2.9g
saturated fat 1.5g	Cholesterol 9mg	Iron 1.0mg
Protein 6.3g	Sodium 240mg	Calcium 148mg

Sugar Snap Peas with Papaya Salsa

1   cup peeled, seeded, and diced papaya
½   cup chopped fresh cilantro
1   tablespoon minced onion
2   teaspoons lime juice
2   teaspoons rice wine vinegar
⅛   teaspoon salt
⅛   teaspoon ground white pepper
1   pound fresh Sugar Snap peas, trimmed

Combine first 7 ingredients in a small bowl; toss gently, and set aside.

Arrange Sugar Snap peas in a vegetable steamer over boiling water. Cover and steam 3 minutes or until peas are crisp-tender, and drain well.

Transfer Sugar Snap peas to a serving bowl. Spoon papaya mixture over Sugar Snap peas in bowl. Serve immediately. Yield: 4 servings (68 calories per 1-cup serving).

Per Serving:

Fat 0.3g	Carbohydrate 13.6g	Fiber 3.9g
saturated fat 0.1g	Cholesterol 0mg	Iron 2.7mg
Protein 3.5g	Sodium 82mg	Calcium 67mg

Savory Sweet Potatoes and Onions

2   medium onions
     Vegetable cooking spray
2   tablespoons brown sugar
⅛   teaspoon pepper
4   medium-size sweet potatoes, peeled and
        thinly sliced
2   tablespoons maple syrup
1   tablespoon white wine vinegar
1   tablespoon margarine, melted
½   teaspoon dried thyme
¼   teaspoon salt
¼   teaspoon pepper

Thinly slice onions, and cut slices in half. Arrange onion in a 13- x 9- x 2-inch baking dish

coated with cooking spray. Sprinkle brown sugar and ⅛ teaspoon pepper evenly over onion in baking dish. Arrange sweet potato slices over onion, and set aside.

Combine maple syrup, white wine vinegar, margarine, thyme, salt, and pepper in a small bowl, stirring well with a wire whisk. Pour maple syrup mixture over sweet potato and onion. Cover vegetables, and bake at 350° for 1 hour or until potato and onion are tender. Serve with a slotted spoon. Yield: 8 servings (179 calories per serving).

Per Serving:

Fat 2.0g	Carbohydrate 38.9g	Fiber 4.5g
saturated fat 0.4g	Cholesterol 0mg	Iron 1.0mg
Protein 2.5g	Sodium 109mg	Calcium 43mg

Leeks—a Well-Kept Secret

Leeks, which look like large green onions, have a unique sweet onion flavor that makes them a delicious vegetable side dish. When you plan to use leeks, keep these tips in mind:

• When shopping for leeks, look for crisp, green tops, and choose the bundle with the longest white stems. This is the usable part of the vegetable.

• Leeks that are larger than 1½ inches in diameter tend to have a stronger flavor and may be a little tough.

• Store unwashed leeks up to 5 days in a zip-top plastic bag in the vegetable bin of the refrigerator.

• Even clean-looking leeks may hide sand and dirt between their leaves. Clean them thoroughly by pulling the leaves apart under cold running water.

Sugar Snap Peas with Papaya Salsa

Layered Vegetable Casserole

See our tips on page 219 about buying, storing, and cleaning leeks.

⅓   cup minced fresh parsley
1½   tablespoons grated Parmesan cheese
¼   teaspoon salt
1   clove garlic, minced
½   pound small round red potatoes, thinly sliced
     Vegetable cooking spray
1   cup sliced zucchini
1   cup sliced yellow squash
1½   cups sliced fresh mushrooms
½   cup chopped leeks
1   (8-ounce) can no-salt-added tomato sauce
¼   cup (1 ounce) shredded part-skim mozzarella cheese

Combine first 4 ingredients in a small bowl, stirring well.

Place potato in an 11- x 7- x 1½-inch baking dish coated with cooking spray. Sprinkle one-fourth of parsley mixture over potato; top with zucchini. Sprinkle one-fourth of parsley mixture over zucchini; top with yellow squash. Sprinkle one-fourth of parsley mixture over squash; top with sliced mushrooms. Sprinkle remaining parsley mixture over mushrooms; top with leeks.

Pour tomato sauce over layered vegetables. Cover with aluminum foil, and vent. Bake at 350° for 45 minutes. Uncover and sprinkle with mozzarella cheese; bake, uncovered, 5 additional minutes or until cheese melts. Yield: 6 servings (80 calories per serving).

Per Serving:

Fat 1.6g	Carbohydrate 13.2g	Fiber 2.1g
saturated fat 0.9g	Cholesterol 4mg	Iron 1.5mg
Protein 4.1g	Sodium 168mg	Calcium 82mg

Jicama, Corn, And Green Pepper Skillet

This vegetable medley is pretty served in peppers. Just blanch sweet pepper halves and use them for serving containers like we did in the picture on page 209.

     Vegetable cooking spray
1   teaspoon olive oil
2½   cups peeled, finely chopped jicama (about 1 pound)
1½   cups finely chopped green pepper
1   cup frozen whole-kernel corn, thawed
½   cup finely chopped onion
½   teaspoon ground cumin
¼   teaspoon salt
¼   teaspoon pepper
2   cloves garlic, minced
½   cup minced fresh cilantro
1   tablespoon capers
     Fresh cilantro sprigs (optional)

Coat a large nonstick skillet with cooking spray; add oil. Place over medium-high heat until hot. Add jicama and next 7 ingredients; sauté 5 minutes or until vegetables are crisp-tender. Add minced cilantro and capers; stir well. Garnish with fresh cilantro sprigs, if desired. Serve immediately. Yield: 4 servings (100 calories per ¾-cup serving).

Per Serving:

Fat 2.0g	Carbohydrate 20.1g	Fiber 2.2g
saturated fat 0.3g	Cholesterol 0mg	Iron 1.8mg
Protein 2.7g	Sodium 380mg	Calcium 29mg

Tortellini-Basil Soup (page 225)

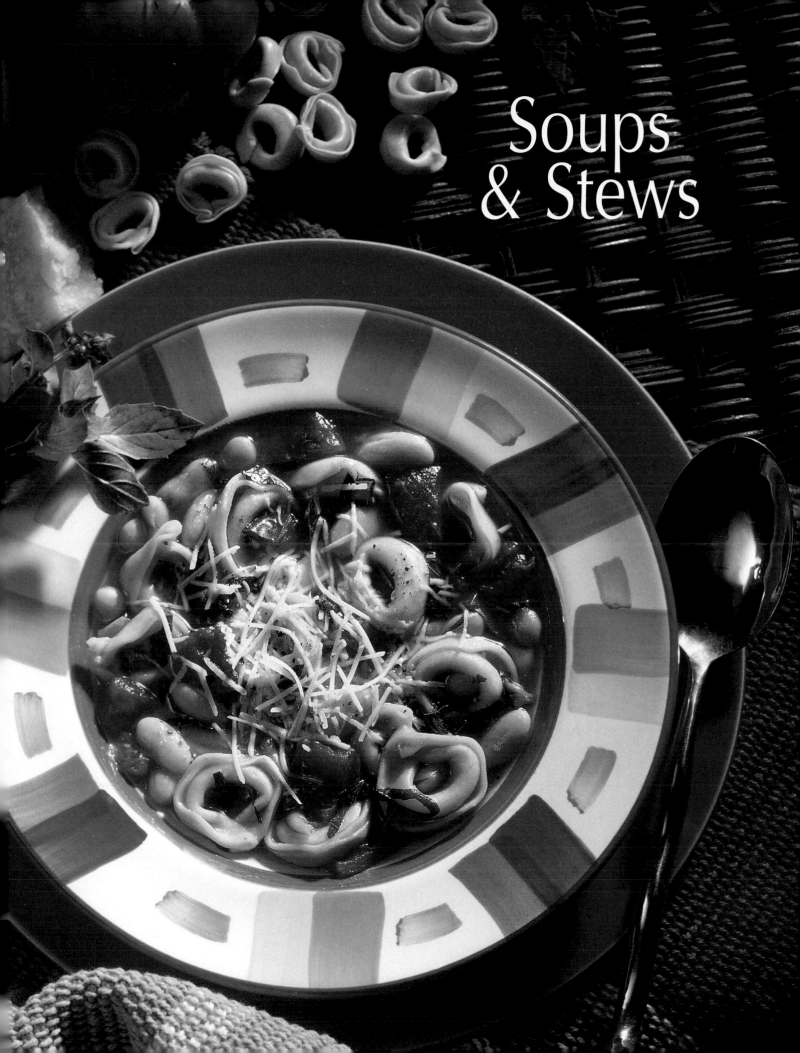

Soups
& Stews

Blushing Pear Soup

*Serve this soup as a refreshing first course
or as a light dessert.*

½   cup sugar
1½ cups water
1½ cups port wine
2   teaspoons grated lemon rind
½   teaspoon lemon juice
3   whole cloves
1   (3-inch) stick cinnamon
6   ripe pears, peeled, cored, and sliced
½   cup reduced-fat sour cream
    Ground cinnamon (optional)

Combine first 7 ingredients in a large Dutch oven. Bring to a boil over medium heat, stirring until sugar dissolves; add pear slices. Cover, reduce heat, and simmer 10 to 15 minutes or until pear is tender. Let mixture cool slightly. Cover and chill.

Remove pear from cooking liquid, using a slotted spoon. Pour liquid through a wire-mesh strainer into a bowl, discarding cloves and cinnamon stick remaining in strainer. Reserve 1½ cups strained liquid; discard remaining liquid.

Place pears in container of an electric blender or food processor; cover and process until smooth. Add sour cream and reserved strained liquid; cover and process until combined. Ladle soup into individual bowls. Sprinkle with cinnamon, if desired. Yield: 4½ cups (142 calories per ¾-cup serving).

Per Serving:		
Fat 2.9g	Carbohydrate 30.4g	Fiber 3.6g
saturated fat 1.5g	Cholesterol 8mg	Iron 0.5mg
Protein 1.2g	Sodium 10mg	Calcium 39mg

Chilled Borscht

*To peel beets after they've been cooked, gently
rub the skin with your fingers. The skin
should come right off.*

2   pounds large fresh beets
     Butter-flavored vegetable cooking spray
1   teaspoon reduced-calorie margarine
2   cups sliced onion
1   cup canned low-sodium chicken broth,
     undiluted
¼   teaspoon salt
¼   teaspoon freshly ground pepper
2½   cups nonfat buttermilk
½   cup low-fat sour cream
½   cup chopped cucumber
¼   cup chopped green onions

Trim stems and roots from beets. Place beets in a large saucepan; add water to cover. Bring to a boil; cover, reduce heat, and simmer 1 hour or until beets are tender. Drain beets, and let cool slightly. Peel beets, and cut into ½-inch-thick slices; set aside.

Coat a large nonstick skillet with cooking spray; add margarine. Place over medium-high heat until margarine melts. Add onion; sauté 10 minutes or until tender.

Place half each of sliced beets, sautéed onion, chicken broth, salt, and pepper in container of an electric blender; cover and process until beet mixture is smooth, stopping once to scrape down sides. Transfer pureed beet mixture to a large bowl. Repeat procedure with remaining beets, sautéed onion, broth, salt, and pepper; add to pureed beet mixture in bowl. Stir in buttermilk. Cover and chill at least 3 hours.

To serve, ladle chilled soup into individual bowls. Top each serving with 1 tablespoon sour cream and 1 tablespoon cucumber; sprinkle evenly with green onions. Yield: 2 quarts (100 calories per 1-cup serving).

Per Serving:		
Fat 3.2g	Carbohydrate 14.4g	Fiber 1.7g
saturated fat 1.4g	Cholesterol 8mg	Iron 0.9mg
Protein 5.1g	Sodium 224mg	Calcium 130mg

Cucumber Vichyssoise

This chilled soup, traditionally made with potatoes and leeks, has a "cool as a cucumber" flavor.

Vegetable cooking spray
1 teaspoon reduced-calorie margarine
3 cups sliced leeks
2 cups sliced onion
2⅓ cups peeled, seeded, and coarsely chopped cucumber
1 cup water
2 cups peeled, cubed baking potato
2 cups canned no-salt-added chicken broth, undiluted
½ teaspoon salt
½ teaspoon ground white pepper
1 cup 1% low-fat milk
   Thinly sliced cucumber (optional)
   Fresh chives (optional)

Coat a large Dutch oven with cooking spray; add margarine. Place over medium-high heat until margarine melts. Add leeks and onion; sauté 15 minutes or until vegetables are tender and golden.

Combine chopped cucumber and water in a small saucepan; bring to a boil. Cover, reduce heat, and simmer 10 minutes.

Add cooked cucumber and cooking liquid, potato, and next 3 ingredients to onion mixture in Dutch oven. Bring to a boil; cover, reduce heat, and simmer 10 minutes or until potato is tender. Remove from heat; let cool 10 minutes.

Transfer cucumber mixture in batches to container of an electric blender or food processor; cover and process until smooth. Pour pureed cucumber mixture into a large bowl. Add milk, and stir well.

Cover and chill thoroughly. Ladle soup into individual bowls. If desired, garnish with cucumber slices and chives. Yield: 2 quarts (90 calories per 1-cup serving).

Per Serving:
Fat 1.4g	Carbohydrate 16.6g	Fiber 1.7g
saturated fat 0.4g	Cholesterol 1mg	Iron 1.1mg
Protein 3.3g	Sodium 211mg	Calcium 71mg

Garbanzo-Lentil Soup

1 cup dried garbanzo beans
5 (14¼-ounce) cans no-salt-added chicken broth
   Vegetable cooking spray
1 teaspoon vegetable oil
1 tablespoon chopped garlic
1¾ cups chopped onion
1¼ cups sliced celery
1 cup dried lentils
1¼ teaspoons freshly ground pepper
1 bay leaf
1 whole clove
2 cups sliced carrot
¼ cup no-salt-added tomato paste
2 tablespoons chopped fresh parsley
2 tablespoons fresh lemon juice
½ teaspoon salt
½ teaspoon hot sauce

Sort and wash garbanzo beans; place beans in a large Dutch oven. Cover with water to depth of 2 inches above beans. Bring to a boil; cover, remove from heat, and let stand 1 hour. Drain beans, and return to Dutch oven; add broth. Bring to a boil; cover, reduce heat, and simmer 1 hour or until beans are tender, stirring occasionally.

Coat a nonstick skillet with cooking spray; add oil. Place over medium-high heat until hot. Add garlic; sauté 1 minute. Add onion and celery; sauté 10 minutes or until vegetables are tender.

Add onion mixture, lentils, and next 3 ingredients to garbanzo beans in Dutch oven. Bring to a boil; cover, reduce heat, and simmer 45 minutes or until lentils are tender.

Add carrot and tomato paste, stirring well. Cover and cook 15 minutes or until carrot is tender. Add parsley and next 3 ingredients; cook, uncovered, until thoroughly heated. Remove and discard bay leaf and clove. Ladle soup into individual bowls. Yield: 9 cups (297 calories per 1½-cup serving).

Per Serving:
Fat 3.2g	Carbohydrate 49.2g	Fiber 7.3g
saturated fat 0.5g	Cholesterol 0mg	Iron 5.4mg
Protein 16.4g	Sodium 265mg	Calcium 86mg

Fresh Corn Chowder

Fresh Corn Chowder

8 ears fresh corn
   Vegetable cooking spray
1 tablespoon margarine
½ cup finely chopped onion
½ cup thinly sliced celery
1 cup peeled, cubed baking potato
1 cup canned vegetable broth, undiluted
1 cup water
3 tablespoons all-purpose flour
2 cups 1% low-fat milk, divided
2 tablespoons minced fresh thyme
1 teaspoon sugar
¼ teaspoon pepper
½ cup seeded, chopped tomato
3 slices turkey bacon, cooked and crumbled

Cut off corn kernels into a large bowl. Scrape milk and remaining pulp from cob, using a small paring knife; set aside.

Coat a Dutch oven with cooking spray; add margarine. Place over medium-high heat until margarine melts. Add onion and celery; sauté until tender. Stir in corn, potato, vegetable broth, and water; bring to a boil. Cover, reduce heat, and simmer 25 minutes or until corn and potato are tender.

Combine flour and ½ cup milk, stirring until smooth. Add flour mixture, remaining 1½ cups milk, thyme, sugar, and pepper to vegetable mixture. Cook over medium heat, stirring constantly, 4 to 5 minutes or until thickened and bubbly.

Ladle chowder into individual bowls. Top each serving with tomato and crumbled bacon. Yield: 9 cups (253 calories per 1½-cup serving).

Per Serving:

Fat 5.4g	Carbohydrate 47.1g	Fiber 6.6g
saturated fat 1.3g	Cholesterol 5mg	Iron 1.5mg
Protein 9.7g	Sodium 275mg	Calcium 116mg

Tortellini-Basil Soup

(pictured on page 219)

4   cups canned low-sodium chicken broth, undiluted
1   (9-ounce) package fresh cheese-filled tortellini, uncooked
1   (15-ounce) can cannellini beans, drained
1   cup chopped tomato
½   cup shredded fresh basil
2   tablespoons balsamic vinegar
¼   teaspoon salt
⅓   cup freshly grated Parmesan cheese
1½   teaspoons freshly ground pepper

Bring broth to a boil in a large Dutch oven. Add tortellini, and cook 6 minutes or until tender. Stir in beans and tomato. Reduce heat, and simmer 5 minutes or until thoroughly heated. Remove from heat; stir in basil, vinegar, and salt.

Ladle soup into individual bowls; sprinkle evenly with cheese and pepper. Yield: 7 cups (185 calories per 1-cup serving).

Per Serving:

Fat 4.1g	Carbohydrate 25.9g	Fiber 1.8g
saturated fat 1.9g	Cholesterol 18mg	Iron 2.6mg
Protein 11.3g	Sodium 409mg	Calcium 153mg

Creamy Tomato-Carrot Soup

¾   cup chopped onion
½   cup chopped carrot
½   cup chopped celery
1½   cups canned low-sodium chicken broth, undiluted
1   (14½-ounce) can no-salt-added whole tomatoes, undrained and chopped
1   cup 1% low-fat milk
2   teaspoons sugar
¼   teaspoon dried thyme
¼   teaspoon dried basil
⅛   teaspoon dried crushed red pepper
1   tablespoon plus 1 teaspoon nonfat sour cream
1   tablespoon plus 1 teaspoon chopped fresh basil

Combine first 4 ingredients in a large saucepan; bring to a boil. Cover, reduce heat, and simmer 20 minutes or until vegetables are tender. Transfer vegetables to container of an electric blender or food processor, using a slotted spoon; reserve liquid in pan.

Add tomato to vegetable mixture in blender. Cover and process until smooth. Return pureed vegetable mixture to saucepan. Add milk and next 4 ingredients; cook until thoroughly heated, stirring frequently.

Ladle soup into individual bowls. Top each serving with 1 teaspoon sour cream and 1 teaspoon chopped basil. Yield: 1 quart (92 calories per 1-cup serving).

Per Serving:

Fat 1.3g	Carbohydrate 15.9g	Fiber 2.0g
saturated fat 0.6g	Cholesterol 2mg	Iron 1.5mg
Protein 4.9g	Sodium 99mg	Calcium 138mg

Roasted Tomato-Shallot Soup

To shave Parmesan cheese into thin slivers,
pull a vegetable peeler across the top of
a wedge of fresh Parmesan.

2   pounds plum tomatoes, cut in half
2   shallots, peeled and cut in half
2   large cloves garlic, cut in half
1   jalapeño pepper, cut in half and seeded
    Vegetable cooking spray
½   (9-ounce) package fresh light cheese-filled
      ravioli, uncooked
2   teaspoons chopped fresh oregano
⅛   teaspoon dried marjoram
1   cup canned low-sodium chicken broth,
      undiluted
1   tablespoon lemon juice
1   teaspoon balsamic vinegar
1   teaspoon sugar
1   ounce shaved fresh Parmesan cheese
    Fresh oregano sprigs (optional)

Combine first 4 ingredients in a shallow baking
pan coated with cooking spray. Bake at 350° for
40 minutes.

Cook ravioli according to package directions,
omitting salt and fat; drain and set aside.

Place roasted vegetables in container of an electric blender or food processor; add chopped
oregano and dried marjoram. Cover and process
until smooth.

Pour tomato mixture into a large saucepan.
Stir in cooked ravioli, chicken broth, lemon juice,
vinegar, and sugar. Cook over medium heat
until thoroughly heated, stirring frequently.
Ladle soup into individual bowls. Top evenly
with cheese. Garnish with oregano sprigs, if
desired. Yield: 1 quart (194 calories per 1-cup
serving).

Per Serving:		
Fat 5.1g	Carbohydrate 29.3g	Fiber 3.9g
saturated fat 2.1g	Cholesterol 27mg	Iron 6.2mg
Protein 10.6g	Sodium 283mg	Calcium 138mg

Oniony Vegetable-Beef Soup

½   pound lean boneless top round steak
    Vegetable cooking spray
1   teaspoon olive oil
1½ cups thinly sliced onion
1   teaspoon sugar
¾   teaspoon salt
1   tablespoon minced garlic
1½ cups water
2   (14¼-ounce) cans no-salt-added beef broth
1   (14½-ounce) can no-salt-added whole
      tomatoes, undrained and chopped
½   teaspoon dried thyme
½   teaspoon pepper
1   bay leaf
1½ cups coarsely chopped cabbage
1   cup chopped celery
1   cup sliced carrot
1   medium-size yellow squash, cut into
      1-inch chunks
1   small zucchini, cut into 1-inch chunks

Trim fat from steak; cut steak into 1-inch pieces.
Coat a Dutch oven with cooking spray; place over
medium-high heat until hot. Add steak; cook
until browned on all sides, stirring frequently.
Remove steak from Dutch oven, and set aside.

Add oil to Dutch oven. Place over medium-high
heat until hot. Add onion; sauté 5 minutes or until
tender. Reduce heat to medium-low; add sugar
and salt. Cook 15 to 20 minutes or until golden,
stirring occasionally. Add garlic; cook 1 minute.

Add beef, water, and next 5 ingredients to
onion mixture. Bring to a boil; cover, reduce heat,
and simmer 1 hour. Add cabbage and remaining
ingredients. Cover and simmer 25 to 30 minutes
or until vegetables are tender. Remove and discard bay leaf. Ladle soup into bowls. Yield: 2½
quarts (79 calories per 1-cup serving).

Per Serving:		
Fat 1.6g	Carbohydrate 9.0g	Fiber 2.0g
saturated fat 0.4g	Cholesterol 13mg	Iron 1.2mg
Protein 6.8g	Sodium 216mg	Calcium 44mg

Oniony Vegetable-Beef Soup

Vegetable-Coconut Soup

Be sure to use light coconut milk in this recipe. It has 65% less fat than regular coconut milk.

Vegetable cooking spray
1½   cups finely chopped onion
1½   cups finely chopped green pepper
 1   tablespoon minced garlic
 2   tablespoons all-purpose flour
 2   teaspoons curry powder
 ¼   teaspoon ground red pepper
 3   (10½-ounce) cans low-sodium
      chicken broth
 2   cups peeled, seeded, and chopped tomato
 1   tablespoon brown sugar
 3   tablespoons fresh lemon juice
 ½   teaspoon salt
1½   cups unsweetened light coconut milk
 1   cup cooked long-grain rice (cooked
      without salt or fat)

Coat a large Dutch oven with cooking spray. Place over medium-high heat until hot. Add onion, green pepper, and garlic; sauté 5 minutes. Add flour, curry powder, and ground red pepper; cook 1 minute, stirring constantly. Gradually add chicken broth, stirring constantly. Add tomato and next 3 ingredients. Bring to a boil; reduce heat, and cook 5 minutes, stirring constantly.

Add coconut milk and rice to vegetable mixture in Dutch oven; cook, stirring constantly, until thoroughly heated. Ladle soup into individual bowls. Yield: 2 quarts (113 calories per 1-cup serving).

Per Serving:

Fat 3.5g	Carbohydrate 18.5g	Fiber 2.3g
saturated fat 2.6g	Cholesterol 0mg	Iron 1.7mg
Protein 3.0g	Sodium 210mg	Calcium 19mg

Harvest Clam Chowder

Instead of using cream as a base for this hearty chowder, we used a combination of low-fat milk and a rich-tasting vegetable puree.

2¼   cups peeled, cubed baking potato
2½   cups canned low-sodium chicken broth,
      undiluted and divided
 1   cup chopped onion
 ¾   cup chopped celery
 ½   cup finely chopped sweet red pepper
 ¼   cup finely chopped carrot
1⅓   cups 1% low-fat milk
 1   (10-ounce) can whole baby clams
 ¼   cup chopped fresh parsley
 ½   teaspoon hot sauce
 ¼   teaspoon coarsely ground pepper

Combine potato and 1½ cups broth in a Dutch oven; bring to a boil. Reduce heat, and simmer, uncovered, 10 to 12 minutes or until potato is tender. Remove half of potato from liquid, using a slotted spoon; set aside. Pour remaining potato mixture into container of an electric blender. Cover and process until smooth; set aside.

Place ½ cup of remaining chicken broth, onion, and next 3 ingredients in Dutch oven. Bring to a boil; reduce heat, and simmer, uncovered, 10 to 15 minutes or until liquid evaporates. Add 1 cup vegetable mixture to potato puree in blender; cover and process until smooth, stopping once to scrape down sides.

Add reserved cubed potato, pureed potato mixture, remaining ½ cup broth, and milk to vegetable mixture in Dutch oven. Bring to a boil; reduce heat, and simmer, uncovered, 8 minutes.

Drain clams, reserving liquid. Add clam liquid, parsley, hot sauce, and pepper to Dutch oven; stir well. Cook, uncovered, 5 minutes. Add clams, and cook 2 additional minutes. Ladle soup into individual bowls. Yield 1½ quarts (126 calories per 1-cup serving).

Per Serving:

Fat 1.7g	Carbohydrate 19.8g	Fiber 2.1g
saturated fat 0.7g	Cholesterol 17mg	Iron 3.3mg
Protein 8.3g	Sodium 352mg	Calcium 111mg

Seafood Gumbo

1 pound unpeeled medium-size fresh
  shrimp
⅓ cup all-purpose flour
  Vegetable cooking spray
2 teaspoons vegetable oil
1½ cups chopped onion
1 cup chopped sweet yellow pepper
½ cup chopped celery
1 tablespoon chopped garlic
2⅓ cups sliced fresh okra (about ⅔ pound)
⅓ cup no-salt-added tomato paste
2 cups water
2 (14½-ounce) cans no-salt-added whole
    tomatoes, undrained and chopped
2 (10½-ounce) cans low-sodium
    chicken broth
1 teaspoon dried thyme
½ teaspoon ground red pepper
½ teaspoon salt
½ pound fresh lump crabmeat, drained
½ cup diced turkey ham
½ cup chopped fresh parsley
2 teaspoons hot sauce
  Fresh parsley sprigs (optional)

Peel and devein shrimp; set aside.

Place flour in a small nonstick skillet. Cook over medium-high heat 8 to 10 minutes or until lightly browned, stirring frequently; set aside.

Coat a Dutch oven with cooking spray; add oil. Place over medium-high heat until hot. Add onion, chopped pepper, celery, and garlic; sauté 15 minutes. Add okra and tomato paste; cook 1 minute, stirring constantly. Add water and next 5 ingredients; bring to a boil. Reduce heat, and simmer, uncovered, 40 minutes.

Combine browned flour and 2 cups cooking liquid from Dutch oven, stirring until smooth. Add flour mixture to Dutch oven, stirring constantly with a wire whisk. Bring to a boil. Reduce heat, and cook, uncovered, 10 minutes. Add shrimp, crabmeat, and ham; cover and cook 3 to 5 minutes or until shrimp turn pink. Stir in parsley and hot sauce. Ladle soup into individual bowls. Garnish with parsley sprigs, if desired. Yield: 3 quarts (188 calories per 1½-cup serving).

Per Serving:		
Fat 3.8g	Carbohydrate 19.1g	Fiber 2.8g
saturated fat 0.8g	Cholesterol 100mg	Iron 3.9mg
Protein 20.1g	Sodium 504mg	Calcium 143mg

"Weighting" to be Young Again

A regular regime of fitness can help turn back the clock, according to recent research. Men and women in their 70s, 80s, and 90s walked faster, climbed stairs more easily, and generally became more physically active after participating in a strength-training program at the Human Nutrition Research Center on Aging at Tufts University. And the best news is that the exercise wasn't strenuous —even programs using simple exercises such as sit-ups and leg lifts produced significant results.

Strength training adds muscle mass, which translates into greater strength and stamina for all types of daily activities, from hauling bags of groceries to lifting grandchildren. It also means you burn calories faster. And the increased metabolic rate from this type of training means keeping unwanted weight gain at bay.

Don't worry about hoisting an enormous barbell; it's easy to do your own strength training at home. Invest in a few hand-held dumbbells, strap on some ankle weights, and do your arm curls and leg lifts during commercial breaks while watching television. It's also a great way to keep you from going to the refrigerator!

Pork and Black Bean Stew

2   cups dried black beans
1   pound lean boneless pork loin
    Vegetable cooking spray
2   teaspoons vegetable oil, divided
2   cups chopped onion
2   cups chopped cabbage
1   cup chopped celery
1   tablespoon minced garlic
1   jalapeño pepper, seeded and minced
2   tablespoons ground cumin
2   teaspoons paprika
1   teaspoon dried crushed red pepper
2   cups water
2   (14¼-ounce) cans no-salt-added
    chicken broth
2   (14½-ounce) cans no-salt-added whole
    tomatoes, undrained and chopped
¾   teaspoon salt
½   cup chopped green onions

Sort and wash beans; place beans in a large Dutch oven. Cover with water to depth of 2 inches above beans; let soak overnight. Drain beans, and set aside.

Trim fat from pork; cut pork into 1-inch cubes. Coat Dutch oven with cooking spray; add 1 teaspoon oil. Place over medium-high heat until hot. Add pork, and cook until browned on all sides, stirring frequently. Remove pork from Dutch oven; set aside.

Add remaining 1 teaspoon oil to Dutch oven. Add 2 cups onion and next 4 ingredients; sauté until tender. Stir in cumin, paprika, and pepper; sauté 1 minute.

Add beans, pork, water, and broth to onion mixture in Dutch oven. Bring to a boil; cover, reduce heat, and simmer 1 hour. Add tomato and salt; cover and cook 1 hour or until beans are tender. Ladle stew into individual bowls. Sprinkle evenly with chopped green onions. Yield: 13½ cups (290 calories per 1½-cup serving).

Per Serving:		
Fat 6.1g	Carbohydrate 38.1g	Fiber 8.0g
saturated fat 1.7g	Cholesterol 30mg	Iron 4.3mg
Protein 21.8g	Sodium 264mg	Calcium 127mg

Chocolate-Mocha Torte (page 240)

Desserts

1. Scoop out a hollow space in side of each pear, using a melon ball scooper.

2. Cut off a thin slice of pear opposite hollowed-out space in each pear so they will sit flat.

3. Place pears on individual serving plates; fill evenly with blackberry pudding.

Elegant Pears with Blackberry Pudding

6	medium-size ripe pears
½	cup sugar
1⅓	cups water
1½	tablespoons fresh lemon juice
1½	tablespoons amaretto
2⅔	cups fresh blackberries
1½	tablespoons margarine
2½	tablespoons all-purpose flour
¾	teaspoon vanilla extract
¼	cup plus 2 tablespoons frozen reduced-calorie whipped topping, thawed
1	tablespoon sliced almonds, toasted

Peel pears, leaving stem ends intact; set aside.

Combine sugar and next 3 ingredients in a Dutch oven; bring to a boil. Carefully place pears in sugar mixture. Cover, reduce heat, and simmer 10 to 15 minutes or until tender. Cool completely in syrup.

Remove pears from syrup, using a slotted spoon; cover pears, and chill thoroughly. Add blackberries to syrup in Dutch oven; place over medium-high heat. Bring to a boil; cover, reduce heat, and simmer 5 minutes or until tender.

Pour blackberry mixture through a wire-mesh strainer into a bowl; press juice mixture with back of a spoon against sides of the strainer to squeeze out liquid. Discard pulp and seeds remaining in strainer. Pour blackberry mixture into Dutch oven. Bring to a boil. Cover, reduce heat, and simmer 10 minutes.

Melt margarine in a large saucepan over medium heat; add flour. Cook 1 minute, stirring constantly with a wire whisk. Gradually add blackberry mixture, stirring constantly. Cook 6 to 8 minutes or until slightly thickened and bubbly. Stir in vanilla; let cool.

Scoop out a hollow space for sauce in side of each pear, using a melon ball scooper. Cut off a thin slice opposite hollowed-out space in each pear so pears will sit flat. Place pears on individual serving plates; fill evenly with blackberry pudding. Spoon 1 tablespoon whipped topping onto each pear, and sprinkle with toasted almonds. Yield: 6 servings (223 calories per serving).

Per Serving:

Fat 5.3g	Carbohydrate 45.4g	Fiber 6.6g
saturated fat 1.4g	Cholesterol 0mg	Iron 0.8mg
Protein 1.6g	Sodium 40mg	Calcium 36mg

Apple-Raisin Crumble

4½   cups peeled, coarsely chopped Rome apple
½   cup raisins
⅓   cup unsweetened apple juice
⅓   cup sugar
2   tablespoons all-purpose flour
½   teaspoon ground cinnamon
¼   teaspoon ground nutmeg
     Vegetable cooking spray
⅔   cup quick-cooking oats, uncooked
¼   cup all-purpose flour
¼   cup firmly packed brown sugar
¼   cup reduced-calorie margarine

Combine first 3 ingredients in a large bowl, tossing gently. Combine ⅓ cup sugar and next 3 ingredients; sprinkle over apple mixture, and toss gently to coat.

Spoon apple mixture into an 8-inch square pan coated with cooking spray. Combine oats, ¼ cup flour, and brown sugar in a small bowl. Cut in margarine with a pastry blender until mixture resembles coarse meal. Sprinkle oat mixture over apple mixture. Bake at 375° for 40 minutes or until apple is tender and oat mixture is lightly browned. Serve warm. Yield: 8 servings (219 calories per serving).

Per Serving:		
Fat 4.5g	Carbohydrate 45.8g	Fiber 3.8g
saturated fat 0.7g	Cholesterol 0mg	Iron 1.0mg
Protein 2.0g	Sodium 59mg	Calcium 21mg

Raspberry Chess Custard

Cornmeal creates a thin, slightly crunchy top layer on the custard filling.

     Vegetable cooking spray
48   fresh raspberries
⅔   cup sugar
1   tablespoon yellow cornmeal
1   tablespoon all-purpose flour
1   cup skim milk
⅔   cup nonfat buttermilk
2   tablespoons margarine, melted
3   egg whites, beaten
1   egg, beaten

Coat 6 (6-ounce) custard cups with cooking spray. Place 8 raspberries in bottom of each cup; set aside.

Combine sugar, cornmeal, and flour in a medium bowl. Add skim milk and remaining ingredients; stir well. Pour into prepared custard cups.

Place custard cups in a 13- x 9- x 2-inch pan. Add hot water to pan to depth of 1 inch. Bake at 350° for 30 to 32 minutes or until a knife inserted in center comes out clean. Remove cups from water, and let cool slightly on a wire rack. Serve warm. Yield: 6 servings (194 calories per serving).

Per Serving:		
Fat 5.2g	Carbohydrate 30.8g	Fiber 1.2g
saturated fat 1.2g	Cholesterol 40mg	Iron 0.4mg
Protein 6.6g	Sodium 163mg	Calcium 127mg

The Fat-Free Fake-Out

Don't be fooled—just because a label says fat free doesn't mean the product is guilt free or calorie free. Manufacturers may use large amounts of carbohydrates and sugar to replace fat in reduced-fat products. And sugar can mean calories—lots of them. Some fat-free products have higher calorie levels than the full-fat products they replace!

The strategy is to treat that fat-free muffin as though it is a full-fat variety. Eat just one, and savor it. In short, you'll keep your fat and calories under control.

Black Bottom Cranberry Pudding

⅔   cup chocolate wafer crumbs (about 12 wafers)
2   tablespoons reduced-calorie margarine, melted
¾   cup sugar, divided
¼   cup plus 2 tablespoons water
2   cups frozen cranberries, thawed
¼   cup seedless raspberry jam
1   cup 1% low-fat milk
2   egg yolks
¼   cup all-purpose flour
5   egg whites
1   teaspoon powdered sugar

Combine chocolate wafer crumbs and margarine, stirring well. Press crumb mixture into bottom of an 8-inch square pan; set aside.

Combine ¼ cup plus 2 tablespoons sugar and water in a saucepan. Bring to a boil over medium heat. Add cranberries, and return to a boil. Reduce heat, and simmer, uncovered, 10 minutes, stirring occasionally. Remove from heat, and stir in jam; let cool. Spoon cranberry mixture into prepared pan.

Place milk in a small saucepan; bring just to a boil over medium heat, stirring occasionally. Beat egg yolks and ¼ cup sugar at high speed of an electric mixer until yolks are thick and pale (about 5 minutes). Gently fold flour into yolk mixture, using a large wire whisk. Gradually stir about ¼ cup hot milk into yolk mixture; add to remaining hot milk, stirring constantly. Cook over medium-low heat, stirring constantly, 1 minute or until thickened. Transfer milk mixture to a large bowl; let cool.

Beat egg whites at high speed of an electric mixer until soft peaks form. Gradually add remaining 2 tablespoons sugar, beating until stiff peaks form. Fold one-fourth of beaten egg white mixture into milk mixture; fold in remaining egg white mixture. Pour egg white mixture over cranberry mixture in pan. Bake at 375° for 20 minutes or until puffed and golden. Sprinkle with powdered sugar. Serve immediately. Yield: 8 servings (210 calories per serving).

Per Serving:
Fat 5.3g
   saturated fat 1.3g
Protein 4.9g
Carbohydrate 36.4g
Cholesterol 62mg
Sodium 113mg
Fiber 0.5g
Iron 0.6mg
Calcium 58mg

Peanut Butter, Pineapple, and Banana Pudding

¼   cup reduced-fat peanut butter spread
24 vanilla wafers
½   cup sugar
2   tablespoons cornstarch
⅛   teaspoon salt
3   cups 1% low-fat milk
2   eggs
1   egg white
2   teaspoons vanilla extract
1   large banana, peeled and sliced
⅓   cup canned crushed pineapple, drained

Spread peanut butter on bottoms of 12 vanilla wafers. Top with remaining wafers; set aside.

Combine sugar, cornstarch, and salt in a medium saucepan; gradually stir in milk. Cook over medium heat, stirring constantly, until mixture comes to a boil; cook 1 additional minute. Remove from heat.

Combine eggs and egg white in a medium bowl; beat well. Gradually stir about one-fourth of hot milk mixture into beaten eggs; add to remaining hot mixture, stirring constantly. Cook over medium heat, stirring constantly, 3 minutes or until thickened. Remove from heat; stir in vanilla, and set aside.

Arrange cookie sandwiches in bottom of a 1-quart casserole; top with banana slices and pineapple. Spoon vanilla mixture over fruit. Cover and chill thoroughly. Yield: 8 servings (241 calories per serving).

Per Serving:
Fat 8.0g
   saturated fat 2.1g
Protein 7.8g
Carbohydrate 35.3g
Cholesterol 66mg
Sodium 190mg
Fiber 0.9g
Iron 0.8mg
Calcium 126mg

Pumpkin Flan

Pumpkin Flan

1 cup sugar, divided
1 (16-ounce) can pumpkin
1 teaspoon pumpkin pie spice
1 teaspoon vanilla extract
½ teaspoon maple extract
½ cup skim milk
¼ cup unsweetened orange juice
1 (12-ounce) can evaporated skimmed milk
4 egg whites, lightly beaten
2 egg yolks, lightly beaten
   Cinnamon sticks (optional)
   Orange rind curls (optional)

Place ½ cup sugar in a saucepan. Cook over medium heat, stirring constantly, until sugar melts and is light brown. Pour melted sugar into a 10-inch pieplate, tilting to coat bottom; set aside.

Combine remaining ½ cup sugar, pumpkin, and next 3 ingredients, stirring well. Add skim milk and next 4 ingredients; stir well. Pour pumpkin mixture into prepared pieplate; place in a large shallow pan. Pour hot water into pan to depth of 1 inch. Bake at 350° for 1 hour and 5 minutes or until a knife inserted in center comes out clean. Remove pieplate from water, and let cool on a wire rack.

Cover and chill at least 4 hours. Loosen edges of flan with a knife; invert onto a rimmed serving plate. If desired, garnish with cinnamon sticks and orange rind curls. Yield: 8 servings (184 calories per serving).

Per Serving:

Fat 1.6g	Carbohydrate 36.0g	Fiber 2.4g
saturated fat 0.6g	Cholesterol 56mg	Iron 1.1mg
Protein 6.8g	Sodium 88mg	Calcium 166mg

Chocolate Mousse

Gelatin adds a firm texture to mousse without adding fat. Most mousses depend on eggs to provide the same firm texture.

1½ teaspoons unflavored gelatin
1 cup 1% low-fat milk, divided
½ cup sugar
2 tablespoons cornstarch
2 tablespoons unsweetened cocoa
⅛ teaspoon salt
2 (1-ounce) squares semisweet chocolate, coarsely chopped
¾ teaspoon vanilla extract
1½ cups frozen reduced-calorie whipped topping, thawed

Sprinkle gelatin over ¼ cup milk in a small bowl; set aside.

Combine sugar and next 3 ingredients in a saucepan. Add remaining ¾ cup milk, stirring until smooth. Cook over medium heat, stirring constantly, until thickened. Add gelatin mixture, stirring until gelatin dissolves. Remove from heat. Add chocolate and vanilla, stirring until chocolate melts. Transfer mixture to a large bowl.

Cover and chill 1½ hours, stirring frequently. Fold in whipped topping. Spoon evenly into individual dessert dishes. Cover and chill until firm. Yield: 6 servings (184 calories per ½-cup serving).

Per Serving:

Fat 5.8g	Carbohydrate 31.4g	Fiber 0.1g
saturated fat 3.7g	Cholesterol 2mg	Iron 0.7mg
Protein 3.5g	Sodium 83mg	Calcium 69mg

Brownie Torte with Grand Marnier Mousse

1 cup sugar
⅔ cup unsweetened cocoa
⅓ cup all-purpose flour
½ teaspoon baking powder
¼ cup vegetable oil
1 teaspoon vanilla extract
4 egg whites, lightly beaten
  Vegetable cooking spray
1 envelope unflavored gelatin
¾ cup cold water
¼ cup sugar
¾ cup unsweetened orange juice
2 tablespoons Grand Marnier or other orange-flavored liqueur
2 cups frozen reduced-calorie whipped topping, thawed

Combine first 4 ingredients in a bowl, stirring well. Combine oil, vanilla, and egg whites in a large bowl. Gradually add cocoa mixture to oil mixture, stirring with a wire whisk. Pour batter into an 8-inch springform pan coated with cooking spray. Bake at 325° for 30 to 35 minutes or until a wooden pick inserted in center comes out clean. Let cool completely on a wire rack.

Sprinkle gelatin over ¾ cup cold water in a small saucepan; let stand 1 minute. Cook over low heat, stirring until gelatin dissolves, about 2 minutes. Add ¼ cup sugar and orange juice to gelatin mixture; cook until sugar dissolves. Transfer mixture to a large bowl. Add liqueur, stirring well. Cover and chill 25 minutes or until consistency of unbeaten egg white.

Beat gelatin mixture at high speed of an electric mixer until light and fluffy. Cover and chill 20 minutes. Fold in whipped topping.

Spoon mousse mixture over brownie in pan. Cover and chill at least 2 hours. Yield: 10 servings (242 calories per serving).

Per Serving:

Fat 8.1g	Carbohydrate 37.1g	Fiber 0.1g
saturated fat 2.6g	Cholesterol 0mg	Iron 1.3mg
Protein 4.6g	Sodium 34mg	Calcium 35mg

Fudgy Mint Brownie Dessert

This minty dessert was voted one of the best light desserts we've tested in our test kitchens.

1¼ cups sugar
½ cup frozen egg substitute, thawed
¼ cup margarine, melted
2 tablespoons water
1 teaspoon vanilla extract
1¼ cups sifted cake flour
1 teaspoon baking powder
⅛ teaspoon salt
¼ cup plus 2 tablespoons unsweetened cocoa
 Vegetable cooking spray
½ cup fat-free hot fudge topping
1 tablespoon Crème de Menthe
2 cups frozen reduced-calorie whipped
 topping, thawed
¼ cup mint-flavored semisweet chocolate
 morsels, finely chopped

Combine first 5 ingredients in a bowl, stirring well. Combine flour, baking powder, salt, and cocoa; add to sugar mixture, stirring well. Spoon batter into a 9-inch square pan coated with cooking spray. Bake at 325° for 25 to 30 minutes or until a wooden pick inserted in center comes out clean. Let cool slightly on a wire rack.

Combine fudge topping and Crème de Menthe in a small saucepan; cook over low heat until thoroughly heated, stirring frequently. Let cool slightly.

Prick brownie several times with a fork or wooden pick. Pour warm fudge mixture over brownie. Let cool completely.

Combine whipped topping and chocolate morsels; spread evenly over brownie. Cover and chill thoroughly. Cut into 12 squares. Yield: 12 servings (249 calories per serving).

Per Serving:

Fat 6.9g	Carbohydrate 44.0g	Fiber 1.0g
saturated fat 2.7g	Cholesterol 0mg	Iron 2.2mg
Protein 3.9g	Sodium 126mg	Calcium 53mg

Hawaiian Bread Pudding

Hawaiian bread is a dense, sweet bread shaped in a round loaf. For a mail-order source, see page 272.

½ cup pineapple marmalade
2 tablespoons unsweetened orange juice
½ (16-ounce) round loaf Hawaiian bread, cut
 into 1-inch cubes
¼ cup golden raisins, chopped
¼ teaspoon ground cinnamon
⅛ teaspoon baking powder
1¼ cups skim milk
1 teaspoon vanilla extract
5 egg whites
¼ cup plus 2 tablespoons sugar
 Vegetable cooking spray
½ cup frozen reduced-calorie whipped
 topping, thawed
2 tablespoons plus 2 teaspoons flaked
 coconut, toasted

Combine marmalade and orange juice, stirring well. Set aside.

Combine bread cubes and next 3 ingredients in a large bowl, tossing well. Add milk and vanilla; stir well. Let stand 10 minutes.

Beat egg whites at high speed of an electric mixer until foamy. Gradually add sugar, 1 tablespoon at a time, beating until stiff peaks form and sugar dissolves (2 to 4 minutes). Gently fold egg white mixture into bread mixture.

Spoon bread mixture into an 11- x 7- x 1½-inch baking dish coated with cooking spray. Bake at 375° for 20 minutes or until puffed and golden. Spoon pudding into individual dessert dishes. Drizzle evenly with marmalade mixture. Top each serving with 1 tablespoon whipped topping and 1 teaspoon coconut. Serve immediately. Yield: 8 servings (246 calories per serving).

Per Serving:

Fat 3.4g	Carbohydrate 46.4g	Fiber 1.4g
saturated fat 1.5g	Cholesterol 11mg	Iron 0.2mg
Protein 6.8g	Sodium 142mg	Calcium 59mg

Cherry Winks Soufflés

Cherry Winks Soufflés

Vegetable cooking spray
⅓ cup dried sweet cherries
⅔ cup hot water
⅔ cup dried apricots
½ teaspoon vanilla extract
4 egg whites
2 tablespoons sugar
⅓ cup semisweet chocolate mini-morsels
¾ cup fat-free hot fudge topping

Coat bottoms of 6 (4-ounce) soufflé dishes with cooking spray; set aside.

Combine cherries and water; let stand 15 minutes. Drain, reserving cherries and juice.

Combine reserved juice and apricots in a small saucepan; bring to a boil. Cover, reduce heat, and simmer 25 minutes. Position knife blade in food processor bowl; add apricot mixture and vanilla. Process 30 seconds or until smooth, scraping sides of processor bowl occasionally. Transfer apricot mixture to a large bowl; set aside.

Beat egg whites at high speed of an electric mixer until foamy. Gradually add sugar, 1 tablespoon at a time, beating until stiff peaks form and sugar dissolves (2 to 4 minutes). Fold about one-fourth of egg white mixture into apricot mixture. Gently fold in remaining egg white mixture. Gently fold in cherries and chocolate morsels.

Spoon egg white mixture evenly into prepared dishes. Bake at 375° for 12 to 15 minutes or until puffed and golden. Serve immediately with hot fudge topping. Yield: 6 servings (228 calories per serving).

Per Serving:

Fat 3.7g	Carbohydrate 48.2g	Fiber 3.2g
saturated fat 1.9g	Cholesterol 0mg	Iron 2.3mg
Protein 5.5g	Sodium 138mg	Calcium 49mg

Cinnamon-Apple Ice Milk

Enjoy a scoop of this creamy, frozen dessert without an ounce of guilt. A ½-cup serving is virtually fat free.

¼   cup ginger ale
3   tablespoons brown sugar
2   tablespoons reduced-calorie maple syrup
2   cups peeled, finely chopped apple
½   teaspoon ground cinnamon
2   cups 1% low-fat milk
1   cup evaporated skimmed milk
⅔   cup sugar
½   cup frozen egg substitute, thawed
1¾   cups marshmallow creme
½   teaspoon brandy extract

Combine first 3 ingredients in a medium saucepan; bring to a boil over medium heat. Add apple; reduce heat to medium-low, and cook 30 minutes or until mixture thickens and most of liquid evaporates, stirring frequently. Stir in cinnamon; set aside.

Combine low-fat milk and next 3 ingredients; beat at medium speed of an electric mixer until smooth. Add marshmallow creme and brandy extract to milk mixture, beating well. (Mixture will not be smooth.)

Pour milk mixture into freezer can of a 2-quart hand-turned or electric freezer. Freeze according

to manufacturer's instructions. Spoon into a 13- x 9- x 2-inch baking dish; stir in apple mixture. Cover and freeze 1 hour or until firm. Scoop ice milk into individual dessert bowls. Serve immediately. Yield: 8 cups (115 calories per ½-cup serving).

Per Serving:

Fat 0.4g	Carbohydrate 25.1g	Fiber 0.5g
saturated fat 0.2g	Cholesterol 2mg	Iron 0.3mg
Protein 3.0g	Sodium 55mg	Calcium 89mg

Caramel-Kahlúa Squares

This sinfully delicious dessert received a top rating from our staff. We polished off every bite!

¼   cup plus 1 tablespoon chocolate wafer crumbs (about 6 wafers)
2   teaspoons reduced-calorie margarine, melted
    Vegetable cooking spray
2   tablespoons Kahlúa or other coffee-flavored liqueur
6   cups vanilla low-fat ice cream, softened
½   cup fat-free caramel-flavored syrup
2   tablespoons strong brewed coffee

Combine chocolate wafer crumbs and margarine, stirring well. Sprinkle half of crumb mixture over bottom of an 8-inch square pan coated with cooking spray.

Stir Kahlúa into softened ice cream. Spread half of ice cream mixture into prepared pan. Combine caramel syrup and coffee; drizzle half of caramel mixture over ice cream mixture. Freeze until firm. Repeat layers with remaining ice cream mixture and caramel mixture. Sprinkle evenly with remaining crumb mixture. Freeze until firm. Yield: 9 servings (201 calories per serving).

Per Serving:

Fat 5.1g	Carbohydrate 34.8g	Fiber 0g
saturated fat 2.5g	Cholesterol 15mg	Iron 0.2mg
Protein 3.5g	Sodium 126mg	Calcium 126mg

1. Sprinkle powdered sugar over top of cake.

2. Cut 1½-inch-wide strips of aluminum foil or wax paper, and place over cake in a checkerboard design.

3. Sprinkle grated chocolate over top of cake.

4. Remove foil strips.

Chocolate-Mocha Torte

(pictured on page 231)

1	(18-ounce) package low-fat devil's food cake mix
1¾	cups water
4	egg whites
	Vegetable cooking spray
½	cup semisweet chocolate morsels
2	teaspoons instant espresso powder
½	cup plain nonfat yogurt
½	cup nonfat cottage cheese
1	tablespoon vanilla extract
2	teaspoons powdered sugar
3	tablespoons grated semisweet chocolate
	Fresh strawberry halves (optional)

Combine first 3 ingredients in a large mixing bowl. Beat at medium speed of an electric mixer 30 seconds. Beat 2 minutes at high speed. Pour batter into 2 (8-inch) round cakepans coated with cooking spray. Bake at 350° for 25 to 30 minutes or until a wooden pick inserted in center comes out clean. Cool in pans on wire racks 10 minutes; remove from pans, and let cool completely on wire racks. Slice each cake layer in half horizontally. (Keep layers covered to prevent drying.)

Place chocolate morsels in top of a double boiler; bring water to a boil. Reduce heat to low; cook until chocolate melts. Remove from heat, and stir in espresso powder. Set aside, and keep warm.

Combine yogurt and cottage cheese in container of an electric blender; cover and process until smooth. Transfer mixture to a small bowl. Gradually add chocolate mixture to yogurt mixture, stirring with a wire whisk until combined. Stir in vanilla.

Place 1 cake layer on a serving plate; spread with one-third of chocolate mixture. Repeat procedure twice with 2 cake layers and remaining chocolate mixture; top with remaining cake layer.

Cover and chill at least 2 hours. Sprinkle powdered sugar and grated chocolate in a checkerboard design over top of cake just before serving. Garnish with strawberry halves, if desired. Yield: 12 servings (221 calories per serving).

Per Serving:

Fat 6.8g	Carbohydrate 39.0g	Fiber 1.3g
saturated fat 2.5g	Cholesterol 1mg	Iron 1.2mg
Protein 5.3g	Sodium 400mg	Calcium 103mg

Triple Ginger Pound Cake

Vegetable cooking spray
1 teaspoon sifted cake flour
¼ cup plus 2 tablespoons margarine, softened
⅔ cup sugar
3 egg whites
2½ cups sifted cake flour
¾ teaspoon baking soda
¼ teaspoon salt
1 teaspoon ground ginger
1 (8-ounce) carton lemon nonfat yogurt
¼ cup finely chopped crystallized ginger
1 tablespoon peeled, minced gingerroot
2 teaspoons vanilla extract

Coat an 8½- x 4½- x 3-inch loafpan with cooking spray; dust pan with 1 teaspoon flour, and set aside.

Beat margarine at medium speed of an electric mixer until creamy; gradually add sugar, beating well. Add egg whites; beat at medium speed 4 minutes or until well blended.

Combine 2½ cups flour, soda, salt, and ground ginger; add to margarine mixture alternately with yogurt, beginning and ending with flour mixture. Mix after each addition. Stir in crystallized ginger, gingerroot, and vanilla.

Pour batter into prepared pan. Bake at 350° for 55 to 60 minutes or until a wooden pick inserted in center comes out clean. Cool in pan on a wire rack 10 minutes. Remove from pan, and let cool completely on a wire rack. Yield: 16 servings (155 calories per serving).

Per Serving:
Fat 4.5g	Carbohydrate 25.4g	Fiber 0.6g
saturated fat 0.9g	Cholesterol 0mg	Iron 1.9mg
Protein 2.9g	Sodium 168mg	Calcium 39mg

Pumpkin-Pecan Pound Cake

Pumpkin adds flavor and moistness to this cake and provides a significant source of beta-carotene, an antioxidant that helps fight disease.

¾ cup margarine, softened
1½ cups firmly packed brown sugar
1 cup sugar
1¼ cups frozen egg substitute, thawed
1 (16-ounce) can pumpkin
⅓ cup bourbon
3 cups all-purpose flour
2 teaspoons baking powder
½ teaspoon baking soda
¼ teaspoon salt
2 teaspoons pumpkin pie spice
¼ cup chopped pecans
Vegetable cooking spray

Beat margarine at medium speed of an electric mixer until creamy; gradually add sugars, beating well. Add egg substitute, and beat well.

Combine pumpkin and bourbon, stirring well. Combine flour and next 4 ingredients; add to margarine mixture alternately with pumpkin mixture, beginning and ending with flour mixture. Mix after each addition.

Sprinkle pecans over bottom of a 10-inch tube pan coated with cooking spray. Spoon batter over pecans. Bake at 325° for 1 hour and 35 minutes or until a wooden pick inserted in center comes out clean. Cool in pan 10 minutes. Remove cake from pan, and cool completely on a wire rack. Yield: 24 servings (213 calories per serving).

Per Serving:
Fat 6.7g	Carbohydrate 35.7g	Fiber 1.3g
saturated fat 1.2g	Cholesterol 0mg	Iron 1.6mg
Protein 3.2g	Sodium 143mg	Calcium 49mg

Banana Pudding Cheesecake

(pictured on page 2)

    Vegetable cooking spray
¼   cup reduced-fat vanilla wafer crumbs
2   (8-ounce) cartons light process cream
      cheese, softened
⅔   cup sugar
½   cup frozen egg substitute, thawed
2   egg whites
1   cup low-fat sour cream
⅓   cup banana cream-flavored cook and serve
      pudding mix
3   tablespoons skim milk
1   teaspoon vanilla extract
1¼ cups peeled, sliced banana
1   teaspoon lemon juice
¾   cup frozen reduced-calorie whipped
      topping, thawed
4   reduced-fat vanilla wafers, cut in half

Coat bottom of an 8-inch springform pan with cooking spray; sprinkle crumbs over bottom.

Beat cream cheese at medium speed of an electric mixer until creamy; gradually add sugar, beating well. Add egg substitute and egg whites; beat well. Add sour cream and next 3 ingredients. Beat at low speed just until blended. Pour mixture into prepared pan.

Bake at 300° for 55 minutes. (Center will be soft but will firm when chilled.) Turn off oven; partially open oven door. Leave cheesecake in oven 20 minutes. Remove from oven, and run a knife around edge of pan. Let cheesecake cool on a wire rack. Cover and chill 8 hours.

Remove cake from pan. Toss banana slices with lemon juice, and arrange over cake. Pipe or spoon whipped topping around edge of cake; insert cookie halves into topping. Yield: 12 servings (206 calories per serving).

Per Serving:

Fat 9.8g	Carbohydrate 24.6g	Fiber 0.5g
saturated fat 5.7g	Cholesterol 30mg	Iron 0.4mg
Protein 6.7g	Sodium 287mg	Calcium 84mg

Lemon Cream Pie

1   cup low-fat cinnamon graham cracker
      crumbs (about 7 crackers)
¼   cup reduced-calorie margarine, melted
¾   cup sugar
¼   cup plus 3 tablespoons cornstarch
⅛   teaspoon salt
1   cup water
⅔   cup nonfat buttermilk
½   cup frozen egg substitute, thawed
2   teaspoons grated lemon rind
½   cup fresh lemon juice
2½ cups frozen reduced-calorie whipped
      topping, thawed
    Lemon zest (optional)
    Lemon rind curls (optional)
    Lemon slices (optional)
    Fresh mint sprigs (optional)

Combine cracker crumbs and margarine; stir well. Press into bottom and up sides of a 9-inch pieplate. Bake at 350° for 8 to 10 minutes or until golden. Remove from oven; let cool on a wire rack.

Combine sugar, cornstarch, and salt in a saucepan; gradually stir in water and buttermilk. Cook over medium heat, stirring constantly, until mixture comes to a boil. Cook 1 minute.

Gradually stir about one-fourth of hot mixture into egg substitute; add to remaining hot mixture, stirring constantly. Cook over medium heat, stirring constantly, 2 minutes or until thickened. Remove from heat; stir in 2 teaspoons lemon rind and lemon juice.

Spoon lemon mixture into prepared crust. Cover; chill thoroughly. Spread whipped topping over filling just before serving. If desired, garnish with lemon zest, lemon rind curls, lemon slices, and fresh mint. Yield: 8 servings (251 calories per serving).

Per Serving:

Fat 7.2g	Carbohydrate 46.4g	Fiber 0.6g
saturated fat 2.6g	Cholesterol 1mg	Iron 0.8mg
Protein 4.1g	Sodium 175mg	Calcium 47mg

Lemon Cream Pie

Chocolate Nougat Pie

1 cup reduced-fat chocolate graham cracker crumbs (about 7 crackers)
3 tablespoons reduced-calorie margarine, melted
1½ teaspoons unflavored gelatin
½ cup cold water
1 (14-ounce) can low-fat sweetened condensed milk
2 (1-ounce) squares unsweetened chocolate
1¾ cups frozen reduced-calorie whipped topping, thawed

Combine cracker crumbs and margarine. Press crumb mixture into bottom and up sides of a 9-inch pieplate. Bake at 350° for 8 minutes. Remove from oven, and let cool on a wire rack.

Sprinkle gelatin over ½ cup cold water in a small saucepan; let stand 1 minute. Cook over low heat, stirring until gelatin dissolves, about 2 minutes. Remove from heat, and let cool.

Combine condensed milk and chocolate in a medium saucepan. Cook over medium-low heat, stirring constantly, until chocolate melts and mixture is smooth. Stir in gelatin mixture, and let cool completely.

Gently fold whipped topping into cooled chocolate mixture. Pour chocolate mixture into prepared crust. Cover and chill 2½ hours or until set. Yield: 10 servings (236 calories per serving).

Per Serving:		
Fat 9.2g	Carbohydrate 35.0g	Fiber 0.3g
saturated fat 3.2g	Cholesterol 5mg	Iron 0.7mg
Protein 5.1g	Sodium 144mg	Calcium 93mg

Almond Biscotti

Crunchy biscotti is made for dunking in coffee. A few of these and your favorite flavored coffee are great for coffee breaks, dessert, or to cap off a fun evening.

2 eggs
1 egg white
¼ cup sugar
¼ teaspoon almond extract
2⅓ cups all-purpose flour
¾ teaspoon baking soda
¼ teaspoon salt
½ cup sugar
¼ cup chocolate wafer crumbs (about 5 wafers)
1 (2-ounce) package slivered almonds, coarsely chopped and toasted
Vegetable cooking spray

Beat eggs and egg white at high speed of an electric mixer 3 minutes. Gradually add ¼ cup sugar, beating at high speed. Add almond extract, and beat 2 additional minutes.

Combine flour and next 4 ingredients in a medium bowl, stirring well; stir in almonds.

Slowly add egg mixture to flour mixture, stirring until dry ingredients are moistened. (Mixture will be very stiff.)

Turn dough out onto work surface, and knead lightly 7 or 8 times. Divide dough in half; shape each half into an 8-inch log. Place logs, 4 inches apart, on a baking sheet coated with cooking spray. Bake at 350° for 40 minutes. Remove from oven, and let cool 15 minutes.

Using a serrated knife, cut each log diagonally into 15 (½-inch-thick) slices; place slices, cut side down, on baking sheet. Reduce oven temperature to 300°, and bake 23 minutes. (Cookies will be slightly soft in center but will harden as they cool.) Remove from baking sheet, and let cool completely on wire racks. Yield: 2½ dozen (75 calories each).

Per Cookie:		
Fat 1.6g	Carbohydrate 13.3g	Fiber 0.5g
saturated fat 0.3g	Cholesterol 15mg	Iron 0.6mg
Protein 2.0g	Sodium 60mg	Calcium 9mg

Molasses Crinkles

¼ cup margarine, softened
¾ cup plus 1½ tablespoons sugar, divided
¼ cup molasses
1 egg
2 cups all-purpose flour
2 teaspoons baking soda
¼ teaspoon salt
1¾ teaspoons ground cinnamon, divided
Vegetable cooking spray

Beat margarine at medium speed of an electric mixer until creamy; gradually add ¾ cup sugar, beating well. Add molasses and egg; beat well.

Combine flour, baking soda, salt, and 1½ teaspoons ground cinnamon in a small bowl, stirring well. Gradually add flour mixture to margarine mixture, beating until blended. Cover dough, and chill 1 hour.

Combine remaining 1½ tablespoons sugar and ¼ teaspoon ground cinnamon in a small bowl, and set aside.

Shape dough into 48 (1-inch) balls; roll balls in sugar mixture. Place balls, 2 inches apart, on cookie sheets coated with cooking spray. Bake at 350° for 8 minutes or until golden. Cool slightly on cookie sheets. Remove from cookie sheets, and cool completely on wire racks. Yield: 4 dozen (48 calories each).

Per Cookie:		
Fat 1.1g	Carbohydrate 8.7g	Fiber 0.2g
saturated fat 0.2g	Cholesterol 5mg	Iron 0.4mg
Protein 0.7g	Sodium 78mg	Calcium 6mg

Orange-Butterscotch Cookies

¼ cup plus 2 tablespoons margarine, softened
½ cup sugar
½ cup firmly packed brown sugar
¼ cup frozen egg substitute, thawed
2 tablespoons skim milk
1 teaspoon grated orange rind
1 tablespoon unsweetened orange juice
1½ cups all-purpose flour
2 teaspoons baking powder
½ teaspoon salt
¼ teaspoon ground nutmeg
⅓ cup butterscotch morsels
Vegetable cooking spray

Beat margarine at medium speed of an electric mixer until creamy; gradually add sugars, beating well. Add egg substitute and next 3 ingredients; beat well.

Combine flour and next 3 ingredients. Add to margarine mixture, stirring just until blended. Stir in butterscotch morsels. Drop dough by level tablespoonfuls, 2 inches apart, onto cookie sheets coated with cooking spray. Bake at 375° for 7 to 8 minutes or until edges are golden. Let cool on cookie sheets 1 minute. Remove from cookie sheets, and let cool completely on wire racks. Yield: 40 cookies (63 calories each).

Per Cookie:		
Fat 2.2g	Carbohydrate 10.0g	Fiber 0.1g
saturated fat 0.6g	Cholesterol 0mg	Iron 0.4mg
Protein 0.7g	Sodium 54mg	Calcium 21mg

Sugar is Sugar is Sugar

Don't be misled by food companies and health food stores that promote fruit juice sweeteners as a healthier alternative to refined sugar. Sugar is sugar, no matter what the source, and there are no nutritional advantages to sweetening a cookie, a cake, or jam with fruit juice. The only way fruit sugar could have an advantage over other varieties would be if it's still in the fruit. Then you'd be getting the fiber and other nutrients along with the sweetness!

Eat Great to Lose Weight

These 21 preplanned menus designed around recipes in this book will help you eat a healthy diet without even thinking about it. Recipes are noted with an asterisk, and page numbers are included for your convenience.

If you're trying to lose weight or just want to consume a steady number of calories, you'll love the way each of these menus is adjusted to fit a 1,200-calorie and a 1,600-calorie eating plan. And substituting food that's not on the menu (for example, a baked sweet potato instead of steamed carrots), is no problem. Just check the Calorie/Nutrient Chart on pages 250 through 262 to find out how many calories the substitution contains.

LOSING WEIGHT SAFELY

Most women can safely lose weight by eating 1,200 calories a day, and most men can do the same at 1,600 calories a day. But you can continue to use these menus after you've lost weight—just alter them to include the number of calories you need to maintain your desired weight.

If the weight comes off slowly and you get impatient, resist the urge to cut more calories to try to lose weight faster. Increase your exercise time instead. Severely restricting caloric intake may rob your body of the nutrients you need to stay healthy. And it can cause your metabolism to slow down to accommodate a limited food supply, which means you're more likely to regain the weight you've lost (and possibly gain more) when you go back to a normal diet.

Breakfast

Day 1

1200 CALORIES			1600 CALORIES	
		BREAKFAST		
1 serving	233	*Warm Peaches and Cream Cereal (p. 24)	1 serving	233
1 slice	78	*Sugared Turkey Bacon (p. 28)	1 slice	78
½ cup	70	Pineapple Juice	½ cup	70
	381			381
		LUNCH		
1 serving	272	*Pizza Milanese (p. 145)	1 serving	272
1 cup	12	Spinach Leaves	1 cup	12
1 tablespoon	25	Fat-Free French Dressing	1 tablespoon	25
	309			309
		DINNER		
1 serving	219	*Saucy Veal Skillet (p. 153)	1 serving	219
1 cup	25	Steamed Broccoli	1 cup	25
½ cup	71	*Garlic Mashed Potatoes (p. 39)	1 cup	143
1 medium	97	Pear	1 medium	97
—	—	*Chocolate Mousse (p. 236)	1 serving	184
	412			668
		SNACK		
—	—	*Pink Passion Cooler (p. 93)	½ cup	48
¼ cup	89	*Sassy Snack Mix (p. 55)	½ cup	178
	89			226
Total 1191			**Total 1584**	
(Calories from Fat: 18%)			(Calories from Fat: 17%)	

Lunch

Dinner

Day 2

1200 CALORIES			1600 CALORIES	
BREAKFAST				
1 serving	124	*Vegetable Omelets (p. 33)	1 serving	124
1 slice	55	Whole Wheat Toast	2 slices	110
1 teaspoon	20	Reduced-Calorie Margarine	2 teaspoons	40
2 teaspoons	19	Reduced-Calorie Strawberry Jam	1 tablespoon	29
½ cup	64	*Spiced Fruit Tea (p. 28)	1 cup	128
	282			**431**
LUNCH				
1 serving	187	*Poached Ginger Chicken (p. 166)	1 serving	187
1 serving	199	*Herbed Rice-Stuffed Tomatoes (p. 182)	1 serving	199
—	—	Green Grapes	1 cup	58
	386			**444**
DINNER				
1½ cups	290	*Pork and Black Bean Stew (p. 230)	1½ cups	290
1 muffin	119	*Confetti Corn Muffins (p. 56)	1 muffin	119
—	—	Vanilla Low-Fat Ice Cream	½ cup	92
—	—	*Caramel-Apple Sauce (p. 200)	2 tablespoons	88
	409			**589**
SNACK				
2 tablespoons	58	*Smoky Cheddar-Pimiento Spread (p. 197)	2 tablespoons	58
6 rounds	69	Melba Rounds	6 rounds	69
	127			**127**
Total 1204			**Total 1591**	
(Calories from Fat: 14%)			(Calories from Fat: 19%)	

Day 3

1200 CALORIES			1600 CALORIES	
BREAKFAST				
1 muffin	148	*Oatmeal-Raisin Muffins (p. 99)	2 muffins	296
½ medium	31	Orange	1 medium	62
1 cup	86	Skim Milk	1 cup	86
	265			**444**
LUNCH				
1 serving	247	*Grilled Spinach and Cheese Sandwiches (p. 190)	1 serving	247
½ cup	10	Celery Sticks	½ cup	10
1 medium	81	Apple	1 medium	81
—	—	*Black Currant and Raspberry Cooler (p. 93)	1 cup	72
	338			**410**
DINNER				
1 serving	157	*Savory Beef Roast (p. 151)	1 serving	157
1 cup	112	*Glazed Brussels Sprouts and Baby Carrots (p. 213)	1 cup	112
1 medium	216	Baked Potato	1 medium	216
1 tablespoon	10	Nonfat Sour Cream	1 tablespoon	10
—	—	Reduced-Calorie Margarine	1 teaspoon	20
	495			**515**
SNACK				
1 cookie	63	*Orange-Butterscotch Cookies (p. 245)	2 cookies	126
½ cup	43	Skim Milk	1 cup	86
	106			**212**
Total 1204			**Total 1581**	
(Calories from Fat: 17%)			(Calories from Fat: 18%)	

Breakfast

Lunch

Day 4

1200 CALORIES			1600 CALORIES	
BREAKFAST				
1 slice	128	*Date-Walnut Bread (p. 97)	2 slices	256
½ medium	38	Grapefruit	½ medium	38
1 tablespoon	12	Nonfat Cream Cheese	2 tablespoons	24
1 cup	86	Skim Milk	1 cup	86
	264			**404**
LUNCH				
1 serving	348	*Roasted Pork Sandwiches with Peach-Onion Chutney (p. 194)	1 serving	348
½ cup	88	*Creamy Coleslaw (p. 56)	¾ cup	133
—	—	Apple Juice	1 cup	117
	436			**598**
DINNER				
1 serving	229	*Greek Beef and Pasta (p. 129)	1 serving	229
1 cup	44	*Mandarin Orange Salad (p. 176)	1 cup	44
1 roll	138	*Whole Wheat Clover Rolls (p. 53)	1 roll	138
1 teaspoon	20	Reduced-Calorie Margarine	1 teaspoon	20
	431			**431**
SNACK				
1 cup	1	Decaffeinated Coffee	1 cup	1
1 cookie	75	*Almond Biscotti (p. 244)	2 cookies	150
	76			**151**
Total 1207			**Total 1584**	
(Calories from Fat: 19%)			(Calories from Fat: 17%)	

Day 5

1200 CALORIES			1600 CALORIES	
BREAKFAST				
1 egg	77	Scrambled Egg	1 egg	77
1 cup	130	*Minted Grapefruit (p. 210)	1 cup	130
1 biscuit	94	*Cranberry Silver Dollar Biscuits (p. 96)	2 biscuits	188
1 slice	30	Turkey Bacon	1 slice	30
	331			**425**
LUNCH				
1½ cups	253	*Fresh Corn Chowder (p. 224)	1½ cups	253
1¼ cups	73	*Chicory and Papaya Salad with Poppy Seed Dressing (p. 176)	1¼ cups	73
—	—	*Whole-Grain-Goodness Bread (p. 104)	1 slice	114
	326			**440**
DINNER				
1 serving	190	*South-of-the-Border Bass (p. 108)	1 serving	190
1 cup	148	*Zucchini-Parmesan Rice (p. 123)	1 cup	148
1 cup	66	Steamed Carrots	1 cup	66
—	—	*Caramel-Kahlúa Squares (p. 239)	1 serving	201
	404			**605**
SNACK				
1 cup	54	*Spicy Tomato Cocktail (p. 34)	1 cup	54
2 cups	61	Popcorn	2 cups	61
	115			**115**
Total 1176			**Total 1585**	
(Calories from Fat: 19%)			(Calories from Fat: 19%)	

Dinner

Dinner

Day 6

1200 CALORIES			1600 CALORIES	
		BREAKFAST		
¾ cup	271	*Swiss Muesli (p. 25)	¾ cup	271
—	—	Banana	1 medium	109
½ cup	56	Orange Juice	½ cup	56
	327			**436**
		LUNCH		
1½ cups	266	*Tuna Pasta Salad (p. 183)	1½ cups	266
5 crackers	60	Unsalted Crackers	6 crackers	72
1 cup	45	Strawberries	1 cup	45
—	—	*Triple Ginger Pound Cake (p. 241)	1 slice	155
	371			**538**
		DINNER		
1 serving	192	*Chicken Breast Dijon (p. 166)	1 serving	192
¾ cup	54	*Roasted Green Beans and Onions (p. 215)	1 cup	72
¾ cup	103	*Brandied Apples (p. 210)	¾ cup	103
		Whole Wheat Rolls	1 each	72
—	—	Reduced-Calorie Margarine	1 teaspoon	20
	349			**459**
		SNACK		
1 cup	150	*Mocha Milk Shake (p. 94)	1 cup	150
	150			**150**

Total 1197

(Calories from Fat: 15%)

Total 1583

(Calories from Fat: 17%)

Day 7

1200 CALORIES			1600 CALORIES	
		BREAKFAST		
1 slice	191	*Chocolate Chip Streusel Cake (p. 25)	1 slice	191
—	—	Turkey Sausage Breakfast Link	1 link	79
½ cup	41	Blueberries	½ cup	41
1 cup	86	Skim Milk	1 cup	86
	318			**397**
		LUNCH		
1 serving	277	*Chicken and Noodles (p. 171)	1 serving	277
1 roll	133	*Potato Pan Rolls (p. 101)	2 rolls	266
1 cup	7	Lettuce	1 cup	7
½ medium	13	Tomato	½ medium	13
1 tablespoon	12	Nonfat Mayonnaise	1 tablespoon	12
	442			**575**
		DINNER		
1 serving	133	*Lobster Tails with Lemon Cream (p. 115)	1 serving	133
6 spears	21	Steamed Asparagus	6 spears	21
½ cup	127	*Roasted Garlic and Onion Risotto (p. 121)	1 cup	253
1 cup	79	*Chocolate-Hazelnut Coffee (p. 72)	1 cup	79
	360			**486**
		SNACK		
1 tablespoon	38	*Chutney Spread (p. 197)	2 tablespoons	76
3 cakes	30	Fat-Free Caramel-Flavored Popcorn Cakes	6 cakes	60
	68			**136**

Total 1188

(Calories from Fat: 19%)

Total 1594

(Calories from Fat: 17%)

Calorie/Nutrient Chart

FOOD	APPROXIMATE MEASURE	FOOD ENERGY (CALORIES)	PROTEIN (GRAMS)	FAT (GRAMS)	SATURATED FAT (GRAMS)	CARBOHYDRATE (GRAMS)	FIBER (GRAMS)	CHOLESTEROL (MILLIGRAMS)	IRON (MILLIGRAMS)	SODIUM (MILLIGRAMS)	CALCIUM (MILLIGRAMS)
Alfalfa sprouts, raw	½ cup	8	1.1	0.2	0.02	1.1	0.6	0	0.3	2	9
Apple											
Fresh	1 medium	81	0.2	0.5	0.08	21.0	4.3	0	0.2	0	10
Juice, unsweetened	½ cup	58	0.1	0.1	0.02	14.5	0.2	0	0.5	4	9
Applesauce, unsweetened	½ cup	52	0.2	0.1	0.01	13.8	1.8	0	0.1	2	4
Apricot											
Fresh	1 each	18	0.4	0.1	0.01	4.1	0.8	0	0.2	0	5
Canned, in juice	½ cup	58	0.8	0.0	0.00	15.0	0.5	0	0.4	5	15
Canned, in light syrup	½ cup	75	0.7	0.1	—	19.0	0.5	—	0.3	1	12
Canned, peeled, in water	½ cup	25	0.8	0.0	0.00	6.2	1.7	0	0.6	12	9
Dried, uncooked	1 each	17	0.3	0.0	0.00	4.3	0.5	0	0.3	1	3
Nectar	½ cup	70	0.5	0.1	0.01	18.0	0.8	0	0.5	4	9
Artichoke											
Whole, cooked	1 each	53	2.6	0.2	0.04	12.4	1.1	0	1.6	79	47
Hearts, cooked	½ cup	37	1.8	0.1	0.03	8.7	0.8	0	1.1	55	33
Arugula	3 ounces	21	2.2	0.5	—	3.1	—	0	—	23	136
Asparagus, fresh, cooked	½ cup	23	2.3	0.3	0.06	4.0	0.9	0	0.6	4	22
Avocado	1 medium	322	3.9	30.6	4.88	14.8	4.2	0	2.0	20	22
Bacon											
Canadian-style	1 ounce	45	5.8	2.0	0.63	0.5	0.0	14	0.2	399	2
Cured, broiled	1 ounce	163	8.6	14.0	4.93	0.2	0.0	24	0.5	452	3
Turkey, cooked	1 ounce	60	4.0	4.0	—	8.0	—	20	—	400	—
Bamboo shoots, cooked	½ cup	7	0.9	0.1	0.03	1.1	0.4	0	0.1	2	7
Banana											
Mashed	½ cup	101	1.1	0.5	0.20	25.8	3.2	0	0.3	1	7
Whole	1 medium	109	1.2	0.5	0.22	27.6	3.5	0	0.4	1	7
Barley											
Dry	½ cup	352	9.9	1.2	0.24	77.7	15.6	0	2.5	9	29
Cooked	½ cup	97	1.8	0.3	0.07	22.2	—	0	1.0	2	9
Basil, fresh, raw	¼ cup	1	0.1	0.0	—	0.1	—	0	0.1	0	3
Bean sprouts, raw	½ cup	16	1.6	0.1	0.01	3.1	0.6	0	0.5	3	7
Beans, cooked and drained											
Black	½ cup	114	7.6	0.5	0.12	20.4	3.6	0	1.8	1	23
Black, canned, no-salt-added	½ cup	100	7.0	0.0	0.00	17.0	6.0	0	1.5	15	48
Cannellini	½ cup	112	7.7	0.4	0.06	20.2	3.2	0	2.6	2	25
Garbanzo (chickpeas)	½ cup	134	7.3	2.1	0.22	22.5	2.9	0	2.4	6	40
Great Northern	½ cup	132	9.3	0.5	0.16	23.7	3.8	0	2.4	2	76
Green, fresh	½ cup	22	1.2	0.2	0.40	4.9	1.1	0	0.8	2	29
Green, canned, regular pack	½ cup	14	0.8	0.1	0.01	3.1	0.9	0	0.5	171	18
Kidney or red	½ cup	112	7.7	0.4	0.06	20.2	3.2	0	2.6	2	25
Lima, frozen, baby	½ cup	94	6.0	0.3	0.06	17.5	4.8	0	1.8	26	25
Pinto, canned	½ cup	94	5.5	0.4	0.08	17.5	2.6	0	1.9	184	44
Pinto, canned, no-salt-added	½ cup	90	5.0	0.5	0.00	17.0	6.0	0	1.5	15	32
Wax, canned	½ cup	14	0.8	0.1	0.01	3.1	0.8	0	0.5	171	18
White	½ cup	127	8.0	0.6	0.15	23.2	3.9	0	2.5	2	65
Beef, trimmed of fat											
Flank steak, broiled	3 ounces	207	21.6	12.7	5.43	0.0	0.0	60	2.2	71	5
Ground, extra-lean, broiled	3 ounces	218	21.5	13.9	5.46	0.0	0.0	71	2.0	60	6
Ground, ultra-lean, broiled	3 ounces	146	20.8	7.0	2.75	1.5	—	72	—	238	—
Liver, braised	3 ounces	137	20.7	4.2	1.62	2.9	0.0	331	5.7	60	6

Dash (—) indicates insufficient data available.

FOOD	APPROXIMATE MEASURE	FOOD ENERGY (CALORIES)	PROTEIN (GRAMS)	FAT (GRAMS)	SATURATED FAT (GRAMS)	CARBOHYDRATE (GRAMS)	FIBER (GRAMS)	CHOLESTEROL (MILLIGRAMS)	IRON (MILLIGRAMS)	SODIUM (MILLIGRAMS)	CALCIUM (MILLIGRAMS)
Beef (*continued*)											
Round, bottom, braised	3 ounces	189	26.9	8.2	2.92	0.0	0.0	82	2.9	43	4
Round, eye of, cooked	3 ounces	156	24.7	5.5	2.12	0.0	0.0	59	1.7	53	4
Round, top, lean, broiled	3 ounces	162	27.0	5.3	1.84	0.0	0.0	71	2.4	52	5
Sirloin, broiled	3 ounces	177	25.8	7.4	3.03	0.0	0.0	76	2.9	56	9
Tenderloin, roasted	3 ounces	173	24.0	7.9	3.09	0.0	0.0	71	3.0	54	6
Beets											
Fresh, diced, cooked	½ cup	26	0.9	0.4	0.01	5.7	0.8	0	0.5	42	9
Canned, regular pack	½ cup	31	0.8	0.1	0.02	7.5	0.7	0	0.5	201	16
Beverages											
Beer	12 fluid ounces	146	1.1	0.0	0.00	13.1	0.7	0	0.1	18	18
Beer, light	12 fluid ounces	95	0.7	0.0	0.00	4.4	—	0	0.1	10	17
Bourbon, brandy, gin, rum, vodka, or whiskey, 80 proof	1 fluid ounce	65	0.0	0.0	0.00	0.0	0.0	0	0.0	0	0
Champagne	6 fluid ounces	135	0.5	0.0	0.00	2.1	0.0	0	0.9	7	5
Club soda	8 fluid ounces	0	0.0	0.0	0.00	0.0	0.0	0	—	48	11
Coffee, black	1 cup	5	0.2	0.0	0.00	0.9	—	0	1.0	5	5
Coffee liqueur	1 fluid ounce	99	0.0	0.1	0.03	13.9	—	0	0.0	2	0
Cognac brandy	1 fluid ounce	69	—	—	—	—	—	—	—	—	—
Crème de menthe liqueur	1 tablespoon	110	0.0	0.1	0.00	12.3	—	0	0.0	1	0
Sherry, sweet	1 fluid ounce	39	0.1	0.0	—	2.0	0.0	0	0.1	4	2
Vermouth, dry	1 fluid ounce	35	0.0	0.0	0.00	1.6	0.0	0	0.1	5	2
Vermouth, sweet	1 fluid ounce	45	0.0	0.0	0.00	4.7	0.0	0	0.1	8	2
Wine, port	6 fluid ounces	279	0.2	0.0	0.00	21.3	0.0	0	0.7	7	7
Wine, red	6 fluid ounces	121	0.4	0.0	0.00	0.5	0.0	0	1.4	18	12
Wine, white, dry	6 fluid ounces	117	0.2	0.0	0.00	1.1	0.0	0	0.9	7	16
Wine cooler											
Berry	12 fluid ounces	210	0.0	0.0	0.00	32.0	0.0	0	—	5	—
Original	12 fluid ounces	180	0.0	0.0	0.00	27.0	0.0	0	—	0	—
Biscuit and baking mix, low-fat	¼ cup	140	3.0	0.5	0.00	40.0	0.0	0	1.1	510	0
Blackberries, fresh	½ cup	37	0.5	0.3	0.01	9.2	5.3	0	0.4	0	23
Blueberries, fresh	½ cup	41	0.5	0.3	0.02	10.2	3.3	0	0.1	4	4
Bouillon, dry											
Beef-flavored cubes	1 cube	3	0.1	0.0	—	0.2	—	—	—	400	—
Beef-flavored granules	1 teaspoon	10	0.5	1.1	0.30	0.5	—	—	—	945	—
Chicken-flavored cubes	1 cube	10	0.2	0.2	—	1.1	—	1	0.1	1152	—
Chicken-flavored granules	1 teaspoon	10	0.5	1.1	0.30	0.5	—	—	—	819	—
Bran											
Oat, dry, uncooked	½ cup	153	8.0	3.0	0.28	23.5	6.0	0	2.6	1	31
Oat, unprocessed	½ cup	114	8.0	3.3	0.62	30.8	7.4	0	2.5	2	27
Wheat, crude	½ cup	65	4.7	1.3	0.19	19.4	12.7	0	3.2	1	22
Bread											
Bagel, miniature, plain	1 each	70	3.0	0.0	0.00	14.0	—	0	0.9	130	—
Bagel, regular-size, plain	1 each	161	5.9	1.5	0.21	30.5	1.2	—	1.4	196	23
Biscuit, homemade	1 each	127	2.3	6.4	1.74	14.9	0.6	2	0.6	224	65
Bun, hamburger or hot dog	1 each	136	3.2	3.4	0.52	22.4	0.1	13	0.8	112	19
Bun, hamburger, reduced-calorie, whole wheat	1 each	80	2.0	1.0	0.00	15.0	1.4	0	—	220	1
Cornbread	2-ounce square	154	3.5	6.0	3.36	21.1	1.2	56	0.7	273	96
English muffin	1 each	182	5.9	3.6	1.93	30.9	0.8	32	1.5	234	41
French	1 slice	73	2.3	0.5	0.16	13.9	0.6	1	0.6	145	11
Light, Italian	1 slice	40	2.0	0.0	0.00	10.0	2.0	0	0.6	120	0
Light, wheatberry or 7-grain	1 slice	40	2.0	1.0	—	7.0	2.8	0	0.7	105	20
Pita, whole wheat	1 medium	122	2.4	0.9	0.10	23.5	4.4	0	4.4	—	39
Pumpernickel	1 slice	76	2.8	0.4	0.05	16.4	1.8	0	0.7	176	26
Raisin	1 slice	66	1.6	0.7	0.16	13.4	0.9	1	0.3	91	18
Rye	1 slice	61	2.3	0.3	0.04	13.0	1.5	0	0.4	139	19
White	1 slice	67	2.2	0.8	0.19	12.6	0.5	1	0.6	127	18
Whole wheat	1 slice	56	2.4	0.7	0.12	11.0	2.1	1	0.5	121	23

FOOD	APPROXIMATE MEASURE	FOOD ENERGY (CALORIES)	PROTEIN (GRAMS)	FAT (GRAMS)	SATURATED FAT (GRAMS)	CARBOHYDRATE (GRAMS)	FIBER (GRAMS)	CHOLESTEROL (MILLIGRAMS)	IRON (MILLIGRAMS)	SODIUM (MILLIGRAMS)	CALCIUM (MILLIGRAMS)
Breadcrumbs											
Fine, dry	½ cup	196	6.3	2.2	0.52	36.7	2.1	2	1.7	368	61
Seasoned	½ cup	214	8.4	1.5	—	41.5	0.3	—	1.9	1590	59
Breadstick, plain	1 each	17	0.4	0.5	—	2.7	—	—	0.2	20	1
Broccoli, fresh, chopped, cooked or raw	½ cup	12	1.3	0.1	0.02	2.3	1.4	0	0.4	12	21
Broth											
Beef, canned, diluted	1 cup	31	4.8	0.7	0.34	2.6	0.0	24	0.5	782	0
Beef, no-salt-added	1 cup	22	0.5	0.0	0.00	1.9	0.0	0	0.0	7	0
Chicken, low-sodium	1 cup	22	0.4	0.0	—	2.0	0.0	0	0.0	4	0
Chicken, no-salt-added	1 cup	16	1.0	1.0	—	0.0	—	—	—	67	—
Vegetable	1 cup	22	0.0	1.1	—	3.3	—	—	0.3	1015	—
Brussels sprouts, fresh, cooked	½ cup	30	2.0	0.4	0.08	6.8	3.4	0	0.9	16	28
Bulgur, uncooked	½ cup	239	8.6	0.9	0.16	53.1	12.8	0	1.7	12	24
Butter											
Regular	1 tablespoon	102	0.1	11.5	7.17	0.0	0.0	31	0.0	117	3
Whipped	1 tablespoon	68	0.1	7.7	4.78	0.0	0.0	21	0.0	78	2
Cabbage											
Bok choy, shredded	1 cup	9	1.0	0.1	0.02	1.5	0.7	0	0.6	45	73
Common varieties, raw, shredded	½ cup	8	0.4	0.1	0.01	1.9	0.8	0	0.2	6	16
Cake, without frosting											
Angel food	2-ounce slice	147	3.2	0.1	—	33.7	0.0	0	0.2	83	54
Pound	1-ounce slice	305	3.6	17.5	10.19	33.7	0.4	134	0.5	245	27
Pound, fat-free	2-ounce slice	147	3.3	0.0	0.00	32.7	0.3	0	0.0	193	21
Pound, chocolate, fat-free	2-ounce slice	140	2.7	0.0	0.00	32.7	1.3	0	0.8	273	11
Sponge, cut into 12 slices	1 slice	183	3.6	5.0	1.48	30.8	0.3	221	0.8	99	44
Yellow, cut into 12 slices	1 slice	190	2.8	7.5	1.92	28.0	0.3	40	0.2	157	79
Candy											
Caramels	1 ounce	108	1.3	2.3	1.87	21.8	0.3	2	0.0	69	39
Fudge, chocolate	1 ounce	113	0.8	3.4	—	21.3	0.1	0	0.3	54	22
Gumdrops	1 ounce	98	0.0	0.2	0.03	24.8	0.0	0	0.1	10	2
Hard	1 each	27	0.0	0.0	0.00	6.8	0.0	0	0.1	2	1
Jelly beans	1 ounce	104	0.0	0.1	0.09	26.4	0.0	0	0.3	3	3
Milk chocolate	1 ounce	153	2.4	8.7	5.13	16.4	—	7	0.4	23	58
Cantaloupe, raw, diced	½ cup	28	0.7	0.2	0.12	6.7	0.9	0	0.2	7	9
Capers	1 tablespoon	4	0.4	0.0	—	0.6	—	0	—	670	—
Carambola (starfruit)	1 medium	42	0.7	0.4	—	9.9	1.5	0	0.3	3	5
Carrot											
Raw	1 medium	31	0.7	0.1	0.02	7.3	2.3	0	0.4	25	19
Cooked, sliced	½ cup	33	0.8	0.1	0.22	7.6	1.4	0	0.4	48	22
Juice, canned	½ cup	66	1.6	0.2	0.05	15.3	1.6	0	0.8	48	40
Catsup											
Regular	1 tablespoon	18	0.3	0.1	0.01	4.3	0.3	0	0.1	178	4
No-salt-added	1 tablespoon	15	0.0	0.0	—	4.0	—	—	—	6	—
Reduced-calorie	1 tablespoon	7	0.0	0.0	—	1.2	—	—	0.0	3	0
Cauliflower											
Flowerets, raw	½ cup	12	1.0	0.1	0.01	2.5	1.2	0	0.3	7	14
Flowerets, cooked	½ cup	15	1.2	0.1	0.02	2.8	1.4	0	0.2	4	17
Caviar	1 tablespoon	40	3.9	2.9	0.07	0.6	0.0	94	—	240	—
Celeriac, raw, shredded	½ cup	30	1.2	0.2	0.06	7.2	1.0	0	0.5	78	34
Celery, raw, diced	½ cup	10	0.4	0.1	0.02	2.2	1.0	0	0.2	52	24
Cereal											
Bran flakes	½ cup	64	2.5	0.4	0.06	15.3	2.7	0	5.6	182	10
Bran, whole	½ cup	104	6.0	1.5	0.12	32.7	14.9	0	6.7	387	30
Corn flakes	½ cup	44	0.9	0.0	0.00	9.8	0.1	0	0.7	140	0
Crispy rice	½ cup	55	0.9	0.1	—	12.4	0.2	0	0.3	103	3
Granola	½ cup	242	5.8	8.9	—	34.7	—	—	1.8	66	29

Dash (—) indicates insufficient data available.

FOOD	APPROXIMATE MEASURE	FOOD ENERGY (CALORIES)	PROTEIN (GRAMS)	FAT (GRAMS)	SATURATED FAT (GRAMS)	CARBOHYDRATE (GRAMS)	FIBER (GRAMS)	CHOLESTEROL (MILLIGRAMS)	IRON (MILLIGRAMS)	SODIUM (MILLIGRAMS)	CALCIUM (MILLIGRAMS)
Cereal (*continued*)											
Granola, with raisins, low-fat	½ cup	181	4.5	3.0	0.00	38.0	3.0	0	2.7	91	—
Granola, without raisins, low-fat	½ cup	165	3.0	2.2	0.00	34.5	3.0	0	2.7	53	—
Puffed wheat	½ cup	22	0.9	0.1	0.01	4.8	0.2	0	0.3	0	2
Raisin bran	½ cup	77	2.7	0.5	—	18.6	3.4	0	3.0	179	9
Shredded wheat miniatures	½ cup	76	2.3	0.5	0.08	17.0	2.0	0	0.9	2	8
Toasted oat	½ cup	44	1.7	0.7	0.13	7.8	0.4	0	1.8	123	19
Whole-grain wheat flakes	½ cup	79	1.9	0.2	0.04	18.6	1.4	0	0.6	150	6
Cheese											
American, processed	1 ounce	106	6.3	8.9	5.58	0.5	0.0	27	0.1	405	175
American, processed, fat-free	¾ ounce	30	5.0	0.0	0.00	3.0	0.0	3	0.0	320	120
American, processed, light	1 ounce	50	6.9	2.0	—	1.0	0.0	—	—	407	198
American, processed, skim	1 ounce	69	6.0	4.0	—	2.0	0.0	15	—	407	198
Asiago	1 ounce	101	7.0	8.0	5.00	0.5	0.0	25	—	342	168
Blue	1 ounce	100	6.1	8.1	5.30	0.7	0.0	21	0.1	395	150
Brie	1 ounce	95	5.9	7.8	4.94	0.1	0.0	28	0.1	178	52
Camembert	1 ounce	85	5.6	6.9	4.33	0.1	0.0	20	0.1	239	110
Cheddar	1 ounce	114	7.0	9.4	5.98	0.4	0.0	30	0.2	176	204
Cheddar, fat-free	1 ounce	40	9.0	0.0	0.00	1.0	0.0	5	0.0	200	200
Cheddar, 40% less-fat	1 ounce	71	5.0	4.1	2.40	6.0	—	15	0.1	195	192
Cheddar, light, processed	1 ounce	50	6.9	2.0	—	1.0	0.0	—	—	442	198
Cheddar, reduced-fat, sharp	1 ounce	86	8.3	5.4	3.15	1.2	0.0	19	0.1	205	251
Colby, reduced-fat	1 ounce	85	8.2	5.5	3.23	0.7	—	19	0.1	163	223
Cottage, dry curd, no-salt-added	½ cup	62	12.5	0.3	0.20	1.3	0.0	5	0.2	9	23
Cottage, nonfat	½ cup	70	15.0	0.0	0.00	3.0	—	5	—	419	60
Cottage, low-fat (1% milkfat)	½ cup	81	14.0	1.1	0.72	3.1	0.0	5	0.2	459	69
Cottage, low-fat (2% milkfat)	½ cup	102	15.5	2.2	1.38	4.1	0.0	9	0.2	459	77
Cottage (4% milkfat)	½ cup	108	13.1	4.7	2.99	2.8	0.0	16	0.1	425	63
Cream, light	1 ounce	62	2.9	4.8	2.86	1.8	—	16	0.0	160	38
Cream, nonfat	1 ounce	24	4.0	0.0	—	1.0	0.0	5	0.0	170	80
Farmer	1 ounce	40	4.0	3.0	—	1.0	—	—	—	—	30
Feta	1 ounce	75	4.0	6.0	4.24	1.2	0.0	25	0.2	316	139
Fontina	1 ounce	110	7.3	8.8	5.44	0.4	0.0	33	0.1	—	156
Goat, semisoft	1 ounce	103	6.1	8.5	5.85	0.7	0.0	22	0.5	146	84
Gouda	1 ounce	101	7.1	7.8	4.99	0.6	0.0	32	0.1	232	198
Gruyère	1 ounce	117	8.4	9.2	5.36	0.1	0.0	31	—	95	287
Monterey Jack	1 ounce	106	6.9	8.6	5.41	0.2	0.0	22	0.2	152	211
Monterey Jack, fat-free	1 ounce	40	9.0	0.0	0.00	1.0	0.0	5	0.0	200	200
Monterey Jack, reduced-fat	1 ounce	83	8.4	5.4	3.15	0.5	—	19	0.1	181	227
Mozzarella, part-skim	1 ounce	72	6.9	4.5	2.86	0.8	0.0	16	0.1	132	183
Mozzarella, whole milk	1 ounce	80	5.5	6.1	3.73	0.6	0.0	22	0.0	106	147
Muenster	1 ounce	104	6.6	8.5	5.42	0.3	0.0	27	0.1	178	203
Neufchâtel	1 ounce	74	2.8	6.6	4.20	0.8	0.0	22	0.1	113	21
Parmesan, grated	1 ounce	129	11.8	8.5	5.40	1.1	0.0	22	0.3	528	390
Parmesan Italian Topping, fat-free, grated	1 ounce	60	8.0	0.0	0.00	8.0	0.0	20	0.0	180	128
Provolone	1 ounce	100	7.2	7.5	4.84	0.6	0.0	20	0.1	248	214
Ricotta, light	1 ounce	20	3.0	1.0	0.60	1.0	—	4	—	20	34
Ricotta, nonfat	1 ounce	20	4.0	0.0	—	2.0	—	3	—	15	48
Ricotta, part-skim	1 ounce	39	3.2	2.2	1.39	1.5	0.0	9	0.1	35	77
Romano, grated	1 ounce	110	9.0	7.6	4.85	1.0	0.0	29	—	340	302
Swiss	1 ounce	107	8.1	7.8	5.04	1.0	0.0	26	0.0	74	272
Swiss, processed, fat-free	¾ ounce	30	5.0	0.0	0.00	3.0	0.0	3	0.0	240	120
Swiss, reduced-fat	1 ounce	85	9.6	5.0	2.78	0.5	—	18	0.1	44	334
Cherries											
Dried	1 ounce	82	1.4	1.1	0.25	18.8	2.6	0	0.5	0	17
Fresh, sweet	½ cup	52	0.9	0.7	0.16	12.0	1.7	0	0.3	0	11
Sour, in light syrup	½ cup	94	0.9	0.1	0.03	24.3	0.1	0	1.7	9	13
Sour, unsweetened	½ cup	39	0.8	0.2	0.05	9.4	1.8	0	0.2	2	12

FOOD	APPROXIMATE MEASURE	FOOD ENERGY (CALORIES)	PROTEIN (GRAMS)	FAT (GRAMS)	SATURATED FAT (GRAMS)	CARBOHYDRATE (GRAMS)	FIBER (GRAMS)	CHOLESTEROL (MILLIGRAMS)	IRON (MILLIGRAMS)	SODIUM (MILLIGRAMS)	CALCIUM (MILLIGRAMS)
Chicken, skinned, boned, and roasted											
White meat	3 ounces	147	26.1	3.8	1.07	0.0	0.0	72	0.9	65	13
Dark meat	3 ounces	174	23.3	8.3	2.26	0.0	0.0	79	1.1	79	13
Liver	3 ounces	134	20.7	4.6	1.56	0.7	0.0	537	7.2	43	12
Chili sauce	1 tablespoon	18	0.4	0.1	0.03	4.2	0.1	0	0.1	228	3
Chives, raw, chopped	1 tablespoon	1	0.1	0.0	0.00	0.1	0.1	0	0.0	0	2
Chocolate											
Chips, semisweet	¼ cup	215	1.7	15.2	—	24.2	0.4	0	1.1	1	13
Sweet	1 ounce	150	1.2	9.9	—	16.4	0.1	0	0.4	9	27
Syrup, fudge	1 tablespoon	62	0.9	2.6	1.55	10.1	0.1	2	0.2	17	24
Unsweetened, baking	1 ounce	141	3.1	14.7	8.79	8.5	0.7	0	2.0	1	23
White, baking	1 ounce	169	1.5	11.9	7.18	14.6	0.0	4	0.0	35	49
Chutney, apple	1 tablespoon	41	0.2	0.0	—	10.5	—	—	0.2	34	5
Cilantro, fresh, minced	1 tablespoon	1	0.1	0.0	0.00	0.3	0.2	0	0.2	1	5
Clams											
Raw	½ cup	92	15.8	1.2	0.12	3.2	0.0	42	17.3	69	57
Canned, drained	½ cup	118	20.4	1.6	0.15	4.1	0.0	54	22.4	90	74
Cocoa powder, unsweetened	1 tablespoon	24	1.6	0.7	0.44	2.6	—	0	0.9	2	8
Coconut											
Fresh, grated	1 cup	460	4.3	43.5	38.61	19.8	11.7	0	3.2	26	18
Dried, sweetened, shredded	1 cup	463	2.7	32.8	29.08	44.0	4.9	0	1.8	242	14
Dried, unsweetened, shredded	1 cup	526	5.5	51.4	45.62	18.8	4.2	0	2.6	30	21
Cookies											
Brownie	2-ounce bar	243	2.7	10.1	3.13	39.0	—	10	1.3	153	25
Chocolate	1 each	72	1.0	3.4	0.90	9.4	0.0	13	0.4	61	18
Chocolate chip, homemade	1 each	69	0.9	4.6	—	6.8	0.2	7	0.3	30	7
Fig bar	1 each	60	0.5	1.0	0.26	11.0	—	—	0.5	60	10
Fig bar, fat-free	1 each	50	0.5	0.0	0.00	11.0	1.0	0	0.2	63	8
Fortune	1 each	23	0.3	0.2	—	5.0	0.1	—	0.1	—	1
Gingersnaps	1 each	36	0.5	1.3	0.33	5.4	0.0	3	0.4	11	14
Oatmeal, plain	1 each	57	0.9	2.7	0.68	7.2	0.4	9	0.3	46	13
Sugar wafers	1 each	47	0.6	2.4	0.48	5.9	0.0	7	0.1	61	4
Vanilla creme	1 each	83	0.8	3.6	—	12.1	—	—	0.4	61	3
Vanilla wafers	1 each	17	0.2	0.9	0.17	2.1	0.0	2	0.1	22	2
Corn											
Fresh, kernels, cooked	½ cup	89	2.6	1.0	0.16	20.6	3.0	0	0.5	14	2
Cream-style, regular pack	½ cup	92	2.2	0.5	0.08	23.2	1.5	0	0.5	365	4
Cornmeal											
Degermed, yellow	1 cup	505	11.7	2.3	0.31	107.2	7.2	0	5.7	4	7
Self-rising	1 cup	407	10.1	4.1	0.58	85.7	—	0	7.0	1521	440
Cornstarch	1 tablespoon	31	0.0	0.0	0.00	7.3	0.1	0	0.0	1	0
Couscous, cooked	½ cup	100	3.4	0.1	0.03	20.8	—	0	0.3	4	7
Crab											
Blue, cooked	3 ounces	87	17.2	1.5	0.19	0.0	0.0	85	0.8	237	88
Imitation	3 ounces	87	10.2	1.1	—	8.7	0.0	17	0.3	715	11
King, cooked	3 ounces	82	16.5	1.3	0.11	0.0	0.0	45	0.6	912	50
Crackers											
Butter	1 each	17	0.0	1.0	—	2.0	—	—	0.1	32	4
Graham, plain	1 square	30	0.5	0.5	—	5.5	—	—	0.2	48	1
Melba rounds, plain	1 each	11	0.4	0.2	—	2.0	—	—	0.1	34	0
Saltine	1 each	13	0.3	0.4	—	2.1	—	—	0.1	43	5
Saltine, fat-free	1 each	10	0.2	0.0	0.00	2.4	—	0	0.1	23	0
Whole wheat	1 each	33	0.7	1.3	0.33	4.7	0.3	0	0.0	60	0
Cranberries											
Dried, whole	1 ounce	85	0.0	0.4	0.14	20.3	1.6	0	0.0	1	3
Fresh, whole	½ cup	23	0.2	0.1	0.01	6.0	0.6	0	0.1	0	3

Dash (—) indicates insufficient data available.

FOOD	APPROXIMATE MEASURE	FOOD ENERGY (CALORIES)	PROTEIN (GRAMS)	FAT (GRAMS)	SATURATED FAT (GRAMS)	CARBOHYDRATE (GRAMS)	FIBER (GRAMS)	CHOLESTEROL (MILLIGRAMS)	IRON (MILLIGRAMS)	SODIUM (MILLIGRAMS)	CALCIUM (MILLIGRAMS)
Cranberries (*continued*)											
Juice cocktail, reduced-calorie	½ cup	22	0.0	0.0	0.00	5.6	—	0	0.0	4	11
Juice cocktail, regular	½ cup	75	0.0	0.1	0.00	19.2	—	0	0.2	5	4
Sauce, sweetened	¼ cup	105	0.1	0.1	0.01	26.9	0.2	0	0.1	20	3
Cream											
Half-and-half	1 tablespoon	20	0.4	1.7	1.08	0.7	0.0	6	0.0	6	16
Sour	1 tablespoon	31	0.5	3.0	1.88	0.6	0.0	6	0.0	8	17
Sour, nonfat	1 tablespoon	10	1.0	0.0	—	1.0	—	0	—	10	—
Sour, reduced-calorie	1 tablespoon	20	0.4	1.8	1.12	0.6	0.0	6	0.0	6	16
Whipping, unwhipped	1 tablespoon	51	0.3	5.5	3.43	0.4	0.0	20	0.0	6	10
Creamer, nondairy, powder	1 teaspoon	11	0.1	0.7	0.64	1.1	0.0	0	0.0	4	16
Croutons, seasoned	1 ounce	139	3.0	5.0	—	18.9	—	—	0.3	—	20
Cucumbers, raw, whole	1 medium	32	1.3	0.3	0.08	7.1	2.4	0	0.7	5	34
Currants	1 tablespoon	25	0.4	0.0	0.00	6.7	0.1	0	0.3	1	8
Dandelion greens, raw	1 cup	25	1.5	0.4	—	5.1	0.9	0	1.7	42	103
Dates, pitted, unsweetened	5 each	114	0.8	0.2	0.08	30.5	3.6	0	0.5	1	13
Doughnut											
Cake-type	1 each	156	1.8	7.4	1.92	20.6	0.5	24	0.5	200	16
Plain, yeast	1 each	166	2.5	10.7	2.60	15.1	0.9	10	0.6	94	15
Egg											
White	1 each	16	3.4	0.0	0.00	0.3	0.0	0	0.0	52	2
Whole	1 each	77	6.5	5.2	1.61	0.6	0.0	213	0.7	66	25
Yolk	1 each	61	2.8	5.2	1.61	0.3	0.0	213	0.6	7	23
Substitute	¼ cup	30	6.0	0.0	0.00	1.0	—	0	1.1	90	20
Eggplant, cooked without salt	½ cup	13	0.4	0.1	0.02	3.2	0.5	0	0.2	1	3
Extract, vanilla	1 teaspoon	15	0.0	0.0	—	1.5	0.0	0	0.0	0	0
Fennel, leaves, raw	½ cup	13	1.2	0.2	—	2.3	0.2	0	1.2	4	45
Figs											
Fresh	1 medium	37	0.4	0.2	0.03	9.9	1.9	0	0.2	1	18
Dried	1 each	48	0.6	0.2	0.04	12.2	3.2	0	0.4	2	27
Fish, cooked											
Cod	3 ounces	89	19.4	0.7	0.14	0.0	0.0	47	0.4	66	12
Flounder	3 ounces	100	20.5	1.3	0.31	0.0	0.0	58	0.3	89	15
Grouper	3 ounces	100	21.1	1.1	0.25	0.0	0.0	40	1.0	45	18
Haddock	3 ounces	95	20.6	0.8	0.14	0.0	0.0	63	1.1	74	36
Halibut	3 ounces	119	22.7	2.5	0.35	0.0	0.0	35	0.9	59	51
Mackerel	3 ounces	134	20.1	5.4	1.53	0.0	0.0	62	0.6	56	11
Mahimahi	3 ounces	93	20.2	0.8	0.20	0.0	0.0	80	1.2	96	—
Perch	3 ounces	100	21.1	1.0	0.20	0.0	0.0	98	1.0	67	87
Pollock	3 ounces	96	20.0	1.0	0.20	0.0	0.0	82	0.2	99	5
Pompano	3 ounces	179	20.1	10.3	3.83	0.0	0.0	54	0.6	65	37
Salmon, sockeye	3 ounces	184	23.2	9.3	1.63	0.0	0.0	74	0.5	56	6
Scrod	3 ounces	89	19.4	0.7	0.14	0.0	0.0	47	0.4	66	12
Snapper	3 ounces	109	22.4	1.5	0.31	0.0	0.0	40	0.2	48	34
Sole	3 ounces	100	20.5	1.3	0.31	0.0	0.0	58	0.3	89	15
Swordfish	3 ounces	132	21.6	4.4	1.20	0.0	0.0	43	0.9	98	5
Tilapia	3 ounces	84	16.0	2.0	—	—	0.0	—	—	45	—
Trout	3 ounces	128	22.4	3.7	0.71	0.0	0.0	62	2.1	29	73
Tuna, canned in oil, drained	3 ounces	168	24.8	7.0	1.30	0.0	0.0	15	1.2	301	11
Tuna, canned in water, drained	3 ounces	111	25.2	0.4	0.14	0.0	0.0	—	2.7	303	10
Flour											
All-purpose, unsifted	1 cup	455	12.9	1.2	0.19	95.4	3.4	0	5.8	2	19
Bread, sifted	1 cup	495	16.4	2.3	0.33	99.4	—	0	6.0	3	21
Cake, sifted	1 cup	395	8.9	0.9	0.14	85.1	—	0	8.0	2	15
Rye, light, sifted	1 cup	374	8.6	1.4	0.15	81.8	14.9	0	1.8	2	21
Whole wheat, unsifted	1 cup	407	16.4	2.2	0.39	87.1	15.1	0	4.7	6	41

FOOD	APPROXIMATE MEASURE	FOOD ENERGY (CALORIES)	PROTEIN (GRAMS)	FAT (GRAMS)	SATURATED FAT (GRAMS)	CARBOHYDRATE (GRAMS)	FIBER (GRAMS)	CHOLESTEROL (MILLIGRAMS)	IRON (MILLIGRAMS)	SODIUM (MILLIGRAMS)	CALCIUM (MILLIGRAMS)
Frankfurter											
All-meat	1 each	138	4.9	12.6	4.63	1.1	0.0	22	0.5	482	5
Chicken	1 each	113	5.7	8.6	—	3.0	—	44	0.9	603	42
Turkey	1 each	103	5.6	8.5	2.65	1.1	—	42	0.8	488	60
Fruit bits, dried	1 ounce	93	1.3	0.0	—	20.0	—	0	0.5	24	—
Fruit cocktail, canned, packed in juice	½ cup	57	0.6	0.0	0.00	14.6	0.8	0	0.2	5	10
Garlic, raw	1 clove	4	0.2	0.0	0.00	1.0	0.0	0	0.1	1	5
Gelatin											
Flavored, prepared with water	½ cup	81	1.5	0.0	—	18.6	0.0	0	0.0	54	0
Unflavored	1 teaspoon	10	2.6	0.0	—	0.0	—	—	—	3	—
Ginger											
Fresh, grated	1 teaspoon	1	0.0	0.0	0.00	0.3	0.0	0	0.0	0	0
Crystallized	1 ounce	96	0.1	0.1	—	24.7	0.2	0	6.0	17	65
Grapefruit											
Fresh	1 medium	77	1.5	0.2	0.03	19.3	1.5	0	0.2	0	29
Juice, unsweetened	½ cup	47	0.6	0.1	0.02	11.1	0.0	0	2.5	1	9
Grape juice, Concord	½ cup	60	0.0	0.0	—	14.9	—	—	0.0	11	4
Grapes, green, seedless	1 cup	114	1.1	0.9	0.30	28.4	2.6	0	0.4	3	18
Grits, cooked	½ cup	73	1.7	0.2	0.04	15.7	—	0	0.8	0	0
Ham											
Cured, roasted, extra-lean	3 ounces	123	17.8	4.7	1.54	1.3	0.0	45	1.3	1023	7
Reduced-fat, low-salt	3 ounces	104	15.3	4.2	—	1.8	—	42	—	658	—
Hominy, white or yellow	½ cup	58	1.2	0.7	0.10	11.4	2.0	0	0.5	168	8
Honey	1 tablespoon	64	0.1	0.0	0.00	17.5	0.0	0	0.1	1	1
Honeydew, raw, diced	1 cup	59	0.8	0.2	0.08	15.6	1.5	0	0.1	17	10
Horseradish, prepared	1 tablespoon	6	0.2	0.0	0.01	1.4	0.1	0	0.1	14	9
Hot sauce, bottled	¼ teaspoon	0	0.0	0.0	—	0.0	—	0	0.0	9	0
Ice cream											
Chocolate, regular	½ cup	147	2.6	7.5	4.62	19.2	0.0	—	0.6	52	74
Chocolate, fat-free	½ cup	100	3.0	0.0	0.00	22.0	0.0	0	0.0	60	80
Vanilla, regular	½ cup	134	2.3	7.2	4.39	15.9	0.0	30	0.0	58	88
Vanilla, fat-free	½ cup	100	2.0	0.0	0.00	22.0	0.0	0	0.0	40	64
Vanilla, gourmet	½ cup	175	2.0	11.8	7.37	16.0	0.0	44	0.1	54	75
Vanilla, low-fat	½ cup	92	2.6	2.8	1.76	14.5	0.0	9	0.1	52	88
Jams and Jellies											
Regular	1 tablespoon	54	0.1	0.0	0.01	14.0	0.2	0	0.2	2	4
Reduced-calorie	1 tablespoon	29	0.1	0.0	—	7.4	—	0	0.0	16	1
No-sugar-added	1 tablespoon	40	0.0	0.0	0.00	10.0	—	0	—	0	—
Jicama, diced	1 cup	49	1.6	0.2	0.07	10.5	0.7	0	0.7	7	18
Kiwifruit	1 each	44	1.0	0.5	0.08	8.9	2.6	0	0.4	0	20
Kumquat	1 each	12	0.2	0.0	0.00	3.1	0.7	0	0.1	1	8
Lamb											
Ground, cooked	3 ounces	241	21.0	16.7	6.91	0.0	—	82	1.5	69	19
Leg, roasted	3 ounces	162	24.1	6.6	2.35	0.0	—	76	1.8	58	7
Loin or chop, broiled	3 ounces	184	25.5	8.3	2.96	0.0	—	81	1.7	71	16
Rib, broiled	3 ounces	200	23.6	11.0	3.95	0.0	—	77	1.9	72	14
Lard	1 tablespoon	116	0.0	12.8	5.03	0.0	0.0	12	0.0	0	0
Leeks, sliced, raw	½ cup	32	0.8	0.2	0.03	7.3	0.6	0	1.0	10	31
Lemon											
Fresh	1 each	22	1.3	0.3	0.04	11.4	0.4	0	0.6	3	66
Juice	1 tablespoon	3	0.1	0.0	0.01	1.0	—	0	0.0	3	2

Dash (—) indicates insufficient data available.

FOOD	APPROXIMATE MEASURE	FOOD ENERGY (CALORIES)	PROTEIN (GRAMS)	FAT (GRAMS)	SATURATED FAT (GRAMS)	CARBOHYDRATE (GRAMS)	FIBER (GRAMS)	CHOLESTEROL (MILLIGRAMS)	IRON (MILLIGRAMS)	SODIUM (MILLIGRAMS)	CALCIUM (MILLIGRAMS)
Lemonade, sweetened	1 cup	99	0.2	0.0	0.01	26.0	0.2	0	0.4	7	7
Lentils, cooked	½ cup	115	8.9	0.4	0.05	19.9	4.0	0	3.3	2	19
Lettuce											
Belgian endive leaves	1 cup	14	0.9	0.1	0.02	2.9	—	0	0.5	6	—
Boston or Bibb, shredded	1 cup	7	0.7	0.1	0.02	1.3	0.4	0	0.2	3	—
Curly endive or escarole	1 cup	8	0.6	0.1	0.02	1.7	0.4	0	0.4	11	26
Iceberg, chopped	1 cup	7	0.5	0.1	0.01	1.1	0.5	0	0.3	5	10
Radicchio, raw, torn	1 cup	10	0.6	0.1	—	1.8	—	0	—	8	8
Romaine, chopped	1 cup	9	0.9	0.1	0.01	1.3	1.0	0	0.6	4	20
Lime											
Fresh	1 each	20	0.4	0.1	0.01	6.8	0.3	0	0.4	1	21
Juice	1 tablespoon	4	0.1	0.0	0.00	1.4	—	0	0.0	0	1
Lobster, meat only, cooked	3 ounces	83	17.4	0.5	0.09	1.1	0.0	61	0.3	323	52
Luncheon meats											
Bologna, all-meat	1 slice	90	3.3	8.0	3.01	0.8	0.0	16	0.4	289	3
Deviled ham	1 ounce	78	4.3	6.7	—	0.0	0.0	—	0.3	—	1
Salami	1 ounce	71	3.9	5.7	2.29	0.6	0.0	18	0.8	302	4
Turkey ham	1 ounce	34	5.5	1.2	0.45	0.3	—	19	0.4	286	2
Turkey pastrami	1 ounce	33	5.4	1.2	0.43	0.1	—	18	0.4	283	2
Lychees, raw	1 each	6	0.1	0.0	—	1.6	0.0	0	0.0	0	0
Mango, raw, chopped	½ cup	54	0.4	0.2	0.05	14.0	1.2	0	0.1	2	8
Margarine											
Regular	1 tablespoon	101	0.1	11.4	2.23	0.1	0.0	0	0.0	133	4
Reduced-calorie, stick	1 tablespoon	50	0.1	5.6	0.93	0.1	0.0	0	0.0	139	3
Fat-free	1 tablespoon	5	0.0	0.0	0.00	0.0	0.0	0	0.0	90	0
Marshmallows, miniature	½ cup	73	0.5	0.0	0.00	18.5	0.0	0	0.4	9	4
Mayonnaise											
Regular	1 tablespoon	99	0.2	10.9	1.62	0.4	0.0	8	0.1	78	2
Nonfat	1 tablespoon	12	0.0	0.0	—	3.0	—	0	0.0	190	—
Reduced-calorie	1 tablespoon	44	0.1	4.6	0.70	0.7	0.0	6	0.0	88	1
Milk											
Buttermilk	1 cup	98	7.8	2.1	1.35	11.7	0.0	10	0.1	257	284
Buttermilk, nonfat	1 cup	88	8.8	0.8	0.64	12.0	—	8	—	256	288
Chocolate, low-fat, 1%	1 cup	158	8.1	2.5	1.55	26.1	0.1	8	0.6	153	288
Chocolate, low-fat, 2%	1 cup	180	8.0	5.0	3.10	25.8	0.1	18	0.6	150	285
Condensed, sweetened	1 cup	982	24.2	26.3	16.77	166.5	0.0	104	0.5	389	869
Evaporated, skim, canned	1 cup	200	19.3	0.5	0.31	29.1	0.0	10	0.7	294	742
Low-fat, 1%	1 cup	102	8.0	2.5	1.61	11.6	0.0	10	0.1	122	300
Low-fat, 2%	1 cup	122	8.1	4.7	2.93	11.7	0.0	20	0.1	122	298
Nonfat dry	⅓ cup	145	14.5	0.3	0.20	20.8	0.0	8	0.1	214	503
Powder, malted, chocolate	1 tablespoon	84	1.1	0.7	—	18.4	—	—	0.3	47	13
Skim	1 cup	86	8.3	0.4	0.28	11.9	0.0	5	0.1	127	301
Whole	1 cup	149	8.0	8.1	5.05	11.3	0.0	34	0.1	120	290
Mint, fresh, raw	¼ cup	1	0.1	0.0	—	0.1	—	0	0.1	0	4
Molasses, cane, light	1 tablespoon	52	0.0	0.0	—	13.3	0.0	0	0.9	3	34
Mushrooms											
Fresh	½ cup	9	0.7	0.1	0.02	1.6	0.5	0	0.4	1	2
Canned	½ cup	19	1.5	0.2	0.02	3.9	—	0	0.6	—	—
Shiitake, dried	1 each	14	0.3	0.0	0.01	2.6	0.4	0	0.1	0	0
Mussels, blue, cooked	3 ounces	146	20.2	3.8	0.02	6.3	0.0	48	5.7	314	28
Mustard											
Dijon	1 tablespoon	18	0.0	1.0	—	1.0	0.0	0	—	446	—
Prepared, yellow	1 tablespoon	12	0.7	0.7	0.03	1.0	0.2	0	0.3	196	13
Nectarine, fresh	1 each	67	1.3	0.6	0.07	16.1	2.2	0	0.2	0	7
Nuts											
Almonds, chopped	1 tablespoon	48	1.6	4.2	0.40	1.7	0.9	0	0.3	1	22
Cashews, dry-roasted, unsalted	1 tablespoon	49	1.3	4.0	0.78	2.8	0.5	0	0.5	1	4

FOOD	APPROXIMATE MEASURE	FOOD ENERGY (CALORIES)	PROTEIN (GRAMS)	FAT (GRAMS)	SATURATED FAT (GRAMS)	CARBOHYDRATE (GRAMS)	FIBER (GRAMS)	CHOLESTEROL (MILLIGRAMS)	IRON (MILLIGRAMS)	SODIUM (MILLIGRAMS)	CALCIUM (MILLIGRAMS)
Nuts (continued)											
Hazelnuts, chopped	1 tablespoon	45	0.9	4.5	0.32	1.1	0.3	0	0.2	0	14
Macadamia, roasted, unsalted	1 tablespoon	60	0.6	6.4	0.96	1.1	0.1	0	0.1	1	4
Peanuts, roasted, unsalted	1 tablespoon	53	2.4	4.5	0.62	1.7	0.8	0	0.2	1	8
Pecans, chopped	1 tablespoon	50	0.6	5.0	0.40	1.4	0.5	0	0.2	0	3
Pine nuts	1 tablespoon	52	2.4	5.1	0.78	1.4	0.1	0	0.9	0	3
Pistachio nuts	1 tablespoon	46	1.6	3.9	0.49	2.0	0.9	0	0.5	0	11
Walnuts, black	1 tablespoon	47	1.9	4.4	0.28	0.9	0.5	0	0.2	0	5
Oats											
Cooked	1 cup	145	6.1	2.3	0.42	25.3	2.1	0	1.6	374	19
Rolled, dry	½ cup	156	6.5	2.6	0.45	27.1	4.2	0	1.7	2	21
Oil											
Canola	1 tablespoon	117	0.0	13.6	0.97	0.0	0.0	0	0.0	0	0
Corn	1 tablespoon	121	0.0	13.6	1.73	0.0	0.0	0	0.0	0	0
Olive	1 tablespoon	119	0.0	13.5	1.82	0.0	0.0	0	0.1	0	0
Peanut	1 tablespoon	119	0.0	13.5	2.28	0.0	0.0	0	0.0	0	0
Safflower	1 tablespoon	121	0.0	13.6	1.24	0.0	0.0	0	0.0	0	0
Sesame	1 tablespoon	121	0.0	13.6	1.92	0.0	0.0	0	0.0	0	0
Okra, cooked	½ cup	26	1.5	0.1	0.04	5.8	0.6	0	0.3	4	50
Olives											
Green, stuffed	1 medium	4	0.0	0.4	—	0.1	—	—	—	290	—
Ripe	1 medium	5	0.0	0.4	0.08	0.3	0.1	0	0.1	35	4
Onions											
Green, chopped	1 tablespoon	2	0.1	0.0	0.00	0.5	0.2	0	0.1	1	5
Raw, chopped	½ cup	32	1.0	0.1	0.02	7.3	1.6	0	0.2	3	17
Cooked, yellow or white, chopped	½ cup	23	0.7	0.1	0.02	5.3	—	0	0.1	2	12
Orange											
Fresh	1 medium	62	1.2	0.2	0.02	15.4	5.8	0	0.1	0	52
Juice	½ cup	56	0.8	0.1	0.01	13.4	0.2	0	0.1	1	11
Mandarin, canned, packed in juice	½ cup	46	0.7	0.0	0.00	12.0	0.1	0	0.4	6	14
Mandarin, canned, packed in light syrup	½ cup	77	0.6	0.1	0.02	20.4	0.1	0	0.5	8	9
Mandarin, canned, packed in water	½ cup	37	0.0	0.0	—	8.4	—	—	0.4	11	—
Oysters, raw	3 ounces	59	6.0	2.1	0.54	3.3	0.0	47	5.7	95	38
Papaya											
Fresh, cubed	½ cup	27	0.4	0.1	0.03	6.9	1.2	0	0.1	2	17
Nectar, canned	½ cup	71	0.3	0.3	0.06	18.1	—	0	0.4	6	13
Parsley, raw	1 tablespoon	1	0.1	0.0	0.00	0.3	0.2	0	0.2	1	5
Parsnips, cooked, diced	½ cup	63	1.0	0.2	0.04	15.1	2.1	0	0.4	8	29
Passion fruit	1 medium	17	0.4	0.1	—	4.2	2.0	0	0.3	5	2
Pasta, cooked											
Macaroni or lasagna noodles	½ cup	99	3.3	0.5	0.07	19.8	1.1	0	1.0	1	5
Medium egg noodles	½ cup	106	3.8	1.2	0.25	19.9	1.8	26	1.3	6	10
Rice noodles	½ cup	138	3.1	1.3	—	28.6	—	0	2.2	—	40
Spaghetti or fettuccine	½ cup	99	3.3	0.5	0.07	19.8	1.1	0	1.0	1	5
Spinach noodles	½ cup	100	3.8	1.0	0.15	18.9	1.4	0	1.8	22	46
Tortellini, fresh, cheese-filled	½ cup	180	8.7	5.3	1.33	24.6	—	27	1.5	147	53
Whole wheat	½ cup	100	3.7	1.4	0.18	19.8	2.5	0	1.0	1	12
Peaches											
Fresh	1 medium	37	0.6	0.1	0.01	9.7	1.4	0	0.1	0	4
Canned, packed in juice	½ cup	55	0.8	0.0	0.00	14.3	0.6	0	0.3	5	7
Canned, packed in light syrup	½ cup	69	0.6	0.0	0.00	18.6	0.4	0	0.5	6	4
Canned, packed in water	½ cup	29	0.5	0.1	0.01	7.5	0.4	0	0.4	4	2
Juice	½ cup	57	0.0	0.0	—	13.6	—	—	—	5	—

Dash (—) indicates insufficient data available.

FOOD	APPROXIMATE MEASURE	FOOD ENERGY (CALORIES)	PROTEIN (GRAMS)	FAT (GRAMS)	SATURATED FAT (GRAMS)	CARBOHYDRATE (GRAMS)	FIBER (GRAMS)	CHOLESTEROL (MILLIGRAMS)	IRON (MILLIGRAMS)	SODIUM (MILLIGRAMS)	CALCIUM (MILLIGRAMS)
Peanut butter											
Regular	1 tablespoon	95	4.6	8.3	1.38	2.6	1.0	0	0.3	79	5
Reduced-fat	1 tablespoon	90	4.0	6.0	1.00	7.5	0.5	0	0.4	70	—
No-salt-added	1 tablespoon	95	4.6	8.3	1.38	2.6	1.0	0	0.3	3	5
Pear											
Fresh	1 medium	97	0.6	0.7	0.03	24.9	4.3	0	0.4	0	18
Canned, packed in juice	½ cup	62	0.4	0.1	0.00	16.0	1.1	0	0.3	5	11
Canned, packed in light syrup	½ cup	71	0.2	0.0	—	19.6	3.1	0	0.3	6	6
Nectar, canned	½ cup	64	0.4	0.2	—	16.1	0.4	—	0.1	1	4
Peas											
Black-eyed, cooked	½ cup	90	6.7	0.7	0.17	15.0	1.5	0	1.2	3	23
English, cooked	½ cup	62	4.1	0.2	0.04	11.4	3.5	0	1.2	70	19
Snow pea pods, cooked or raw	½ cup	34	2.6	0.2	0.03	5.6	2.2	0	1.6	3	34
Split, cooked	½ cup	116	8.2	0.4	0.05	20.7	2.3	0	1.3	2	14
Sugar Snap, cooked or raw	½ cup	42	2.7	0.2	0.04	7.5	2.6	0	2.1	4	43
Peppers											
Chile, hot, green, chopped	1 tablespoon	4	0.2	0.0	0.00	0.9	0.2	0	0.1	1	2
Jalapeño, green	1 medium	4	0.2	0.0	0.00	0.9	0.2	0	0.1	1	2
Sweet, raw, green, red, or yellow	1 medium	19	0.6	0.4	0.05	3.9	1.2	0	0.9	2	4
Phyllo pastry, raw	1 sheet	57	1.3	1.1	0.17	10.0	—	0	0.6	92	2
Pickle											
Dill, sliced	¼ cup	4	0.2	0.1	0.02	0.9	0.5	0	0.4	553	10
Relish, chopped, sour	1 tablespoon	3	0.1	0.1	—	0.4	0.2	0	0.2	207	4
Sweet, sliced	¼ cup	57	0.2	0.2	0.04	14.1	0.4	0	0.5	276	5
Pie, baked, 9-inch diameter, cut into 8 slices											
Apple, fresh	1 slice	409	3.3	15.3	5.22	67.7	3.5	12	0.8	229	37
Chocolate meringue	1 slice	354	6.8	13.4	5.38	53.8	0.5	109	1.2	307	130
Egg custard	1 slice	248	7.3	11.6	4.07	28.6	0.3	149	0.9	229	129
Peach	1 slice	327	3.2	11.0	2.74	55.1	0.8	0	1.0	339	35
Pecan	1 slice	478	5.8	20.3	4.31	71.1	0.5	141	2.4	324	51
Pumpkin	1 slice	181	4.0	6.8	2.24	27.0	0.8	61	1.1	210	78
Pimiento, diced	1 tablespoon	4	0.2	0.1	0.01	1.0	—	0	0.3	3	1
Pineapple											
Fresh, diced	½ cup	38	0.3	0.3	0.02	9.6	1.2	0	0.3	1	5
Canned, packed in juice	½ cup	75	0.5	0.1	0.01	19.6	0.9	0	0.3	1	17
Canned, packed in light syrup	½ cup	66	0.5	0.2	0.01	16.9	0.6	0	0.5	1	18
Juice, unsweetened	½ cup	70	0.4	0.1	0.01	17.2	0.1	0	0.3	1	21
Plum, fresh	1 medium	35	0.5	0.4	0.03	8.3	1.3	0	0.1	0	3
Popcorn, hot-air popped	1 cup	23	0.8	0.3	0.04	4.6	0.9	0	0.2	0	1
Poppy seeds	1 tablespoon	47	1.6	3.9	0.43	2.1	0.5	0	0.8	2	127
Pork, cooked											
Chop, center-loin	3 ounces	204	24.2	11.1	—	0.0	0.0	77	0.9	59	5
Roast	3 ounces	204	22.7	11.7	4.07	0.0	0.0	77	1.0	59	8
Sausage link or patty	1 ounce	105	5.6	8.8	3.06	0.3	0.0	24	0.3	367	9
Spareribs	3 ounces	338	24.7	25.7	10.00	0.0	0.0	103	1.5	79	40
Tenderloin	3 ounces	141	24.5	4.1	1.41	0.0	0.0	79	1.3	57	8
Potatoes											
Baked, with skin	1 each	218	4.4	0.2	0.05	50.4	3.6	0	2.7	16	20
Boiled, diced	½ cup	67	1.3	0.1	0.02	15.6	1.2	0	0.2	4	6
Potato chips											
Regular	10 each	105	1.3	7.1	1.81	10.4	1.0	0	0.2	94	5
No-salt-added	10 each	105	1.3	7.1	1.81	10.4	1.0	0	0.2	1	5
Fat-free, made with real potatoes	10 each	37	1.0	0.0	0.00	7.7	0.7	0	0.3	60	0
Pretzel sticks, thin	10 each	25	0.5	0.5	—	4.4	0.0	—	0.3	83	4
Prunes											
Dried, pitted	1 each	20	0.2	0.0	0.00	5.3	0.6	0	0.2	0	4
Juice	½ cup	91	0.8	0.0	0.00	22.3	1.3	0	1.5	5	15

FOOD	APPROXIMATE MEASURE	FOOD ENERGY (CALORIES)	PROTEIN (GRAMS)	FAT (GRAMS)	SATURATED FAT (GRAMS)	CARBOHYDRATE (GRAMS)	FIBER (GRAMS)	CHOLESTEROL (MILLIGRAMS)	IRON (MILLIGRAMS)	SODIUM (MILLIGRAMS)	CALCIUM (MILLIGRAMS)
Pumpkin											
Canned	½ cup	42	1.3	0.3	0.18	9.9	2.0	0	1.7	6	32
Seeds, dry	1 ounce	153	7.0	13.0	2.46	5.0	0.6	0	4.2	5	12
Radish, fresh, sliced	½ cup	10	0.3	0.3	0.01	2.1	0.3	0	0.2	14	12
Raisins	1 tablespoon	27	0.3	0.0	0.01	7.2	0.5	0	0.2	1	4
Raisins, golden	1 tablespoon	31	0.4	0.1	0.02	8.2	0.5	0	0.2	1	5
Raspberries											
Black, fresh	½ cup	33	0.6	0.4	0.01	7.7	5.0	0	0.4	0	15
Red, fresh	½ cup	30	0.6	0.3	0.01	7.1	4.6	0	0.3	0	14
Rhubarb											
Raw, diced	½ cup	13	0.5	0.1	0.02	2.8	0.4	0	0.1	2	52
Cooked, with sugar	½ cup	157	0.5	0.1	0.01	42.1	—	0	0.3	1	196
Rice, cooked without salt or fat											
Brown	½ cup	110	2.5	0.9	—	23.2	0.3	1	0.5	1	8
White, long-grain	½ cup	108	2.0	0.1	—	24.0	0.5	0	0.9	0	10
Wild	½ cup	83	3.3	0.3	0.04	17.5	—	0	0.5	2	2
Rice cake, plain	1 each	36	0.7	0.2	0.00	7.7	0.1	0	0.2	1	1
Roll											
Croissant	1 each	272	4.6	17.3	10.67	24.6	0.8	47	1.1	384	32
Hard	1 each	156	4.9	1.6	0.35	29.8	0.1	2	1.1	312	24
Kaiser, small	1 each	92	3.0	1.8	—	16.0	0.1	—	1.3	192	7
Plain, brown-and-serve	1 each	82	2.2	2.0	0.34	13.7	0.1	2	0.5	141	13
Whole wheat	1 each	72	2.3	1.8	0.51	12.0	0.8	9	0.5	149	16
Rutabaga, cooked, cubed	½ cup	29	0.9	0.2	0.02	6.6	0.9	0	0.4	15	36
Salad dressing											
Blue cheese	1 tablespoon	84	0.4	9.2	—	0.3	0.0	0	0.0	216	3
Blue cheese, fat-free	1 tablespoon	16	0.0	0.0	0.00	4.0	0.0	0	0.0	120	0
Blue cheese, low-calorie	1 tablespoon	59	0.9	5.8	1.40	0.8	—	11	0.1	171	24
Cucumber, fat-free, reduced-calorie, creamy	1 tablespoon	8	0.0	0.0	0.00	2.0	0.0	0	0.0	100	0
French	1 tablespoon	96	0.3	9.4	—	2.9	0.0	8	0.1	205	6
French, low-calorie	1 tablespoon	20	0.0	0.0	0.00	4.0	—	0	—	120	—
Italian	1 tablespoon	84	0.1	9.1	—	0.6	0.0	0	0.0	172	1
Italian, no-oil, low-calorie	1 tablespoon	8	0.1	0.0	—	1.8	0.0	0	0.0	161	1
Ranch-style, fat-free	1 tablespoon	16	0.0	0.0	0.00	3.0	0.0	0	0.0	150	0
Thousand Island	1 tablespoon	59	0.1	5.6	0.94	2.4	0.3	—	0.1	109	2
Thousand Island, low-calorie	1 tablespoon	24	0.1	1.6	0.25	2.5	0.2	2	0.1	153	2
Salsa, commercial	1 tablespoon	3	0.1	0.0	—	0.5	—	—	0.0	42	1
Salt, iodized	1 teaspoon	0	0.0	0.0	0.00	0.0	0.0	0	0.0	2343	15
Sauces											
Barbecue	2 tablespoons	23	0.5	0.5	—	4.0	0.2	0	0.3	255	6
Caramel, fat-free	2 tablespoons	110	0.0	0.0	0.00	27.0	1.0	0	0.0	70	0
Hot fudge, light	2 tablespoons	90	2.0	0.0	0.00	23.0	2.0	0	0.8	90	32
Tartar, regular	2 tablespoons	143	0.3	15.2	2.35	1.4	0.1	14	0.2	426	6
Sauerkraut, canned	½ cup	22	1.1	0.2	0.04	5.0	1.3	0	1.7	780	35
Scallops, raw, large	3 ounces	75	14.3	0.6	0.07	2.0	0.0	28	0.2	137	20
Sesame seeds, dry, whole	1 teaspoon	17	0.5	1.5	0.21	0.7	0.1	0	0.4	0	29
Sherbet											
Lime or raspberry	½ cup	104	0.9	0.9	—	23.8	0.0	0	0.0	67	39
Orange	½ cup	135	1.1	1.9	1.19	29.3	0.0	7	0.1	44	52
Shortening	1 tablespoon	113	0.0	12.6	2.36	0.0	0.0	0	0.0	0	0
Shrimp											
Fresh, cooked, peeled, and deveined	3 ounces	84	17.8	0.9	0.25	0.0	0.0	166	2.6	191	33
Canned, drained	3 ounces	102	19.6	1.7	0.32	0.9	0.0	147	2.3	144	50

Dash (—) indicates insufficient data available.

FOOD	APPROXIMATE MEASURE	FOOD ENERGY (CALORIES)	PROTEIN (GRAMS)	FAT (GRAMS)	SATURATED FAT (GRAMS)	CARBOHYDRATE (GRAMS)	FIBER (GRAMS)	CHOLESTEROL (MILLIGRAMS)	IRON (MILLIGRAMS)	SODIUM (MILLIGRAMS)	CALCIUM (MILLIGRAMS)
Soup, condensed, made with water											
Chicken noodle	1 cup	75	4.0	2.4	0.65	9.3	0.2	7	0.7	1106	17
Chili, beef	1 cup	170	6.7	6.6	—	21.4	1.4	13	2.1	1035	43
Cream of chicken	1 cup	117	2.9	7.3	2.07	9.0	0.1	10	0.6	986	34
Cream of chicken, low-salt, reduced-fat	1 cup	80	2.0	2.5	1.00	11.0	—	10	0.3	480	0
Cream of mushroom	1 cup	129	2.3	9.0	2.44	9.0	0.4	2	0.5	1032	46
Cream of mushroom, low-salt, reduced-fat	1 cup	70	2.0	3.0	1.00	9.0	—	10	0.0	480	16
Cream of potato	1 cup	73	1.7	2.3	1.22	11.0	—	5	0.5	1000	20
Onion	1 cup	58	3.7	1.7	—	8.2	—	0	0.7	1053	27
Tomato	1 cup	85	2.0	1.9	0.37	16.6	0.5	0	1.7	871	12
Vegetable, beef	1 cup	78	5.4	2.0	0.83	9.8	0.2	5	1.2	956	17
Soy sauce											
Regular	1 tablespoon	8	0.8	0.0	0.00	1.2	0.0	0	0.3	829	2
Low-sodium	1 tablespoon	6	0.0	0.0	0.00	0.0	—	0	0.0	390	—
Reduced-sodium	1 tablespoon	8	0.8	0.0	0.00	1.2	0.0	0	0.3	484	2
Spinach											
Fresh, torn	1 cup	12	1.6	0.2	0.03	2.0	2.2	0	1.5	44	55
Canned, regular pack	½ cup	22	2.3	0.4	0.00	3.4	1.1	0	1.8	373	97
Cooked	½ cup	21	2.7	0.2	0.04	3.4	2.4	0	3.2	63	122
Squash, cooked											
Acorn	½ cup	57	1.1	0.1	0.03	14.9	1.2	0	1.0	4	45
Butternut	½ cup	41	0.8	0.1	0.02	10.7	1.2	0	0.6	4	42
Spaghetti	½ cup	22	0.5	0.2	0.05	5.0	1.0	0	0.3	14	16
Summer	½ cup	18	0.8	0.3	0.06	3.9	1.4	0	0.3	1	24
Squid, raw	4 ounces	104	17.7	1.6	0.41	3.5	0.0	264	0.8	50	36
Strawberries, fresh	1 cup	45	0.9	0.6	0.03	10.5	3.9	0	0.6	1	21
Sugar											
Granulated	1 tablespoon	48	0.0	0.0	0.00	12.4	0.0	0	0.0	0	0
Brown, packed	1 tablespoon	51	0.0	0.0	—	13.3	0.0	0	0.5	4	12
Powdered	1 tablespoon	29	0.0	0.0	0.00	7.5	0.0	0	0.0	0	0
Sunflower kernels	¼ cup	205	8.2	17.8	1.87	6.8	2.4	0	2.4	1	42
Sweet potatoes											
Whole, baked	1 each	103	1.7	0.1	0.02	24.3	3.0	0	0.4	10	28
Mashed	½ cup	172	2.7	0.5	0.10	39.8	4.9	0	0.9	21	34
Syrup											
Chocolate-flavored	1 tablespoon	49	0.6	0.2	0.00	11.0	—	0	0.3	12	3
Corn, dark or light	1 tablespoon	60	0.0	0.0	0.00	15.4	0.0	0	0.8	14	9
Maple, reduced-calorie	1 tablespoon	30	0.0	0.2	0.00	7.8	0.0	0	0.0	41	0
Pancake	1 tablespoon	50	0.0	0.0	0.00	12.8	0.0	0	0.2	2	20
Taco shell	1 each	52	0.7	2.8	—	5.9	—	—	—	62	—
Tangerine											
Fresh	1 medium	38	0.5	0.1	0.02	9.6	1.6	0	0.1	1	12
Juice, unsweetened	½ cup	53	0.6	0.2	0.02	12.5	0.1	0	0.2	1	22
Tapioca, dry	1 tablespoon	32	0.0	0.0	—	8.4	0.1	0	0.2	0	2
Tofu											
Firm	4 ounces	164	17.9	9.9	1.43	4.9	1.4	0	11.9	16	232
Soft	4 ounces	60	7.0	3.0	—	2.0	—	0	1.4	5	100
Tomato											
Fresh	1 medium	26	1.0	0.4	0.06	5.7	1.6	0	0.6	11	6
Cooked	½ cup	30	1.3	0.3	0.04	6.8	0.9	0	0.7	13	10
Dried	1 ounce	73	4.0	0.8	0.12	15.8	—	0	—	594	31
Dried, packed in oil	1 ounce	60	1.4	4.0	0.54	6.6	—	0	—	75	0
Juice, regular	1 cup	41	1.8	0.1	0.02	10.3	0.9	0	1.4	881	22
Juice, no-salt-added	1 cup	41	1.8	0.1	0.02	10.3	0.9	—	1.4	24	22
Paste, regular	1 tablespoon	14	0.6	0.1	0.02	3.1	0.7	0	0.5	129	6
Paste, no-salt-added	1 tablespoon	11	0.5	0.0	—	2.6	—	—	0.2	6	4
Sauce, regular	½ cup	37	1.6	0.2	0.03	8.8	1.8	0	0.9	741	17

FOOD	APPROXIMATE MEASURE	FOOD ENERGY (CALORIES)	PROTEIN (GRAMS)	FAT (GRAMS)	SATURATED FAT (GRAMS)	CARBOHYDRATE (GRAMS)	FIBER (GRAMS)	CHOLESTEROL (MILLIGRAMS)	IRON (MILLIGRAMS)	SODIUM (MILLIGRAMS)	CALCIUM (MILLIGRAMS)
Tomato *(continued)*											
Sauce, no-salt-added	½ cup	40	1.2	0.0	—	9.2	1.6	—	—	24	—
Stewed, canned	½ cup	30	0.9	1.1	0.20	5.2	0.2	0	0.4	187	10
Whole, canned, peeled	½ cup	22	0.9	0.0	—	5.2	0.8	—	0.5	424	38
Whole, canned, no-salt-added	½ cup	22	0.9	0.0	—	5.2	0.8	—	0.5	15	38
Tortilla											
Chips, plain	10 each	135	2.1	7.3	1.05	16.0	0.2	0	0.7	24	3
Corn, 6" diameter	1 each	67	2.1	1.1	0.12	12.8	1.6	0	1.4	53	42
Flour, 6" diameter	1 each	111	2.4	2.3	0.56	22.2	0.9	0	0.8	0	27
Turkey, skinned, boned, and roasted											
White meat	3 ounces	134	25.3	2.7	0.87	0.0	0.0	59	1.1	54	16
Dark meat	3 ounces	159	24.3	6.1	2.06	0.0	0.0	72	2.0	67	27
Sausage link or patty	1 ounce	55	6.1	3.2	1.00	0.5	—	20	—	296	—
Smoked	3 ounces	126	20.4	4.9	1.45	0.0	0.0	48	2.3	586	9
Turnip greens, cooked	½ cup	14	0.8	0.2	0.04	3.1	2.2	0	0.6	21	99
Turnips, cooked, cubed	½ cup	14	0.6	0.1	0.01	3.8	1.6	0	0.2	39	17
Veal, cooked											
Ground	3 ounces	146	20.7	6.4	2.59	0.0	—	88	0.8	71	14
Leg	3 ounces	128	23.9	2.9	1.04	0.0	—	88	0.8	58	5
Loin	3 ounces	149	22.4	5.9	2.19	0.0	—	90	0.7	82	18
Vegetable juice cocktail											
Regular	1 cup	46	1.5	0.2	0.03	11.0	0.5	0	1.0	883	27
Low-sodium	1 cup	48	2.4	0.2	—	9.7	—	—	1.7	48	34
Venison, roasted	3 ounces	134	25.7	2.7	1.06	0.0	—	95	3.8	46	6
Vinegar, distilled	1 tablespoon	2	0.0	0.0	0.00	0.8	0.0	0	0.0	0	0
Water chestnuts, canned, sliced	½ cup	35	0.6	0.0	0.01	8.7	0.4	0	0.6	6	3
Watercress, fresh	½ cup	2	0.4	0.0	0.00	0.2	0.4	0	0.0	7	20
Watermelon, raw, diced	1 cup	51	1.0	0.7	0.35	11.5	0.9	0	0.3	3	13
Wheat germ	1 tablespoon	26	1.7	0.7	0.12	3.7	1.1	0	0.5	1	3
Whipped cream	1 tablespoon	26	0.2	2.8	1.71	0.2	0.0	10	0.0	3	5
Whipped topping, nondairy, frozen	1 tablespoon	15	0.1	1.2	1.02	1.1	0.0	0	0.0	1	0
Wonton wrappers	1 each	6	0.2	0.1	0.03	0.9	0.0	5	0.1	12	1
Worcestershire sauce											
Regular	1 tablespoon	12	0.3	0.0	0.00	2.7	0.0	0	0.0	147	15
Low-sodium	1 tablespoon	12	0.0	0.0	0.00	3.0	—	0	—	57	—
Yeast, active, dry	1 package	20	2.6	0.1	0.01	2.7	2.2	0	1.1	4	3
Yogurt											
Coffee and vanilla, low-fat	1 cup	193	11.2	2.8	1.84	31.3	0.0	11	0.2	150	388
Frozen, low-fat	½ cup	99	3.0	2.0	1.41	18.0	—	10	—	35	100
Frozen, nonfat	½ cup	82	3.4	0.0	0.00	18.1	—	0	—	60	129
Fruit varieties, low-fat	1 cup	225	9.0	2.6	1.68	42.3	0.2	9	0.1	120	313
Plain, low-fat	1 cup	143	11.9	3.5	2.27	16.0	0.0	14	0.2	159	415
Plain, nonfat	1 cup	127	13.0	0.4	0.26	17.4	0.0	5	0.2	173	452
Zucchini											
Raw, sliced	½ cup	9	0.7	0.1	0.02	1.9	0.3	0	0.3	2	10
Cooked, diced	½ cup	17	0.7	0.1	0.01	4.1	0.5	0	0.4	3	14

Dash (—) indicates insufficient data available.

Source of Data: Computrition, Inc., Chatsworth, California. Primarily comprised of *Composition of Foods: Raw, Processed, Prepared.* Agriculture Handbook No. 8 Series. United States Department of Agriculture, Human Nutrition Information Service, 1976-1993.

Recipe Index

Almonds
  Asparagus with Blue Cheese and
    Almonds, 71
  Biscotti, Almond, 244
  Moons, Almond, 69
Appetizers
  Canapés, Caponata, 63
  Chicken Drummettes with
    Pineapple Sauce,
    Teriyaki, 88
  Chicken Kabobs, Curried, 88
  Chips, Crispy Oriental, 91
  Crab Cakes, Louisiana, 86
  Dips
    Green Chile Dip, 196
    Pepper Dip, Roasted, 84
    Two-Bean Salsa,
      Southwestern, 84
  Granola Squares, Peanut
    Butter, 198
  Italian Appetizer Skewers, 90
  Mushrooms, Chinese Stuffed, 90
  Mushrooms, Greek, 91
  Mussels in Tomato-Wine
    Sauce, 87
  Pizza Snacks, Spicy, 196
  Pizza Wedges, Peppy, 91
  Potato Skin Snacks, Crispy, 197
  Salmon with Fresh
    Asparagus, 86
  Shrimp Toast, 67
  Shrimp with Creamy Honey-
    Mustard Sauce, Spiced, 85
  Shrimp with Santa Fe Dip,
    Chilled, 85
  Snack Mix, Sassy, 55
  Snack Mix, Sugar and Spice, 198
  Spreads
    Cheddar-Pimiento Spread,
      Smoky, 197
    Chutney Spread, 197
    Garlic and Cheese Spread, 78
    Trout Spread, Smoked, 84
  Tomato-Cheese Melts, 196
  Turkey-Spinach Pinwheels, 89
  Zucchini Wedges, Baked, 89
Apples
  Applesauce, Blueberry, 28
  Baked Apples, Honey-, 45
  Brandied Apples, 210
  Crumble, Apple-Raisin, 233
  Ice Milk, Cinnamon-Apple, 239
  Risotto, Sausage and Apple, 174

  Sandwiches, Ham and
    Apple, 193
  Sauce, Caramel-Apple, 200
  Sauce, Creamy Apple-Wine, 203
Artichoke and Portabella
    Mushroom Mélange, 211
Asparagus
  Blue Cheese and Almonds,
    Asparagus with, 71
  Creamy Chive Sauce, Asparagus
    with, 211
  Rolls, Scallop, Mushroom, and
    Asparagus, 118
  Salmon with Fresh Asparagus, 86

Bananas
  Cheesecake, Banana Pudding, 242
  Pudding, Peanut Butter,
    Pineapple, and Banana, 234
Barley
  Autumn Grains, 124
  Sauté, Barley-Vegetable, 120
Beans
  Bake, Spicy Sausage and
    Bean, 174
  Black Beans, Grilled Vegetables
    with Pasta and, 140
  Black Beans, Polenta with,
    Spicy, 141
  Casserole, Cajun Beans and
    Rice, 142
  Chili, Hearty Three-Bean, 55
  Green
    Basil, Green Beans with, 43
    Italian Green Beans, 64
    Roasted Green Beans and
      Onions, 215
  Mexicali Pasta and Beans, 128
  Salad, Southwestern Bean and
    Pasta, 183
  Salsa, Southwestern Two-
    Bean, 84
  Seasoned Potatoes and
    Beans, 216
  Soups
    Chickpea and Tomato
      Soup, 41
    Garbanzo-Lentil Soup, 223
    White Bean and Tomato
      Soup, 77
  Stew, Pork and Black Bean, 230
  White Beans, Tuna with Roasted
    Tomato, Onion, and, 113

Beef
  Roasts
    Cranberry Pot Roast with
      Roasted Acorn Squash, 152
    Savory Beef Roast, 151
  Salad, Mexican Beef, 37
  Soup, Oniony Vegetable-
    Beef, 226
  Steaks
    Ale, Steak with, 150
    Beef Rolls, Curried, 148
    Flank Steak, Grilled Spicy, 149
    Gingered Beef and Peppers, 68
    Greek Beef and Pasta, 129
    Stir-Fried Beef and Greens, 149
Beef, Ground
  Meat Loaf, Jerk, 148
  Pizza, Inside Out, 191
Beets
  Borscht, Chilled, 222
Beverages
  Alcoholic
    Cocoa, Creamy Amaretto, 82
    Coffee, Irish, 59
    Margarita, Orange-Lime, 93
    Mint Juleps, 50
  Black Currant and Raspberry
    Cooler, 93
  Cider, Cranberry-Orange, 31
  Coffee, Chilled Mexican, 37
  Coffee, Chocolate-Hazelnut, 72
  Gingered Tropical Smoothie, 93
  Piña Colada Freeze, 94
  Pink Passion Cooler, 93
  Shake, Mocha Milk, 94
  Tea, Orange-Lemon, 62
  Tea, Spiced Fruit, 28
  Tomato Cocktail, Spicy, 34
Biscuits
  Cranberry Silver Dollar Biscuits, 96
  Sweet Potato Biscuits, Nutty, 96
Blackberries
  Fresh Berries with Creamy Peach
    Topping, 34
  Pudding, Elegant Pears with
    Blackberry, 232
Blueberries
  Applesauce, Blueberry, 28
  Muffins, Blueberry, 98
  Vinegar, Blueberry-Mint, 207
Bok Choy
  Ginger and Water Chestnuts, Bok
    Choy with, 212

Bok Choy (continued)
  Lo Mein, Chicken and
    Vegetable, 129
  Slaw, Asian Cabbage, 178
Breads. See also specific types.
  Date-Walnut Bread, 97
  Rosemary Sweet Bread, 97
  Scones, Cranberry-Walnut, 81
  Yeast
    Black Bread, Russian, 102
    Breadsticks, Basic, 99
    Breadsticks, Sesame-
      Poppy, 101
    Breadsticks, Sweet Anise, 100
    Chocolate Bread, 105
    Flat Breads, Italian-Style, 105
    Focaccia, Garlic-Rosemary, 106
    Focaccia, Mozzarella and Sun-
      Dried Tomato, 106
    Focaccia, Onion, 106
    Focaccia with Garlic and
      Cheese Spread,
      Rosemary, 78
    Grain Bread, Hearty, 104
    Rolls, Dillweed, 34
    Rolls, Potato Pan, 101
    Whole-Grain-Goodness
      Bread, 104
Broccoli
  Lemon, Broccoli with, 39
  Sesame Broccoli, 212
Brussels Sprouts and Baby Carrots,
  Glazed, 213

Cabbage
  Coleslaw, Creamy, 56
  Slaw, Asian Cabbage, 178
  Slaw, Spicy, 61
Cakes
  Cheesecake, Banana
    Pudding, 242
  Pound
    Ginger Pound Cake,
      Triple, 241
    Pumpkin-Pecan Pound
      Cake, 241
  Streusel Cake, Chocolate
    Chip, 25
  Streusel Cake, Cornmeal and
    Prune, 79
  Torte, Chocolate-Mocha, 240
  Torte with Grand Marnier
    Mousse, Brownie, 236
Carrots
  Glazed Brussels Sprouts and
    Baby Carrots, 213
  Soup, Creamy Tomato-
    Carrot, 225

Casseroles
  Baked Vegetable Macaroni and
    Cheese, 126
  Cajun Beans and Rice
    Casserole, 142
  Layered Vegetable Casserole, 220
Cauliflower with Pimiento-Olive
  Vinaigrette, 214
Cereals
  Peaches and Cream Cereal,
    Warm, 24
  Swiss Muesli, 25
Cheese
  Asparagus with Blue Cheese and
    Almonds, 71
  Chicken with Tomato Cream
    Sauce, Parmesan, 71
  Crêpes, Raspberry-Cheese, 72
  Dressing, Parmesan-
    Peppercorn, 188
  Enchiladas, Stacked Rice and
    Cheese, 146
  Flounder, Easy Parmesan, 108
  Focaccia, Mozzarella and Sun-
    Dried Tomato, 106
  Macaroni and Cheese, Baked
    Vegetable, 126
  Manicotti, Spinach and
    Cheese, 127
  Melts, Tomato-Cheese, 196
  Mostaccioli with Fresh Tomatoes
    and Goat Cheese, 126
  Muffins, Sausage-Cheese, 26
  Platter, Fruit and Cheese, 176
  Pork Chops with Apple Stuffing,
    Brie-Filled, 159
  Pot Stickers, Cheese, 137
  Rice, Zucchini-Parmesan, 123
  Sandwiches, Grilled Spinach and
    Cheese, 190
  Soufflé with Tomato Sauce,
    Eggplant Parmesan, 134
  Spread, Garlic and Cheese, 78
  Spread, Smoky Cheddar-
    Pimiento, 197
  Squash, Cheddar-Stuffed, 217
  Tart, Potato-Cheese, 136
Cherries
  Sauce, Lamb Chops with
    Cherry, 156
  Soufflés, Cherry Winks, 238
Chicken
  Breast Dijon, Chicken, 166
  Breasts with Marmalade,
    Chicken, 170
  Curry, Southeast Asian
    Chicken, 172

Drummettes with Pineapple
  Sauce, Teriyaki Chicken, 88
Garlic-Ginger Chicken, 169
Kabobs, Curried Chicken, 88
Lemon Chicken and
  Potatoes, 64
Lo Mein, Chicken and
  Vegetable, 129
Malaysian Chicken, 171
Moroccan Chicken and
  Orzo, 130
Noodles, Chicken and, 171
Orange-Basil Chicken, 47
Parmesan Chicken with Tomato
  Cream Sauce, 71
Pizza, Skillet Chicken, 164
Poached Ginger Chicken, 166
Pot Pie, Country Chicken, 168
Salads
  Curried Chicken Salad
    Platter, 184
  Roasted Chicken and
    Vegetable Salad, 52
Sandwiches, Barbecued
  Chicken, 191
Sandwiches, Chicken Caesar, 192
Skillet, Chicken and Saffron
  Rice, 169
Thai Spring Rolls with
  Chicken, 165
Chili, Hearty Three-Bean, 55
Chocolate
  Beverages
    Cocoa, Creamy Amaretto, 82
    Coffee, Chilled Mexican, 37
    Coffee, Chocolate-
      Hazelnut, 72
    Milk Shake, Mocha, 94
  Bread, Chocolate, 105
  Brownie Dessert, Fudgy
    Mint, 237
  Cakes and Tortes
    Brownie Torte with Grand
      Marnier Mousse, 236
    Mocha Torte, Chocolate-, 240
    Streusel Cake, Chocolate
      Chip, 25
  Ice Cream, Caramel-Brownie
    Chunk, 62
  Mousse, Chocolate, 236
  Pie, Chocolate Nougat, 244
  Pudding, Chocolate-Mocha, 39
  Sauce, White Chocolate-Irish
    Cream, 201
Chowders
  Clam Chowder, Harvest, 228
  Corn Chowder, Fresh, 224

Chutney
    Fruit Chutney, Curried, 206
    Peach-Onion Chutney, Roasted
        Pork Sandwiches with, 194
    Spread, Chutney, 197
Clam Chowder, Harvest, 228
Coleslaw. *See* Cabbage or Salads.
Cookies
    Almond Biscotti, 244
    Almond Moons, 69
    Molasses Crinkles, 245
    Orange-Butterscotch
        Cookies, 245
    Peanut Butter Granola
        Squares, 198
Corn
    Chili-Corn Mashed Potatoes, 217
    Chowder, Fresh Corn, 224
    Relish, Spicy Tomato-Corn, 206
    Salad, Southwestern Corn and
        Pepper, 179
    Salad, Zesty Corn, 74
    Skillet, Jicama, Corn, and Green
        Pepper, 220
Cornbreads
    Cakes, Corn, 138
    Muffins, Confetti Corn, 56
    Sandwiches, Cornbread-
        Turkey, 195
Cornish Hens, Tropical, 172
Crab
    Cakes, Louisiana Crab, 86
    Cakes with Lemon Sauce,
        Seasoned Crab, 114
    Stone Crab Claws with Creamy
        Dijon Dressing, 185
Cranberries
    Biscuits, Cranberry Silver
        Dollar, 96
    Cider, Cranberry-Orange, 31
    Pot Roast with Roasted Acorn
        Squash, Cranberry, 152
    Pudding, Black Bottom
        Cranberry, 234
    Scones, Cranberry-Walnut, 81
    Whitefish with Cranberry-Pine
        Nut Dressing, Whole, 114
Crêpes
    Crêpes, 72
    Raspberry-Cheese Crêpes, 72
Cucumbers
    Relish, Cool Cucumber, 156
    Vichyssoise, Cucumber, 223
Curry
    Beef Rolls, Curried, 148
    Chicken Curry, Southeast
        Asian, 172

Chicken Kabobs, Curried, 88
Chicken Salad Platter,
    Curried, 184
Fruit Chutney, Curried, 206
Custards
    Pumpkin Flan, 229
    Raspberry Chess Custard, 233

Date-Walnut Bread, 97
Desserts. *See also* specific types.
    Chocolate
        Brownie Dessert, Fudgy
            Mint, 237
        Mousse, Chocolate, 236
        Pudding, Chocolate-Mocha, 39
        Torte, Chocolate-Mocha, 240
        Torte with Grand Marnier
            Mousse, Brownie, 236
    Frozen
        Caramel-Kahlúa Squares, 239
        Cinnamon-Apple Ice Milk, 239
        Ice Cream, Caramel-Brownie
            Chunk, 62
        Sorbet, Watermelon, 75
    Fruit
        Apples, Honey-Baked, 45
        Apple-Raisin Crumble, 233
        Banana Pudding
            Cheesecake, 242
        Cherry Winks Soufflés, 238
        Cranberry Pudding, Black
            Bottom, 234
        Orange Slices with Grand
            Marnier, 43
        Pear Tart, Cinnamon-, 59
        Pears, Blushing Poached, 64
        Pears with Blackberry
            Pudding, Elegant, 232
        Pineapple, and Banana
            Pudding, Peanut Butter, 234
        Raspberry-Cheese Crêpes, 72
        Raspberry Chess Custard, 233
        Strawberries and Yogurt, 48
        Strawberry Crunch Parfaits, 53
    Sauces
        Caramel-Apple Sauce, 200
        Sherry Sauce, 200
        Vanilla Custard Sauce, 200
        White Chocolate-Irish Cream
            Sauce, 201

Eggplant
    Caponata Canapés, 63
    Italian Eggplant and Rice, 214
    Soufflé with Tomato Sauce,
        Eggplant Parmesan, 134
Eggs
    Frittata, Christmas, 81

Omelets, Vegetable, 33
Strata, Sourdough and
    Mushroom, 30
Enchiladas
    Rice and Cheese Enchiladas,
        Stacked, 146
    Turkey Enchiladas, 173

Fish. *See also* specific types and
    Seafood.
    Bass, South-of-the-Border, 108
    Catfish Sandwiches, Oven-
        Fried, 193
    Flounder, Easy Parmesan, 108
    Halibut Provençal, Baked, 42
    Mahimahi with Pineapple,
        Grilled, 108
    Orange Roughy in Chunky
        Tomato Sauce, 110
    Salmon, Seasoned Alaskan, 30
    Salmon with Fresh Asparagus, 86
    Salmon with Yellow Tomato
        Salsa, Poached, 110
    Sole with Lemon Cream Sauce,
        Vegetable-Filled, 111
    Swordfish, Herb-Grilled, 74
    Tilapia in Corn Husks, 112
    Trout Spread, Smoked, 84
    Tuna Pasta Salad, 183
    Tuna with Roasted Tomato,
        Onion, and White
        Beans, 113
    Whitefish with Cranberry-Pine
        Nut Dressing, Whole, 114
Fruit. *See also* specific types.
    Berries with Creamy Peach
        Topping, Fresh, 34
    Chutney, Curried Fruit, 206
    Compote, Spiced Fruit, 82
    Platter, Fruit and Cheese, 176
    Poached Dried Fruit, 41
    Tea, Spiced Fruit, 28
    Vanilla-Glazed Fruit, 26

Granola
    Squares, Peanut Butter Granola, 198
    Swiss Muesli, 25
Grapefruit
    Dressing, Orange-Grapefruit, 187
    Minted Grapefruit, 210
Gumbo, Seafood, 229

Ham and Apple Sandwiches, 193

Jicama
    Salad, Citrus-Jicama, 37
    Skillet, Jicama, Corn, and Green
        Pepper, 220

Kabobs
Appetizer Skewers, Italian, 90
Chicken Kabobs, Curried, 88
Lamb Kabobs, Grecian, 156
Pork and Potatoes, Grilled, 159
Shrimp and Sausage,
Skewered, 61
Shrimp, Southwestern
Grilled, 117

Lamb
Chops, Italian Lamb, 158
Chops, Marinated Broiled
Lamb, 45
Chops with Cherry Sauce,
Lamb, 156
Kabobs, Grecian Lamb, 156
Smothered Lamb,
Hungarian, 155
Lasagna
Vegetable Lasagna, Garden, 139
Vegetable Lasagna, Roasted, 128
Lemon
Broccoli with Lemon, 39
Chicken and Potatoes,
Lemon, 64
Lobster Tails with Lemon
Cream, 115
Pie, Lemon Cream, 242
Sauce, Lemon, 114
Sauce, Lemon-Ginger, 202
Sauce, Vegetable-Filled Sole with
Lemon Cream, 111
Tea, Orange-Lemon, 62
Vinegar, Strawberry-Lemon, 207
Lentils
Pie, Lentil Shepherd's, 142
Potpourri, Hearty Lentil, 215
Salad, Warm Lentil, 45
Soup, Garbanzo-Lentil, 223
Lobster Tails with Lemon Cream, 115

Muffins
Blueberry Muffins, 98
Corn Muffins, Confetti, 56
Oatmeal-Raisin Muffins, 99
Sausage-Cheese Muffins, 26
Mushrooms
Crostini on Greens,
Mushroom, 41
Greek Mushrooms, 91
Linguine with Exotic
Mushrooms, 125
Mélange, Artichoke and
Portabella Mushroom, 211
Popover Squares,
Mushroom, 135

Rolls, Scallop, Mushroom, and
Asparagus, 118
Strata, Sourdough and
Mushroom, 30
Stuffed Mushrooms, Chinese, 90
Mussels in Tomato-Wine Sauce, 87
Mustard
Chicken Breast, Dijon, 166
Dressing, Dijon-Herb, 187
Dressing, Stone Crab Claws with
Creamy Dijon, 185
Sauce, Spiced Shrimp with
Creamy Honey-Mustard, 85
Sauce, Veal Roast with Mustard
Cream, 155

Noodles
Chicken and Noodles, 171
Szechuan Noodles with
Shrimp, 132

Oatmeal-Raisin Muffins, 99
Onions
Focaccia, Onion, 106
Relish, Grilled Veal Chops with
Peach-Onion, 154
Rings, Crispy Onion, 215
Risotto, Roasted Garlic and
Onion, 121
Roasted Green Beans and
Onions, 215
Salad, Orange and Onion, 69
Sandwiches with Peach-Onion
Chutney, Roasted Pork, 194
Sauce, Tarragon-Onion, 203
Savory Sweet Potatoes and
Onions, 219
Soup, Oniony Vegetable-
Beef, 226
Tuna with Roasted Tomato,
Onion, and White Beans, 113
Oranges
Beverages
Cider, Cranberry-Orange, 31
Margarita, Orange-Lime, 93
Tea, Orange-Lemon, 62
Chicken, Orange-Basil, 47
Cookies, Orange-
Butterscotch, 245
Dressing, Orange-Grapefruit, 187
Salads
Citrus-Jicama Salad, 37
Mandarin Orange Salad, 176
Onion Salad, Orange and, 69
Slices with Grand Marnier,
Orange, 43
Orzo, Moroccan Chicken
and, 130

Pancakes, Silver Dollar, 27
Papaya Salad with Poppy Seed
Dressing, Chicory and, 176
Papaya Salsa, Sugar Snap Peas
with, 219
Pastas
Beef and Pasta, Greek, 129
Cavatappi with Turkey and Basil-
Cilantro Pesto, 131
Chicken and Vegetable Lo
Mein, 129
Gemelli, Roasted Vegetables
with, 125
Linguine with Exotic
Mushrooms, 125
Manicotti, Spinach and Cheese, 127
Mexicali Pasta and Beans, 128
Mostaccioli with Fresh Tomatoes
and Goat Cheese, 126
Orecchiette with Fresh Vegetables
and Herbs, 127
Orzo, Moroccan Chicken
and, 130
Salad, Southwestern Bean and
Pasta, 183
Salad, Tuna Pasta, 183
Soup, Tortellini-Basil, 225
Toss, Three-Pepper Pasta, 124
Vegetables with Pasta and Black
Beans, Grilled, 140
Peaches
Cereal, Warm Peaches and
Cream, 24
Chutney, Roasted Pork
Sandwiches with Peach-
Onion, 194
Fresh Berries with Creamy Peach
Topping, 34
Relish, Grilled Veal Chops with
Peach-Onion, 154
Spiced Peaches and
Pineapple, 210
Peanut Butter Granola Squares, 198
Pears
Elegant Pears with Blackberry
Pudding, 232
Poached Pears, Blushing, 64
Puree, Rutabaga and Pear, 217
Salad, Pear and Watercress, 77
Salad, Stuffed Pear, 178
Soup, Blushing Pear, 222
Tart, Cinnamon-Pear, 59
Peas with Papaya Salsa, Sugar
Snap, 219
Peppers
Appetizer Skewers, Italian, 90
Dip, Roasted Pepper, 84

Peppers (continued)
Gingered Beef and Peppers, 68
Medley, Four-Pepper, 216
Pasta Toss, Three-Pepper, 124
Potato-Stuffed Peppers, 135
Roasted Peppers, Spinach
Gnocchi with, 143
Salad, Southwestern Corn and
Pepper, 179
Skillet, Jicama, Corn, and Green
Pepper, 220
Skillet, Pork and Pepper, 38
Pickles and Relishes
Cucumber Relish, Cool, 156
Peach-Onion Relish, Grilled Veal
Chops with, 154
Tomato-Corn Relish, Spicy, 206
Pies and Pastries
Chicken Pot Pie, Country, 168
Chocolate Nougat Pie, 244
Lemon Cream Pie, 242
Lentil Shepherd's Pie, 142
Tart, Cinnamon-Pear, 59
Pineapple
Mahimahi with Pineapple,
Grilled, 108
Poached Pineapple, 210
Poached Pineapple in Yukon
Jack, 31
Pudding, Peanut Butter,
Pineapple, and Banana, 234
Sauce, Pineapple, 88
Spiced Peaches and
Pineapple, 210
Pizza
Chicken Pizza, Skillet, 164
Inside Out Pizza, 191
Milanese, Pizza, 145
Primavera, Pizza, 144
Snacks, Spicy Pizza, 196
Wedges, Peppy Pizza, 91
Polenta
Black Beans, Polenta with
Spicy, 141
Sun-Dried Tomatoes, Polenta
with, 120
Pork. See also Ham.
Chops
Brie-Filled Pork Chops with
Apple Stuffing, 159
Skillet, Pork and Pepper, 38
German Pork with
Sauerkraut, 158
Grilled Pork and Potatoes, 159
Roasts
Basil-Scented Pork Roast with
Zucchini Pesto, 161

Loin Roast, Peppercorn-
Crusted Pork, 160
Mesquite-Smoked Pork with
Texas Caviar, 162
Salad, Warm Sesame Pork, 184
Sandwiches with Peach-Onion
Chutney, Roasted Pork, 194
Stew, Pork and Black Bean, 230
Potatoes
Gnocchi with Roasted Peppers,
Spinach, 143
Grilled Pork and Potatoes, 159
Lemon Chicken and Potatoes, 64
Mashed Potatoes, Chili-
Corn, 217
Mashed Potatoes, Garlic, 39
Oven-Roasted Potato Slices, 43
Rolls, Potato Pan, 101
Peppers, Potato-Stuffed, 135
Salad, Baked Potato, 179
Seasoned Potatoes and
Beans, 216
Skin Snacks, Crispy Potato, 197
Potatoes, Sweet
Biscuits, Nutty Sweet
Potato, 96
Savory Sweet Potatoes and
Onions, 219
Tart, Potato-Cheese, 136
Vichyssoise, Cucumber, 223
Prune Streusel Cake, Cornmeal
and, 79
Puddings. See also Custards.
Blackberry Pudding, Elegant
Pears with, 232
Bread Pudding, Hawaiian, 237
Chocolate-Mocha Pudding, 39
Cranberry Pudding, Black
Bottom, 234
Peanut Butter, Pineapple, and
Banana Pudding, 234
Pumpkin
Flan, Pumpkin, 235
Pound Cake, Pumpkin-
Pecan, 241

Raisins
Crumble, Apple-Raisin, 233
Muffins, Oatmeal-Raisin, 99
Raspberries
Cooler, Black Currant and
Raspberry, 93
Crêpes, Raspberry-Cheese, 72
Custard, Raspberry Chess, 233
Rice
Autumn Grains, 124
Cakes, Mexican Rice, 122

Casserole, Cajun Beans and
Rice, 142
Enchiladas, Stacked Rice and
Cheese, 146
Herbed Rice-Stuffed
Tomatoes, 182
Italian Eggplant and Rice, 214
Pilaf, Mediterranean Rice, 123
Pilaf, Simple Rice, 48
Pilaf, Vegetable, 145
Risotto, Roasted Garlic and
Onion, 121
Risotto, Sausage and Apple, 174
Skillet, Chicken and Saffron
Rice, 169
Zucchini-Parmesan Rice, 123
Rolls. See also Breads.
Dillweed Rolls, 34
Potato Pan Rolls, 101
Whole Wheat Clover Rolls, 53
Rutabaga and Pear Puree, 217

Salad Dressings
Dijon-Herb Dressing, 187
Garlic Dressing, Creamy, 187
Orange-Grapefruit Dressing, 187
Parmesan-Peppercorn
Dressing, 188
Pesto Dressing, Creamy, 188
Piquant Dressing, 178
Poppy Seed Dressing,
Creamy, 187
Tarragon Dressing, 188
Salads
Bean and Pasta Salad,
Southwestern, 183
Chicken
Curried Chicken Salad
Platter, 184
Roasted Chicken and
Vegetable Salad, 52
Citrus-Jicama Salad, 37
Corn and Pepper Salad,
Southwestern, 179
Corn Salad, Zesty, 74
Fruit
Mandarin Orange Salad, 176
Orange and Onion Salad, 69
Papaya Salad with Poppy Seed
Dressing, Chicory and, 176
Pear and Watercress Salad, 77
Pear Salad, Stuffed, 178
Platter, Fruit and Cheese, 176
Green
Baby Greens with Toasted
Sesame Croutons, 180
Italian Green Salad, 180

Salads, Green (continued)
    Mixed Greens with Balsamic
        Vinaigrette, 58
    Mushroom Crostini on
        Greens, 41
    Lentil Salad, Warm, 45
    Mexican Beef Salad, 37
    Pork Salad, Warm Sesame, 184
    Potato Salad, Baked, 179
    Shrimp and Spinach Salad, 186
    Slaws
        Cabbage Slaw, Asian, 178
        Creamy Coleslaw, 56
        Spicy Slaw, 61
    Stone Crab Claws with Creamy
        Dijon Dressing, 185
    Tabbouleh-Vegetable Salad, 181
    Tomatoes, Herbed Rice-
        Stuffed, 182
    Tuna Pasta Salad, 183
Salmon
    Asparagus, Salmon with
        Fresh, 86
    Poached Salmon with Yellow
        Tomato Salsa, 110
    Seasoned Alaskan Salmon, 30
Salsas
    Papaya Salsa, Sugar Snap Peas
        with, 219
    Two-Bean Salsa,
        Southwestern, 84
Sandwiches
    Catfish Sandwiches, Oven-
        Fried, 193
    Chicken Caesar Sandwiches, 192
    Chicken Sandwiches,
        Barbecued, 191
    Cornbread-Turkey
        Sandwiches, 195
    Ham and Apple Sandwiches, 193
    Pizza, Inside Out, 191
    Pork Sandwiches with Peach-
        Onion Chutney,
        Roasted, 194
    Spinach and Cheese Sandwiches,
        Grilled, 190
    Tomato-Cheese Melts, 196
    Vegetable Confetti on Dark Rye,
        Peppery, 190
Sauces. See also Desserts/Sauces and
    Salsas.
    Apple-Wine Sauce, Creamy, 203
    Cocktail Sauce,
        Southwestern, 202
    Dillweed-Horseradish Sauce, 203
    Herb Sauce, Creamy, 205
    Lemon-Ginger Sauce, 202

    Lemon Sauce, 114
    Marinade, Mexican Meat, 207
    Peppercorn Sauce, Creamy, 161
    Pesto, Zucchini, 161
    Pineapple Sauce, 88
    Tarragon-Onion Sauce, 203
    Tomato Sauce, Hearty, 205
    Vinaigrette Sauce, 202
Sausage
    Bake, Spicy Sausage and
        Bean, 174
    Muffins, Sausage-Cheese, 26
    Risotto, Sausage and Apple, 174
    Skewered Shrimp and
        Sausage, 61
Scallops
    Rolls, Scallop, Mushroom, and
        Asparagus, 118
    Shells with Vegetable-Cream
        Sauce, Scallops in, 117
Seafood. See also specific types and
    Fish.
    Gumbo, Seafood, 229
Shrimp
    Chilled Shrimp with Santa Fe
        Dip, 85
    Salad, Shrimp and Spinach, 186
    Skewered Shrimp and
        Sausage, 61
    Southwestern Grilled Shrimp, 117
    Spiced Shrimp with Creamy
        Honey-Mustard Sauce, 85
    Szechuan Noodles with
        Shrimp, 132
    Toast, Shrimp, 67
Snacks. See Appetizers.
Soufflés
    Cherry Winks Soufflés, 238
    Eggplant Parmesan Soufflé with
        Tomato Sauce, 134
Soups. See also Chili, Chowders,
    Gumbo, Stews.
    Borscht, Chilled, 222
    Chickpea and Tomato Soup, 41
    Garbanzo-Lentil Soup, 223
    Pear Soup, Blushing, 222
    Tomato-Carrot Soup,
        Creamy, 225
    Tomato-Shallot Soup,
        Roasted, 226
    Tortellini-Basil Soup, 225
    Vegetable-Beef Soup,
        Oniony, 226
    Vegetable-Coconut Soup, 228
    Vichyssoise, Cucumber, 223
    White Bean and Tomato
        Soup, 77

Spinach
    Gnocchi with Roasted Peppers,
        Spinach, 143
    Manicotti, Spinach and
        Cheese, 127
    Pinwheels, Turkey-Spinach, 89
    Salad, Shrimp and Spinach, 186
    Sandwiches, Grilled Spinach and
        Cheese, 190
    Wilted Spinach with Cheese Pot
        Stickers, 136
Squash. See also Zucchini.
    Cheddar-Stuffed Squash, 217
    Roasted Acorn Squash, 152
Stews. See also Chili and Soups.
    Pork and Black Bean Stew, 230
    Seafood Gumbo, 229
Strawberries
    Fresh Berries with Creamy Peach
        Topping, 34
    Parfaits, Strawberry Crunch, 53
    Vinegar, Strawberry-Lemon, 207
    Yogurt, Strawberries and, 48

Tomatoes
    Cocktail, Spicy Tomato, 34
    Focaccia, Mozzarella and Sun-
        Dried Tomato, 106
    Marinated Tomatoes,
        Tangy, 75
    Melts, Tomato-Cheese, 196
    Mostaccioli with Fresh Tomatoes
        and Goat Cheese, 126
    Mussels in Tomato-Wine
        Sauce, 87
    Orange Roughy in Chunky
        Tomato Sauce, 110
    Parmesan Chicken with Tomato
        Cream Sauce, 71
    Poached Salmon with Yellow
        Tomato Salsa, 110
    Polenta with Sun-Dried
        Tomatoes, 120
    Relish, Spicy Tomato-Corn, 206
    Sauce, Hearty Tomato, 205
    Soufflé with Tomato Sauce,
        Eggplant Parmesan, 134
    Soup, Chickpea and
        Tomato, 41
    Soup, Creamy Tomato-
        Carrot, 225
    Soup, Roasted Tomato-
        Shallot, 226
    Soup, White Bean and
        Tomato, 77
    Stuffed Tomatoes, Herbed
        Rice-, 182

Tomatoes *(continued)*
    Tuna with Roasted Tomato,
        Onion, and White Beans, 113
    Zucchini and Tomatoes, 48
Tuna
    Pasta Salad, Tuna, 183
    Roasted Tomato, Onion, and
        White Beans, Tuna with, 113
Turkey
    Bacon, Sugared Turkey, 28
    Cavatappi with Turkey and Basil-
        Cilantro Pesto, 131
    Enchiladas, Turkey, 173
    Pinwheels, Turkey-Spinach, 89
    Risotto, Sausage and Apple, 174
    Sandwiches, Cornbread-
        Turkey, 195
    Sausage and Bean Bake, Spicy, 174
    Sausage-Cheese Muffins, 26
    Sausage, Skewered Shrimp
        and, 61
    Snacks, Spicy Pizza, 196

Veal
    Chops with Peach-Onion Relish,
        Grilled Veal, 154
    Ragoût of Veal, 58
    Roast with Mustard Cream
        Sauce, Veal, 155

Shanks with Red Wine, Veal, 153
Skillet, Saucy Veal, 153
Vegetables. *See also* specific types.
    Baked Vegetable Macaroni and
        Cheese, 126
    Casserole, Layered
        Vegetable, 220
    Confetti on Dark Rye, Peppery
        Vegetable, 190
    Corn Cakes with Creamy
        Vegetable Topping, 138
    Gemelli, Roasted Vegetable
        with, 125
    Grilled Vegetables with Pasta and
        Black Beans, 140
    Lasagna, Garden
        Vegetable, 139
    Lasagna, Roasted
        Vegetable, 128
    Lo Mein, Chicken and
        Vegetable, 129
    Omelets, Vegetable, 33
    Orecchiette with Fresh Vegetables
        and Herbs, 127
    Pilaf, Vegetable, 145
    Salad, Roasted Chicken and
        Vegetable Salad, 52
    Salad, Tabbouleh-Vegetable, 181
    Sauté, Barley-Vegetable, 120

Scallops in Shells with Vegetable-
    Cream Sauce, 117
Sole with Lemon Cream Sauce,
    Vegetable-Filled, 111
Soup, Oniony Vegetable-
    Beef, 226
Soup, Vegetable-Coconut, 228
Vinegars
    Blueberry-Mint Vinegar, 207
    Bouquet Garni Vinegar, 208
    Peppercorn-Chive Vinegar, 208
    Strawberry-Lemon Vinegar, 207

Walnuts
    Biscuits, Nutty Sweet Potato, 96
    Bread, Date-Walnut, 97
    Scones, Cranberry-Walnut, 81
Watermelon Sorbet, 75
Wontons
    Cheese Pot Stickers, 137
    Chips, Crispy Oriental, 91

Yogurt, Strawberries and, 48

Zucchini
    Pesto, Zucchini, 161
    Rice, Zucchini-Parmesan, 123
    Tomatoes, Zucchini and, 48
    Wedges, Baked Zucchini, 89

Subject Index

Alcohol
  computer analysis of, 13
  heart disease and intake of, 11
American College of Obstetricians
    and Gynecologists
    (ACOG), 182
American College of Sports
    Medicine, 139
American Heart Association, 11
Apples, benefits of eating, 212
Aromatherapy, 16
Asparagus, 211
Atherosclerosis, vegetarian
    diet and, 12

Beef, choosing lean cuts of, 151
Beets, peeling, 222
Blood cholesterol levels. *See*
    Cholesterol, blood.
Bok choy, 129, 178
Bone density, strength training
    and, 113, 139
Box aerobics, 75
Breadsticks, shaping, 100
Broccoli, benefits of eating, 212
Brussels sprouts, 213

Calcium
  daily amounts of, 12, 13
  increasing intake of, 12
  osteoporosis and, 12
  sources of, 12
Calorie/Nutrient Chart, 250
Calories
  burning, 131, 169
  daily amounts of, 13
  fat-free products and, 233
  for weight loss, 13
Cancer
  fruit and vegetable intake
    and, 212
  reducing risk of, 10
Carbohydrates, daily amounts
    of, 13
Chicory, 176
Cholesterol, blood, 79
  diet and, 26
  exercise and, 26
  genetic profile and, 26
  medicine and, 11
  older adults and, 11
  saturated fat intake and, 11

Cholesterol, dietary
  daily amounts of, 13
  eggs and, 79
  heart disease and, 79
  reducing level in food, 21
  sensitivity to, 79
Circuit training, 75, 139
Computer nutritional analysis, 13
Computers, health and fitness
    information services
    on, 164
Cranberry juice, benefits of
    drinking, 212
Cross training, recommendations
    for, 81

Dairy products
  as calcium source, 12
  fat content of milk, 94
  low-fat substitutions for, 21

Egg white powder, 19
Eggs, dietary cholesterol in, 79
Energy bars, 194
Exercise. *See also* Flexibility
    exercises, Strength training,
    and Stretching.
  aerobic, 75, 139
  agility and, 10
  benefits of, 85, 10
  benefits of during
    pregnancy, 182
  bone strength and, 10
  calories burned
    during, 131, 169
  cancer and, 10
  cooling down and, 124
  cycling, 10
  diabetes and, 10
  heart disease and, 10
  muscle strength and, 10
  older adults and, 10
  osteoporosis and, 10
  reduced depression and, 10
  running, 10
  signs of overtraining, 203
  spas and, 115
  tennis, 10
  vigorous workouts, 10
  walking, 10
  warming up and, 124
  weight control and, 85

Exercise equipment
  in-line skates, 43
  stationary bicycles, 193

Facial, 16
Fat, body, 10
  losing, 85, 113
Fat, dietary, 13, 94
  calories in, 233
  content in milk, 94
  counting grams of, 13
  daily amounts of, 13
  reduced-fat cooking and, 21
Fiber
  daily amounts of, 13, 121
  increasing intake of, 121
  increasing water intake
    and, 121
  sources of, 121, 134
  types of, 121
Fitness, types of classes, 75
Flexibility exercises, 124
  types of, 141
Fruit juice, 245
Fruits, benefits of eating, 212

Garlic, benefits of eating, 212
Gnocchi, making, 143
Granola, muesli, 25
Grid Nutrients. *See* Nutrients.

Hawaiian bread, 237
  mail-order source for, 272
Heart disease
  fruit and vegetable intake
    and, 212
  reducing risk of, 10, 11, 12
  sodium intake and, 68
  weight gain and, 52
  wine intake and, 11
Heart rate. *See also* Maximum
    heart rate and Target
    heart rate.
High blood pressure
  reducing, 68
  weight gain and, 52

In-line skating, safety tips
    for, 43
International Association of Fitness
    Professionals, 55, 75
Iron, daily amounts of, 13

Lamb, choosing lean cuts of, 151
Leeks, 219
  buying, 219
  cleaning, 219
  storing, 219
Lifestyle, positive changes
    in, 16, 17
Luncheon meats, 19
  sodium content of, 19

Margarine, fat-free alternatives, 18
Massage, 16
Maximum heart rate, to
    determine, 58
Meal planning, 246
Meals, balanced, 246
Meats, 151. *See also* specific
    types.
Metabolism, 246

National Institute of
    Health, 12
National Sporting Goods
    Association, 193
Nutrients. *See also* specific types.
  calculation of, 13
  computer analysis of, 13
  daily amounts of, 13

Osteoporosis, 12
  exercise and, 10
  strength training and, 113

Pasta
  capellini, 149
  gemelli, 125
  orecchiette, 127
  tripolini, 128
Pork, choosing lean cuts of, 151

Potatoes
  mail-order source for
      specialty, 272
  nutrient content of, 216
  varieties of, 216
Protein, daily amounts of, 13
Pumpkin, 241

Recipe modification, 21
Rice
  Arborio, 121
  basmati, 123

Salt. *See* Sodium.
Saturated fat, daily amounts
    of, 13
Self-improvement, 16
Sodium
  daily amounts of, 13
  heart disease and, 68
  low-fat products and, 21
  reducing intake of, 68, 168
Spas
  fitness programs and, 115
  Spa-Finders, 115
  Spa-Trek, 115
Stationary bicycling, 193
Step aerobics, 75
Strength training
  aging and, 229
  benefits of, 113, 229
  bone density and, 113
  improving stamina and
      agility, 229
  muscle mass and, 10
Stretching
  benefits of, 55
  recommendations for, 55

Stone crab claws, method for
    cracking, 185
Sugar, 245

Tai chi chuan, 141
Target heart rate, to determine, 58
Tarragon, 188
Tomatoes
  benefits of eating, 212
  seeding, 89

U.S. Department of Agriculture, 13

Veal, choosing lean cuts of, 151
Vegetables, benefits of eating, 212
Vegetarian lifestyle
  benefits of, 12
  meatless burgers, 18
Vinegars
  making flavored, 208
  using flavored, 22

Walking
  benefits of, 10, 11
  shoes, 18
Water
  increasing intake of, 179
  monitoring intake of, 179
  working out in, 75
Weight control, 13
  aging and, 52, 229
  calorie requirements for, 13, 246
  exercise and, 246
  guidelines for, 52
  metabolic rate and, 113
  positive attitude and, 148
Weight training, 139

Yoga, 141

Acknowledgments and Credits

Oxmoor House wishes to thank the following individuals and merchants:

Annieglass, Santa Cruz, CA

Bridges Antiques, Birmingham, AL

Bromberg's, Birmingham, AL

Carolyn Rice Art Pottery, Marietta, GA

Charlotte & Company, Birmingham, AL

Christine's, Birmingham, AL

Fioriware, Zanesville, OH

Fitz & Floyd/Omnibus International, Dallas, TX

Mr. and Mrs. Roy Gilbert, Jr., Birmingham, AL

The Holly Tree, Birmingham, AL

Lace in Stone, Santa Cruz, CA

Lamb's Ears, Birmingham, AL

Maralyn Wilson Gallery, Birmingham, AL

Potluck Studios, Modena, NY

Table Matters, Birmingham, AL

Taitu, Dallas, TX

Union Street Glass, Oakland, CA

Villeroy & Boch, New York, NY

Photography and photo styling by Oxmoor House Staff:

Photographers: Ralph Anderson and Jim Bathie
Photo Stylists: Kay E. Clarke and Virginia R. Cravens

Additional photography:
Josh Gibson: page 177

Additional photo styling:
Iris Crawley O'Brien: pages 27, 224

Mail-order sources:
To request an order form for Hawaiian Bread, send a self-addressed stamped envelope to:
    King's Hawaiian Bakery West, Inc.
    Consumer Affairs Dept.
    P.O. Box 7879
    Torrance, CA 90504

For specialty potatoes contact:
    Frieda's, Inc.
    4465 Corporate Center Drive
    Los Alamitos, CA 09720-2561
    1-800-421-9477